Sugarcoated Ethics

SUGARCOATED ETHICS

Children's Literature and Atlantic Enslavement

Courtney Weikle-Mills

Johns Hopkins University Press

Baltimore

2 4 6 8 9 7 5 3 1

Johns Hopkins University Press
2715 North Charles Street
Baltimore, Maryland 21218
www.press.jhu.edu

A catalog record for this book is available from the British Library.

Library of Congress Cataloging-in-Publication Data

Names: Weikle-Mills, Courtney author
Title: Sugarcoated ethics : children's literature and Atlantic enslavement /
Courtney Weikle-Mills.
Description: Baltimore : Johns Hopkins University Press, 2026. | Includes
bibliographical references and index. | Summary: "A transnational and
transoceanic literary history that moves across English-speaking locales of
the Atlantic, Sugarcoated Ethics traces the stories that British and US
children's books, as well as Afro-Caribbean storytelling traditions, tell about
the ethical responsibilities demanded by immediate and distant transatlantic
relationships. This book treats transatlantic circulation-of people, ideas, goods,
and books-not only as an impetus for children's literature's explorations of
ethics, but also as a site for ethical and unethical actions, with real impacts"—
Provided by publisher.
Identifiers: LCCN 2025039849 | ISBN 9781421454450 paperback |
ISBN 9781421454467 ebook
Subjects: LCSH: Slavery in literature | Children's literature—Moral and ethical
aspects | Children's literature, American—History and criticism | Children's
literature, English—History and criticism | Children's stories, West Indian
(English)—History and criticism | BISAC: LITERARY CRITICISM / Semiotics
& Theory | LITERARY CRITICISM / Subjects & Themes / Historical Events |
LCGFT: Literary criticism
Classification: LCC PN1009.5.S58 W45 2026
LC record available at https://lccn.loc.gov/2025039849

EU GPSR Authorized Representative
LOGOS EUROPE, 9 rue Nicolas Poussin, 17000, La Rochelle, France
E-mail: Contact@logoseurope.eu

To Ryan and Soren,
who are consistently loving, kind, and ethical

CONTENTS

The longer I exist in the world, the more my gratitude magnifies. I could not have written this book without my husband, Ryan Mills, whom I lovingly thank for talking me through my arguments and reading ethical theory with me. I thank my son Soren Mills for being unfailingly positive and loving when the work felt long and hard.

I am grateful for Marah Gubar for her encouraging mentorship and brilliant ideas; among other insights, she is responsible for pointing out I could use the noisy and silent eggs as metaphors in chapter 2. I am lucky to have a tremendous colleague in Tyler Bickford; he offered valuable feedback and is a fantastic coconspirator when it comes to Children's Literature Program initiatives at Pitt, as is our new colleague, Lidong Xiang. I thank my (current and former) Pitt colleagues Laura Lovett, Gayle Rogers, Amy Murray Twyning, Shalini Puri, Don Holmes, Marcus Rediker, Lara Putnam, Benjamin Parris, and Stephanie Espie for their encouragement and assistance as I worked on this book. I thank Jonathan Arac and David Marshall for supporting my work with a Humanities Center Fellowship, and the attendees at a colloquium there for their questions (especially Dan Kubis and Zach Horton). I extend appreciation to Veronica Dristas and Allyson Delnore for connecting me to the Global Studies and European Studies Centers at Pitt, and for supporting efforts to make our children's literature program more global. I am grateful for insights from my graduate students (scholars in their own right) who encountered parts of the book in progress, including Sreemoyee Dasgupta (who shared her copy of *Kathataranga* with me), Rachel Maley, Shawna McDermott, Amanda Awanjo, Christine Case, Kirsten Paine, Gabriela Lee, and Hebah Uddin.

I thank my editors at Johns Hopkins, including Matthew McAdam. I am incredibly grateful for the incisive feedback of two anonymous readers. I thank Carrie Waterson for copyediting the book, Edith Saint Preux for coordinating production, Phoebe Oathout for answering my questions as I prepared the manuscript, and Kathy Patterson for providing the index.

I relied on the invaluable help of librarians and archivists as I completed my research. I am grateful to Tom McCullough of the Moravian Archives; Donald Wieand and Andrew McLeod of the Moravian Historical Society; Clare Withers of Pitt's Elizabeth Nesbitt Collection; Mary Jones of the Heinz History Center; Fiona Hartley-Kroeger and Suzan Alteri of the Baldwin Library of Historical Children's Literature at the University of Florida; Laurie Taylor and Chelsea Dinsmore of the Digital Library of the Caribbean; Carlyle Best of the West India Collection at the University of the West Indies, Barbados; Ingrid Thompson of the Barbados Department of Archives; Harriet Pierce of the Barbados Museum and Historical Society; Marilyne Walker of the National Library Services, Barbados; Beverly Borton of Codrington College Library; Lucy McCann of the Bodleian Libraries at Oxford University; Phaedra Casey and Tace Fox of the British Foreign and School Society Archives at Brunel University; Laura Wasowicz and Brianne Barrett of the American Antiquarian Society; Andrea Immel of the Cotsen Children's Library at Princeton University; Joanne Schwartz of the Osborne Collection of Early Children's Books; Caitlin Goodman of the Friends Historical Library at Swarthmore College; Penny Ramon and Kristina Krasny of the Lilly Library; Lara Unger of the University of Michigan; and Marta Crilly of the Burns Library at Boston College. I thank the British Library for providing me access to materials there.

I build on the work of scholars who have come before me in dealing with childhood as it relates to the Caribbean, including Karen Sands O'Connor, Colleen Vasconcellos, and Chris Bischof (all of whom were kind enough to reply to my emails), as well as Lissa Paul (who asked me great questions at conferences). I thank Brigitte Fielder, Emily Murphy, Karen Sánchez-Eppler, Jacqueline Reid-Walsh, Allison Giffin, Lucia Hodgson, and Jared Gardner, as well as my students, for organizing conference panels with me, which were helpful in working out my arguments. I am grateful to Jan Susina and Jessica Straley for answering my questions about Lewis Carroll. I profusely thank Nina Christensen and Charlotte Appel, who invited me to Aarhus University in Denmark to speak about the Danish St. Croix sections, and Xu Derong, Zhu Ziqiang, and Jiang Jianli, who brought me to China to talk about the Bengali *Sandford and Merton*. I end by thanking my colleagues in the Children's Literature Global Network, including Murphy (who helped generate sources for my conclusion), Xu, M. O. Grenby, Kimberly Reynolds, Vanessa Joosen, Emma-Louise Silva, and Ritwika Roy. You inspire me as I look to the future of the field.

Sugarcoated Ethics

Enslavement and the Relational Ethics of Children's Literature

In August 1836, a prolific British colonial printer, Henry James Mills of Trinidad, ran an advertisement featuring an ample offering of books for youth, reflecting the innovations of nearly a century of commercial development of children's literature in English. The ad begins with a list of schoolbooks, containing *Vyse's Spelling Book* and *Goldsmith's Grammar of Geography*, before moving on to nursery books, including *Barbauld's Lessons for Children, Boy's Own Book*, and *Abbott's Fireside*. Mills touts a full Family Library and ends with the reminder that "Children's Books in great variety" can be had at his printshop.[1]

In the column beside the book advertisement appears a very different list involving children: those for whom enslavers were trying to claim compensation following the 1833 abolition of enslavement in the British colonies, which took effect in 1834, freeing children under six and instituting a four-year apprenticeship period for those over six. Eighty-one children are represented by numbers beside enslavers' names, without reference to names, ages, genders, languages, or national origins. The accompanying notice declares that compensation has been denied because these youth were born to women illegally imported, presumably after the British abolition of the slave trade in 1807, but notes that the children have not been "condemned" and prompts enslavers to submit evidence of their so-called property.[2] Although the clerical tone buries the cruelty of these children's circumstances in colonial bureaucracy, the juxtaposition with the book ad is jarring.

Taking the historical correspondence between the early commercial development of English-language children's literature and the most active era of Atlantic enslavement as its starting point, *Sugarcoated Ethics* is about the interrelations between the two cultures of childhood indicated by these notices. Although the gap between the childhoods they evoke seems wide, there are numerous points of intersection. With the institution of slavery and related industries contributing substantially to white British and US incomes, enslavement produced a key part of the disposable income that allowed upper- and middle-class families to purchase books for their offspring, providing an economic basis for English children's literature's commercial rise and proliferation. These investments in the slave economy shaped the stories that appeared in children's books from the beginning, as authors considered how to represent the growing dependence on enslaved people and the products they produced.[3] White children's contact with the system of slavery was used as a rationale for literary lessons. Thomas Day's *The History of Sandford and Merton* (1783–1789), which I discuss later in this introduction, inaugurated a motif of child characters supposedly cleansed of this connection through ethical retraining.

Enslavement also had a major impact on how children's literature and the connected concept of childhood circulated. Enslaved youth—whether they survived the middle passage or were born in the colonies—were denied the protections associated with white upper- and middle-class childhood. In *Stolen Childhood* (1998), Wilma King argues that they "had virtually no childhood because they entered the workplace early . . . These experiences made them grow old before their time."[4] Yet childhood was part of what William Boelhower refers to as the Atlantic world's "inseparable cargo of plants, animals, commodities, peoples, skills, languages, races, and ideas," and it took on new meanings as it was applied in colonial contexts.[5] The newspaper list demonstrates the importance and precarity of enslaved youth following the abolition of the slave trade, when mothers and babies became key to enslavers' plans to continue using enslaved people's labor.[6] Some turned to illegal importing, as the newspaper notice documents, but they also escalated an existing practice of using mass sexual violence to replicate their workforce. As Sasha Turner and Colleen Vasconcellos argue, this enslaver strategy assigned enslaved youth special value *as children*.[7]

As abolition gained steam and ameliorations were proposed, some enslavers portrayed themselves as benevolent parents, a claim that complexly intersected with efforts in the English-speaking Caribbean to indoctrinate enslaved youth with education designed to control future generations. Although education was available to only a small fraction of the enslaved, the missionaries providing such an education, some of whom opposed enslavement, brought thousands of children's books to the colonies. Teaching enslaved youth and, later, emancipated children meant attempting to transform them into colonizers' idea of ethical beings by promoting a European habitus, using books like Isaac Watts's *Divine Songs* (1715) and Peter Parley's *Tales of Europe* (1828). Meanwhile, as Ebony Elizabeth Thomas has argued, "Black storytelling traditions exist in the shadows" of children's literature.[8] Although what Thomas (after Kevin Young) calls "shadow books" are "lost along the way," extant traces reveal how enslaved Africans and their descendants countered increasing colonizer interest in youth.[9]

Considering a range of books and story forms from the Atlantic world, this book investigates how young people, Black and white, learned about their ethical obligations and were invited to engage in ethical critique in the contexts of enslavement and colonization.[10] Ethical traditions among enslaved and free Africans are robust, if difficult to access as presented to children. Meanwhile, although the institution of slavery was commonly rationalized by white Europeans and Americans, enslavement was an ethical crisis in its divergence from the ideals of freedom and reciprocity coming to be celebrated in political and economic discourse. Some writers for youth responded to these contradictions. However, the formation of commercial English children's literature within a culture of enslavement and around an audience considered not fully rational results in many responses that are sanitized or sugarcoated.

Sugarcoating sometimes means literally fetishizing sugar while obscuring enslaved people's relationship to its production. For example, the title character of John Newbery's *The Renowned History of Giles Gingerbread* (1764)—a book possibly written by the pioneering bookseller himself—voraciously consumes a book made of gingerbread. Eating perennially raises questions about the ethics of food production. The book as food motif accurately reflects white child readers' status as potentially destructive consumers within an Atlantic economy powered by slave labor. Yet the book spares them from learning that the raw materials the gingerbread contains were grown and processed by enslaved people. By normalizing feeding young bodies with ginger and sugar (in the form of molasses), Giles Gingerbread sidesteps engagement with families' growing reliance on foreign goods and the humans forced to produce them. Newbery's slogan, "Trade and Plumb Cake Forever, Huzzah!" makes a similar dodge, capturing how the landmark press's activities are underwritten by a blithe mentality regarding the extraction of sweet products through enslavement.

This kind of sugarcoating continues today. For example, Thomas, Debbie

Reese, and Kathleen T. Horning critique Emily Jenkins's *A Fine Dessert* (2015) and Ramin Ganeshram's *A Birthday Cake for George Washington* (2016) for submerging the painful realities of enslavement within stories of Africans creating sweet treats for their enslavers.[11] These books seem designed to generate basic empathy for enslaved domestics but avoid giving young readers a full understanding of the massive theft of enslaved people's labor in the sugar production process or the institutional structures and public support that allowed this to happen.

But strikingly, sugarcoating does not manifest only in avoidance. Children's literature, especially of the early period, is a genre that concerns itself with relational ties and often positions itself *as* a relation.[12] As a result, some early children's books by white authors address the ethical crisis of enslavement as a relational crisis, or a crisis of connection. Characterizing a widespread institution in terms of relationships fosters further simplification, but it also activates relational ideas associated with childhood, including interdependency and openness to unknown people and futures—concepts that have become key to modern formulations of relational ethics. This means that children's books sometimes offer more relevant responses to enslavement than the so-called universal ethics that dominated at the time, based on sunny notions that a Christian God has designed a reciprocal world or on restrictive views of humanity that frame "slavery" as a metaphor for hardships faced by white Europeans and Americans.[13] Anticolonial, antiracist, and anti-ageist scholars have critiqued these universal ethics for failing to solicit care for others, gestures that do sometimes appear in children's books.[14] Yet the relational ethics of children's texts show how enslavement curtails acts of caring, contorting relationality into simplified, sanitized, and pathological forms. As Parvati Raghuram points out, "The meaning, nature and value of care are all deeply racialized," because "slavery and colonialism defined who cared and who received care."[15] In ways that also seem right to characterize as sugarcoating, relational responses to enslavement often react to this crisis by *narrowing* ethical responsibility.

Narrow ideas of relationality persist in the present, even as thinkers from multiple disciplines are recovering what Sarada Balagopalan calls "devalued relationalities," or ways of being that emphasize vulnerability, reciprocity, and caregiving, to address "rising racialized inequalities."[16] Evasions of relationality, too, are rife in our current world. As Simone Drichel has written, "What often marks our psychic entanglements, as much as our political relationships, is not an affirmation but a disavowal of relationality . . . Arguably, then, what is at stake in the contemporary relational turn . . . is the pressing question of what gets in the way of this promise and leaves us facing relationality's pathological alternatives instead."[17] In *Sugarcoated Ethics*, I historicize by discussing the pathological alternatives *to*, as well as problematic versions *of* relation and relationality, that emerge in children's literature alongside occasionally more radical and transformative relational possibilities. My history begins in Britain but is transatlantic and finally global in scope, moving along the circuits by which products and ideas related to enslavement traveled to draw attention to their wide impact on children's culture.

White-authored texts contain many of the seeds of distorted relational dynamics that continue to impede attempts to address the legacies of enslavement, including the harms of the global capitalist economy enslavement helped to build. In this introduction and chapter 1, I address a core early children's book motif—beginning with *Sandford and Merton* and influencing Frances Hodgson Burnett's Golden Age texts *A Little Princess* (1905) and *The Secret Garden* (1910–1911)—that attempts to make white youth ethical beings by purifying them of contact with enslavement and colonization. *Sandford and Merton* enlists a formerly enslaved adult in this process, to whom the white child protagonist is made complexly accountable, but the overall dynamic establishes what Anne Helen Petersen has called "white rituals of civility," which prioritize peace between white friends and relatives over confrontations that address racial harms.[18] By promoting the idea that witnessing enslavement literally makes white children frail, this motif also begins to shape what Robin DiAngelo calls "white fragility," or a lack of stamina for addressing racial violence.[19] Indeed, the premise of these books is based on white fragility and hypocrisy, as authors see white children as uniquely susceptible to harm and downplay violence to enslaved children. An escalation of this evasiveness appears in fictions of benevolent enslavers, discussed in chapter 2, which suggest that false versions of congeniality and interracial collaboration can improve the slave system.

Books encouraging relationality as a spur to activism in white children, discussed in chapter 3, no longer evade ethical engagement but shade into colonialism and white saviorism, aligning with Lissa Paul's argument that even antislavery children's books often contribute to enslaved people's disempowerment.[20] As I discuss in chapter 4, white saviorist attitudes make way for colonial interventions that limit ethical responsibility to securing enslaved and formerly enslaved children's access to books. Book producers, however, rarely tackle the appropriateness of children's books for Afro-Caribbean readers. These children's experiences, which I attempt to reconstruct, are crucial to studying the ethics of English-language children's literature.

The idea that ethics demanded intervening in enslaved and colonized children's situations fed into the global circulation of children's books in the nineteenth century. Books by white writers about enslaved African characters, as I discuss in chapter 5, become part of the global-imperial children's literature trade, circulating to Malaysia, Singapore, China, South Africa, Egypt, and elsewhere to spread expectations of assimilation and respectability. These publishing networks lead to what Emer O'Sullivan calls "the imbalance of international exchange" when it comes to children's literature, in which hegemonic British and US stories erase others.[21] The overall arc of the book points to the increasing impingement of universal versions of ethics on relational ones and the universalization of pathological relations.

Yet forgotten materials in the archives offer significant critique. These include stories, songs, and writing calling for direct and responsive relational justice, such as folktales told by enslaved Afro-Caribbean women about persecuted heroines (chapter 2), protest songs by Afro-Caribbean workers (this introduction and chapter 3), and intergenerational US activist writing supporting African American newspapers (chapter 3). Materials such as these reflect traditions that free and enslaved Africans kept alive and show how Anglo ideas of childhood were not received passively but morphed as they interacted with African American and Afro-Caribbean cultures. Édouard Glissant theorizes that the diaspora is defined by a "poetics of relation" attesting (in Betsy Nies and Melissa García Vega's summation) to the "interconnection of all phenomena and the futility of domination."[22]

As Paul points out, even a cursory glance at historical records shows a "glaring" disconnect between "the courageously sustained resistance of enslaved people . . . and their fictional counterparts."[23] Additionally, I suggest, ethical interventions can be found in storytelling and musical traditions, anticipating Fred Moten's reframing and expansion of ethics to include the aesthetics of Black life.[24] As a white US scholar invested in ethics, I see doing my part to recover such materials as a responsibility that comes with researching this topic, and I build on the work of Michelle H. Martin, Brigitte Fielder, Nazera Wright, Kate Capshaw, Karen Sands O'Connor, Thomas, Paul, and others who have bridged the fields of Black studies and children's literature. I do this research as what Martin calls "crossover scholarship . . . written about groups to which the scholar does not belong" as a "a short-term solution to a long-term and historically grounded problem"—namely, that

BIPOC scholars are structurally disadvantaged within academia.[25] Reflecting on historical patterns is only one piece of this work; in my professional life, I am committed to making academia a welcoming place for difference. Part of this is recognizing that I am not the first or final authority on the African American and Afro-Caribbean materials in my project; I aim to amplify conversations begun by scholars of color (stretching back to Maud Cuney-Hare, who appears later in this introduction) and to make space for more scholarship from these communities, which is needed to achieve greater nuance and draw on lived understanding.

There are materials in the archive for allies, even if they do not become the dominant ways that early English children's literature deals with relationality. Radical alternatives by white British and US writers include an absurd animal story satirizing British hypocrisy on enslavement (chapter 1), which may have influenced Lewis Carroll's use of sea creatures to draw attention to unethical consumption in *Alice's Adventures in Wonderland* (1865), and US Quaker street cry narratives, which draw on the long tradition of books based on street vendors' calls to encourage youth to be conscious consumers during the transatlantic sugar boycott (chapter 3).

There are also more fundamentally radical potentials within children's literature that emerge through its relational orientation, even if they are laced with pathological strains. I introduce what I argue are the relational aspects of early children's literature in English, using Anna Laetitia Barbauld's writing for youth as well as Day's *Sandford and Merton*. Barbauld was an innovator of dialogues for young readers, which became a pervasive format.[26] *Sandford and Merton* is an early example of long-form children's fiction that has had a large, if underappreciated, influence on children's literature criticism. Jacqueline Rose uses the book as a key piece of evidence in her argument that children's literature uses the child "to mediate, or resolve" the contradictions of a degenerate modern world.[27] Rose does not examine the text as a response to enslavement, even though, as Kimberley Reynolds points out, Day is clearly motivated by antislavery campaigns.[28] I address this tension in the book's critical reception to begin a discussion of children's literature's significant, but restricted, engagements with ethical relationality in the context of enslavement.

Early materials created by Afro-Caribbean people, by contrast, deserve more representation in children's literature and childhood studies.[29] I use transhistorical research methods underutilized in the children's literature field to discuss the protest song "Queen Mary" (1880), currently taught to young people in St. Croix, showing how woman-centered musical traditions use relational structures to prompt intergenerational ethical action. Together, these texts showcase the range of relational possibilities I want to discuss when it comes to the intertwined histories of enslavement and youth.

Children's Literature as a Relational Genre

Relation and relationality are at the heart of the children's literature field, with many scholars continuing to engage with Rose's argument that children's literature "hangs on . . . the impossible relation between adult and child" or proposing alternate theories of relation.[30] Although Rose is often criticized, many of her arguments remain convincing; she perceives, for instance, that "children's literature" claims to be *for* people who do not usually control its contents and do not exist as a unified group. Children's literature's dogged organization around an implied, idealized relation between young people and adults invites the question, is children's literature an ethical relation? Although Rose criticizes scholars for building scholarship on the question of what book "does the child most good?" she seems motivated by (broadly framed) ethical concerns like how adult desires around "the child" aim to circumvent "social inequality" by collapsing difference, even beyond the adult-child relationship.[31] Children's books not only fail to adequately relate to young people, she proposes, but also contain strategies for deceptively simplifying the world on behalf of the child and through a fantasy of childhood innocence.

While Rose confines her discussion of children's literature's circumvention of power dynamics to class and colonialism, representations of enslavement reflect similar desires to simplify, resolve contradictions, and shore up power structures. Indeed, we might identify enslavement as the most significant crisis of contradiction in the vicinity of children's literature's development that would prompt such simplification, making it a key (though unacknowledged) context for Rose's observations. That *Sandford and Merton* is one of Rose's main texts supports this point. Revisiting texts featuring white children's interactions with enslaved people shows that their authors were more willing to wrestle with ethical difficulties—including children's *lack* of innocence within the Atlantic economy—than Rose acknowledges, a point Marah Gubar has made about their depictions of adult-child relations.[32]

Although Rose is skeptical that children's books can do more than "take in" readers construed as passive, the majority of early texts incorporate relational structures and model interactive exchanges, which Rose claims get lost as children's literature moves toward a realist aesthetic.[33] Through dialogues, storytelling, and frame narratives, early texts frequently *belabor* rather than "totally erase[]" the "question of who is talking to whom, and why," as Rose argues that paradigmatic children's books do.[34] We could read these relational structures as even more overt attempts to capture the child by including a child voice, but they also suggest an openness to relating (and encountering relational messiness) that might temper the idealization of an impossible adult-child relation. Depictions of such interactions, though fictive, often do not erase but *introduce* and foreground contradictions; for instance, in chapter 4 I discuss a dialogue in which the child voice brings up enslavement, which the adult voice addresses insufficiently.

For an example of how relational messiness appears in early children's literature, we might turn to the "conversational primer," which Jessica Wen Hui Lim identifies as a genre Barbauld pioneered using an interactive narrator with "the persona of the parent-author" or "affectionate parent-teacher."[35] Such figures come about because children's book writers assume that young people need to learn ethical ways of behaving through relationships rather than rational deliberation or rules. In this respect, they draw on but amend the work of Enlightenment philosophers like John Locke and Jean-Jacques Rousseau. These thinkers argue in favor of a universal ethics available via reason but consider children incapable of full rationality and in need of ethical education from teachers and parents. Thus Locke, in *Some Thoughts Concerning Education* (1693), claims that children should learn ethics "more by practice than rules"—in other words, relationally.[36]

Rousseau, a significant figure in Rose's argument that children are vehicles for easing contradictions, advocates that children be trained by a tutor who can orchestrate relational stresses, leading to ethical realizations. As depicted in *Émile* (1762), these realizations are framed by the tutor as universal truths, a dynamic feeding into Rose's claims about children's utility in restoring a purportedly natural order in the face of modern strife. Yet the universal lessons are complicated by relational ones, for instance, when Émile's tutor encourages him to plant beans in a plot the gardener is already using, knowing they will be dug up. Although the tutor means to illustrate the (naturalized) concept that (prior) labor begets property, he exploits the child's supposedly natural curiosity to initiate the lesson. The lesson is thus about conflict brought on by different people's natural drives and the resulting sense of injustice shared by Émile and the gardener (both of whom, Marianna Papastephanou and Zelia Gregoriou point out, read as dispossessed colonial figures).[37] In dealing with this conflict, Émile develops sensitivity to others and learns to compromise, showing that the seemingly rigid claims of property can be mediated with conversation.

In many children's books, a gap between universal/rational rules and ethical learning through relationships similarly creates openings for components of relational ethics to emerge, including an interdependence and mutual vulnerability that rise to ethical obligations and an attitude of openness that allows ethical decisions to emerge spontaneously in interaction.[38] Alongside irrationality and innocence, these qualities inform the versions of childhood that appear in children's literature; openness, for instance, takes shape in a motif Clémentine Beauvais calls the "mighty child," who "might do something . . . the adult does not anticipate."[39]

Building on the philosophical traditions, narrators based on friendly relatives and relational narrative devices, like dialogues, pervade early children's books and do not, I propose, evaporate but create a persistent (if sometimes deemphasized) relational awareness that resurfaces throughout children's literature's history. Books featuring friendly narrators reappear, for example, in contemporary teen books like Kate Bornstein's *Hello Cruel World* (2006), which Gabrielle Owen argues engage in "a more ethical relationality" by featuring "a person speaking to another person."[40] When it comes to early books, it is worth pointing out that reading was more of a social event than it typically is now. Even if early writers do not go so far as to directly "acknowledg[e] the situatedness of [their] thoughts and perspective," as in the books Owen discusses, relational structures emphasize listening to others and thereby implicitly pose questions of ethical relationality, which proliferate beyond the adult-child relationship.[41]

Most children's books of this early period are not ultimately concerned with the relationship between adults and children but aim to initiate young people into a world of broader social connections and responsibility. Barbauld's *Lessons for Children* (original editions 1778–1808, revised edition 1841) aims to help its young readers understand, in Lim's words, that "human relationships are the basis undergirding the daily consumption of material objects."[42] When the child (Charles) asks the parent-teacher-narrator (Mama) for something to eat, this dialogue unfolds, beginning with Mama:

> But the bread is not baked.
> Then bid Christopher Clump heat his oven and bake it—
> But the loaf is not kneaded.

Then bid little Margery take the dough and knead it—
But the flour is not ground.
Then take it to the mill, and bid Roger the miller grind it—
But the corn is not threshed [etc.].[43]

Charles is made to understand that he relies on other people for his sustenance. Lim claims the dialogue teaches that "to be human is to consume and to become a material part of the social network of production and labour," in other words, to be interdependent.[44]

This is not to say that Barbauld includes all the economic relations that children are in, or that these relations are depicted fully accurately or ethically. Charles grows imperious in his commands, especially when the workers are female. There is sugarcoating, in that social connectivity is taught via an idealized local manufacturing process rather than distant processes involving enslaved workers. Yet the focus on interdependence means that weak relational links in the economic supply chain become apparent. Barbauld teaches awareness of the transatlantic economy one page earlier when Mama asks whether Charles knows "what sugar comes from?"[45] Reflecting poor relationality, she does not give him a chance to respond but provides an answer: "Sugar comes from a cane . . . they squeeze the juice out, and boil it a great deal, and that makes sugar."[46] "They" refers to enslaved people, but they are not named, their enslavement is obscured, and their treatment remains unaddressed. Barbauld has Mama monologue here, rather than open a conversation. Still, the logic dictates that if bread requires relationships—and their attendant messiness if someone is unacknowledged (or mistreated)—so does sugar.

The ethical implications of interconnectedness resurface in Barbauld's later six-volume collaboration with John Aiken, *Evenings at Home* (1793), which offers an explicitly critical take on the global economy. To chart global relationality, the authors amend a widely influential image of transnational commerce expressed in Joseph Addison's "The Royal Exchange" (1711). Visiting the place where foreign goods are imported into England, Addison characterizes trade as "mutual intercourse" ethically designed by a deified Nature: "Nature seems to have taken a particular Care to disseminate her Blessings among the different Regions of the World, with an Eye to this mutual Intercourse and Traffick among Mankind, that the Natives of the several Parts of the Globe might have a kind of Dependance upon one another, and be united together by their common Interest."[47] Addison's statement was so influential that I return to it as a touchstone throughout this book.[48] Even as it presents an undeniable consciousness of human interconnection, it ignores realities of trade in Addison's lifetime, meaning that it is detached, decontextualized, and universalized, without ethical implications.[49]

We can contrast Addison's celebratory language with the explanation of global trade in Karl Marx and Friedrich Engels's *Communist Manifesto* (1848) just over a century later: "The need of a constantly expanding market for its products chases the bourgeoisie over the whole surface of the globe. It must nestle everywhere, settle everywhere, establish connexions everywhere . . . In place of the old wants, satisfied by the productions of the country, we find new wants, requiring for their satisfaction the products of distant lands."[50] Marx and Engels perceive that the connections created by commerce have been the product of colonial greed and exploitation, rather than any natural tendency toward reciprocity or peace.[51]

Aiken and Barbauld amend Addison's account of trade as global cooperation to give a more realistic account of global inequities, with corresponding ethical demands. In a section they call the "globe-lecture," they emphasize the "active industry" of people, rather than "nature": "Nature does not drop her fruits into their mouths, but offers them as the price of labour. Human wants are many . . . but the human powers fully exerted are equal to the demand . . . What the land does not yield itself, its inhabitants by their active industry procure from the remotest parts of the globe. When we drink tea, we sweeten the infusion of a Chinese herb with the juice of a West Indian cane."[52] Departing from Addison's notion of nature ex machina, they suggest that the needs of British manufactures for raw materials requires "friendly intercourse" with other nations.[53] Aiken and Barbauld note that Europeans aim to "render all countries and climates familiar to them" to carry out imperial ambitions, anticipating Marx and Engels's contention that the bourgeoisie "establish connexions" everywhere.[54] But because nature has been dropped as the invisible force ensuring mutual benefit, there is no illusion of mutuality; rich countries dominate trade.[55]

Although these relationships are instrumental, they demand ethical consideration. Barbauld and Aiken conclude that "no part of the world is void of our human brethren, who, amid all the diversities of character and condition are yet all *men*."[56] This ethical exploration results in an openness to difference, a hallmark of relational ethics: "We are too apt to look at the differences of mankind, and to undervalue all those who do not agree with us . . . But who are we—and what cause have we to think ourselves right, and all others wrong?

Can we imagine that hundreds of millions of our species in other parts of the world are left destitute of what is essential to their well-being, while a favoured few like ourselves are the only ones who possess it?"[57] The appreciation of difference, in this case, does not translate into active care. The passage argues against a Western style of charitable intervention and hinges on a capitalist fantasy regarding equality of opportunity: "The road to virtue and happiness is alike open to all."[58]

Inequality returns, however, via references to enslavement. In a story called "The Wanderer's Return," the white narrator, who loses his liberty during his travels, mentions seeing enslaved Africans in the West Indies and witnessing parents selling their children in the East Indies. On the surface, the story can be read as minimizing ethical responsibility, since the man regains his freedom and returns home with a "clear conscience" despite not doing anything to respond to the atrocities he witnesses.[59] Yet the story raises awareness that might lead to future action; Michelle Levy points out that Barbauld and Aiken make "the monstrous nature" of colonization and enslavement "apparent to children, as the state's activities are identified with criminality."[60] As Beauvais argues, children's greater access to the future means that authors often leave room for potentiality, which she frames as "the paradoxical adult desire to ask the child didactically for an unpredictable future."[61] In holding open the problem of global ethics in a world powered by enslavement, we might understand these authors as motivated by desires beyond simplification and avoidance: ethical desires to solve difficult problems and care for their offspring by trying to make the world a better place. Such relationally focused desires have been the focus of modern feminist care ethicists; Carol Gilligan, for instance, claims that experiences of caring, especially for children, yield ethics focusing on "responsibility" and "relationship."[62]

Responsibility is a key term in Barbauld's adult political writing. In the years before writing *Evenings at Home*, Barbauld lambasted Parliament for insufficiently addressing enslavement in *Epistle to William Wilberforce Esq. on the Rejection of the Bill for Abolishing the Slave Trade* (1791) and wrote an anti-war book, *Sins of Government, Sins of the Nation* (1792), in which she claims that citizens are responsible for the unethical actions of their government and have an obligation to demand change. We might read her children's books as increasingly pursuing this responsibility. Aiken, meanwhile, encouraged his children to reflect on the ethical implications of their consumption. His daughter Lucy was one of the child participants in the transatlantic sugar boycott (discussed in chapter 3). The problematic relations created by enslavement and trade, for these authors, mean turning to youth to seek an ethical future.

Recentering Enslavement in Early Children's Literature

Openness needs to be an opening to others as well as an opening to the future. Black feminist care ethicists, as Wesley C. Jacques notes, draw attention to how care differs depending on one's "relation to power," meaning that *listening* to people with different positionalities is important, as is becoming aware of the power dynamics that impede this work.[63] Day's *Sandford and Merton* experiments with approximating not just the voice of the child but the voice of the other, requiring reflection on how power shapes such experiments.

Like Barbauld's *Lessons, Sandford and Merton* employs a format that foregrounds relation—in this case, stories told by an English tutor, inserted within a frame narrative of a white creole child's ethical training after returning to mainland Britain from Jamaica. In the frame narrative, the sickly protagonist, Tommy Merton, has failed to develop an ethical worldview because he has been spoiled by his status-conscious mother and enslaved "servants," making him unfit for British society.[64] After Tommy encounters a hearty English boy named Harry Sandford, Tommy's parents send him to Harry's teacher, Mr. Barlow, who becomes the reader's teacher too. Barlow is the main source of the text's inset fables and nonfiction lessons. Storytelling, we might note, encourages listening to others—and the frame narrative models interaction between listener and teller. Later, the text incorporates stories from a man formerly enslaved by the Spanish in Brazil, known (problematically) in the text as the "grateful Black."

With Barlow's lessons, Day initially seems to solve the text's overt problem—that relational ethical teaching has failed because relations in the British colonies do not enforce the manners of the metropole—by turning to a universal and rational ethics. These teachings reflect a bourgeois capitalist worldview. Echoing Addison, he teaches the boys that "one country frequently produces what another does not; and . . . by exchanging their different commodities, the people of both may live more conveniently than they did before."[65]

Barlow's lessons about the world inform Rose's account of the text as a prototypical children's book anticipating the "adventure story," which she perceives is driven by "a belief in childhood as something which is able to by-pass the imperfections of the civilized world."[66] To derive this influential formula for thinking about children's books, Rose claims that Day is inspired by Rousseau's attempt in *Émile* to imagine a version of childrearing to counter the process whereby "God makes all things good; man meddles with them and they become evil."[67] She writes, "The objective of [Day's] story is to bring the classes together, and to put right the degeneracies of Merton's previous genteel education by setting him to work on the land."[68] Day, however, makes a crucial alteration to Rousseau's generalized idea of social corruption by grounding the text in Tommy's exposure to British enslavement. Conceits that recall *Émile*, such as a scene where Tommy learns to garden, address not basic conflicts arising from the social idea of property but his corrupt reliance on the labor of others. This reliance causes weakness—an idea reinforced in Barlow's stories and culminating in the story of the grateful Black, where that weakness incurs ethical debt.

By choosing not to discuss enslavement in the text, Rose overestimates the degree to which Day is invested in a return to natural innocence via the child, as Tommy is always already the child of enslavers. Imagining a scenario in which such a child might become an ethical being, the book *does* "by-pass" some of the imperfections of society in ways that I will discuss. Even so, the text does not settle these imperfections using innocence. Rather, interdependence and openness emerge, though radical forms are tangled with pathological ones. These relational concepts drive the interactions with the grateful Black, who offers a negative take on the same economy that Barlow describes, highlighting the need for relational listening to temper platitudes deriving from a narrow employment of rationality.

The depiction of this relationship, I argue, resonates with discussions of interdependence and vulnerability in contemporary ethical texts such as *Giving an Account of Oneself* (2005), in which Judith Butler builds on the theories of Emmanuel Levinas (discussed in more detail below) to outline the intertwined experiences of self and other that lead to ethical awareness. With its reference to accounting for one's actions in narrative form, Butler's title plays with a convention of eighteenth-century writing for children, epitomized by Isaac Watts's poem "Against Idleness and Mischief" (more commonly known as "How Doth the Little Busy Bee"). Like the insect that "improve[s] each shining hour," Watts directs children to keep a ledger-like record of the ethically sound ways they have used their time to show God when they die.[69] While Watts's poem emphasizes the speaker's individual report to a universal, rational, and patriarchal divine judge, Butler argues that an account of oneself responding to the "rhetorical condition for responsibility" should be addressed to another human and consider whether both are "sustained and altered."[70] Watts's idea of a balanced ethical ledger influences many children's books, but Butler's version is arguably more relevant to *Sandford and Merton*. Tommy does not merely build up knowledge and good actions, nor does he revert to a naturally innocent state; he must be altered and must account for this transition with the grateful Black.

Day and Butler share an interest in vulnerability as a catalyst for ethics. An interest in children's experience of the world created by adults underlies Butler's theory, contrasting with Rose's emphasis on adult desires for children. Butler unintentionally addresses a question that plagues those of us who teach about the ethical impacts of children's literature, how can children's literature affect readers if children do not always understand or relate to it? Butler argues, by way of Levinas and Jean Laplanche, that ethical responsibility resembles the enigmatic messages that children imbibe from the adult world. While this "experience of being imposed upon" might seem to "destroy[] the potential for agency," "it delineates a physical vulnerability from which we cannot slip away . . . but which can provide a way to understand that none of us is fully bounded, utterly separate, but, rather, we are in our skins, given over, in each other's hands, at each other's mercy."[71] This vulnerability, Butler claims, "grounds our responsibility."[72] Young people are pulled into ethical relation though contact with a world in which they lack full understanding or power.

The theme of vulnerability appears in a more literal way at the beginning of Day's text. Upon returning to England, Tommy is thrown into a realization of his physical vulnerability when a snake coils around his leg. On one level, this event conveys Tommy's dangerous lack of knowledge about the English landscape and fauna, as the native-born Harry saves him. This weakness, because it results from contact with the institution of slavery, can be read as a literal version of white fragility. White creole children's frailty, as I discuss in chapter 1, appears in several books as a reason to restore their connection with white British families and land. Day uses physical vulnerability, however, to start Tommy on the path toward becoming an ethical person, as Tommy meets Barlow through Harry. The pattern repeats in Tommy's encounter with the grateful Black, who saves him from being gored by a bull. The later scene uses vulnerability in a way closer to Butler's imagining, to catalyze ethical relation.

Vulnerability illustrates interconnectedness and humans' dependence on others; it also dovetails with openness, which in *Sandford and Merton* results from having to reexamine one's ideas and behavior. Even before the grateful

Black's appearance, the text's structure as a dialogical interaction opens a chance for Tommy to make mistakes and for the seeming universality of Barlow's lessons to be amended based on the specific needs of people Tommy encounters. For example, Barlow chides Tommy for ordering around a child dressed in rags, pointing out that his viewpoint is not logically consistent: "Then if your clothes should wear out and become ragged, every gentleman will have a right to command you?"[73] Duly shamed, Tommy resolves to help the child by giving him silk clothes. Barlow commends Tommy for embodying another supposedly universal virtue: charity. Yet this incident reveals shortcomings in an abstract approach to ethics; Tommy's gift leads the boy to be beaten and robbed. By featuring relational messiness (between Tommy and the boy, Tommy and Barlow) and a lack of understanding of the full context by both child and teacher, Day makes the point that specific relations are more important than rational rules when determining ethics.[74]

In looking at the outcomes of ethical behavior, not just its rationale, Day interacts with debates related to utilitarianism, a movement connected to proto-relational ethicists such as Francis Hutcheson, as well as reformers like Jeremy Bentham, who published his *Introduction to the Principles of Morals and Legislation* (1789) the same year Day finished the last installment of *Sandford and Merton*.[75] The ethical values of actions, for Bentham, are determined by their specific ends, including their capacity to produce pain or pleasure.[76] Bentham's emphasis on physical-emotional senses was counterintuitive to many educators at the time, including, to an extent, Day. They worried that making ethics dependent on sensory motivations would not solidify children's commitment to ethical behavior that was difficult or painful.[77] Because Tommy is the spoiled child of an enslaver, Barlow is eager to teach him that discomfort is nothing to fear; a favorite story of Barlow's teaches the "elevated method of thinking," defined as the "inclination to sacrifice our own pleasures . . . to the well-being of others."[78] However, building on the other-consciousness of this passage, Barlow moves toward teaching that pleasure and pain are ways to measure ethical relationships, claiming that "every benevolent person feels the greatest pleasure in doing good."[79]

Bentham too eschews a narrow focus on the senses to outline the ethical stakes of pleasure and pain as driving relationality. Specifically, he uses enslavement as an example of the ethical obligation to prevent pain not only in oneself but also in others: "The French have already discovered that the blackness of the skin is no reason why a human being should be abandoned without redress to the caprice of a tormentor. It may one day come to be recognized that the number of legs, the villosity of the skin, or the termination of the os sacrum are reasons equally insufficient for abandoning a sensitive being to the same fate . . . The question is not Can they reason? nor Can they talk? but, Can they suffer?"[80] Bentham's relation of human and animal suffering recalls comparisons between enslaved people and animals in children's books such as Sarah Trimmer's *Fabulous Histories* (1786) and *The Slave's Friend* (1836–1839), as discussed by Brigitte Fielder and Spencer Keralis.[81] But although many children's texts treat care for familiar animals (for instance, birds in cages) as the *entry* points for ethical awareness, extending metaphorically to *people* who have been othered, Bentham's version proposes a different trajectory whereby opposition to enslaved people's suffering opens ethical engagement along a chain of nearly infinite, not fully knowable otherness, extending to animals without a sacrum.[82] In this way, Bentham's work anticipates Levinas's argument for ethics as "first philosophy" in *Totality and Infinity* (1961), which lays the ground for modern relational ethics by arguing that ethical responsibility is based on the origin of human subjectivity in a prerational encounter with an other that is infinitely unknowable. Levinas's ethical theory focuses on relationships with (human) strangers as a paradigm because, in his view, these relationships do not proceed from identification or result in reciprocity but invite generosity that is unlimited.

Sandford and Merton, like Bentham, uses human-animal comparisons in a way that emphasizes relationship across difference, though Day at first emphasizes reciprocity rather than unlimited ethical responsibility. Barlow retells several animal fables, but the first and most elementary is "Androcles and the Lion," in which an enslaved man runs away and encounters a lion with a thorn in his paw. After helping the lion, Androcles gets recaptured and sentenced to death. The lion in the arena of punishment happens to be the same lion Androcles helped. The animal refuses to kill Androcles, leading to his pardon. In addition to making the Bentham-like point that awareness of one form of suffering opens the potential to see suffering among others, the story offers the subtle argument that the downtrodden act ethically because they are intimately aware of suffering.[83] This view informs Day's portrayal of the grateful Black, a stranger laden with otherness—though the man's story complicates the simplistic ideal of reciprocity in the lion fable, drawing attention to ethical situations that are not reciprocal.

The grateful Black section contains contradictory insinuations about gratitude, reciprocity, and debt, which point to tensions between a transformative and a pathological version of relationality. When we meet the grateful

Black at a bullbaiting Tommy attends with his friends, he is panhandling. Tommy wants to give him some money, but only Harry has enough to give. Following the initial meeting, a bull nearly tramples Tommy after escaping its rope. Mimicking the snake scene, Harry jumps in front of the bull but is almost gored to death, meaning that his superior strength is not enough to save him. Instead, both children are saved when the grateful Black deftly taunts the bull. This scene in some sense mirrors the earlier scene's emphasis on knowledge: the grateful Black understands Spanish ways (implied to be violent) and therefore the bull. There is also an Addison-like current of reciprocity, in that the man acts out of gratitude for the donation—though an exchange of gratitude for money is rarely equal, as money is a discrete measurable currency and gratitude potentially unending.

The text moves beyond this limited idea of reciprocity to draw attention to colonial power differentials and the need for just interactions on a global scale. In a follow-up scene, the grateful Black offers a scathing critique of white British society. As with Barlow, Day seems to base the man's view of the economy on the "Royal Exchange," but his version emphasizes Britons' one-sided dependence on people in other parts of the world: "Nature has, in every country, furnished the human species with all the qualities necessary for their preservation. In this country, and many others which I have seen, there are thousands who live, like birds in cages, upon the food provided by others, without doing anything for themselves. But they should be contented with the happiness they enjoy (if such a life can be called happiness), and not despise their fellow-creatures, without whose continual assistance they could not exist an instant."[84] In contrast with animal stories that use birds in cages as metaphors for the enslaved, white British people are the "birds in cages," having imprisoned themselves by their reliance on others. (This reversal repeats in another book in my study, Sarah Schoonmaker Baker's 1859 *Babes in the Basket*.) Notably, the "assistance" that enslaved people provide is not a discrete event but a "continual" support, so vast that it cannot be repaid or even quantified.

The theme of not being able to repay reappears at the text's conclusion in ways that amplify the critique but tread into safer relational territory. Anticipating Levinasian ethics, the grateful Black, who is clearly an ethically sound person, suggests that his responsibility to others is limitless, saying Tommy is "extremely welcome to all I have done; I would at any time risk my own safety to preserve one of my fellow-creatures."[85] Although he claims he has been repaid by Tommy and his family's "kindness," Tommy is forced to admit,

"That is not enough."[86] Tommy initially implies he can make up the difference with money but remembers he has none of his own. This inability seems convenient for those who would wish to tie up contradictions; as a child, Tommy cannot pay, but his father could. Yet as one enslaver's recompense would not end enslavement, the text relies on children to see that accountability has not yet happened and that the grateful Black has helped Tommy without hope of repayment—a truly unselfish ethical act. It is only when Tommy is made deeply, experientially conscious of his dependence on the grateful Black that he transforms into an ethical person, with the text commenting that his "heart expand[s]."[87] After this change, the text concludes with Tommy reflecting on his resolution "to consider all men as his brethren and equals."[88]

This transformational ethics is sugarcoated, however, in that the text has absorbed pathological understandings of interrelatedness from the slave system. The appellation "grateful Black," while to some degree ironic given the comments on Europeans' dependence on enslaved Africans, insinuates a permanently unequal power dynamic in which the Black man inherently *owes* the white children something, in a way that too closely resembles stories of benevolent enslavers and their "grateful slaves" that were circulating in this period.[89] Black people are more often depicted as taking ethical responsibility for white children than the reverse—even if they were, in truth, strangers—while white people were not always thought to be ethically responsible even for blood relatives, an idea I unpack in later chapters.

The grateful Black alters Tommy more than Tommy alters him, and Tommy's openness to alteration at all is in tension with a desire to settle the relationship and make it a reciprocal transaction, an iteration of Addison's peaceful global commerce on a micro scale. In this context, as Raghuram insists, care is "situated and non-innocent," as well as "risky."[90] Diverging from a Levinasian perspective, the burden of ethical action is put onto the other. Finally, Tommy's only available metaphor for mutuality is brotherhood, which relies on familiarity and sameness as a precondition for caring, foreclosing any real engagement with difference. Marilisa Jiménez García points out that such metaphors in the context of colonization and enslavement often function as "a means of imagining a politically dependent relationship."[91]

There is further sugarcoating here in that we do not ever come face to face with the horrors of British enslavement or directly confront Tommy's family's reliance on that institution for their wealth. Not only does Mr. Merton not pay the grateful Black, but Tommy's family also retains its stake in the slave system, an outcome we will see is common even in children's books that problematize the enterprise. The text tries, in a Rosian sense, to tie up a contradiction: the need to solve the ethics of enslavement while acknowledging the institution will continue operating. But if we bracket the insinuations of gratitude, the text also suggests that white Europeans cannot atone for their dependence on enslavement without changing dramatically.[92] If there is an adult desire expressed here, it is for children to enact change. This idea of the child as a vehicle for ethical expansion takes many forms in children's literature, including colonial ones, but it ideally requires openness to the experiences of the other.

Although Day ends with contradictions and (comparative) openness, later texts such as Barbara Hofland's *Matilda, or the Barbadoes Girl* (1816) and A. Selwyn's *The Little Creoles* (1820) (discussed in chapter 1) make the child's rehabilitation from enslavement a slicker process, amplifying subtle references to the magic of the British mainland that appear in Day's text. The narrative formulation that Day introduces culminates in *The Secret Garden*, which represents a scaling up of the formula to respond to broader colonial conditions. To consider a different facet of this global context, I revisit Day's text in chapter 5 by analyzing a Bengali translation that reconfigures the story of the grateful Black. For now, it is enough to note the push and pull between idealistic, critical, and pathological forms of relationality that intersect in *Sandford and Merton*, demonstrating the multiple threads that the difficult relations of childhood and enslavement bring together, which intertwine throughout this study.

Afro-Caribbean Ethics for Youth: Fragments of the Fireburn

In addition to arguing for the significance of enslavement to early children's literature's formulations of ethics, this book investigates the contributions of enslaved and free Africans to children's and youth culture. Compared to white British and US books outlining ethics for children, eighteenth- and nineteenth-century African American and Afro-Caribbean ethical teachings for youth are difficult to access because of the biases of the archive. While Joseph Roach and Diana Taylor have argued that scholars studying the Atlantic world might consider the role of embodied archives (i.e., people) and performances in preserving traditions, written evidence is often the standard of proof when considering historical subjects.[93] Saidiya Hartman, Marisa Fuentes, and Lisa Lowe have grappled with when it makes sense to fill in the gaps in the written archive.[94] My perspective is that an ethical approach requires recognizing absences but also piecing together as much of the picture as we can.

Kate Capshaw and Anna Mae Duane's collection *Who Writes for Black Children?* (2017) does substantial work in identifying how eighteenth- and nineteenth-century African American youth act "as readers, as curators, and as producers of print culture."[95] Enslaved youth with access to books were "the exception not the rule," especially when it comes to books produced by Africans in the Americas, but as Angela Sorby points out, history yields examples of enslaved adults creating texts for young people. For instance, Lucy Skipwith turned the Ten Commandments into rhyming couplets and asked for copies to distribute to enslaved children.[96] I build on these investigations into Black children's reading while exploring what these children themselves wrote, recovering what I can about writing by African American antislavery youth (chapter 3) and the conditions of Afro-Caribbean children's reading and copywork (chapter 4).

Along with tracing children's and adults' interactions with print culture where possible, Audra Diptee and David V. Trotman have suggested that scholars consider nontraditional sources when investigating childhoods in the Caribbean, including music, dance, and play, which have the "potential to offer access" to ideas that were "articulated in arenas that remained largely outside of colonial control."[97] When it comes to the ways that enslaved and free African youth were taught about ethics, it makes sense to consider the robust, intergenerational Afro-Caribbean culture of storytelling and singing, which was often intended, as Colleen Vasconcellos points out, for ethical education.[98]

This body of material is relevant to contemporary discussions following from Moten's book *The Universal Machine (consent not to be a single being)* (2018), which presents a sustained critique of Western ethical frameworks.[99] Moten responds to moments, usually considered aberrations in Levinas's work, where Levinas seems to suggest that people in non-Western cultures—namely, people dancing and singing at a funeral in Africa—are not fully ethical or serious, and that Judeo-Christian culture has a unique ethical orientation and potential to shape world history in the direction of ethics. Moten argues that such a predisposition toward hierarchy taints Levinas's understanding of the relation between the ethical subject and the other.

Moten instead emphasizes relations, epitomized by Black experience, that he labels "thingly": characterized by hybridity, interdependence, difference, openness, vulnerability, and refusal of mastery.[100] Playing on Levinas's "ethics as first philosophy," Moten proposes a way of engaging with ethical problems that he calls "sound before ethics."[101] With this intervention, he gestures toward responses to suffering that cannot be fully cordoned off from other parts of life as ethics but nonetheless have ethical significance. Improvisational practices and aesthetics of Black life illustrate the meaningful responses that emerge in embodied experiences and creative expressions. Such a capacious understanding of ethics is valuable for tracing ethical perspectives among enslaved African youth and parents. Storytelling, dance, and music, in addition to voicing anticolonial critique, surface as activities with a radical relational orientation.

A challenge is that many sources of these cultural forms are contemporary rather than historical, requiring scholars to engage with processes of preservation and memory. In this section, I introduce a method I use throughout this book of combining past and present materials to reconstruct Afro-Caribbean ethical teaching with an analysis of "Queen Mary," a protest song that emerged in the nineteenth century (possibly originally during enslavement). Performed in recent years by Afro-Caribbean schoolchildren, the song features the qualities of interdependence, openness, and refusal of mastery that Moten emphasizes, overlapping with the components of relational ethics I have been tracing. It conveys a belief in interdependence in its emphasis on collective action. The element of openness comes in the song's positioning of the protest, which must have involved deliberate planning, as directly responsive and improvisational. In addition to refusing to be mastered themselves, those engaging in the action are prompted to listen and relate rather than seek knowledge or mastery of the situation by asking questions. This relational posture makes the song adaptable to new circumstances, a feature that becomes even more apparent when we reconstruct the faint traces of its transmission over time.

The best-known version of "Queen Mary" commemorates the Fireburn, an 1878 labor riot in Danish St. Croix resulting from tensions initiated by the Labor Act of 1849, which introduced rules restricting Afro-Caribbean workers' bargaining ability following abolition on the English-speaking Danish islands. Such restrictions were perceived as uncomfortably similar to enslavement and especially threatening to young people's freedom. Because of the limited opportunities resulting from an economy focused on sugar as a monocrop, as well as high fees imposed by the government for travel papers, many of the island's Afro-Caribbean residents still lived and worked on plantations for low wages but lacked the minimal rations of enslavement. In 1878, the Central Sugar Factory, subsidized by the Danish government, opened near Christiansted and began paying higher wages, but the Labour Act allowed workers to change their employers only once per year, preventing many workers from benefitting.

That year, on Contract Day, a group gathered to demand better working conditions. The initially peaceful protest escalated when a rumor spread that a laborer had died in police custody. The workers set fire to plantations, sugar mills, and parts of the town of Frederiksted, with the goal of burning the government seat of Christiansted, the site of Bassin Jailhouse (Bassin being another name for the town). Among the leaders of the protests were three women referred to as "queens," Mary Thomas, Axeline Elizabeth Salomon, and Mathilda McBean, plus another woman, Susannah Abrahamsen, known as "Bottom Belly." These events led the governor-general of the Danish West Indies to declare a "state of siege."[102] More than eighty people were killed, including many workers. Another forty people were arrested—and the queens were sent to jail in Denmark. The protests, nevertheless, were effective; workers no longer had to sign yearly contracts, and after 1882, several estates were divided into small parcels of land that workers could buy, resulting in steady employment providing cane for the Central Sugar Factory.

Unsurprisingly, many European onlookers of the time did not view these events as ethically motivated, despite the positive outcome for the workers. An article in the Danish *Illustrated Times* suggests that the protesters were motivated by "evil passions."[103] Newspaper reports focus on white victims, including "women and children" who escaped to St. Thomas.[104] A chapbook published in Denmark, translated by the Arbejdermuseet (Worker's Museum), uses the dangers to white families as an ethical barometer, focusing on supposed violence to (abstract) children by the protesting "men":

> Look here how it burns
> Father, mother, taking flight
> The child raises his hands
> Towards a negro who is Black
> But he tears the little ones to pieces
> Oh! He is vile![105]

Although the queens are not mentioned in these texts, Mary Thomas's postriot prison records reveal she had been previously jailed for "abusing her child," a situation the museum suggests must be contextualized in light of colonizers' views that "European-Caribbeans had to 'teach' African-Caribbeans

TABLE I.1

"Queen Mary" (excerpt, dated 1880 by Arbejdermuseet)	"Queen Mary" (excerpt, dated 1848 by Maud Cuney-Hare)
Queen Mary, oh where you gon' go burn? Queen Mary oh where you gon' go burn? Don't ask me nothin' at all. Just give me the match and oil. Bassin Jailhouse, ah there the money there . . . Queen Mary, oh where you gon' go burn? Queen Mary, oh where you gon' go burn? Don't ask me nothin' at all. Just give me the match and trash. Bassin Jailhouse, ah there the money there . . . We gon' burn Bassin come down, And when we reach the factory, we'll burn am level down	Queen Mary say Bang-a-Lang-a, Bang-a-Lang, Bang-a-Lang, Mary say Bang-a-Lang-a, Cum out 'er yard, Bang-a-Lang. Oh, Queen Mary, will you hab a glass o' wine? Queen Mary, Wha' way we gwine burn? We gwine burn dare, gwine burn down Wes' End; We gwine burn down; all de way gwine burn down [. . .]

how to raise their children properly."[106] As we will see throughout this study, women and girls are targeted for various kinds of colonial control because of their role in biological and social reproduction; the recent use of the "Queen Mary" song with children suggests the female protester is remembered for her positive advocacy for her people's future.

The "Queen Mary" song in its current form, according to the Arbejdermuseet, can be dated to around 1880, but, intriguingly, an article in *The Crisis* by the trailblazing African American musicologist Maud Cuney-Hare from April 1933 records a different song with the same title and similar lines.[107] A comparison is shown in table I.1. Cuney-Hare posits that the song dates from the 1848 rebellion that led to the end of enslavement in the Danish Caribbean and that it may even derive from a previous slave rebellion in 1759.

It is possible that in her quest to "chronicle what the Negro and his music have been to the ages" (as Carter G. Woodson put it), Cuney-Hare or her informant mistook the date of the song she records, as she mentions Mary's transfer to Denmark, an event that happened in 1882.[108] However, Cuney-Hare had traveled to the Caribbean, and her records may also reflect residents' memories or mythologies related to the song. Either way, the different versions capture the importance of variation and adaptability in Afro-Caribbean musical traditions. In a 2005 interview, Jamaican poet and educator Louise

Bennett-Coverley refers to the technique of composing "new and topical words to old folk tunes," a possible method for transmitting "Queen Mary."[109] The existence of multiple Queen Mary songs—and possibly multiple female protesters called Mary conglomerated into a connected mythology over time— suggests that improvisation was a tool for transferring relational skills to new contexts and new generations.[110]

Framing the song as advancing a relational pedagogy—and as responding to historical forms of European pedagogy—is helpful in considering what it means in its historical and contemporary contexts. The question-and-answer format resembles teaching formats used by colonial educators, including Moravian missionaries, who used a book called *Questions and Answers* around the time of the 1848 rebellion in St. Croix (discussed in chapter 4). The 1880 "Queen Mary" refrain "don't ask me nothing at all," rejects the top-down, knowledge-based education that serves a colonial hierarchy in favor of experiential knowing workers have gained about how the system works, which can inform direct, protective, and retributive action.

The song is structured as a call and response, an interactive compositional technique deriving from West African culture. Asking Mary what to do and where to burn models a relational posture of listening for a person's (or community's) specific needs. While Mary emerges as a leader, there is an insistence on interdependence, as Mary urgently needs materials from listeners to do her work. Mary's actions express an underlying belief that freedom is a universal right, as well as what Leonard Harris calls an "insurrectionist ethics."[111] Yet the song does not emphasize overarching principles; rather, it provides an open, modifiable framework of interaction that can be applied to the needs of a particular situation.

The situation has continued to evolve. Even though the archive does not yield an unbroken genealogy from the past to the present, the 1880 song has become a vehicle for teaching cultural history to children, who participate in remembering and reembodying its revolutionary relational ethics. The shift from the "you" in the song's initial questioning, referring to Queen Mary, to the "we" at the end of the 1880 song opens space for listeners to join in the collective ethical action the song describes. This action stretches over generations, yielding an ethos that can be applied to new situations. Tami Navarro argues that the transmission has created an exchange in which "Queen Mary and the hearers of this song engage in a joint enterprise for Black freedom over space and time."[112] Children are important beneficiaries of the history the song represents, as well as torchbearers carrying its message forward.

Clear de Road: A Virgin Islands History Textbook (1983) substantiates that the song and related story yield intergenerational lessons, beginning its Fireburn chapter by pointing out that young people were present at the protests and have told the story to their descendants.[113] A fictional grandparent tells the story to his granddaughter, who responds by observing that "our struggles are not yet over."[114] A version of the 1880 song appears in the textbook with the cue to sing it "heavily accented and menacing," to embody the spirit of protest.[115]

From at least the 1990s, the song has been performed and recorded by schoolchildren. *Zoop! Zoop! Zoop! Traditional Music and Folklore of St. Croix, St. Thomas, and St. John* (1993) includes a recording of the song sung by young voices.[116] More recently, a YouTube video depicts an elementary school choir performing the song at the United Virgin Islands Friendship Day Celebration, under the direction of Neomie Toussaint-Williams.[117] The children act out the song, several of them carrying paper torches. Reflecting their continuation of Mary's activism, they use a variation of the "we" line that concludes the original song, answering in the first person: "Bassin Jailhouse, where *I* going to burn." This line change correlates with La Vaughn Belle and Jeannette Ehlers's choice to name their commemorative statue of Queen Mary in Denmark *I Am Queen Mary*.[118] This version of relationality (including interisland friendship) involves recognizing a past-present collectivity and intersubjectivity, opening space for new individuals within a long history of activism. Other combinations of past and present Afro-Caribbean materials (discussed in chapters 2 and 4) deepen our understanding of children's role in genealogies of ethical learning and resistance.

Continuing the pattern of this introduction, the chapters that follow interweave analyses of literary and cultural forms for children from the Atlantic world, tracing their engagement with enslavement and elements of relationality. Chapter 1, "Early Children's Literature and White Civility," expands on my discussion of *Sandford and Merton* to consider children's books that depict enslavement as a "crisis of connection" but constrain the resolution of these crises to the preservation of civility in white relationships. This notion of a limited responsibility proved attractive to those lobbying for enslavers' interests and gave rise to lasting children's literature formulas. A more radical framework emerges in a little-known book, *The Lobster's Voyage to the Brazils* (1808), which satirizes Britain's Abertura dos portos trade agreement with Brazil, which allowed the nation to continue profiting from enslavement after the abolition of the slave trade the previous year. This book anticipates Lewis Carroll's attention to the destructive politics of consumption in *Alice's Adventures in Wonderland* (1865).

Chapter 2, "Afro-Caribbean Stories in the Battle over Childhood," focuses on fictions of benevolence among enslavers and how enslaved people countered these false narratives by telling Anansi stories, folktales with origins in West Africa named after a shape-shifting trickster spider deity who often—though not always—appears in the tales. Starting from a suspect reference in which enslaver Matthew Lewis compares an Afro-Caribbean storyteller to "Little Goody Two Shoes," a schoolteacher in a Newbery children's book, I consider what the folktales he records from his plantation might have meant, both for promoting enslavers' interests after the abolition of the slave trade and transmitting enslaved women's strategies for resistance. Through his appropriation of the stories, Lewis advances a fantasy of enslaver and enslaved working toward allegedly ethical ends, with children as beneficiaries. Looking beyond Lewis's relational distortions, I argue that the stories reveal how female storytellers called out colonizers' narrow understanding of ethical responsibility.

Chapter 3, "Taking Responsibility for the Other in Sugar Boycott Books," considers how the children's books created during the first large-scale modern consumer protest movement—the sugar boycott—depart from the images of invasion and contamination of the family that appear in adult protest books, building instead on genres imagining connections with people and processes understood as other: the street cry narrative (depicting exotic strangers and goods in the marketplace) and it-narrative (told in the voice of personified products of manufacture). While these texts insist that consumption requires ethical awareness, responsibility to the other becomes entangled with colonialism. Conversely, the activism of a Juvenile Anti-Slavery Society founded by Black children in Pittsburgh exhibits a different sort of strategic consumption: positively supporting the work of African American periodicals.

Chapter 4, "The Ethics of Circulation in the Enslaved and Colonized West Indies," considers how the notion of responsibility for others across distance yielded colonial aspirations to intervene in Afro-Caribbean children's lives. The assumption that children's literature was a moral good narrowed questions of ethical relationality to matters of book distribution and access. I identify the universal vision of childhood embraced by would-be influencers in the Caribbean—the hard-laboring schoolchild—and attempt to recover the impact of this vision on historical children. I track how this ideal thwarted relational approaches to children's literature development by investigating how US Moravian educators in the Danish Caribbean moved from using books tailored to local contexts to English books imagined to be universally applicable to youth around the globe. Conversely, manuscript materials, including a hand-drawn map created by Afro-Caribbean teacher, show how local cultures push against this incursion of the global.

In chapter 5, "Traces of Atlantic Relations in Early Global Children's Literature," I track the circulation of English-language children's literature that promoted an ethics informed by Atlantic enslavement, starting with the Religious Tract Society's circulation of children's books about enslaved Africans to Asia. I then investigate how limited visions of global relationality inform Frederick Warne's Round the Globe Library, a series predating Warne's better-known release of Golden Age books by Burnett and others. The series contains Baker's *The Babes in the Basket* (1859), featuring an Afro-Caribbean woman based on a doll in her daughter Louise's dollhouse. Baker's book diverges from objectification of enslaved people by humanizing the doll but subsumes the Black woman's needs in a progressive fantasy of incorporation, anticipating white feminist fixations on Black respectability. Although I notice traces of ethical relationality in these texts, the focus on universal ethics results in a far less relational version of global children's literature than might have been. Madhusudan Mukhopadhyay's *Kathataranga*, a Bengali translation of *Sandford and Merton*, offers a chance to consider anticolonial counternarratives.

My conclusion, "Relating Ethically in the Archives," reflects on a question that runs through the book: how to take a relational perspective when studying the past. Archives often reflect the preferred stories of the powerful; for instance, records of post-emancipation colonial educators tout the educational failure of formerly enslaved people, a racist argument aiming to lighten the ethical responsibility of colonizers. Yet archives are also spaces of difference, and traces of other viewpoints exist. I discuss how an image hanging in the Codrington College library in Barbados and an archive of Anansi stories told by children point to storytelling, music, and dance as ethical resources.

When working from an ethos of relationality, it follows that connections might begin to emerge that point to many areas of the world and of study—too many for one scholar to cover. However, embracing unlimited difference aligns closely with my scholarly aspirations. Relationality, after all, emerged to challenge universalizing ethical frameworks. Theodor Adorno, as summarized by Butler in *Giving an Account of Oneself*, points out that postures of universality emerge when collective ethical consensus can no longer be counted on—in other words, when people become aware of diversity. Because the collective ethos is no longer shared, it can "impose its claim to commonality only through violent means."[119] Such a statement is pertinent to the history of English-language children's literature and its global transmission.

A genuinely principled ethics of relationality must push back against the violence that compels everyone to adopt the ethics of colonizing cultures. This book will illustrate how British and US children's literature frequently present simplified, even saccharine, ethical frameworks. In doing so, it aims to cultivate a more direct engagement with the histories of enslavement and colonization, one rooted in listening to the diverse experiences of those most affected. For instance, while Afro-Caribbean storytelling traditions are a small part of my study, their influence expanded significantly after Caribbean independence movements and continues to thrive through writers of color who are charting new paths in children's literature. It is my hope that the field will fervently support scholars who study these interventions, charting a truly relational future for children's literature studies.

CHAPTER 1

Early Children's Literature and White Civility

The institution of slavery, with its circulation of people and products to and from the Americas, was a major context for the development of children's literature in English—both in terms of the scale of the development and the kinds of stories told.[1] Some of the earliest impacts of British enslavement on children's books are reflected in the first English-language novel specifically dedicated to children, Sarah Fielding's *The Governess* (1749), which depicts a kind, gentle girl named Jenny Peace creating harmony among her misbehaving boarding-school classmates and teaching them how to be ethical, peaceful people. Little remarked upon by scholars is that Jenny is attending the school because her guardian aunt Mrs. Newman has gone to Jamaica to tend the family's estate. As Jenny tells it, "After my mamma's death, my Aunt Newman, my father's sister, took the care of me; but being obliged to go to Jamaica, to settle some affairs relating to an estate she is possessed of there, she took with her my Cousin Harriet, her only daughter, and left me under the care of the good Mrs. Teachum till her return."[2] This context suggests that Jenny's tuition is funded at least partially by the sale of Jamaican products, making her tenure at the school—and her pacifist lessons—dependent on slave labor.[3]

Beyond this short description, only the sketchiest account is given of Jenny's aunt.[4] Cousin Harriet is described in even sketchier detail (I make what I can of her later). Yet Fielding had a habit of conveying much information in small details. Given her penchant for allegorical names—Jenny Peace, Mrs. Teachum, Dolly Friendly—the most meaningful aspect of the description of Jenny's relatives might be their name, Newman, though what Fielding considers new about them is ambiguous. Likely, Newman signifies the relative newness of the aunt's activities: owning property in the West Indies, producing goods there, and traveling to the colonies to attend to one's business.[5]

To be sure, the British had been working to colonize Jamaica since Oliver Cromwell ordered its invasion in 1655, but infighting in the colonial government and near constant defense against the Spanish, French, and (most freshly for Fielding) a group of escaped Africans and Indigenous people known as Maroons meant that attempts to profit from the island were frequently interrupted.[6] The eighteenth century saw the emergence of a stronger colonial government and the rise of the sugar industry as Jamaica's main source of income, which meant a greater reliance on enslavement and increases in plantation size with greater need for oversight. Jenny's aunt may have been there for this purpose, making her a participant in what was rapidly becoming a new way of life for British and American people of means and raising questions about the impact of this way of life on the ethical values passed to children.

Many of our critical paradigms for how enslavement shaped English literature's ethical positions relate to novels for an adult audience. Most significantly, Edward Said's analysis of Jane Austen's *Mansfield Park* (1814) contends that a similar offstage plot, in which heroine Fanny Price's wealthy uncle Sir Thomas Bertram goes to tend the family's failing estate in Antigua, ties British ethical values to "colonial possessions."[7] The novel, Said argues, blends recognition of this context with its avoidance. Fanny is mistreated in her relatives' home until Sir Thomas returns from improving the estate, implying that peaceful relations must be grounded in the management strategies emerging from colonial "possession of territory."[8] Beyond this prioritizing of white domestic tranquility over the well-being of the enslaved, ethical violations cannot be discussed without threatening family harmony. Fanny's attempts to speak with Sir Thomas about enslavement yield "dead silence," suggesting to Said that "in order more accurately to read works like *Mansfield Park*, we have to see [these texts] . . . as resisting or avoiding that other setting" to preserve white families' peace, even if it cannot be repressed fully.[9]

This tension between recognition and avoidance of enslavement is a common thread in early children's books like *The Governess* that focus on peaceful relationships between white friends and family while alluding to a broader sphere of ethical relationality or responsibility. A useful term for describing versions of ethics based on seemingly positive values like peacefulness and harmony in conflation with whiteness is "white civility," defined by Daniel Coleman as a "structurally ambivalent" British cultural practice that "involves the creation of justice and equality" and "simultaneously creates borders to the sphere in which justice and equality are maintained."[10] This ambivalence, Coleman argues, results from the association of the "moral-ethical concept of a (relatively) peaceful order" with "the temporal notion of civilization as progress" central to "the colonial mission."[11] White civility has some deceptive hallmarks of relationality, like an emphasis on interconnectedness that prioritizes collective harmony and may pride itself on a welcoming (if condescending) attitude toward difference; however, it is not open to friction, conflicts, or unexpected demands, meaning that it is not responsive to injustice as experienced by people outside of the privileged group.

The Governess reflects a struggle between an ethics based on white civility and a fundamental relationality that perceives the injustice of enslavement. Unlike Austen's novel, in which Bertram returns to influence his niece, Fielding's text does not depict any contact between Jenny and her aunt, making a Said-like reading in which Jenny's ethics derive from the management of her aunt's colonial possessions unsatisfying. Instead, Jenny's deceased mother is her model for an ethics based on connecting one's well-being with that of others. Building on her mother's teachings, Jenny's ethics insist on a fundamental relationality, which Simone Drichel explains (via Niobe Way, Alisha Ali, Carol Gilligan, and Pedro Noguera's book *The Crisis of Connection*) as the notion that "humans are inherently responsive and relational beings," responsible for the well-being of those around them.[12] Drichel argues that relationality "challenges the Cartesian conception of discrete, self-founding subjects—so stubbornly persistent in the Western imagination—and instead asserts the primacy of relationships in the constitution of subjectivity."[13] The influence of Jenny's mother further connects her ethical proficiencies to the experience of maternal care, anticipating feminist care ethics.

For Drichel, challenges to or interruptions of relationality create a "crisis of connection" (again, language that she borrows from Way et al.), which she identifies with modern fantasies of individuality and what she views as their inevitable result: a feeling of loneliness and deprivation. *The Governess*, though written many centuries before Drichel's analysis, is also preoccupied with crises of connection, beginning with a fight between schoolgirls. Jenny is determined to do "the good work of making all her companions friends," offering herself as an ethical model.[14] Her version of selfhood is founded on the importance of others' happiness to her own. Peace, understood in relational terms, is built into her very name.

In this context, Jenny's connections to the Atlantic economy—with its wars and brutal treatment of enslaved people—may seem startling considering the text's representation of her as the poster girl for peace, albeit a pacifism that manifests as peace of mind. We might be reminded, however, that trade was heralded in the eighteenth-century English press as a means to promote peaceful relationships among nations, including in the passage from Joseph Addison's "The Royal Exchange" (1711) cited in my introduction.[15] Addison's vision of global trade as a guarantor of peaceful relationships between cultures had tremendous influence and afterlife, including in children's books, though his view of trade is exclusionary and fictive. Trade set Britain at constant war with other colonizing nations, and the establishment of larger plantations in Jamaica served as a catalyst for the Maroon wars.

Although there is no Fanny Price in Fielding's text to expose the hypocrisy of global ethics that do not take enslavement into account, there are indications that Fielding's vision of trade was not so sunny. Like many of her contemporaries writing novels for adult or mixed-age audiences, she leaves out that enslaved people were exploited, dehumanized, and abused for the profit of British families, but a studious look at the text reveals its fixation on uneasy ethical issues posed by emerging British lifestyles dependent on the labor of enslaved people: the increasing economic value of consumer desire with its attendant dangers and excesses, the treatment of servants and enslaved people (along with the nationalistic need to insist that *Britons* will never be enslaved), the blurring of boundaries between humans and objects, and the injustice of captivity. Even though the text is set in an insular community of girls and the worst aspects of enslavement happen off stage, these elements suggest that *The Governess* assumes some of the ethical burden of the relational web that it sets up with reference to Jenny's relatives.

Nonetheless, Jenny's relationships with enslaved people do not get equal treatment with other connections she makes in the text. In her advocacy for peace, Jenny is most disturbed by the crisis of connection between the girls at her school. This limited relationality coheres with her mother's lessons, which prompt her to prioritize her relationship with her brother over her pet cat. By incorporating limits to ethical response, *The Governess* begins to fashion an ethics of white civility. As we will see, Fielding takes the crisis of transatlantic enslavement and distills it into comparatively simple scenarios: family members being separated and reunited, boarding schoolgirls becoming friends. With such plots, she creates ways of working with the challenges that enslavement and colonization posed to ethical relationships that other British authors would find workable, having a lasting impact on books that would become Golden Age classics. In Frances Hodgson Burnett's *A Little Princess* (1905), a similar heroine develops an ethical code at her boarding school, with comparable failures of perception.

Though they are briefly mentioned, Jenny's aunt and cousin initiate another tradition that would become a mainstay of English children's literature. Stories like Thomas Day's *The History of Sandford and Merton* (1783–1789) (discussed in my introduction)—pairing English child characters with children, often relatives, who hail from the colonies—would become staples of children's literature by the early nineteenth century. By the time the most famous book of this type, Burnett's *The Secret Garden*, was published in serialized form in 1910, multiple books had worked out a set of conventional plot dynamics based on familial relationships strained by trade and empire-related travel. Texts like Barbara Hofland's *Matilda; or The Barbadoes Girl* (1816) and A. Selwyn's *The Little Creoles* (1820) represent characters more fully connected to the West Indian colonies, which arguably precede India and Africa as the locus of alterity in British children's books.

These books expose children to racial difference but more fully adopt the values of white civility by limiting ethical obligation to crises of connection within white families. Their approach to Atlantic relationality is recuperative, knitting back together families (and, in some cases, literally, humans) that are fractured by transatlantic trade. They do this by enshrining white childhood as a plastic state easily molded by children's books and what turns out to be their key topos, the English climate and seasons. Anticipating Burnett's *The Secret Garden*, texts guided by this idea depict the reacclimatization of the white creole child to ensure peaceful interaction with family members, at best leaving enslaved children to suffer in the margins. At worst, they advocate the embrace of enslaver practices and racial categories by the British mainland population as a solution to the crises of connection involving white families.

A more profound representation of the relational crises brought on by enslavement and related transatlantic trade, I argue, appears in *The Lobster's Voyage to the Brazils* (1808), which presents a dystopian vision of the connections between British civil life and the Atlantic world in the form of an absurd children's "papillonnade," Mary V. Jackson's name for animal narratives capitalizing on the popularity of William Roscoe's *The Butterfly's Ball and the Grasshopper's Feast* (1802).[16] *The Lobster's Voyage* features sentient sea animals who forge unequal, aggressive interpersonal connections while using each other as objects and food. The ambivalent depiction of animal sentience, in contrast to Jenny's mother's rejection of the pet cat, makes for a radical confrontation with enslavement as an ethical crisis. Lewis Carroll's exposure to the genre, I argue, might have influenced his disturbing, comical meditations on consumption in *Alice's Adventures in Wonderland* (1865). The sea creatures of *The Lobster's Voyage* and *Alice* engage with the unethical exercise of power and objectification underlying transatlantic slave economics, which the other texts in this chapter sugarcoat, simplify, and sidestep.

The Limits of Jenny's Peace

We can apprehend *The Governess*'s investment in a crisis of connection from its first pages, which give "an account of a fray, begun and carried out for the sake of an apple: in which are shown the sad effects of rage and anger."[17] The apple in question is the biggest in the barrel, which causes the girls to long for it with "desiring Eyes."[18] Jenny Peace has been entrusted to divide the apples and when the girls accost her with their errant desire, she throws the apple over the fence. The girls respond by getting into a pigtail-pulling brawl. Their governess, Mrs. Teachum, who is absent during the fight, gives the girls an unspecified punishment and withdraws. But Jenny is determined to "bring her School-Fellows to be heartily reconciled."[19]

Although the details may be antiquated, this fight for the biggest, shiniest item feels thoroughly recognizable—perhaps because we live in the consumerist world that eighteenth-century Britons were beginning to build. Other authors, most notably Maria Edgeworth in "The Purple Jar," address consumer desires in children with lessons prompting them to resist the pressure to buy shiny products. But while Edgeworth focuses on an isolated incident of consumer disappointment, Jenny's reasoning resembles scholarship like Drichel's that points out the high cost to well-being when people focus on economic wants to the detriment of relational obligations. She exhorts her schoolmates, "Don't you lie awake at nights, and fret and vex yourself, because you are angry with your school-fellows? Are not you restless and uneasy, because you cannot find a safe method to be revenged on them, without being punished yourself?"[20] Jenny's answer to the problem is self-interested—far from a sufficient course in ethics—but it articulates the relational concept of interconnectedness in its insistence that the well-being of individuals is connected to that of others: "Whereas by endeavouring to please and love each other, the End is Happiness to ourselves, and Joy to everyone around us."[21] The text reinforces this message by having each girl, beginning with

Jenny, narrate the change to her emotional health following her newfound understanding of interconnectedness.

As with *Sandford and Merton* (discussed in the introduction), the text uses a relational format, emphasizing listening to others' voices, experiences, and stories to promote responses that are grounded in specific contexts. Jenny's autobiographical tale foregrounds her mother's role in establishing her sense of relationality, which is done by cultivating an atmosphere of "perfect Love and Harmony" between Jenny and her brother.[22] Although Jenny's mother promotes what Enlightenment thinkers were coming to see as rational and universal ethical rules, such as avoiding lying, she teaches Jenny and her brother to resolve conflict by "exerting to . . . prefer the other's pleasures to our own," an endeavor that requires attentive listening and awareness of context.[23] With its context-dependent understanding of ethics, Jenny's autobiography anticipates utilitarianism, as well as feminist arguments that ethical awareness arises from the experience of caring and being cared for, especially by mothers and mothering persons. As Mary Jeanette Moran notes, the body of thought organized under the rubric of feminist care ethics understands selfhood as relational and "prioritize[s] the creation and sustenance of relationships between people" over abstract principles.[24]

Jenny's maternal training is effective in prompting her to define herself in relational terms and strengthening her sense of compassion, but she and her mother come into conflict when Jenny's pet cat is stolen and tortured to death. Jenny comments that she "seemed to miss part of myself in its Absence."[25] After the cat's mistreatment, her mother initially affirms that "Sentiments of Good-nature and Compassion" are "strongly implanted, they will extend their Influence even to the least Animal" (anticipating similar sentiments by Jeremy Bentham, discussed in my introduction).[26] But when Jenny's inability to help the cat causes "inconsolable" sadness, Jenny's mother stops listening and imposes limits on ethical obligation by directing Jenny to privilege her relationships with her family.[27] Jenny must cheer up so that she can avoid a different crisis of connection: not being "fit to converse with" her brother and do her duty to her family by being a "Companion and Delight."[28]

Although this shift from cat to brother follows a program of extending one's caring to wider concentric circles, a feature of the stoic educational philosophy Pamela L. Cheek sees as underlying the text, it feels like a narrowing, given that the cat must be abandoned in the process.[29] Introducing limits to relationality is a significant move at a time when British people were investing in enslavement. The avoidance of suffering to keep harmony within a family presents a logic of white civility, a phenomenon Anne Helen Petersen argues prioritizes peace between white friends and family by sidestepping suffering and injustice.[30] Jenny's mother's ethical limits run in tension with Jenny's difficulty in getting over her cat, bringing tortured beings whose situation one cannot immediately change into the ethical purview of the text. This broader relationality persists in *The Governess* through subtle references to enslavement.

It is, indeed, within this narration about Jenny's duty to her immediate family that we learn of her West Indian connections, raising questions about the relationship between her ethical worldview and the institution of slavery. We might begin our inquiry into the significance of these connections by asking a simpler question: Why must Jenny go to boarding school at all, rather than travel to Jamaica? There are a few reasons why it might have been considered inappropriate to bring extra children to the West Indies. The most obvious is the mortality rate. Susan Dwyer Amussen reports that in addition to the many enslaved Africans who died in the Caribbean, "Europeans carried no resistance to tropical diseases and died of them in great numbers."[31] Another reason is that schooling was less available than in England, although (as I discuss in chapter 4) schools and reading material were more available in the West Indies than English children's books acknowledged. Neither of these reasons explains why Jenny stays and Cousin Harriet goes. The only reason given is that Harriet is her aunt's "only Daughter," which suggests that affection, finances, or the line of inheritance plays a role.[32] As Daniel Livesay has argued, the family arrangements that emerged from British involvement in the Caribbean caused a number of families to consider which members were privileged, exposing fault lines of gender, race, and class—though it is not entirely clear who is privileged here.[33]

It *is* clear whose *story* is privileged, suggesting that ethics for children came to be situated at a remove from enslavement and colonialism to allow for some level of distance and deniability. Jenny Peace becomes a fixture of English children's literature, while Cousin Harriet is a weakly presented double, even if the pairing of Jenny and Harriet has echoes in better-known pairings such as Day's Tommy Merton / Harry Sandford and Burnett's Mary Lennox / Dickon Sowerby.[34] Though gendered female in important ways, Jenny resembles the easygoing Moor child, Dickon, of *The Secret Garden*, and the peaceable country boy, Harry, of *Sandford and Merton*, who are contrasted with Tommy and Mary. Like Jenny, these characters are taught ethics by nurturing English country mothers rather than servants or enslaved people, whose care was devalued when it came to ethical development, reinforcing Parvati Raghuram's point that "the meaning, nature and value of care are all deeply racialized."[35] (Jenny's relationship with her aunt, meanwhile, is replayed somewhat in Burnett's pairing of Sara Crewe with her Africa-venturing father Captain Crewe in *A Little Princess*, which I discuss later, though Jenny has a much easier time at boarding school.) By juxtaposing Jenny to a child who goes to the Caribbean, the text anticipates a motif connecting ethical behavior in British children to geographical immobility and racialized Anglo civility.

Jenny's narrative prominence, and Harriet's lack thereof, indeed has less to do with the inconvenience of taking a child to the Caribbean than with what Elizabeth Dillon calls the logic of "social reproduction," or reproduction of the social relations of capitalism, which feminist Marxists have shown to be in an unstable relationship with biological reproduction.[36] Dillon argues that social reproduction in the eighteenth century was strongly shaped by the Atlantic economy, in which colonizers strove to keep production separate from consumption—the paradigmatic example being the sugar industry. She notes that the enslaved labor force and relations of production in the Caribbean had to be reproduced for its industries to survive, but the cultural traditions seen as worthy of reproduction were those of the metropole, whose inhabitants' "lives primarily register[ed] as consumption."[37] She suggests that "while race slavery was designed to eradicate the possibility of social reproduction among black populations . . . the colonial plantation world was viewed as inimical to white [creole] social reproduction as well."[38] Born in England, Harriet is not literally a creole—a white or mixed-race person born in the Caribbean—but it is the immobile Jenny who gets to have an influence on the kinds of childhoods created by British children's literature. Jenny, indeed, is prolifically reproductive; after encouraging the girls at the school to copy her demeanor, she writes letters to produce the same results in subsequent students, mimicking the way that the children's book, as a new bourgeois commercial invention, tried to affect its readers by inspiring emulation.

One reason that white creole culture was coming to be considered unworthy of reproduction in children is that creoles were considered too close to the incivilities that came with the extraction of labor from enslaved people. As Amussen points out, British people in the Caribbean were learning to be enslavers, an education that rubbed off on their children.[39] Many English children's books took the view that such an environment was damaging for white children and aimed to contain these abusive behaviors to the adult generation directly involved in managing the enslaved, while nonetheless ensuring that those involved in those practices were accepted at home. Such containment, as we will see, was considered part of the business.

Jenny does not need this containment. However, the ethical problems posed by British enslavement find their way into the text. Although no real enslaved people are mentioned (the text's fairy-tale version of enslavement will be considered later), Jenny's emphasis on relationality calls attention to the treatment of servants, yielding conventions replayed in later texts about British enslavement. The most troublesome character, Sukey, has ethical deficiencies deriving from crises of connection that emerge when people wield economic power over others, which would later come to be associated with white creoles, such as Tommy Merton, educated by enslaved and enslaving women. Sukey was spoiled as a child, largely by her nurse, and taught violence from a young age: "When I was but Four Years old, if ever any thing crossed me, I was taught to beat it, and be revenged of it, even tho' it could not feel."[40] Fielding's insinuation that being cared for by a servant instead of a mother stifles children's ethical impulses derives from racist and classicist ideas about servant women, later applied to enslaved women.

Sukey's education in unrestrained passion and violence toward objects transfers to her treatment of people. She confesses that she regularly beat one of her servants: "I had a little Play-fellow, in a Child of one of my Papa's Servants, who was to be entirely under my Command. This Girl I used to abuse and beat, whenever I was out of Humour . . . I thought the Distance between us was so great, that I never considered that she could feel."[41] In addition to suggesting that "distance" in station is not an excuse for abandoning ethical obligations, this scene makes Sukey an early version of what would come to be a common type in children's literature: a white creole child who has witnessed the institution of slavery and needs to be reformed. This type appears in *Sandford and Merton* and later texts on both sides of the Atlantic, including in the character of Henrique, Little Eva's cousin, in Harriet Beecher Stowe's *Uncle Tom's Cabin* (1852). The fact that this scene occurs without Sukey having ever witnessed enslavement indicates the projection at work in British attempts to disassociate themselves from such behavior. The aristocracy had a long-established tradition of mistreating servants before going to the Americas.

Reflecting the evolving fiction of white civility, *The Governess* casts these dominating behaviors, which British enslavers and their children were developing in the context of enslavement, as *other* by insisting that Sukey's behavior is not appropriate for an English girl, especially among her equals. Because her bad behavior to servants unfolds in England, rather than Jamaica, Fielding relies on nationalistic sentiments to back up her disapproval, dodging the implications of the nation's growing reliance on a slave-based economy. In characterizing Sukey's dilemma as an issue of confusing her maid with an object, Fielding suggests that *English* persons, however abject, can be disidentified from objects and, by extension, from enslaved people. Englishness, in other words, was meant to be cut off from the dehumanizing aspects of British enslavement.[42] In this sense, the scene that opens the book, in which the girls become so identified with an apple that they are willing to fight for it becomes a parable of not relating with objects too strongly and of non-self-objectification. An opposite sort of food narrative, we will see, appears in *The Lobster's Voyage to the Brazils*, where the animal characters shift from sentient beings to objects to food during their transatlantic travels.

Yet if a major thrust of the text is to resist identification with objects, or viewing others as objects, many aspects of the book counteract this message. The apple scene is seemingly a lesson in Lockean self-possession, in that the girls emerge from a state of war and consent in "one voice" to form a peaceful society together. John Locke's model of contractual governance is based on the intertwining of (what he frames as natural) individual rights with the preservation of property, including property in the self. In *The Governess*, the property—the apple—is not protected; it disappears before the contract is made. Jenny points out that the girls' adoption of peaceful behavior will allow them to better preserve their property in the future. Their property in themselves, secured by their civil treatment of others, becomes most important because it is the security of this property through civility that gives them the ability to reflect on their conditional future property.

Metaphorically and actually, though, these basic forms of property possible to possess as an English girl cannot be separated from the property that Jenny's aunt goes to manage: the human kind. For Locke, property in oneself gains its foremost significance in comparison with the condition of enslavement—one is defined through the other.[43] Yet in the transatlantic economy, multiple forms of property circulate and can be turned into each other. When money from a slave estate buys boarding school tuition, which buys apples, tossing the apples over the fence becomes a refusal to acknowledge the chain of possession that undergirds one's training in self-possession more than a renunciation of it. We see another version of this refusal to acknowledge the connection between self-possession, enslavement, and wealth in the passive way that the text describes Aunt Newman's travel. She is "obliged to go" (it is not clear by whom), a phrase that obscures Newman's responsibility for the exploitative practices that go with owning colonial property, as well as the benefits she reaps. The roundabout grammar, "to an estate she is possessed of," makes Newman the object of the estate as much as it is an object of hers, hinting at an entanglement of selfhood, property, and enslavement.

Allowing for these kinds of disassociation, the objects producing consumer desire in the book are conspicuously organic English products (apples, milk) or frivolous items referencing longer-established Middle Eastern trade routes. Nanny Spruce's desire for "finery" inhibits her ability to love her schoolmates, because they are just as fine and she no longer stands out.[44] The most troublesome item is Betty Ford's "scarlet damask," a type of Middle Eastern cloth named after Damascus, a city on the silk road.[45] In an embedded fairy tale, "The Princess Hebe," the evil, vaguely Orientalized fairy Brunetta has an attachment to "gaudy furniture."[46] Conversely, a trip to a dairy farm shows it to be idealistically run by an old English woman and her daughter. Although the representation of commercial exchange seems to offer a clear-cut value system in which Middle Eastern trade products are gauche and English products scrubbed of controversy, the connections between English tradespeople and ethically compromised transatlantic trade are conveyed by the treat served alongside the farmers' humble offerings: sugar. The source of the sugar, unlike the cream and the damask, is not commented on, but Britain's reliance on the West Indies for this good was climbing; the Caribbean would supply 90 percent of the nation's sugar by the end of the century.

Although *The Governess* omits any representation of Caribbean production, British colonizers and Afro-Caribbeans *did* reproduce—biologically, socially, and economically. Amussen notes that the social relations that emerged from enslavement "returned to England along with the sugar that became the colonies' primary export."[47] Even if the text largely keeps the peace by obscuring the colonial sources of products, enslavement appears in the most prominent tale that Jenny tells: "The Story of the Cruel Giant Barbarico, the Good Giant Benefico, and the Little Pretty Dwarf Mignon." This story about an enslaved person (albeit set in Wales rather than the Caribbean) makes the text's most dramatic argument about the violence ensuing from a lack of awareness of relationality. It toggles, however, between two ways of thinking about enslavement, as an unjust form of captivity requiring liberation and a trial producing virtues that aid in developing white rituals of civility.

Set in an exoticized Welsh mountain landscape with a veneer of fantasy that the text casts as code for the emotional life of upper- and middle-class English girls, the tale is a cross between a slave uprising and a prototype of the "grateful" or "faithful slave" trope. This trope features a fictional enslaved person who patiently suffers, carries out a rescue of his enslavers, and chooses to serve a supposedly benevolent master. The main character, the "patient slave," is named Mignon, "stolen" as a child and kept by Barbarico, a giant described as "most miserable as well as the most wicked Creature."[48] The giant engages in "insufferable Slavery," because he fails to understand how his happiness is dependent on others.[49]

These events seem to indicate a clear stance against enslavement; in a one-man rebellion, Mignon strangles Barbarico with a "magic Fillet" he finds in his dungeons.[50] Yet the text strangles itself in relating this event. The inscription on the fillet reads (in part):

Wouldst thou from the Rage be free

Of the Tyrant's Tyranny . . .

PATIENCE bids, make no Delay:

Haste to bind him, haste away.[51]

The strangeness of "Patience" bidding Mignon to make haste only makes sense in relation to Mrs. Teachum's insistence, which she makes Jenny relay to the girls, that the fairy tale be read allegorically, the incongruous moral being that "by Patience you will overcome all Difficulties."[52] When we consider enslavement as a referent, the message is mixed: haste is required to overcome its extreme injustice, but patience marks the virtuous person who civilly accepts a subordinate place in the hierarchy until incremental change can be made or the hardship ends naturally. There is a tension between the need to protect others and the need to discard emotions that threaten civil behavior and ties. The text does not settle on a clear ethics or temporality when it comes to enslavement; Mignon seeks a "speedy Deliverance" but waits until another character, Fidus, has been captured, to attempt his rescue of both.[53]

While we could read Fielding's story of enslavement as reflecting a common philosophical practice of using "slavery" as a metaphor while ignoring actual enslaved people, it is worth remembering that Fielding names a historical context for her novel in sending Jenny's aunt to Jamaica. Fielding was writing soon after the conclusion of the First Maroon War in 1839–1840, in which British enslavers in Jamaica "negotiated treaties with the [largely antislavery] Maroon communities" that required them to accept the slave system, transforming "longtime rebels into the King's most loyal friends" and making it safe for women like Jenny's aunt to travel there.[54] Until the eruption of the Second Maroon War in the 1790s, the Maroons became "Britain's favored blacks" who "to conserve the king's order . . . captured and shot slaves who ran away or led rebellions in Jamaica."[55] The text's representation of Mignon as a heroic enslaved person affords some sympathy for antislavery rebellion, but the text also supports the transformation of rebellion into (more patient) endurance and survival—perhaps a version of the qualified support for the downtrodden that Coleman names as a feature of white civility.

Given this context, it is significant that the rebel Mignon becomes the subject of Benefico, a noble giant who inspires voluntary fealty through kindness.[56] In both name and attitude, Benefico anticipates a character type that would become popular in texts rationalizing enslavement in the 1780s and 1790s: the benevolent enslaver, a figure whose gentleness supposedly renders enslavement—sometimes euphemized as servitude—benign.[57]

The text compares the girl listeners more closely with Benefico than the smaller Mignon, implying that their ethical obligations as English girls involve their power over others and the need to act benevolently. After Mrs. Teachum intervenes to make sure the tale is not a vehicle for subversive fantasy, Jenny conveys *her* moral: "Whenever you have any Power, you must follow the Example of the Giant *Benefico*, and do Good with it."[58] Little girls did not have power over many people, except servants and the enslaved; Sukey's story of beating her servant directly follows this story. The idea that English girls must use their power civilly, we will see, is replayed later in *Matilda; or the Barbadoes Girl*, where it would explicitly refer to power over enslaved people.

White civility, however, is primarily designed not to minimize harm to those with less power but to ease relations between white family members and associates. Enslavement is transformed through allegory into the need for British girls to be free of angry passions. In this sense, it matters that Jenny is telling the tale to the girls at the school so they can get along with each other by adopting compatible ways of dealing with emotions, rather than inviting them to reform their behavior at home or abroad. Reflecting this context, the ethical questions surrounding Mignon's treatment get transformed when the text clarifies his familial relationship to Fidus's lover, Amata; he is revealed to be the long-lost brother of this British woman. To the extent that he is a rebelling slave, his rebellion can be couched as that of a Briton wrongfully put upon by Barbarico, exercising the supposed freedom of his blood, rather than that of a Maroon.[59] The story's setting in Wales rather than Jamaica connects Mignon to other Welsh giant-slaying heroes, such as Jack the Giant Killer and King Arthur, who by this point had been claimed by the English. Mignon, by implication, is part of the (white) British national family and therefore considered worthy of benevolent governance rather than barbaric enslavement. Jenny Peace is a Benefico-like figure, but her ending is similar to Mignon's: after reconciling the girls, she goes back to her aunt's English estate where the rift in her family occasioned by the trip to the West Indies is shown to be small and easily mended.[60] The impulse to consider characters who could be interpreted as creole as white and as family would be taken up in other children's books.

The limited relational ethics of Jenny Peace get reprised in a Golden Age classic of children's literature: Burnett's *A Little Princess*. The main character, Sara Crewe, plays a similar role to Fielding's heroine: she is an orphan (for the majority of the story), tells fairy tales, is an ethical example for her fellow boarding school students, and develops stoic practices for disciplining her feelings, which allow her to act like a little soldier while being "a princess inside."[61] Unlike Jenny, Sara was born in the (East Indian) colonies, yet the text has a similar opening gambit for explaining her arrival at school; she cannot travel with her father and must return to England for school because "the climate of India [is] very bad for children."[62] Although her mother died when she was born, she shares with Jenny a penchant for settling quarrels among the other girls, without ever making herself "disagreeable."[63]

Written more than a decade and a half after Fielding's novel, *A Little Princess* covers similar ethical ground. A key plotline asserts that child servants (at least those born in England) are worthy of kind treatment; Sara insists to her unkind teacher Miss Minchin that Becky, the "bounden slave" who works in the school, is, like her, a "little girl."[64] Sara's sympathies, like Jenny's, extend to the poor and animals, even her doll. Sara explains her desire to do charity to friends and strangers alike by declaring that she is "one of the populace," or the common people, even if she aspires to the manners of a princess.[65]

Burnett broaches, in a similarly minimal way, the topic of ethical obligations to people at a distance. In the chapter "The Other Side of the Wall," Sara asserts that she has taken ethical responsibility for the "Indian gentleman," Mr. Carrisford, who lives next door, saying, "I have adopted him for a friend. You can do that with people you never speak to at all. You can just watch them, and think about them and be sorry for them, until they seem almost like relations."[66] Despite this extension of (pity-centered) ethical connection, in which the wall poses questions about how ethical responsibility functions across cultural barriers and physical distance, the text narrows the child's relationality by pointing out that the neighbor is not Indian but English and by making Carrisford a guardian appointed by Sara's father. What seems like caring for a person removed from family and duty turns out to be the narrative's anticipation of a quasi-familial connection. If this message were not clear enough, Sara states to the neighbor's pet monkey, "You ought to be fondest to your own family; and I'm not a *real* relation."[67]

The narrowing of ethical responsibility means that a major plot point of Burnett's text, Sara's inheritance of a fortune from a diamond mine, remains at a distance from the heroine's ethical concerns. Workers in such mines, often youth, suffered in extremely dangerous conditions, and many died in the course of their employment. The real-life corollary of Sara's "adopted friend," Mr. Carrisford, was Cecil Rhodes, a diamond magnate, head of De Beers Consolidated Mines, and eventual South African prime minister, who became involved in South African politics to enact policies that eliminated Black Africans' property and voting rights, forcing them into indentured labor. Rhodes's policies formed the basis of apartheid. Given this connection, it is fitting that Sara develops an obsession with aristocratic prisoners, such as Marie Antoinette, who were held in the Bastille during the French Revolution. The text ends with Sara declaring that her diamond mine money will allow her to give "bread to the populace," of which she is no longer a part, a corollary to the lack of ethical awareness attributed to Antoinette through the phrase "let them eat cake."[68] Though she believes she can feel for others "through a wall," Sara cannot relate to the diamond miners. By this time, a tradition of British children's literature had set precisely this kind of ethical limit. Indeed, scenarios that limit ethical significance to proximate friends and family have become an implicit part of the basic structure of many children's books, especially for young readers, which means they often evade tensions related to race and other differences that are not easily assimilated.

Not-So-Secret Gardens

The Governess anticipates the next generation of children's books, which also focus on ethics in the family but deal more directly with children's exposure to the institution of slavery. As Livesay has shown, a significant number of British people's experiences in this period more closely resembled those of Harriet than those of Jenny, in that they had direct experiences with British enslavement and family connections with African and mixed-race persons. Amussen notes that "the traffic between the West Indies and England was two-way, with many [people] spending some years in Jamaica or Barbados and then returning to England."[69] Precisely because the Caribbean was not considered a good place for children's education, white children and a small but significant number of mixed-race children born to enslaved women (largely through sexual violence) were sent to mainland Britain for educational purposes. Livesay argues that over the course of the eighteenth century, mixed-race children were increasingly ostracized from their British families—a trend he connects to families' attempts to adjust to "the turbulent economic fluctuations brought about by merchant capitalism, political upheaval, and regular warfare abroad," which raised concerns about these children's lack of economic connections.[70] Children's books reflect these narrowing versions of relationality.

Even as mixed-race children were increasingly rejected within families, the larger trend in Britain was one of increasing awareness of cultural difference and the impact of the colonies on British life. Writers managed this impact by writing children's literature about creole children, envisioned as white children able to be reintegrated back into British families with ethical training. The foremost book of this type, Day's *Sandford and Merton* (discussed in the introduction), more directly than *The Governess*, introduces what would become a long-standing plot formula for narrowing the ethical obligations brought about by British enslavement.

Day's characterization of Tommy Merton as a Jamaica-born creole "spoiled" by his mother and cruel to his African "servants" follows from Fielding's Sukey and anticipates later texts that expand the formula to deal with the colonies at large, especially Burnett's *The Secret Garden* (1911). Like Tommy, Burnett's colonial child Mary Lennox begins the text weak, impulsive, and arrogant. Mary's parents die, causing her to be sent to England, where, like Tommy, she must change her ways. Tommy's educational program involves him working in the garden of his rural tutor, Mr. Barlow, anticipating Mary's horticultural cure a century later. Both texts disavow the influence of the colonies and celebrate a rosy version of rural English childhood based on the virtues of pastoral life. Both suggest that colonialism and enslavement, along with bad parents, have negative effects on children that could cause a crisis in connection if not remedied. And in both, the crisis in connection deemed most important (other than in Day's grateful Black section) involves disruptions to the child's relationships with white family members and is solved by the reintegration of the child back into mainland Britain. Even though en-slavement was illegal in British colonies by the time Burnett was writing, it is telling that there is no corollary to the grateful Black beyond a brief men-tion of the death of Mary's Ayah in Burnett's text; suffering involving colo-nized people has been deprioritized.

In Day's texts and others that predate *The Secret Garden*, it is implied that this reintegration of the child into a domestic sphere of relation is part of the business of Atlantic trade. The grateful Black reflects Day's stance against enslavement in his private life and adult writings—which show him to be, as Karen Sands O'Connor notes, "a firm abolitionist."[71] Yet Tommy's education is fully embraced by his father, an absentee landlord and enslaver. At the end of the grateful Black section, when Tommy's father collects him from Bar-low's care, he declares, "I have heard . . . such an account of your present behavior, that the past is entirely forgotten; and I begin to glory in owning you for a son."[72] Mr. Merton delights in how Barlow has softened his domi-neering, overtly racist son into someone more palatable to civil English sen-sibilities. Simultaneously, Merton extends his ownership of human beings to his son—a statement that creepily resonates with the reality of mixed-race children who belonged to their father-owners and may not have been recog-nized as relatives. Merton's embrace implies that Tommy's reeducation is not in conflict with his father's unsavory way of making money, so long as his son does not bear the marks of the business.[73]

A simplified version of Day's plot thus proved useful to those with busi-ness interests in the West Indies. More closely anticipating Burnett's book, Barbara Hofland's *Matilda; Or the Barbadoes Girl* (1816, US edition 1817) fea-tures a white creole girl who returns to England to be replanted and "pruned" of her abusive, spoiled behaviors. An extant copy in Oxford's Bodleian Library includes the stamp of the West India Committee, a lobbyist group formed in 1780 to promote enslaver interests, suggesting that readers considered the book useful to this initiative.[74] The committee's seal of approval suggests that the recuperation of English children from the Caribbean was considered an important part of its operations.[75]

Like many of the girls in *The Governess*, Matilda characteristically suffers from "peevishness," which the text attributes to a combination of her rela-tionships with enslaved people and her lack of ethical training. She "indulged in the free exercise of a railing tongue, and even of a clawing hand, towards the numerous negro dependents that swarmed in her father's mansion, over whom she had exercised all the despotic sovereignty of a queen, with the capriciousness of a petted child, and thereby obtained a habit of tyranny over all whom she deemed her inferiors."[76] This animal metaphor—of Matilda as queen bee and enslaved people as a swarm—presents a greater entanglement of enslaver and enslaved than we see in other animal metaphors used to teach children about enslavement, such as those featuring pets as metaphors for the enslaved. However, the goal is not to promote compassion along a chain of otherness, as in Jeremy Bentham's image discussed in the introduction, but to disentangle the white child from the chain.

Matilda's British relations are the key to her disentanglement. Matilda and an enslaved woman named Zebby come to live with Matilda's father's friend, Mr. Harewood, along with his wife and children. The Harewood family attempts to change Matilda's behavior toward Zebby, mainly to avoid offending the families' finer sensibilities. Matilda's youth is a key factor in her extrication; she is childish for her years and does not fit into the Harewood family, but "she [is] a child of an acute mind, excellent capacity . . . and being at an age when the mind expands quickly, it [is] no wonder that she soon [gives] evident marks of improvement."[77] Showing her recuperation, Matilda becomes an honorary member of the family, then an official member through her marriage to eldest son, Edmund.

As in *The Secret Garden*, where the garden is a metaphor for the child, the English climate and seasons figure prominently in Matilda's reeducation.[78] Matilda is, indeed, described as a metaphorical garden: "There were still many points in which the errors of her Barbadoes education were but too visible, and which called for the pruning hand of a sensible and pious friend."[79] While creoles and Africans alike are described as "indolent," the longer Matilda stays in England, the livelier she becomes, a change attributed to "the climate."[80] Experiencing and reading about the seasons are equally important. In one scene, Matilda is surprised to see snow.[81] Harewood's daughter Ellen lends her "a little book where you will see a description of a place of ice, and of whole mountain of snow, called Glaciers."[82]

As Chimamanda Ngozi Adichie points out in her TED Talk, "The Danger of a Single Story," the English climate and seasons made their way into colonial children's reading as iconic features of children's literature.[83] Because English-language literature became ubiquitous via colonialism and cultural imperialism, colonial and postcolonial children often experience it as essential to childhood, despite their own different experiences. Adichie recounts that when she began writing, her characters "played in the snow . . . and they talked a lot about the weather: how lovely it was that the sun had come out."[84]

Yet the problem is even deeper than Adichie suggests. The way that the seasons figure in *The Barbadoes Girl* indicates that they are not an innocuous feature of British children's literature that only becomes dangerously monolithic when children's literature spreads elsewhere; rather, the seasons ward off stories of colonial exploitation and traumatic childhoods happening elsewhere. The notion that white creole children can be molded into better versions of themselves by the seasons, furthermore, anticipates a eugenic sensibility in which the child's plasticity, as Jules Gill-Peterson argues, comes to be connected with "an abstract form of whiteness," while people of color are imagined to be static and unchangeable.[85]

A test of Matilda's plasticity comes later in the text, when rich boys try to play a trick on her using hail. This scene culminates a narrative thread about Matilda's faults: She likes dainty food, described as "sweet things and trash," "eating the entirety of 'any delicacy ... provided for the company,'" and munching on "almonds, figs, gingerbread, biscuits, or comfits" continually.[86] As Britain was a primary consumer of products of the colonies, including the sugar in these treats, there is projection in this depiction of the creole child's faults. Matilda does not just consume the food; it takes over her body in over-the-top ways, making her a personification of slave-enabled consumerism. The text makes the key to avoiding gluttony an understanding of seasonal variations that comes from being in England. We know that Matilda has improved when her mother visits and is surprised to see her serving a custard rather than eating it, but we know she is *cured* of her gluttony when she resists eating the boys' fake ice comfits, knowing them to be snowballs in disguise. Knowledge of English climate allows her to adopt civilized ways of interacting.

The text moves from this attempt to project consumption onto the creole child to a general edict, declaring that such behavior "renders young people hateful in their appearance since nothing can be more unladylike or disagreeable than the circumstance of being called to speak when your mouth is full, or displaying the greediness of your appetite, by cramming between meals, stealing out of a room to fill your mouth in the passage, or silently moving your jaws about, as if you had got the mumps."[87] Although Matilda and Zebby (who gets sick from overconsumption) are the ones with an excessive eating problem in the text, this passage betrays that English readers are also guilty of these faults. As O'Connor has noted, creole children in stories are often "given negative traits common to childhood—only exaggerated."[88]

Beyond this projection when it comes to gluttony, the text puts the creole child at the center of its ethical lessons. Matilda's domineering behavior toward Zebby becomes merely a troubling aspect of her personality that needs to be pruned to make her socially acceptable. In a frequently illustrated scene, Matilda demands (ginger?) beer and when it does not come fast enough, throws it in Zebby's face (fig. 1.1).[89] A test of Matilda's reformation comes when Zebby, in a state of delirium, overturns a bowl of hot broth on Matilda. Matilda passes the text's ethical test by assuring Zebby of her forgiveness and writing to her mother in Jamaica to make sure that Zebby is not blamed. Meanwhile, it is never considered that Zebby be admitted into civil society, though a gut-wrenching moment shows the family comforting Zebby before she is assured of Matilda's forgiveness, saying "in old England every servant [has] law and justice as much on their side as their master."[90] While this discussion seems to hint at the potential for a version of relationality with Zebby included, it is used to illustrate Matilda's remaining distance from her white British relatives and her need to emulate their greater civility.

The family's concern for Zebby does not extend to making her an equal. Given the stamp by the West India Committee, the text's position on enslavement is surprisingly critical, but the resolution offered by its moral center, Mr. Harewood, is "the emancipation of all the blacks, who will . . . become diligent servants and happy householders; no longer the slaves of tyrants, but the servants of upright masters"—in other words, benevolent rulers like Benefico.[91] This was likely a position acceptable to the committee because Harewood insisted, mirroring Fielding's emphasis on Mignon's patience, that "the emancipation of the slaves takes place gradually, and by that means enables people to collect their money."[92] In the interim between *The Governess* and *The Barbadoes Girl*, gradual emancipation had become a favored way to end enslavement and would guide antislavery discussions with the formation of the Society for the Mitigation and Gradual Abolition of Slavery Throughout the British Dominions in 1823.

The Barbadoes Girl was written at a time (which I describe in more detail in chapter 2) when enslavers thought they might be able to preserve their power in the face of abolitionist challenges through ameliorative improvements, accompanied by indoctrination of enslaved youth. Harewood's vision of making "friends" of the enslaved hints at a belief that the transformation of children like Matilda could usher in an era of supposedly ethical enslavement. That *The Barbadoes Girl* circulated in mainland Britain suggests that its publisher thought it would improve enslavers' political situation.

The aim was for British children to accept the legacies of enslavement and

Figure 1.1. Illustration labeled "Miss Hanson throwing a glass of Beer in Zebby's face," from Barbara Hofland, *Matilda, Or the Barbadoes Girl. A Tale for Young People*. London: A. K. Newman and Co., 1816. Courtesy of Toronto Public Library.

civilly relate to enslavers, as much as to reform creole children. The climactic scene in which Matilda demonstrates her transformation by avoiding the ice comfits marks a transition to a new conflict involving her relationships with other children living in England. Unlike the Harewoods, these children are objectified, as if their cruelty can be explained by a disconnect from the English landscape caused by (feminized) commercial influences. In addition to being tormented by rich boys, Matilda is targeted by a girl bully, Miss Holdup, described as "an automaton figure" and a "bedizened doll."[93]

The introduction of Holdup suggests that whatever Matilda's connection to enslavement (her family relies on enslaved people for "agriculture and domestic labour"), there are crimes with more worrying consequences, because they harm white children's civil relationships with each other.[94] Another girl remarks to Holdup: "I don't doubt, Miss [Matilda] Hanson . . . can tell you exactly how much pain is necessary to kill a slave, how many stripes a child can endure, and how long hunger, beating, and torturing, may be applied without producing death."[95] When Holdup says that she has heard enough, the girl claims that British "children amuse themselves in Barbadoes with sticking pins into the legs of little children, dropping scalding sealing-wax upon their arms, and cutting lines and stars in their necks with knives and scissars [*sic*]."[96]

Rather than inviting outrage about violence against enslaved children, the text redirects the reader's outrage to the pain these words will cause for the rehabilitated Matilda, as well as the social rift they will create by disrupting interactions between white people. This scene demonstrates, however, that white civility preserves peace by asserting white fragility, which Robin DiAngelo defines as a "discomfort" with "racial stress" that works to protect "white advantage."[97] Mr. Harewood comes to Matilda's rescue by stating, "I have this very evening heard words applied to the heart of an unoffending individual, *more painful than the lash,* and seen looks directed against her, *more torturing than any of the hateful operations you have mentioned.*"[98] With this assertion that mean looks can be "more torturing" than cutting enslaved children comes Matilda's ultimate recuperation; she runs into Mr. Harewood's arms and seeks refuge. Matilda's acceptance by this paternal figure, and her integration into this solidly British family as a child, is arguably more important than the text's denouement, which narrates her marriage to Edmund. Matilda afterward serves as governess to another Harriet, who is from an enslaver family but has lost her fortune (possibly due to the abolition of the slave trade in 1807). Although Harriet has Matilda's "same errors," at only six years old she has not yet been fully corrupted.[99] With Harriet as the future, *The Barbadoes Girl* substitutes concerns about the enslaved with an obligation to enslavers' progeny.[100]

This would prove to be a popular formula. Published just four years later, A. Selwyn's *The Little Creoles* (1820) follows a similar pattern of recuperating West Indian children, while encouraging those in mainland Britain to accept aspects of racial categorization and slave management developed in the Caribbean. The text begins with two white creole children's arrival to their British cousins' home following the death of their father, a Jamaican merchant. Like Tommy Merton and Matilda, Francis and Blanche are excessively weak and fragile, requiring replanting.

As this opening suggests, the text is primarily concerned about the white progeny of enslavers, though the fact of racial difference within some transatlantic families is played for suspense when the children's cousins, Grace, Rowland, and Augustus, argue over whether the arriving children might be Black Africans. Historical children traveling from the West Indies, indeed, were not necessarily white. Livesay has argued that Black-appearing mixed-race children were sometimes accepted into white families for educational purposes without qualms until late in the eighteenth century. However, *The Little Creoles* reflects Livesay's conclusion that mixed-race children were increasingly excluded from families. After a teasing moment where an enslaved child, Juba, gets out of the coach first and the boys think they are vindicated, Grace is proven right. The main characters are white, so much that one of them is named Blanche. As if Blanche's name were not enough to indicate their whiteness, the text fetishizes their "fair complexion."[101]

The lesson is clear: family members are white, and relations between white and Black people are limited to relations between enslaver and enslaved. An obsession with such "racial thinking," Hazel V. Carby notes, arose in part because "colonial rulers . . . feared the stark imbalance in the [Caribbean] population because of the prospect of black rebellion" and became interested in clear racial divisions so they could "constantly calculat[e] the ratio of black to white bodies."[102] *Little Creoles* makes the case that racial distinctions reinforcing the subjugation of people with dark skin need to be accepted in mainland British families, even if the Somerset case (1772) has declared by this time that the law did not support enslavement in mainland Britain.[103]

As in *Sandford and Merton* and *The Barbadoes Girl*, the creole children are replanted in England, though in this case there are no bad behaviors to be pruned. Instead, Blanche and Francis are *literally* fragile from their contact with the institution of slavery; they are described as "a delicate looking boy, half dead with cold, and a sleeping child enveloped in a boat-cloak."[104] They are particularly vulnerable to the cold climate: they are frostbitten, they cannot walk on snow, Blanche almost "perishes" one day when the boys take her out without a coat, and Grace teases Francis for not knowing that England is not always snowy until she remembers that he cannot have had access to "natural history" in the West Indies.[105] The idea that West Indian children were unaware of variations in climate is untrue. Natural histories about England (and elsewhere) were available in the West Indies, often in lieu of information about Caribbean children's own environment. However, the orphans get stronger as they experience English seasons for the first time, both in reality and in books, which are conflated. A major improvement to their lives is the ability to read the elevated language the seasons have inspired in British writers such as Anna Laetitia Barbauld.

Yet Francis and Blanche's transformation from potential Afro-Caribbean creoles and fragile waifs into civil white family members is less important than the changes their English boy cousins must make, which get yoked to the imagery of seasonal change. The central female character, Grace, is a Jenny Peace–like figure who joins with the creoles to resolve the crisis in connection brought on by the family's transatlantic separation and to assist the figurative rebirth of the boy cousins. For Rowland, this rebirth is heralded by accidental physical debilitation: he loses his looks and sight from playing with explosives: "So dreadfully was her brother's face disfigured, that [Grace] could scarcely discern a trace of his well-known features."[106]

This event is narratively connected to the text's commentary on enslavement—namely, to Rowland and Augustus's maltreatment of the cousins and the enslaved Juba. Rowland's disfigurement signifies his brutality and his punishment for the brothers' cruel behavior, a textual element that connects the abuses of enslavement and colonization to the British family at home. The boys' viciousness is presented as highly ironic, given the Somerset case had included language about the freedom inherent in the British soil. The brothers treat Juba violently by pelting him with snowballs, then respond to Francis's indignation by pointing out that Juba is free as soon as he "sets his foot on English ground."[107] The brothers seem unaware of the irony of hitting Juba with material dusting that ground and Francis retorts that "no slave was ever treated so ill on my father's estate, as you have used my poor Juba to-day."[108]

As in *The Barbadoes Girl*, the scene seems to express concern about violence against enslaved children. However, it ultimately advances the dubious claim that British West Indian practices attached to enslavement are comparatively humane and ethical when set against the actions of those who have not experienced enslaver culture. The emphasis is less on Juba's mistreatment than on the fact that Francis, Rowland, and Augustus cannot agree about how he should be mistreated. The message: West Indian enslavers know better—and observers in mainland Britain need to accept enslavers' perspectives.

The relational ethical dilemmas occasioned by enslavement are thereby transformed into dilemmas impacting people who can be construed as family and as white. In the end, healing means knitting together the families and bodies of the white characters. Rowland recovers his sight only after his creole cousin, Francis, reads to him. This event is accompanied by the change of seasons from winter to spring, like Colin's recovery in *The Secret Garden*. The scenes of Mary and Colin reawakening a garden and conjuring "white" magic to heal their hearts and bodies in *The Secret Garden* are prefigured by the ending of *The Little Creoles*, where "Spring now advanced, and the little Creole [Francis] had the pleasure of seeing the snow melt away and the leaves and flowers make their appearance."[109]

The Animal Atlantic

Although many children's texts of this era fail to adequately address the horrifying realities of British enslavement and Atlantic trade, their extreme cruelty and dehumanization make a surprising appearance in the resplendently odd *Lobster's Voyage to the Brazils* (1808), a book that anticipates the strange violent fantasy underworld of Carroll's *Alice in Wonderland* (1865). *Lobster's Voyage* is part of the genre Jackson calls "papillonades": books that draw on the success of Roscoe's *The Butterfly's Ball, and the Grasshopper's Feast* (1802) and feature mock epics about anthropomorphic animals that satirize British society. Roscoe's publisher, J. Harris, released several titles capitalizing on Roscoe's poem. Richard De Ritter notes that "[Catherine Ann] Dorset's The Peacock 'At Home' . . . established the basic template to which subsequent works adhered . . . [A]fter hearing of the butterfly's ball, an animal or a certain species (lions, elephants, horses, or flowers, for instance) decide to host their own gathering. Invitations are sent, responses are received. The poem provides a description of the gathering . . . before concluding with a speech or moral."[110] The genre reinforces British rituals of civility, but with indication of the violence that is usually buried or excluded within civil discourse; Daniel Froid argues that Dorset's books establish "a world in which ritual must be observed, and normative rules obeyed, in order to maintain harmony," but "subtle predator-prey jokes hint at a darker world" of class-based conflicts, injustice, and mistreatment.[111]

This dynamic of civility paired with underlying callousness gets linked to enslavement in two sea-based papillonades released by Harris in 1808, *The Feast of the Fishes; Or, the Whale's Invitation to his Brethren of the Deep* (1808), attributed to Theresa Tyro (likely a pseudonym) and *The Lobster's Voyage to the Brazils*, whose author is not named.[112] De Ritter analyzes *The Feast of the Fishes*, focusing on a disturbing scene in which the shark declines the flying fish's invitation because he is already "following in a slave ship's wake."[113] De Ritter argues that the book's "grotesque implication" that the shark is feeding on the bodies of enslaved people who have been thrown overboard "is glossed over by the language of politeness," though images of sharks and slave ships were also used critically in abolitionist rhetoric beginning in 1780.[114]

Beyond the integration of a crude fact into polite language, the tone of the reference is difficult to gauge, due to the text's blend of comedy with instruction. On the one hand, De Ritter notes, the book does not sugarcoat enslavement, casting its child reader as "far from an innocent who must be shielded from acts of injustice and brutality."[115] On the other, the book does not provide "sympathy-provoking detail" or ethical instruction, leading De Ritter to conclude that readers are "invited to participate in the almost gleeful flippancy with which the poem alludes to the barbarism of the slave trade."[116] Whether *The Feast of the Fishes* normalizes the dehumanization of enslaved people by making it a source of flippant humor or offers a damning critique of polite society as profiting from racial violence, its vulgarity challenges white civility's attempts to bury, sidestep, or disidentify with the atrocities of enslavement.

The Lobster's Voyage also relies on crude and disturbing humor but directs that humor pointedly at British hypocrisy by satirizing a specific moment in the history of slave-related transatlantic trade: the Portuguese adoption of the Abertura dos portos policy in November 1807, which opened the potential for Britain to trade directly with the slave-driven economy of Brazil. The policy derived from events occurring at the outset of the Peninsular War. When Napoleonic forces invaded Portugal because of its alliance with Great Britain, Portugal's Prince Regent John transferred his court to Brazil under the protection of the British navy before he could be deposed by the Napoleonic army. When John arrived in Brazil, he aided British commerce by opening trade between Brazil and Nações Amigas, or "friendly nations," which recalls the sunny phrasing of Addison's "Royal Exchange." The resulting economic boom for Brazil meant a significant increase in slave labor and British profit from it, despite the abolition of the British slave trade a few months earlier in April 1807 (the Strangford Treaty of 1810 would grant Britain further special trading privileges with Brazil). Although these events gave Britain leverage to encourage the Portuguese to limit their slave trade, they also demonstrate the seeming inescapability of the trade and the hypocrisies of the government in allowing British merchants to profit from a trade that had been outlawed.

The book represents this history by having Lobster—a "Gentleman" whose nationality is initially unknown—join a Portuguese fleet for the Brazils, recruiting others to come along.[117] The story immediately references enslavement through an image of sea animals caught in traps:

> The Miss PRAWNS, who, escp'd from the net of the rakers,
>
> Had themselves hardly clear'd from the surge and the breakers,
>
> Came wriggling along, just to hear the good news,
>
> And there sat as demure as young Owls or Sea-mews.[118]

Referencing the British abolition of the trade, the prawns are freed only to learn of new circumstances that inhibit their freedom: the Lobster's desire to manipulate them into joining his ill-conceived, economically motivated voyage.

Building on the drama of this opening, *The Lobster's Voyage* addresses a larger context of war. A vague reference to the Second Maroon War in the 1790s appears when a "crab" from Jamaica comes "reeling and wheeling, crawl'd down from a hill."[119] But the date of the text—and its depiction of a Portuguese fleet to Brazils—suggest that Lobster joins the "voyage" of Prince Regent John. Prince John's proxy in the text, the Travell'r Jack-Herring, pitches participation in the voyage—with its attendant risks—in commercial terms:

> [S]ince to Brazil he intended to go,
>
> Their orders in trade he requested to know;
>
> And, as Partners in Co., 'twas his humble opinion,
>
> Would make pleasant the tour thro' the wat'ry dominion.[120]

As with *The Governess*, the central source of suspense in the story is not initially politics or economics, but the well-being of a teenage girl. Miss Sprat, a "miss in her teens," volunteers to accompany Jack-Herring to the Brazils, being that the Miss Prawns are too young. A debate ensues in which "Counsellor MUSCLE object[s] her youth" while Lobster declares "Though for Miss he'd no private affection . . . Yet with both he would go, and afford 'em protection."[121] The section wrestles with Sprat's ability to make decisions in a situation that stretches the bounds of civil interaction. Muscle attempts to control Sprat's location and counteract her decision to go. Sprat does not speak again, only curtseys politely, which means that it is Lobster who applies the muscle and makes the decision: "the LOBSTER was known for the strength of his claw, / And whatever he said, was receiv'd as a law."[122] This imposition of force over civility implies that once one has left the boundaries of Britain, voluntary wishes and social rituals are no longer the basis by which one's fate is decided. They are decided instead by who has the power in its limited definition as military prowess and physical brawn—and unlike the girls in *The Governess* or even the enslaving Matilda, who is said to have used a "clawing hand" against the people she enslaves, Sprat does not ever have power. The Lobster's claw represents the force, violence, and war that propel the transatlantic economy.

Although we might suspect the danger to Sprat to be characterized in sexual ways, it is only loosely so. Herring gives her a sly look; the Lobster says he will keep her safe "in his conjugal breast."[123] The more significant danger lurking in the Atlantic is that Sprat will become food. Lobster gives her instructions for avoiding the whale, the shark, and Lord Turbot, who might "cram you in his throat."[124] At first, Sprat manages to participate in the world of consumption. They stop to have dinner with some fish, who makes "dainties" including "Snail-broth" and "Custards serv'd up in a rich PORCELAIN Shell."[125] It is not enough for these characters to eat, as animals do for survival; they consume luxury items, analogs of British merchants accumulating wealth from the deal with Portugal. Sentient animals understood as food, conversely, are linked with Afro-Caribbean culture. A fish "dropped from a West-India packet" dances a jig but is deemed in a footnote to be good "food."[126] The food threat ultimately hangs over the dance in general, as the whole place becomes a stew pot: "so small is the Ball-Room, so many intrude, / That the gold-coated CARP truly dreads to be stew'd."[127]

Personifying animals who were considered food and giving them Caribbean nationalities implies a connection between food and enslaved persons. This connection is meant on some level to be humorous, but it confronts us with more complications to white civility than the slave ship reference in *Feast of the Fishes*. Where in Tyro's text the whale uses following the slave ship as an excuse not to go to the ball, in *The Lobster's Voyage* polite society is inseparable from destructive consumption. Those who are consumed appear in the texts as persons, rather than being referenced by a vague insinuation that does not recognize the sentience of the eaten. This food-animal metaphor also differs from abolitionist writing that casts the enslaved as caged birds or pets, which Spencer Keralis describes as part of a broader "sentimental displacement of human affection away from human objects within the family and toward domesticated animals."[128] Whereas Jenny Peace's mother demands that she limit her ethical sphere by forgetting her cat, abolitionist writers wanted to expand children's ethical sphere by using animal abuse as a gateway to understanding ethical relationality with enslaved humans. As Keralis writes, "Animal imagery . . . is particularly prevalent in texts marketed to children," because abolitionists imagined that if they were unsuccessful in changing adult minds, they might be able to teach children new ways of relating.[129] However, pet metaphors afford white authors an easy framework for proposing minor changes to enslaved people's treatment while failing to question white supremacy. Keralis, drawing from Yi-Fu Tuan, explains that pet making is "an exercise in power which compels its object . . . to conform to specific behavioral standards in order to receive affectionate attention and material support from its master."[130]

The text's food-animal metaphors instead show how slave-driven capitalism leads to the annihilation of sentient beings as part of its basic functioning. Christina Sharpe's analysis of the slave ship *Zong*, from which enslaved people suffering from malnutrition, dehydration, and overcrowding were thrown overboard to preserve the chance of getting insurance money, prompts the realization that such images are not only metaphors but instead reference disturbing truths (merely insinuated by *Feast of the Fishes*). Sharpe writes, "There have been studies done on whales that have died and have sunk to the seafloor. These studies show that within a few days the whales' bodies are picked almost clean by benthic organisms . . . My colleague Anne Gardulski tells me it is most likely that a human body would not make it to the seafloor intact."[131] *The Lobster's Voyage* offers no way out of such horrors, a reflection of how the Abertura dos portos ensured British capitalism's continued connections to enslavement even as Britain outlawed the trade. Eating, unlike mistreating pets, is not optional—and abstaining from seafood or meat, like abolishing the slave trade, cannot grind the system to a halt. Stories of human-like animals who become food capture the brutal incivility underlying every-

Figure 1.2. Illustration labeled "The Collation," from *The Lobster's Voyage to the Brazils.* London: Printed for J. Harris, 1808. Courtesy of Lilly Library, Indiana University.

day activities in the Atlantic world. At the same time, the everydayness of eating presents an avenue for plausible deniability, since humans regularly excuse eating sentient beings as a necessary and unavoidable kind of violence.

Other elements represent the objectification of enslaved people and exploitation of their labor. At another dinner, a turtle "spread[s] her broad back for a table" (fig. 1.2).[132] The text is ambiguous as to whether this act is voluntary or forced. Although this turtle is a minor character, presented without context, her subordination has haunting significance considering the history of the turtle industry, which was "a distinctive maritime commerce" carried out by British people in the Caribbean through the exploitation of Indigenous people.[133] Early explorers to the Caribbean observed that turtles were prevalent. They became an object of consumer fixation beginning in the eighteenth century, with shells used for jewelry, combs, and book bindings. They were also a source of food on ships and in luxury kitchens. Lynn B. Harris explains that those profiting from turtle hunting "were known to hire or capture Miskito Indians to serve aboard their ships" making it unclear to outside observers whether specific hunters had "joined the crew of a vessel willingly."[134]

The turtle and other characters in *The Lobster's Voyage* thus reflect real circumstances and their implications for people in the Caribbean. In this remarkably honest portrayal of Atlantic life, being a British consumer does not immunize one against being objectified, which makes a powerful point about the interrelationship among participants in the Atlantic economy. Nearly all the animals are forced to cede their status as independent beings. For the seeming civility of dinners and dances, there is the constant danger that characters might become forced into an inhumane relation because of the relentless force of consumption. They might become the food on someone else's plate, the bones in someone else's belly.

At their destination, the practice of dining upon others catches up with Lobster, Jack-Herring, and Sprat. As the text ends:

> The Gen'ral [Lobster] was caught, bought, and brought to the Kitchen
> Of the Portuguese Regent, but recently landed—
> To the fat Cook en chef he was suddenly handed.[135]

The Lobster manages to avoid being cooked only by revealing his Englishness, which means he has enough disidentification with enslavement and importance to the prince's Brazilian deal to save him:

> When he told them in accents so gentle, so clear
> That "on *Albion's* shores he was hatch'd, and came hence
> Just to catch a side-glance of their amiable prince" . . .
> He is heard: he receives soon his warrant of grace
> And with shouts is proclaim'd the first KING of his race.[136]

Herring and Sprat, conversely, do become food:

> For leaving his *Mentor*, JACK HERRING was flung
> In a Fisherman's Boat, dried, salted, and hung:
> On the grid-iron, SPRAT her last sigh did exhale;
> And, sweet Ladies, this line puts an END to my tale.[137]

The ending's humor works by keeping Sprat within the realm of stories told about young women—inviting readers to poke fun at the feeble females who die at the end of cautionary seduction tales—and by foregrounding that she is not a human but a fish, always from a human view destined for the grill, a violent activity frequently excused by its commonness.[138] In this sense, the text provides a possible escape, or catharsis through humor, to counter the hypocrisies and cruelties that underlie its narrative. In its simultaneous denial and acknowledgment that Sprat is in the same category as "sweet ladies," the joke provides comic relief, while venturing a truth about how the marriage market and Atlantic trade both made sentient beings into consumable objects. Being an English gentleman is the only thing that can save a person from this fate, but the saying that Englishmen are always free is also made into a joke, revealing the absurdity of the idea that being born (or replanted) on English soil supposedly exempts one from the grim consequences of Atlantic enslavement and trade.

Possibly *The Lobster's Voyage* proved too political for children. While most texts in Harris's series were published multiple times in London and the United States, the *Lobster* appears to have been published in only one 1808 edition. The book has an important afterlife, however, in that it anticipates Carroll's chapter "The Lobster's Quadrille," in *Alice in Wonderland* (1865), as well as motifs of eating that run through his writing, often involving sea creatures.

Although there is no known record of Carroll reading *The Lobster's Voyage*, he had at least one and probably many encounters with the papillonade genre. J. Harris was still advertising *The Butterfly's Ball* and *The Peacock at Home* in the 1840s, when Carroll was a young person, followed by other firms. Dean and Son, of London, advertised a "colored sixpenny toy book" and George Routledge a "toy book" version "for little readers."[139] There is evidence that Carroll knew Roscoe's poems and enjoyed them. He wrote in his diary about seeing a Christmas pantomime adaptation called *The Butterfly's Ball and the Grasshopper's Feast, or Harlequin and the Genius of Spring* at the Theatre Royal Haymarket in January 1856, noting that it was "very good."[140] The adaptation used Roscoe's poem as inspiration for a plot involving a Wasp trying to sneak into the kitchen before the gathering to poison the food and being chased away, resonating with anxieties around eating and dangerous kitchen scenes in *The Lobster's Voyage* and *Alice*. Numerous print versions of *The Butterfly's Ball* appeared in the 1860s as Carroll was working on *Alice in Wonderland*, some with illustrations resembling Carroll's imagery and John Tenniel's illustrations.[141] Carroll was familiar with the illustrator of Harris's *Butterfly's Ball* and *Lobster's Voyage*, William Mulready, viewing his work at exhibitions in 1857 and 1864, the latter as Carroll was working with Tenniel on illustrating *Alice*.[142]

F. J. Harvey Darton in *Children's Books in England* (1932) proposes that Roscoe's poem might have inspired specific rhythms in Carroll's work.[143] More broadly, Carroll draws on the underlying predator-prey dynamics of the papillonades, which threaten polite exchanges and evoke the politics of consumption. These themes take their most profound expression in passages involving sea creatures. In "The Lobster's Quadrille," two talking animals, the Gryphon and the Mock Turtle, call Alice's attention to a "pretty dance" that small sea creatures do on the shore amid the waves, with lobsters for partners.[144] As in *The Lobster's Voyage*, the animals' cultural activities are overshadowed by the threat of being eaten; when asked whether she has seen a "lobster" and a "whiting," Alice only just keeps herself from blurting out that she sees them at dinner.[145] The animals do not accept this objectification; when Alice describes the fish as covered with "crumbs," the Mock Turtle objects that the water would wash the crumbs off.[146]

Instead, they sing a song about the quadrille, with the refrain "will you, won't you, will you, won't you, won't you join the dance?" requesting a different sort of relation.[147] Although the song does not announce a clear ethical intervention, recalling Fred Moten's idea of "sound before ethics" (discussed in my introduction), we might read this song as a disruption of the binaries that inform colonial relationships. Alice is keen to view the lobster through a subject-object binary, but the dancing lobsters occupy an in-between state resembling Moten's concept of the thingly, a hybrid, indeterminate position that includes aspects of both the subject and object but is ultimately neither. The dance, a corollary to Moten's image of Africans dancing at a funeral, happens despite the death-driven economies of enslavement and consumption. It does not propose a traditional ethics based on moral or immoral actions toward others, but it offers an ethics of resistance opposing the hierarchical and cleanly differentiated terms through which Alice wants to define the lobsters.

Alice does not join the dance, however. When the Gryphon orders Alice to recite a poem, she utters a poem that tries to force the thingly lobsters into being food objects: "'Tis the voice of the Lobster; I heard him declare, / 'You have baked me too brown, I must sugar my hair'" (fig. 1.3).[148] Although illustrated by Tenniel with a large claw similar to the Lobster in *Lobster's Voyage*, Carroll's Lobster is stripped of the power to resist, covered over with words that evoke enslavement, "brown" and "sugar." He can only remind us he is a sentient being by mentioning his hair, trimming his belt, and (in Tenniel's illustration) looking at a mirror, presumably to groom himself. (Later illus-

Figure 1.3. John Tenniel illustration from *Alice's Adventures in Wonderland*. Courtesy of Gettysburg College, Musselman Library, Special Collections, *Alice's Adventures in Wonderland* by Lewis Carroll (1832–1898), p. 157, found on Internet Archive.

trators of Carroll's work have produced Lobsters that look like the *Lobster's Voyage* illustrations, including a 1996 version by Peter Weevers, which vests the Lobster with a soldier's coat reminiscent of Mulready's depiction.) As Tenniel's version of the Lobster made into a food item insinuates, Alice—and, by implication, human consumers in Britain—cannot recognize sentience beyond that of white Europeans that is not reducible to an object for digestion.[149] The mirror subtly implies that this is as much about themselves as about others—that they too might be objectified through this logic.

The scene culminates with the Mock Turtle singing "in a voice choked with sobs" a song about turtle soup that resembles a seller's cry:

> Beautiful soup, so rich and green!
> Waiting in a hot tureen!
> Who for such dainties would not stoop!
> Soup of the evening, beautiful Soup!
> . . . Beau—ootiful Soo—oop!
> Beau—ootiful Soo—oop!
> Soo—oop of the e—e—evening,
> Beautiful, beautiful Soup![150]

In the voice of the Mock Turtle, what sounds at first like an advertisement becomes a heartbreaking song depicting violence, murder, and mourning. As with *The Lobster's Voyage*, this chapter is meant in some sense to be humorous—after all, the character is not even a turtle, but a mock turtle, an imaginary creature named after a soup (made of brains and organ meat). Yet it is perhaps even more disturbing that the Mock Turtle is a creature named after a dish; he represents a dynamic that equates *sentient, talking, human-like* beings with objects to be exploited. Unlike the Lobster, who appears infrequently and unemotionally in illustrations over time, the Mock Turtle, beginning with Tenniel, appears as a cute, shelled figure with cow face and ears, often with tears running down its face. The image cries out for emotional response.

Although lobster was a meat widely available in Europe and the Americas, the Mock Turtle is part of the same history of Caribbean commodities as sugar and turtle meat, in that mock turtle was an alternative that became popular owing to the unsustainability of the turtle industry and the overconsumption of turtles. Lynn Harris explains:

> In the nineteenth century, turtle soup and dishes became wildly popular as
> high cuisine restaurants from Kingston to London, Philadelphia and New York
> added it to the menu of assorted gourmet delicacies, while social elites served
> turtle dishes at private parties hosted in their homes. A leading soup maker in
> London was John Lusty Ltd. . . . [which] brought live turtles both from the West

Indies and Ascension Island in the South Atlantic . . . Mock turtle soup used a
calf's head, a time consuming and skilled preparatory task, termed *tête de veau*,
to imitate the costly green turtle soup . . . Three hundred years after the arrival
of European explorers and settlers, the turtle, like other New World animals,
became a quintessential Caribbean commodity for the Victorian elite.[151]

Considering this history, the sales pitch of the Mock Turtle's song is laughable, in that the character is trying to pass off its soup as the real article. Yet it speaks to the relentlessness of consumer desire for Caribbean products. There is not enough to go around, and, the song implies, these unsatisfied cravings mean that the destruction will not stop with beings—and people—considered other. Domestic things, familiar things, will be caught in the gaping maw.

Beyond the anthropomorphized animals, the Lobster and Mock Turtle scenes downplay connections between animal and human suffering. The only human character in the Lobster scene, Alice, is firmly identified as eater, not eaten. Yet the dynamics of Atlantic consumption shape a pervasive motif in Carroll's work involving British children in danger of being devoured. In the "Pig and the Pepper" chapter of *Alice*, the Duchess refers to a baby as a "pig" while getting him dangerously close to a stew pot and kitchen implements.[152] Before the baby turns into a pig before Alice's eyes, losing her sympathy, Alice refers to it as a "star-fish," connecting to the sea imagery of *The Lobster's Voyage* and its parallels in Carroll's work.[153]

Marah Gubar argues that this motif of potential child-eating conveys Carroll's worries about the damage possible within child-adult relationships.[154] Yet, rather than using adult-child relations to narrow the scope of relational crisis, Carroll keeps the metaphors of eating as exploitation afloat, refusing to give them a single referent. In another relevant scene where Carroll plays with multiple referents, Alice believes that she has "somehow fallen into the sea," before realizing that she is swimming in her own tears.[155] This realization is not disavowal of the salty water as a sea, as Alice goes on to meet both a mouse (whom she initially thinks might be a walrus) and a huge group of tropical and water fowl, whom Tenniel illustrates in a group with other sea creatures, including a lobster and a crab. This representation of salty water as a floating signifier draws connections between the realms of the familial and transoceanic.

Moving among these different contexts, Alice's various scales allow a consideration of exploitative power on multiple levels (she compares herself to a telescope, a device that can see near *and* far, before producing the sea of tears in the first place).[156] Like the satirical *Lobster's Voyage*, Carroll overlays the family-squabble-like interactions of the animals with transnational political operations by having them argue about William the Conqueror, who as the first Norman king of England represents a history of transnational conquest, occupation, and settlement. Although a competing narrative to the drive of competition and consumption appears at the end of the tears-as-sea scene with the animals running a race in which "everyone wins," it ends with the animals choking on the comfits that Alice gives them as prizes.[157]

Other books and media, particularly in the Americas, keep the metaphor of eating more closely tied to enslavement and its effects. To my knowledge, no genealogy exists between Carroll's scenes of child eating and gag films like Thomas Edison's *The Gator and the Pickaninny*, which shows a Black child being eaten by (and then rescued from the mouth of) a gator and which Kyla Wazana Tompkins uses to pose the question, "How does a film of a Black child being eaten become legible to audiences?"[158] Yet underlying the Lobster and Mock Turtle scenes is the similar idea of "bodies inscribed with the marks of race and food."[159] As Tompkins points out, animals share with "racially minoritized subjects" a history of being considered "less social, less intellectual and, at times, less sentient."[160] Carroll's animals are reliably other enough that their transformation into food is not directly threatening to white readers, but they are not so other that the scenes escape presenting consumption as sad and disturbing. In the context of enslavement, this feeling of being disturbed seems a firmer ground for ethics than the depictions in *The Governess* and creole books—though one that lacks direction on how to act.

———

In the next chapter, I turn to a different location in the web of Atlantic slavery: the enslaved and colonized Caribbean, where enslavers tried to construe the institution of slavery as ethical and benevolent. Enslaved storytellers, I argue, work against these fictions by depicting the dangers to children and their relationships in enslavement, advancing their own ethical strategies. Their stories act as counterpoints to those I have considered here.

CHAPTER 2

Afro-Caribbean Stories
in the Battle over Childhood

While visiting his Jamaican estate in 1815, British enslaver and gothic writer Matthew Lewis wrote a letter—to an unknown correspondent—in which he compared an enslaved female storyteller to at least one character from children's literature. The letter recounts that he has called the woman Little Goody Two Shoes, a name he claims is mis-repeated throughout the plantation.[1] In a crude attempt at writing dialect and humor, Lewis translates the enslaved Africans' version of the name as "Goosee Shoo-Shoo."[2]

Lewis's main reference can be easily discerned: *The History of Little Goody Two-Shoes* (1765) was a children's book published and sold by John Newbery, in which a Cinderella-esque heroine loses her parents and home, becoming so poor that she owns only one shoe. Her luck changes when a gentleman gives her *two* shoes. She learns to read, becomes a teacher, and eventually marries another gentleman, acquiring a "coach and six."[3] Lewis's unlikely description of the enslaved storyteller as a "lady, who . . . trots about with her marvelous budget [bag]" probably derives from a scene in which Goody teaches poor children to read using a bag of letters.[4] As Judith Terry points out, the moniker is also reminiscent of another children's character, Mother Goose.[5]

The rest of the letter presents a lively tale attributed to Goosee as a specimen of Afro-Caribbean storytelling. Lewis uses the woman's supposed resemblance to Goody Two Shoes to advance his view that enslaved people's stories are like the "quaint old *nursery* tales . . . that we all more or less, remember: such as 'Jack the Giant-killer,' 'Cinderella,' 'Little Red Riding-hood,' etc."[6] The comparison raises a lot of questions, some relational, some ethical, some basic. Who was this woman called Goosee? Were her stories *really* for children? If so, what might they tell us about the ethical pedagogies of the enslaved?

It is important to acknowledge that Lewis's letter does not (and cannot) provide a transparent window into Afro-Caribbean storytelling. As with British descriptions of the spiritual practices known as Obeah, his account "entangles historical fact in colonial fantasy."[7] There are many things that will likely remain unknown about Goosee and her tale. To answer an immediate question, she is not readily identified from the enslaved women on Lewis's estate.[8] Instead, she resembles Saidiya Hartman's Venus, a catchall name for enslaved women about whom "what we know . . . amounts to 'little more than a register of her encounter with power' " and whose memory tells us "rather about the violence, excess, mendacity, and reason that seized hold of their lives, transformed them into commodities and corpses, and identified them with names tossed-off as insults and crass jokes."[9]

Although Lewis's description of Goosee participates in the practice of sexualizing enslaved women that gave rise to the Venus stereotype, his nickname is unusual. Goody Two Shoes is not a love goddess but a pedagogue. The name nonetheless shares with Venus a certain irony. Just as it is cruel to call an enslaved woman, who had a high likelihood of being sexually assaulted, by the name of a divine seductress, it is cruel to name an enslaved woman after a schoolteacher, as most were not permitted to educate their children in any sustained way. The name gives clues as to Lewis's motivations. Although Lewis professes to care about the well-being of women on his plantation—for what we can discern are self-serving motives—his writing about the enslaved African storyteller avoids ethical obligations, at least as far as Goosee is concerned. Instead, he uses the character to fraudulently profess a common interest with enslaved women in the well-being of the future generation, predicated on a dubious idea of himself as a benevolent enslaver, a rhetorical trope through which enslavers responded to abolitionist activism by contriving the paradoxical prospect of ethical enslavement. Childhood and children's literature played important roles in reforms that sought to remake the image of enslavement, offering legitimation and means of control.

The letter ultimately expresses ambivalence about whether Goosee and her stories are fit for children—and this ambivalence attests to the volatile politics around childhood that inform Lewis's description of the enslaved storyteller. He depicts the woman dedicating the story to her "piccaninnies," a name used (oftentimes derogatorily) for children of African descent. But he also remarks that the closest "piccaninny" was "a fellow above six feet."[10] The letter goes on to lampoon the tale by calling it not just a "pretty story," as

British printers and booksellers often referred to children's books, but a "pretty pretty story," a jocular reference to the previous paragraph in which he gives salacious details about Goosee's "dapper red petticoat" and "shining black throat."[11] Drawing on the Venus stereotype, Lewis claims that he finds Goosee "irresistible."[12] He concludes the letter with a very different designation of her tales as "facetiae," a word signifying humor and sometimes pornography.[13]

In delegitimizing Goosee as an agent of ethical education, Lewis's letter is driven by his desire to claim the woman's stories—and the task of ethically training enslaved children—as his own. The pretty story is not just a "pretty pretty story," but what he calls "my pretty pretty story," one he "made her" recite.[14] Lewis essentially enacts the scenario, described in chapter 1, that wealthy British people wanted to avoid for themselves and their children, in which people are rendered into objects. His hungry gaze at Goosee's throat and petticoat might remind us of Sprat's ending in *The Lobster's Voyage*. Lewis presents Goosee as a sort of exotic doll that he can pick up and move as he likes (I discuss a more explicit literary convergence of an Afro-Caribbean woman and doll in chapter 5).

As much as anything, the letter sets up a literary venture for him. He promises to release a collection of what he calls "Nancy stories" (a bastardization of "Anansi stories," the Akan term for a tradition of folktales originating in West Africa), as part of "a sort of journal," presumably the autobiographical travelogue *Journal of a West India Proprietor*, written around the same time as the letter but published posthumously in 1834.[15] The *Journal* is composed mainly of diary entries recounting Lewis's visits to Jamaica in 1815–1816 and 1817–1818. Four more stories of the sort Goosee tells are interspersed throughout, with sparse commentary and no attribution. Goosee is absent—if indeed she was ever present, since the letter carries out several forms of distortion and caricature. Lewis's fantasy of the enslaved woman as a storybook heroine has been abandoned.

Although it makes sense that Lewis would erase the storyteller when appropriating her work, the abandonment of the Goosee framing and the backhanded praise in the letter hint at his apprehensions about Afro-Caribbean women's storytelling, allowing us to consider how these storytellers addressed childhood, relationality, and ethics. To the extent that the story Lewis attributes to Goosee draws from an Afro-Caribbean tale, what might her story—and those included in the *Journal*—tell us about how enslaved people responded to enslavers' vicious treatment, including that which underwrote so-called enslaver benevolence, and engaged in ethical instruction? What happens when we think of Afro-Caribbean youth as part of the audience for the stories recorded in the letter and *Journal*, even though we access them through their secondary presentation to a white, European, and presumably adult audience?[16]

Scholars of children's literature have been reluctant to consider nineteenth-century stories told by enslaved people as representing material for or even about children. However, the field has long been working from an outdated assumption that childhood was not applied to or used by enslaved Africans. Cynthia James, in her important essay on the development of Jamaican and Trinidadian children's literature, claims that "West Indian society . . . did not specifically place children in a category separate from adults . . . The need for community in the face of adverse conditions, and the near absence of 'childhood' knitted together old and young."[17] She argues that Anansi stories did not become children's literature for Afro-Caribbeans until they were used in early twentieth-century schoolbooks, where they lacked "the cultural and stylistic features that are inherent in their Creole orality."[18]

James's claim is based on reasonable assumptions: Enslavement is difficult to reconcile with childhood, and in many cases, it is condescending to classify folktales told to a mixed-age audience as children's stories. There are, furthermore, obstacles to identifying an enslaved child audience for these tales. Lewis mentions that very young children spent time with old women but never depicts them listening to stories.[19] Enslaved youth were generally forced to labor starting around age five, so it is unclear when they could have listened—though this is also true of adults. But even if we cannot use Lewis's text to locate children at the scene of storytelling, updates in the historical understanding of enslaved childhoods invite a shift in how we read stories told in this location and time.

Building on groundbreaking studies on enslaved youth by Wilma King, Marie Jenkins Schwartz, Cecily Jones, and Audra Diptee, books on Jamaica by Sasha Turner and Colleen Vasconcellos argue that the concept of childhood strongly informed enslaver views between the abolition of the transatlantic slave trade in 1807 and the abolition of British enslavement in 1833, which took effect in 1834. Young people had been captured and sold as part of the slave trade from the beginning, as documented in multiple autobiographies, including Olaudah Equiano's *The Interesting Narrative of the Life of Olaudah Equiano* (1789), in which the author is kidnapped at age eleven. Enslaved adults, however, were favored because of their ability to work harder and longer. Yet in the period from 1807 to 1833, in which enslavement continued to be a central part of Britain's economy but no new enslaved people could be lawfully imported, children became desirable because of slave codes tying the condition of the child to that of the mother.[20] This period coincides with the time that Lewis's work was written and published. As S. Turner points out, British abolitionists even advocated enslaved women's childbearing as a means to end the trade by proposing that enslaved youth could take the place of new enslaved adults. This devil's deal intensified enslaver interest in youth, who were no longer considered useless by-products of adult enslavement but valuable investments.

The enslaver concept of childhood did not have many of the features coming to be associated with white childhood during the same period—namely, protection—but it overlapped in that enslaved children were considered especially trainable and important to the future. Vasconcellos shows that after abolitionists succeeded in ending the trade, "ideas of child worth . . . shifted as planters realized the need for change in the . . . treatment of the women and children on their estates."[21] Casting themselves as benevolent enslavers, they made marginal adjustments to pregnant women's and children's diets, as well as access to medical care, to increase their productivity. Some introduced educational schemes designed to make youth obedient. To be clear, these measures were not benevolent. Enslavers proposed the oxymoronic idea of ethical enslavement to secure the longevity of the enterprise—and they were trying to reassert control after multiple rebellions among the enslaved. It is best to understand so-called improvements targeting youth as part of what Diptee and David V. Trotman have called the "battle over childhood and youth" "at the heart of the colonial enterprise."[22]

Vasconcellos recognizes the importance of storytelling to this battle in her claim that enslaved people "likely taught their children moral lessons through stories."[23] This chapter builds on this claim, arguing that enslaved people adapted narratives within a broader tradition of African-derived storytelling to counter the increased violence and indoctrination directed toward children following the end of the slave trade and to instill ethics based on relational care, resilience, respectability, and resistance.[24] We can identify Lewis's declaration that Goosee's stories are "nursery tales" as an attempt to co-opt narratives that were, in their original form, hostile to his presence. It is worth noting that Anansi stories are now considered a part of children's culture. The editors of *Anansesem*, the principle Caribbean children's magazine until it folded in 2020, claim that their publication continued "the tradition . . . that began when Anansi stories first took root in the Caribbean . . . [T]hey are a kind of foundation."[25] The stories collected by Lewis allow us to establish a genealogy for the tales as children's literature, even as we should not accept Lewis's fantasy of the enslaved storyteller telling nursery stories as defined by a European oral or print tradition or conclude that all Anansi stories were (or are) children's literature.

Given Lewis's exploitative relationship with enslaved people, looking for the intentions of the enslaved in his work comes with risks. This chapter offers an interpretive method for mining texts by white writers for insight about the cultures they are involved in oppressing, using a metaphor from one of the unattributed Anansi stories in Lewis's *Journal.* In this story, retold in later children's books from the African diaspora, including Robert San Souci's *The Talking Eggs* (1989) and Obi Onyefulu's *Chinye* (1994), the heroine is advised to move past loud *talking* eggs in the henhouse to collect those that are silent. Researchers interested in the history of enslavement cannot avoid encountering the loud opinions of colonizers like Lewis, but we can examine their motives and, when appropriate, refuse to carry these viewpoints forth, instead repurposing their texts as starting points for uncovering the views of those who have been silenced. Positioning Goosee's story among other historical sources, I consider how enslaved storytellers taught children about objectification, leveraged images of abjection, and imagined potential subjecthood.[26]

By characterizing nineteenth-century Afro-Caribbean storytellers as offering fantastical tales that, like Hartman, "imagine a free state . . . as [an] anticipated future," we can understand these stories as contributing to the ongoing project of freedom over time.[27] I propose that Afro-Caribbean folk stories remained a lasting means to teach young people about colonial violence that impacted them. In contrast to the stories discussed in chapter 1, which limit the ethical imperatives and crises of Atlantic relationality to white families, these stories represent racially blended families, showing them to be the result of unethical relations. Two of the unattributed folktales in Lewis's *Journal,* when read in this historical context, protest what was rapidly becoming enslavers' strategy of securing future slaves by sexually assaulting enslaved women. The emphasis of the stories is not on the mothers but on the enslaved girls who were the product of these practices, demonstrating the intergenerational reverberations of sexual abuse.

As disfavored progeny, these girls face retaliatory violence from their relatives but triumph in the end through both respectability and resistance. I place these materials in a historical context recognizing how enslaved girls contested their situation, showing how these fantastical narratives have historical validity, not always in offering straightforwardly factual accounts but in developing ethical strategies safeguarded over generations.[28] By recognizing how the stories propose intergenerational possibilities for opposing colonialism and enslavement, we can identify how they not only present alternative histories but also invent futures in which Afro-Caribbean girls are cared for and valued. To determine the lasting impact of these tales, I follow Diptee and Trotman's helpful suggestion that to combat the paucity of our archives, we must gather insight from contemporary sources that are product of cultural interactions dating from long before their production. Searching for traces of the folktales reveals that, over time, such stories blended into the figure of Black Cinderella. Encapsulated by reggae artist Errol Dunkley's assertion that the Black woman is "always the Cinderella," the Black Cinderella tradition registers an answer to Lewis's attempt to possess Goosee and a challenge to colonial legacies that still try to impose European stories onto Afro-Caribbean people. The history that gives rise to Black Cinderella, like the history of Goosee Shoo Shoo, is characterized by gaps and silences, but piecing it together traces how Afro-Caribbean people have used childhood—especially girlhood—to teach and demand ethical conduct, beginning during enslavement.

A Two Shoe Method

The story of Goody Two Shoes relates the entire (fictional) history of her life, but what, if anything, can we know about Goosee Shoo Shoo, a figure who is shrouded in the past, dispossessed of a name, and obscured by a colonial gaze? As Simon Gikandi argues, in many cases "the only existing records [are] those committed to slaves' subjection."[29] Enslavers "sought to assert their authority through relentless record keeping . . . And thus . . . the archive of the slaver established statements whose major role was to fix the African as an object, as chattel, as property."[30] To consider one example, Lewis's enthusiastic attention to enslaved people's births in his *Journal*, though presented as the result of better treatment, shows that he designates their children as property and is invested in owning them for the foreseeable future. One entry registers awe in seeing one woman hold up child, saying, "Him nice lilly neger for Massa!"[31] It is hard to tell whether this event happened and, if it did, what it meant. Lewis wields more power than usual writers of narrative in determining how his subjects appear on the page, because he has both the power to command them and a monopoly on their representation. Yet, as Gikandi argues, "the major lesson we have learned from subaltern studies is that this control and regulation, which seeks to remove all traces of difference or resistance, still leaves in its wake important signs of that which it tries to control or erase."[32]

Reading childhood in white-authored texts like Lewis's requires what I call, after Goosee, a "two-shoe" method. First, we must recognize that enslaved childhood was a site of intense colonial interest. Enslavers like Lewis had multiple, sometimes competing, goals when it came to children, including introducing European ideologies, appropriating rituals of the enslaved as evidence of enslaver-friendly practices, and denying enslaved people the humanizing elements associated with childhood. Second, we must unearth Afro-Caribbean people's resistance to these efforts, including practices showing care toward children and fostering their socialization, which though never fully accessible in the colonizers' texts, appear in traces.

Putting these two ways of reading together without assimilating them has the effect, which Gikandi advocates, of "displacing the archive, depriving it of the claim to be a constellation of signs that will lead us to the event itself, and thus also exposing it as a series of stories told to account for a set of events whose meaning was contested then and now."[33] Such an approach is appropriate when it comes to enslaved childhood, which S. Turner frames as a "deeply contested area" in which enslavers, abolitionists, missionaries, and parents "made divergent claims about [children's] future roles."[34] What we can seek in Lewis's text, if not a direct rendering of Anansi stories as enslaved Africans told them, are clues to the conflicts being waged over childhood, which Lewis attempts to conceal under the rubric of benevolent enslavement.

To my mind, the benefits of this approach outweigh its risks, but its risks must be acknowledged, keeping in mind Marah Gubar's argument that talking about children's literature is a "risky business" in which our fear of being wrong sometimes leads us to dismiss valuable evidence.[35] One risk of seeking Afro-Caribbean understandings of childhood and children's literature in this text is that Lewis's work does not provide full access to the original teller or context. He does what a responsible scholar would not want to do, positing that the stories function like "nursery stories"—and, by extension, children's literature—because they look like children's literature to him. To counter this problem, we must not forget that Lewis's biases may have caused him to misinterpret, translate, or even rewrite the stories to fit his worldview and definition of children's literature. We can outline what his investments likely were, using what we know about enslaver attitudes—and set aside some of his assertions as noisy eggs.

Not seeking children's literature in this text would arguably have greater risks. Histories of children's literature attending to sources outside of Europe and the United States—especially oral sources—are in the minority. Despite the argument, made most thoroughly by Gubar, that children's literature is best understood as a fluid category rather than a unified print tradition distinct from oral transmission—and Sarada Balagopalan's argument that "the idea of 'multiple childhoods' is [no longer] something that researchers within the field of childhood studies require to be convinced about"—scholars still marginalize sources, like folktales, that do not bear the marks of a print culture tradition of children's literature.[36] For this reason, considering evidence of diverse perspectives becomes all the more valuable. It is important to corroborate our interpretations, when possible, with sources representing the experiences of enslaved people. At the same time, we must recognize that folk stories contain multiple layers of meaning, many only accessible to the immediate audience, and some nuances will be lost to history.

We can begin to apply this two-shoe method to Lewis's work by consulting his *Journal* for clues about enslaver attitudes toward children, which we can use to contextualize his comments about Goosee and her story. Upon his arrival to Jamaica on November 10, 1815, Lewis includes part of a conversation with a Mr. S——, a planter in the "May-Day Mountains" of Jamaica. Reporting S's opinions in dialect, Lewis says the man believes that "'hedicating the negroes is the only way to make them appy; indeed, in his umble hopinion, hedication his hall in hall!"[37] The dialect is the only indication of Lewis's perspective: that he is not taking S entirely seriously. However, Vasconcellos and S. Turner have discovered that enslavers, who often vehemently opposed education efforts, were coming to hold more favorable sentiments about enslaved children's education during the period when Lewis was writing.

Missionary organizations (as I discuss in chapter 4) had been endeavoring for decades to educate enslaved children for the purposes of conversion, sometimes with the collaboration of Afro-Caribbean locals.[38] The records of such organizations draw on religious ideas of childhood and often refer to enslaved youth as children.[39] Enslavers largely resisted these efforts, particularly prior to the abolition of the slave trade. After the trade was outlawed in 1807—a long process beginning in the 1790s and building on the Amelioration Act of 1798—they became interested in enslaved youths' survival (not their happiness, as S claims) because they could no longer buy adults. They assigned children greater monetary value and offered them marginally better care. These reforms build on literary imaginings of benevolent slaveholders, the most famous being Maria Edgeworth's "The Grateful Negro" (1804). Edgeworth's story, which juxtaposes "two planters; whose methods of managing their slaves were as different as possible," argues for a warped form of ethical relationality, in which an irremediable slave system makes enslavers and enslaved interdependent, so that good management is necessary to ensure the optimal stability and functionality of the system.[40] The title character, an evolution of Thomas Day's grateful Black and Fielding's Mignon, appreciates his enslaver's good treatment so much that he saves him from a plotted rebellion. Such fictions of gratitude imagine the beneficial outcome of ethical reforms.

To repeat, these reforms were not benevolent. They allowed enslavers to rationalize separation of mothers and children and made children vulnerable to indoctrination in the form of enslaver-friendly education. According to S. Turner, enslavers "feared that enslaved children's attachment to their parents would make children rebellious and lazy. Enslavers . . . embraced the idea that children were malleable characters, and that it was up to them to mold enslaved youths into what they imagined they would become."[41] Enslavers viewing themselves as benevolent were more likely to align with missionary organizations than in prior years and, according to Vasconcellos, "carefully used religious instruction to enhance their social control."[42] As I discuss in chapter 4, missionaries boasted to an umbrella organization, the British and Foreign School Society (BFSS), that thousands of enslaved children participated in their programs, a large number that represents only a fraction of the overall population of enslaved Africans.

Some enslavers were skeptical, fearing, as Mary Turner puts it, that "missionaries would teach the slaves not only the Christian virtues of industry and obedience but also that God made all men equal."[43] Others, however, imagined education as a last stand against the outright abolition of enslavement and insurance that they would maintain their dominance if the institution of slavery were abolished. They also wanted to keep from alienating a British government interested in amelioration; M. Turner suggests that the "considerations that had led to the planters to extend a degree of toleration" to missionaries "carried ever greater weight" after the end of the Napoleonic Wars in 1815, because they wanted to maintain the protection of the sugar industry in the British government's trade deals (including the Abertura dos portos discussed in chapter 1).

His ridicule of Mr. S notwithstanding, Lewis participates in this pro-teaching phenomenon. He reports meeting with educators throughout the *Journal*, including Anglicans and Moravians. He claims to be open to the work of both, though he favors the established church and claims he will give them priority access to the young people he enslaved. There may be more to this preference than Lewis admits; M. Turner notes that Anglicans serving in Jamaica were closely aligned with enslavers and not very involved in education, but the prospect of Anglican teaching was "used more than once . . . by the planters and the West India Committee to brighten the slave owners' image."[44] In turn, as Rebecca Schneider demonstrates, enslavers feared dissenting missions were teaching "subversive ideology."[45] Lewis nonetheless goes to a neighboring estate to ask a Moravian minister "what progress had been made" and discovers that "the Moravian has . . . agreed, to give up an hour every day for the religious instruction of the negro children on that property."[46] He comments that he "should certainly request him to extend his labours to [his estate at] Cornwall" if he were not giving priority to the Church of England.[47]

Enslavers specifically expressed concerns about instruction beyond Christian teachings, including in reading and (especially) writing. Lewis, however, discusses expanding Christian education by combining it with reading instruction: "It appears, indeed, to me, that the only means of giving the negroes morality and religion must be through the medium of education . . . There is not a single negro among my whole three hundred who can read a line; and what I suppose to be wanted on West-Indian estates is not an importation of missionaries, but of schoolmasters on Dr. Bell's plan, if it could by any means be introduced here with effect."[48] Other times, he claims that he has asked free Black people about their reading practices, suggesting that he approves of their learning to read. Lewis's support was fickle, however. He expresses qualms about education to island officials, including the need for "extreme delicacy" to prevent "danger to the island."[49] Such reservations acknowledge enslaved people's use of literacy for resistance. As Haley North shows, even a small number of literate enslaved people could catalyze resistance by spreading "information in the newspapers or other written communication about rebellions happening elsewhere."[50] Runaways also used writing skills to forge manumission documents and tickets used by enslavers to control mobility, which North suggests had heightened implications after 1807 due to the inability to replenish enslaved workers.[51]

Perhaps because of such fears, Lewis did not implement schooling on his plantation. He instead trumpets his program of educating the children he enslaved through informal interactions like christenings, about which he flip-pantly reflects, "I think nobody will be able to accuse me of neglecting the religious education of my negroes: for I have not only promised to baptize all the infants, but, meeting a little black boy this morning, who said that his name was Moses, I gave him a piece of silver, and told him that it was for the sake of Aaron; which, I flatter myself, was planting in his young mind the rudiments of Christianity."[52] Such actions likely had little effect, if any, for the hundreds of children on Lewis's estates. He claims also to read to the people he enslaved for a short time, though his reason for writing about this seems to be so he can poke fun at their misunderstanding, such as a time when an enslaved person supposedly conflates him with God.[53] Another time, he tries his hand at a nursery rhyme to discourage the people he enslaved from running away, which he again turns into a sexual joke:

> Peter, Peter was a black boy;
> Peter him pull foot one day:
> Buckra girl, him Peter's joy;
> Lilly white girl entice him away . . .
> Oh! Peter, Peter was a bad boy; Peter was a runaway.[54]

As he includes the poem in the *Journal* without comment, we cannot tell whether he recited it to children, though he does mention a few instances of enslaved people running away. S. Turner suggests that "traditional means of protest, such as running away" were common ways parents and children responded to enslavers' "investment in child-rearing."[55]

Historians have used such protests to gauge enslaved Africans' views on childhood. According to S. Turner, enslaved families also rebelled by attacking "symbols of white power."[56] In this fraught context of child stealing and indoctrination, we can identify storytelling as another front in the attack: a means to reassert authority over child rearing and encode lessons on how to resist. Vasconcellos argues that Anansi tales provided a (largely underground) education to enslaved children: "As in many West African societies, folklore was and still is a tool used in daily life to teach children respect, caution, bravery, courage, perseverance, and morality . . . [R]einvented folklore traditions educated a new generation of children . . . that was born into slavery."[57] Given increased enslaver attention to youth in the years Lewis was writing, we can frame the stories told on his plantation as attempts to counter this attention.

Goosee's Abject Child

It is within this fraught context that Lewis aligns the cultural work done by an enslaved female storyteller with the work done by Goody Two Shoes and children's literature. The ideological underpinnings of the comparison begin to surface when we notice that in Newbery's book Goody begins her story at odds with a rich landowner, becomes an asset to the parish as a teacher, and finally marries another gentleman. Such a story might have been meaningful to Lewis because, according to his *Journal*, the women on his estate frequently resist him. They carry out what he calls a "petticoat rebellion" in which some women refuse to carry trash and a "fierce young devil" named Whaunica tries to strangle Lewis's agent.[58] Lewis disciplines the group and reports on a different occasion—seemingly with relish—that the women have begun to call him "husband."[59] Lewis's version of relation when it comes to these women depends not on ethical responsibility to them but his claim to ownership, framed through a patriarchal understanding of familial cooperation between husband and wife.

The Goosee letter advances a complementary fantasy of cooperation and directs it toward what Lewis (pathologically) frames as an ethical end: enslaver-friendly education, with the child as beneficiary. By naming the storyteller after a motherly schoolteacher, comparing her story to "nursery tales," and announcing that he "shall endeavor to collect" these stories, Lewis implies that they share a quasi-parental investment in the next generation.[60] Although no child listeners appear in the letter, the Goody comparison wistfully implies that enslaved youth can be taught with the same tool they are taught with in England: children's literature.[61]

To the extent that Lewis could appropriate Goosee's tale for a European audience, he probably meant the nursery tale label as an accolade. While pedagogues dismissed fairy tales as fodder for children in the eighteenth century, they were enjoying new vogue due to their favor among Romantic poets like Samuel Coleridge and Charles Lamb. Lewis's gothic writing fits into this literary milieu—and his letter draws on long-standing conventions of using "uneducated, garrulous, and often older women as storytellers to excuse or justify the presentation of low material to a presumably more sophisticated audience."[62] Yet Lewis also relies on an emerging bourgeois definition of children's literature as disciplinary and moralistic, which in the colonies was used for control under the guise of promoting universal virtue ethics.[63] He even forces a moral into Goosee's story, as we will see. Children's literature is a concept by which Lewis seizes the Anansi stories and assigns them with his own value, securing the economic value of his estate.

Lewis is not ultimately very specific in his comparison of Goosee's tales to children's stories, failing to draw tight connections between Anansi stories and *Goody Two Shoes* or the nursery stories he mentions. He implies instead that children's literature is a moralistic form, which can impose a narrow set of ethics favorable to colonizers and enslavers. Lewis is hardly alone in defining children's literature this way, but his employment of a moral framework allows us to see how such definitions of children's literature serve the needs of the British in a colonial context. The insistence on ethical platitudes such as avoiding lying and working hard as key elements of children's literature may stem not only from the importance of these values to classical liberal theories of society but also from the heavy influence that the economic and ideological needs of colonization and trade were having on English-language children's literature. As I discuss in chapter 1, stories featuring unruly child characters from the colonies who need to be disciplined became staples of children's literature by the early nineteenth century. This colonial-inflected disciplinary function of children's literature, as I will discuss further in chapter 4, informed the work of British and US missionaries in the Caribbean, who imported thousands of English-language books into the Caribbean to Anglicanize Afro-Caribbean children during and after enslavement.[64]

That Lewis is not interested in a real partnership or recognition of Goosee as an author-educator becomes apparent through his eventual presentation of Goosee as very different from her namesake. He not only sexualizes the enslaved woman but also depicts her as overly interested in tobacco and liquor, saying that "a glass of rum, or a roll of *backy*, is sure to unpack Goosee Shoo Shoo's budget"—a phrase that extends the innuendo.[65] So doing, Lewis questions her abilities as teacher, clearing the way for enslavers' influence and instigating what Lara Putnam has noted is a pervasive trope of Afro-Caribbean parenting as deficient.[66] The hypersexualization of enslaved women served enslaver strategies for increasing their labor force, while suppressing these women's creation of culture. As Elizabeth Dillon writes, "The excessive sexuality and allure of the [creole] woman is thus coupled with a discourse of degeneracy[,] . . . one that insists that for all of the sexual fecundity of the tropical geography and the tropical body, sanctioned reproduction cannot occur at this site."[67] Lewis's happiness in being called "husband" notwithstanding, he claims in another section that enslaved women do not understand that sexual relationships with white men are not equivalent to marriage. This condescending remark diminishes enslaved women as relationally unfit, while betraying Lewis's cluelessness regarding the possibility that the women might be trying to make the best of a nonconsensual sexual relationship.[68]

The tale Lewis retells in the Goosee letter, featuring a young man birthed without a head, may have been appealing to him because it feeds the myth of Afro-Caribbean reproductive incompetence and the need for outside intervention. The mother makes multiple attempts to heal her son in consultation with an owl, but each attempt fails because she is reluctant to share the full details of his condition. As a result of her half truths, the owl is able to give the child only animal heads, including the head of an "ass."[69] The boy is unhappy because these heads frighten the princess whom he wishes to marry. He eventually gets a better head by petitioning the girl's father, the king, who fashions it out of a gold piece, a drop of brandy, and other "shinee" baubles.[70] The couple marries and lives happily with "plenty rum an backy."[71]

The events in the story mirror incidents Lewis describes happening on his estate. He records frustration with low survival rates among infants—a detail that points to resistance among enslaved Africans for, as S. Turner explains, "enslaved mothers understood the importance of their children to planters, and took extreme measures, including infanticide" to prevent separation.[72] As part of his self-fashioning as a benevolent slaveholder, Lewis claims to offer incentives to mothers, such as hospital stays after birth, but suspects them of taking advantage of what he considers an indulgence and complains of their negligence toward their children. The king, as a benefactor to the mother and child, resembles how Lewis depicts his attempts to increase his plantation's fruitfulness. He claims he has given a "scarlet girdle" to all mothers with a "silver medal" for each infant still "alive and well on the fourteenth day."[73]

Building on this white savior dynamic, Lewis claims that Goosee does not include a moral in her story because she is satisfied by the king giving the young man and princess rum and tobacco—and essentially is in a stupor because she has been given these items herself. Since Lewis "takes care" that Goosee has "her due share of [these] . . . highly-prized articles," he becomes the corollary to the king.[74] Just as the king emerges as a better friend to the boy than his mother, Lewis casts himself as a better teacher than Goosee by inserting a moral into the story: "in justice to my favourite, I must really be allowed to observe for her, that people who may have the misfortune to be born without heads, may be assured that telling lies will prove the very worst cement for preserving heads of any description in a proper and becoming situation."[75]

Although presented jokingly, this bland moral resembles the enslaver-friendly ethical truisms promoted in English schoolbooks imported into the Caribbean. For example, in 1819 the *Kingston Chronicle* ran an ad for *Murray's English Reader*, a book that promoted an English canon with writers considered "excellent in . . . moral character and tendency" (see my further discussion in chapter 4).[76] Among its lessons, the book proscribes "dishonesty" and blames "poverty" on the vices of the poor.[77] Enslavers had reason to promote this message: having truthful servants who believed they were at fault for their misery discouraged rebellion. Lying, conversely, could be an effective means of resistance.

Beyond the reasons Lewis might have been interested in the story, what might we glean about enslaved Africans' views of childhood? Goosee's tale is striking for its contrast with accounts in which enslaved women wished for their children to die rather than live as slaves, suggesting that it offers wishful fantasies of the care children deserved. The tale squares with traditions of Black storytelling that function, as S. R. Toliver argues, "to teach, to heal, to bring life" "despite the horrors of state-sanctioned violence."[78] Ebony Elizabeth Thomas proposes that storytelling has been a way "to dream of Afro-futures," providing a "vehicle for cultural transmission . . . and, maybe most importantly, a source of hope."[79] The story mother's concern for her child happens to accord with Lewis's desires, because he relied on enslaved children to shore up his estate, but it is not likely that the mother and Lewis would have agreed about what was needed to keep children from being metaphorically headless. The mother's hope for the boy to marry the king's daughter bespeaks higher goals, unattainable unless he were freed. Anticipating feminist care ethics' emphasis on "particular others" over "universal principles," Goosee's emphasis is not on freedom as a universal right, though she may have indeed supported such a right, but on the specific situation of a child and the circumstances that inhibit his mother's care.[80]

As such, Goosee's tale, unlike those I discuss later, does not offer advice to achieve the goal of freedom. Instead, it conveys poetic truths about the dehumanizing effects of enslavement. In truth, the boy hovers between life and death, for who could live without a head? In contrast to Lewis's depiction of Goosee as an object of colonial desire and the Afro-Caribbean child as a creature whose head is bestowed by a benevolent master, Goosee's child approaches the abject, which Julia Kristeva defines as a horrific figure representing the breakdown of distinction between subject and object.[81] The abject is that which is radically excluded from the symbolic order, as well as from social participation. The child in the story represents a truth that enslavers were trying to sidestep and with which enslaved women were all too familiar; the person rendered into property cannot be made whole through so-called benevolent enslavement. The person rendered into property is a horror.

Headlessness and other shocking experiences that cannot be spoken about are common themes in stories associated with the African diaspora. In a story from Lewis's *Journal* discussed in the next section, the heroine meets two women without heads and says "nothing."[82] A similar scene appears in John Steptoe's *Mufaro's Beautiful Daughters* (1987), a Cinderella story derived from an African folktale. The application of this African storytelling convention in a Caribbean context gestures to the unspeakable challenges facing enslaved children. Goosee, through Lewis, describes the headless boy: "him no talk— him no hear—him no see—him no yammee (eat)," a poignant description of the subaltern, technically living but denied the basic requirements of life and personhood.[83]

The mother's silences regarding her son's condition attest to the difficult-to-process realities of being born into slavery: How to explain that a child has never been given the chance to have an intact identity? Recent writing about Caribbean childhoods sheds light on silence as a placeholder for children's unspeakable experiences. Derek Walcott writes in "Another Life," the "child hears nothing, hears everything / that the historian cannot hear, the howls / of all the races that crossed the water."[84] This "nothing" acknowledges the pain that cannot be put into words. And yet the story speaks. Poignantly, the head the boy gets is made of objects—shiny baubles and alcohol—rather than recognizable markers of personhood. This makeshift head fashions him into a legible figure who is able to be married and participate in the economy of "rum and backy" as a consumer rather than the consumed—but the head's composition remains an acknowledgment that in the transatlantic economy people are not independent of the goods and money being exchanged.

Lewis reinforces Goosee's story of dispossession by erasing the enslaved storyteller in his published *Journal*, removing the story of the headless boy and preserving only disembodied, disconnected stories. It is strange, Terry notes, that "though Lewis characteristically used the same material in the *Journal* as in his letters, this lively account . . . was omitted."[85] The omission seems to have been prescient. Although Lewis died in 1818 on a ship to England from Jamaica, the *Journal* was not published until 1834, the year that the abolition of slavery in the British Empire took effect. Enslavers again became averse to children, Vasconcellos explains, because the transitional four-year apprenticeship system required them to provide for people they had enslaved without the expectation of future labor. Other stakeholders, like missionaries, remained invested in Afro-Caribbean children's education, but the economic incentives for a fantasy of collaboration between enslavers and enslaved had evaporated. In the face of this new reality, Goosee would have been a lot less irresistible.

Black Cinderella

The unattributed stories in Lewis's *Journal* nonetheless yield important insights, especially when connected to later Afro-Caribbean storytelling and musical traditions. Two stories allow us to trace the faint beginnings of Black Cinderella, a contemporary figure used in Jamaican culture to highlight the lasting impact of colonial ideologies on girls and to recognize their importance as ethical actors. Lewis perhaps included these persecuted heroine stories because they support his notion that the Anansi tales were "nursery tales" and, additionally, offered exotic descriptions of Obeah. Yet there is evidence that they were recorded faithfully. Two picture books, *The Talking Eggs* and *Chinye*, retell the folktales found in Lewis's text using different African and African American sources.[86]

What English speakers call "Cinderella" is, of course, not just an English-language story. Maria Tatar writes, "When we say the word 'Cinderella,' we are referring . . . to an entire array of stories with a persecuted heroine," including the Chinese story of *Yeh Shen* (618–907 CE), which long predates the best-known European versions by Giambattista Basile, Charles Perrault, and the Grimm brothers.[87] Early folklore studies, such as one by William Bascom in 1972, did not locate this tale type in Africa.[88] However, Bascom's study is almost certainly incomplete; the Greek historian Strabo offers fragments of an Egyptian tale featuring a lost sandal and search for its wearer, though without the story of the girl's persecution and magical transformation.[89] *The Talking Eggs* and *Chinye*, though recorded later than Lewis's *Journal*, suggest the likelihood of other African predecessors, which may or may not have blended with European versions by the time Lewis was writing.

Securing the exact origin of the tales, in my view, is less important than considering how they accrue meanings with specific tellings and contribute to an evolving tradition. As Harry G. Lefever points out, "Afro-Caribbean tales are a complex mixture of both Old World cultural survivals and New World cultural experiences."[90] The context of life on Lewis's plantation can help us contemplate what stories of persecuted heroines might have meant to enslaved Africans, especially when supplemented by Mary Prince's narrative about her life on a similar island from around the same time. Although their tellers do not call these heroines "Cinderella," they use their tales to critique racism and enslavement, anticipating the resistant ways that later Afro-Caribbean artists claim Cinderella as a figure. By connecting early and later examples of this motif, I do not mean to imply that Afro-Caribbean experience is unchanging—a tendency in interpretations of African diasporic folklore that Hazel V. Carby critiques—or to foreclose analysis of nuances in the contemporary usages that move beyond colonial history.[91] Rather, I suggest that persecuted heroine stories are tools for calling attention to situations in which there is a mismatch between experiences and ethical ideals, and for imagining restoration or reparation. They are an especially powerful means of exposing the lie of benevolent enslavement and the violence of enslavers' attempts to reproduce and indoctrinate their workforce after the abolition of the slave trade. They have come to protest lingering injustices against Afro-Caribbean girls.

The problem faced by most persecuted heroines is that their treatment is out of step with their worth because of changes in their family situation, requiring that the heroine be elevated to restore equilibrium. The sexual violence that was amplified with the end of the slave trade adds new dimensions to stories of a daughter's disinheritance and abuse. Characterizing the violence of enslavement as interfamilial, the persecuted heroine stories in Lewis's text respond to the dismantling and reconfiguration of families in enslavement and denounce the unethical sexual treatment of enslaved women that increased once purchasing humans from Africa became illegal. As Patricia Glinton-Meicholas points out, "The universal subject of wicked second spouses, guardians and step-parents occurs frequently in . . . Caribbean-area canons. Trials by ordeal, especially at the hands of abusive step-mothers, are common."[92] Intriguingly, the stories in Lewis's text center on the impact of sexual violence on girls, rather than adult women, even though enslavers would not have been very interested in this distinction.[93] This emphasis on girlhood insinuates that the ethical realignment that the stories imagine will happen in the next generation.

Later folktales and reggae songs, as we will see, explicitly lay claim to Cinderella. Some new forms continue to address the legacies of sexual violence in enslavement, while others challenge the remnants of white colonial educational investments in children that, I have argued, intensified with the abolition of the slave trade. As education historian Shirley Gordon notes, Caribbean schools continued to advance white imperial interests even after the success of Jamaican independence in 1962.[94] Children encountered Cinderella not just as the rags-to-riches tale that has variants from many cultures but as the specific story of a white European girl named Cinderella. Resonances between the stories Lewis recounts, an intermediate folktale from the early twentieth century, and later resistant musical art forms allow us to see how Afro-Caribbean people have imagined liberation from colonial legacies through girls.[95]

The first persecuted heroine story collected in Lewis's *Journal* begins thus: "Two sisters had always lived together on the best terms; but on the death of one of them, the other treated very harshly a little niece . . . [and] made her a common drudge."[96] The mistreated girl breaks a water jug and is ordered to leave home as punishment. After encountering a headless woman, as mentioned in the previous section, she meets with an old woman who tells her she can find magic eggs in the henhouse by ignoring the eggs that speak and gathering the silent ones. Once collected, the silent eggs turn into "a water jug exactly similar to that which she had broken," "a whole large sugar estate," and "a splendid equipage," similar to Charles Perrault's pumpkin carriage.[97] The aunt then sends *her* daughter to the henhouse, but she is impolite and takes the three loudest eggs. The first contains nothing; the second, a snake; and the third, an old woman without a head, who scolds her for her rudeness and sends her home with empty shells.[98]

Blended families like this one took on racially charged meanings during enslavement, as we can glean from the autobiographical *History of Mary Prince, a West Indian Slave* (1831). Prince describes her childhood, spent enslaved to a white family: "I was made quite a pet of by Miss Betsey, and loved her very much . . . we used to play together with Miss Betsey, with as much freedom almost as if she had been our sister."[99] She begins to understand her difference from Betsey when her master's wife dies and she is made to labor.

An experience Prince has with her enslavers uncannily mirrors the challenge that the story heroine faces, even though the latter is never explicitly marked as an enslaved person: "One day a heavy squall of wind and rain came on suddenly, and my mistress sent me round the corner of the house to empty a large earthen jar. The jar was already cracked with an old deep crack that divided it in the middle, and . . . it parted in my hand."[100] Unlike story girl's punishment, Prince's penalty does not bring rewards; she is whipped with a hundred lashes. The folk story therefore does not depict the whole of real life but acknowledges the challenges that children were facing and provides an imaginative escape into a speculative world.

Enslaved and enslavers' children not only were sometimes lumped together as youth but also were part of the same biological families. Several of Lewis's overseers, including his bookkeeper, had children with enslaved women. Admitting that these children usually followed the condition of their mothers, Lewis observes that "(if slaves) [they] are always honoured by their fellows with the title of Miss."[101] Twelve children listed as "mulatto" or "quadroon" in Lewis's Slave Registers in 1817 possibly fit into this category.[102] He also indicates that enslaved women and their progeny faced violence by offhandedly telling a story about women being "kicked in the womb" by bookkeepers at several plantations.[103] Making an offensive joke about women being kicked in the belly from one end of the island to the other, Lewis does not acknowledge the likely possibility that this area of the body was targeted because of pregnancy or reflect on how these stories might thwart his efforts to increase his enslaved population. His flippancy instead conveys indifference to the violence that was undoubtedly part and parcel of controlling more than 1,000 people on his estates. Prince, for her part, tells the story of a pregnant woman killed by her enslaver. The existential threats to the mixed-race children on Lewis's plantation resemble those the niece faces in the story, though he gives no sign that he understands how the common practice of enslaving mixed-race children put him and other enslavers in the position of wicked stepparents.

Lewis seems to have been interested in the story, rather, because of its potential to teach polite behavior. He pairs it with another Anansi tale in which children get punished for theft, commenting that "a moral is always an indispensable part of a Nancy story"—an odd assertion given that *he* inserts the moral into Goosee's story.[104] We can make further guesses about his motives for including the tale by considering what he may have added to it. Lewis's version resembles contemporary renditions of African tales, such as *The Talking Eggs* and *Chinye*, though the latter features gourds instead of eggs. But in these versions, the ultimate reward is gold, not a sugar estate. By implying that the best prize would be to own a plantation rather than a transferable currency, Lewis's version advances a fantasy of European culture, including enslavement, as the pinnacle of achievement. This ending serves enslaver interests by suggesting *both* that one can transcend one's situation with polite behavior—taking only the eggs one is invited to take—and that being an enslaver is the highest station, unreachable if enslaved.

Cultivating politeness and respectability is also a strategy among the enslaved for reclaiming humanity, one that Nazera Wright has found to be associated with girlhood in an African American context. Other elements of the story mirror aspects of African American girlhood documented by Wright: There is insinuation that the girl at its center is "prematurely knowing" owing to sexual violence against enslaved women (though in this case she is the product, not the immediate target, of the violence), and she becomes an idealized beacon of hope for her race.[105] The tale, like those told by the nineteenth-century African American women in Wright's study, claims that girls can transcend their circumstances through respectable behavior. Wright astutely points out that respectability, nevertheless, is a strategy with limitations—it restrains girls even as they are liberated.

A second persecuted heroine story in Lewis's text turns toward violent resistance rather than respectability, reminding us that Jamaica saw individual and group uprisings throughout the eighteenth and nineteenth centuries. This history makes no direct appearance but underpins the storyteller's vision of protest against the unethical treatment and unwholesome relations of enslavers. In the tale, another orphan struggles against her "aunt," who is determined to steal her inheritance. The story hints that racial difference causes this scorn. The girl sings, "Ho-day poor me, O! . . . They call me neger, neger! / They call me Sarah Winyan, O!"[106] The girl runs away and defeats her aunt with the help of her half brothers, who chop the tiger with whom the aunt is conspiring to bits.

Lewis seems oblivious that the violence in the story might be a response to the enslavement of children, presenting it as an example of the dangers of practicing Obeah.[107] Yet the story accords with Afro-Caribbean ethical strategies for coping with family-destroying practices by offering an alternative configuration of family as a group who might aid each other's survival. As Vasconcellos explains, enslaved people often lived in "kin-like" groups based on their shipmates on the Middle Passage.[108] Lewis's *Journal* recalls one enslaved man telling him another man was his "relation" because their fathers were "shipmates."[109] The champions of this story take these connections a step further to become brothers and sisters in resistance.

The resistant understandings of the family in stories like this one provide an important complement to stories of creole families in British children's literature. For instance, in A. Selwyn's *The Little Creoles* (discussed in chapter 1), the white creole characters, Blanche and Francis, are Cinderella-like figures with an uncertain position in their extended family, in some ways mirroring the situation of the mixed-race children who were not enslaved. Yet the text sidesteps the ethical questions presented by enslavers' sexual violence, including mixed-race children's potential inclusion within families, by making a clear division between white and Black characters. While the initially frail Blanche and Francis experience a rise like Cinderella in that they acquire good health and literacy, the main transition comes when their white English cousins Rowland and Augustus accept the white creole children's (erroneous) assertion that enslavers and enslaved are knitted together by bonds of benevolent care. This acceptance accompanies a physical transition; like the stepsisters in the version of Cinderella recorded by the Grimms, Rowland loses his eyesight. He only regains his sight when the white creole Francis reads to him.

The Cinderella-esque stories collected by Lewis, by contrast, present enslavement through a lens of interfamilial oppression, pushing against the violence of Europeans' selective extension of their concepts of family and childhood to enslaved Africans. That Anansi stories are associated with resistance is not a new idea; Emily Zobel Marshall uses the phrase "Anansi tactics" to describe the ways Afro-Caribbeans challenged their oppressors.[110] But such arguments have rarely focused on children as participants. Vasconcellos counters this omission with court records showing that children turned to "theft, violence, vandalism, arson," and murder to resist.[111] Lewis and Vasconcellos both recount stories of teenage girls poisoning their enslavers, which have added meaning when we consider the likely onset age of sexual violence. In the "Nancy story" collected by Lewis, the girl protagonist also asserts her power violently, though Lewis distances the tale from historical incidents of Afro-Caribbean resistance by comparing the aunt to an Angolan queen, who engaged in "pounding little children in a mortar with her own hands."[112] This image nonetheless foregrounds violence done to children and children's resistance. (In my concluding chapter, I argue that Anansi stories figure into Afro-Caribbean children's resistance on another front: the standardization pressures of colonial education.)

Anansi stories eventually blended with children's stories arriving to the Caribbean from England. A representative 1851 advertisement in the *Antigua Weekly Times* hawks "Story Books. For the Young," including "Cinderella."[113] During the post-emancipation period, the European story of Cinderella also gained prominence through the theater; a production was staged in Jamaica in 1873 by the visiting troupe the Holland company to a mixed-race audience.[114] We might rightly see the importation of British books and performances as colonial attempts to drown out Afro-Caribbean stories; Louise Bennett-Coverley famously made this critique after she saw a pantomime performance of Cinderella performed by the Little Theatre Movement, a Jamaican theatrical company, in 1947. She composed a poem noting that everyone was white and wondered whether "is Englan or is Jamaica me deh."[115] However, Afro-Caribbean people borrowed elements of these stories to critique colonial violence and communicate about resistance.

Martha Beckwith, a groundbreaking folklorist who wrote the "the first folklife study" of Africans in the Americas and was the first to hold a chair in folklore at a US university, includes a Cinderella tale in her collection of Anansi stories from rural Jamaica in 1924. This story more strongly associates its central girl character with sexual violence and offers a fuller rationale for resistance than we see in the Lewis stories.[116] Unlike Lewis, Beckwith used an ethnographic method, in which she aimed to write down the exact language of tales.[117] Told by Maud Baker of Dry River, the story in Beckwith's collection features a heroine who is *named* Cinderella after the European heroine, though the tale does not strongly resemble the most popular versions circulating in Europe.[118] Cinderella lives with her godmother, who warns that she must not enter a certain room. She disobeys and sees a pot boiling with blood and no fire underneath. When the godmother questions Cinderella, she, like the earlier heroines, says she saw "nothing."[119] But the godmother cuts out her tongue for not telling the truth. A king finds Cinderella naked in the woods and takes her home, where she bears his children unwed. The godmother steals the babies, putting cats into the bed instead. When a third child is born, the godmother plasters blood on Cinderella's mouth, making her appear cannibalistic.[120] Cinderella is condemned, but the godmother appears with the children and restores Cinderella's tongue. The king then marries Cinderella.

Henrice Altink has offered the sole substantial interpretation of this story, which connects it to early twentieth-century anxieties about Caribbean children being raised by extended families.[121] Although it is important to recognize that Afro-Jamaican experience had changed significantly from the time of enslavement, and there are likely nuances related to the specific period, this interpretation does not account for the godmother stealing the children or for the extreme violence of her relationship with Cinderella. The bloody pot, which brings menstruation to mind, as well as the godmother's punishments, evoke a history in which sexual maturation and pregnancy are dangerous because children are stolen to be enslaved. The godmother hints at the fate of enslaved children by leaving a cat—slang for the notorious "cat-o-nine-tales" used as punishment—in their place. Politeness in the form of saying "nothing," in this case, offers no protection. By bloodying Cinderella's mouth, the godmother conjures the threat of infanticide, a real form of resistance for enslaved women.

Additionally, the bloody pot references mythology surrounding the Maroon Rebellion of 1728–1740. Queen Nanny, an Ashanti woman who successfully led the rebels against the British, reportedly "placed a large cauldron on the corner of a narrow mountain path near the edge. The pot was said to be boiling even though there was no fire beneath it. British soldiers . . . would curiously look inside, fall in and die."[122] The story preserves this key image from Jamaican resistance in cultural memory. Additionally, the godmother, like the mother in Goosee's tale, provides a context-specific relational form of maternal care. Although she seems at first to be an evil aunt, she shape-shifts into the rebelling Nanny who works secretly to undermine the king's power. Her violent maneuvers, though horrifying from the perspective of the Christian ethics colonizers were trying to universalize, respond helpfully to the situation and succeed in getting Cinderella recognized as the king's legitimate wife. The ending of the tale reflects the end of enslavement through the return of a voice to Black Cinderella. A possible moral: she must not say nothing. She must speak.

Jamaican independence offered more freedom to speak not just against interfamilial violence toward children but against the legacy of colonial educational efforts that began in the period I have been tracing. The reggae song "Black Cinderella," written in 1972 by then twenty-one-year-old Jamaican artist Errol Dunkley counters the ways in which the persecuted heroine had become associated with whiteness. According to the *Jamaica Gleaner*, Dunkley got the idea for the song from his colonial education: "I go to school hearing about this Cinderella story, this pretty Cinderella as a white girl who do the washing and cleaning. But when you check it, is the Black woman who is always the Cinderella. She do the washing and cleaning and look after the children and the white woman too."[123] The song's refrain calling for Black Cinderella and asserting that she "cannot be far away" implies that Afro-Caribbean girls who are precious but undervalued are ubiquitous.[124] Dunkley provides an alternate education that continues the tradition of the persecuted daughter tales in attempting to correct the imbalance between status and worth.

Another reggae artist, Sister Carol, who goes by the stage name Black Cinderella, was thirteen when Dunkley's song was released. She says she "liked the song and felt that he spoke to me personally."[125] In her 1984 song by the same title, she critiques the European heroine's reliance on outside intervention and suggests that Black girls have had to rely on inner sources of strength: "me never have no fairy god-mother / only di blessin' from a fi mi sweet Jah Jah [my sweet God]."[126] From this ethical center, Carol reenvisions Cinderella's ball as a space for race and class equality, where people can dance whether they are "purple, brown, or blue," wearing fancy shoes or not.

Although there is no direct connection to the stories in Lewis's text, what little we know about the children on Lewis's estate suggests that they too used singing to undermine colonizer logic. Lewis mentions them obnoxiously screaming a song with the words, "we varrry well off," after he comes.[127] The loud volume hints that the children were aware of Lewis's interest in them and responded to it with irony. Finding reverberations of resistant musical traditions across time allows us to amplify these children's resistance.

Such musical forms of resistance have recently given way to Caribbean Cinderella picture books, including San Souci's *Cendrillon: A Caribbean Cinderella* (1998), which received the 2018 Phoenix Picture Book Award from the Children's Literature Association (ChLA). Although a beautiful book worthy of this distinction, it is disappointing that it has largely not been viewed as part of a longer Afro-Caribbean history. We have come a long way from Lewis claiming that Goosee's tales are "nursery tales," yet ChLA's newsletter announcing the award primarily identifies *Cendrillon* as "a fanciful version of Perrault's 'Cinderella,'" even though San Souci's own description is more nuanced.[128] His author's note claims the book is based on "[Jean] Turiault's nineteenth-century *Creole Grammar*," which loosely follows "Perrault's Cinderella," as well as Patrick Chamoiseau's *Creole Folktales*.[129] In addition, San Souci, like Dunkley, insists that Cinderella was an Afro-Caribbean working woman, a washerwoman from Martinique. As children's literature scholars, we might encourage readers to use *Cendrillon* as an entry point into the tradition of persecuted heroines in Afro-Caribbean storytelling.

———

Recognizing a history of childhood and children's literature in which Afro-Caribbean people participated is an important step toward an ethical future for children's literature studies. In my next chapter, I discuss what a more ethical relationality meant for British and US writers in the eighteenth and nineteenth centuries by focusing on what are arguably the first activist children's books: those discouraging children from buying products associated with the slave trade. In turn, I investigate troubling fantasies that become a major thread within children's literature, promoting the idea that consumption can be innocent, even within an economy characterized by exploitation.

Taking Responsibility for the Other in Sugar Boycott Books

"Christmas" (1836), a poem for youth by US author Elizabeth Margaret Chandler, reflects the full integration of transatlantic products into white children's lives by the early nineteenth century:

> Mother, when Christmas comes once more,
> I do not wish that you
> Should buy sweet things for me again,
> As you were used to do:
>
> The taste of cakes and sugar-plums
> Is pleasant to me yet,
> And temptingly the gay shops look,
> With their fresh stores outset.
>
> But I have learn'd, dear mother,
> That the poor and wretched slave
> Must toil to win their sweetness,
> From the cradle to the grave.[1]

With its description of shop windows decorated to attract children's eyes, the poem shrewdly expresses that goods made by enslaved people were not only a driving force of consumerism but also a centerpiece of family and children's culture.

Twenty-first-century readers, beyond detecting the avoidance implied by the poem's euphemisms ("win their sweetness") and the not-entirely-correct insinuation that white children reside at a distance from enslavement, will recognize the limitations of promoting an individual solution to a structural economic problem. But although such solutions have become all-too-common responses to ethical problems involving overconsumption, they were novel in Chandler's time. By eliciting children's allegiance to people outside of the family and disrupting views of parent-child interactions as innocent and isolated from the economic system, the poem represents a fuller engagement with the ethical crisis of enslavement than many previous children's books. It unmasks white children's location within the transatlantic economy as the end point for slave products and a family culture centered on white civility and childhood innocence as a shelter from unethical relations.

Chandler's work derives from the first large-scale consumer resistance movement, the free-labor movement, or sugar boycott. First organized by US Quakers, this movement led to mass boycotts of products made by enslaved workers, especially sugar.[2] The ultimately international campaign had periods of intensive public participation in Britain and the United States in the 1790s and 1820–1840s. Children's authors such as Chandler, Anna Laetitia Barbauld, Priscilla Wakefield, Charlotte Townsend, Amelia Opie, and Hannah More, as well as many young people, participated. Activists involved children in the movement because families were the main consuming units for slave products. Many also, like Chandler, recognized the growing urge to make childhood into an especially sweet time of life as a force driving consumption.

This insight was astute; Dennis Denisoff confirms that the "dominant modern concepts of the child . . . arose in Western society at roughly the same time and place" as consumer culture.[3] This twin emergence is no coincidence. Both consumer culture and childhood innocence derive from the rise of middle-class wealth—much of which came from enslavement-related ventures—and the wider affordability of consumer goods made possible by the exploitation of African labor. Additionally, building on the insularity of the children's books I discuss in chapter 1, childhood was coming to be understood as a position within transatlantic capitalism identified with consumption rather than production. Through this alliance, childhood and consumption were both construed as unknowing and guiltless. As one marker of this fruitful union, childhood portraits from this period signify innocence by displaying objects such as dolls, whips, and sweets—the latter two with clear ties to the slave economy.

The free-labor activist books for children that I discuss in this chapter work against notions of consumer innocence by foregrounding children's responsibility to the producers of goods. In so doing, they reverse the trend of children's books such as *The Governess* (1749) and *The Little Creoles* (1820) (discussed in chapter 1), which limit children's ethical responsibility to the sphere of the family. They espouse a broader idea of ethical relationality anticipating Emmanuel Levinas's argument that ethics are founded on the limitless call of responsibility to the other. Accordingly, they offer a lesson that remains difficult to teach: that young people should make sacrifices for strangers geographically or socially removed from their spheres of interaction, on a global scale.

Differently than Sarah Fielding, who in *The Governess* emphasizes Jenny Peace's maternal ethical training, Chandler depicts a close relationship between a white child and mother but foregrounds how the emotional and material exchanges of this relationship are founded on slave labor. By depicting her speaker resisting the emotional pressures of this relationship, Chandler offers her own quasi-maternal and quasi-feminist ethical training that positions the child within a wider relational network including enslaved people whom the speaker does not see face to face and therefore requires the author's intervention to learn about.[4] The poem manages the intensity of the poem's ethical imperative by circling back to the speaker's relationship with her "dear mother," but only after estranging the speaker from the usual modes of family relation and securing a commitment to unseen others.

The novelty of a relational ethics based on such a commitment to the other dogged the free-labor movement at large, resulting in frequent returns to family-centered rhetoric. I perceive a split between what I label the movement's *ethical* wing and its *protective* wing. The ethical wing believed that consuming products made by enslaved people would compromise Anglo-American children's *morals* with the unacceptable cost of those items for distant children and adults, while those in the protective wing emphasized that products produced by enslaved people would contaminate the *bodies* of consumers.[5] These differing expressions of consumer worry around childhood have persisted into the twenty-first century. Charlotte Sussman suggests that the sugar boycott gave rise to a pervasive image of the "domestic body in constant danger from a poisonous world"—an image recognizable in ongoing consumer movements responding to toxic chemicals in food and other products, many led by white parents on behalf of their children.[6] By comparison, consumer movements based on *ethical* imperatives and commitments to the other, such as ethical veganism and labor protests, attract fewer people than movements targeting real and imagined contaminants, such as pesticides, GMOs, fatty foods, and vaccines.

The works I discuss in this chapter represent early explorations of these dynamics. Children's literature about the sugar boycott largely avoids the protective stance found in works for an adult or mixed-age audience, landing decidedly in the ethical camp. Chandler's work illustrates this divide. Her poems for adult women, such as "Oh Press Me Not to Taste," use images of pollution wherein the groans, sighs, and blood of enslaved people mix with the products they produce, a dynamic that Jessica Conrad argues relies on sensations of "horror."[7] Yet in her poems with child speakers, such as "The Sugar-Plums," included in William Lloyd Garrison's *Juvenile Poems: For the Use of Free American Children, of Every Complexion* (1835), she avoids contamination imagery, instead giving children imaginary contact with enslaved laborers:

> Perhaps some poor slave child, that hoed up the ground,
>
> Round the cane in whose rich juice your sweetness was found,
>
> Was flogg'd, till his mother cried sadly to see,
>
> And I'm sure I want nobody beaten for me.[8]

Children's boycott literature therefore allows us to consider how authors attempted to foster readers' ethical commitments to people conceived as distant or different.

One strategy follows the lead of the Wedgwood china company and its popularization of the slogan "Am I Not a Man and a Brother?" by collapsing responsibility for those inside and outside of the family and framing the latter in relational terms. Such a collapse represents a significant shift away from earlier texts that confined children's ethical responsibility to a narrowly defined family, though it continues to insist on a sentimental recognition of sameness as a condition for caring. As white antislavery activists challenged paternal metaphors used to excuse enslavement, they sometimes turned to lateral relational concepts, such as brotherhood, to envision assimilation.

Familial metaphors, however, were not the main strategy employed by children's writers; they also repurposed genres that frame alterity as a constituent part of the transatlantic economy. Street cry narratives, or compilations of street sellers' lyrical calls and jingles, published by Quakers reimagine the genre's encounters with exotic strangers and goods in the marketplace to make children aware of product origins, while abolitionists hack it-narratives (stories told in the voice of personified products of manufacture that transcend the scale of human interaction) to connect consumer objects to laborers. These disruptive repurposings of children's genres imply that Anglo-American traditions of children's literature had failed to rise to the ethical demands of enslavement. They substitute new book products challenging ethics founded on specious notions of benevolence or reciprocity and introduce possibilities for reimagining the transatlantic economy through the relational ethics of interconnectedness.

Following Simone Drichel's lead, this book has been tracing cases not only where relational ethics appear in children's literature, but also where children's books advance pathological versions of relationality. Children's sugar boycott books, though they avoid contamination rhetoric, are not free of white saviorism, appropriation of Black voices and images, and so-called remedies to injustice that slot enslaved and free Africans into new subservient roles. Their ethical aims, in some cases, align with the British Empire as an agent of assimilation. In this sense, the books anticipate Fred Moten's argument (discussed in my introduction) that a Levinasian ethics emphasizing responsibility for the other is compatible with colonization.[9]

Even more pernicious pathological alternatives appear in later books that use childhood innocence to purify consumption of its destructive aspects.[10] After enslavement ends but exploitation of African labor in the Americas continues, narratives about sugar production use childhood innocence to neutralize critique. Ultimately, the sugar boycott produced varying levels of engagement among its (primarily white) child audience. Meanwhile, the evidence we have about free Black children's antislavery activism indicates that they went beyond the passive strategies devised by the sugar boycott to positively support African American intellectual culture and alternatives to European colonization.

Rather than tell a narrative of progress, then, I identify the contours of consumer activism, disruptive capitalism, and recuperation of slave products on both sides of the Atlantic. It is instructive, for instance, to compare the longevity of street cry books in Britain, where they are not connected to the radical anti-consumerist tradition I discuss, to their relative insignificance as a lasting children's genre in the United States. As the critical tradition faded and new developments like steam technology changed labor relations, British and US children's writers attempted to sell a fantasy of the economy's reinvention, even as material changes to workers' conditions were minimal.

Ethical Versus Protective Uses of Childhood in the Sugar Boycott

Written at the height of the free labor movement, Andrew Burn's *Second Address to the People of Great Britain* (1792), a sensational boycott book for adult audiences, promotes hysterical images of insulated consumers unaware that they are being contaminated by slave products. Such images build, to some degree, on the eighteenth-century writings of the first abstainer from slave goods on record, Quaker Benjamin Lay, whose book, *All Slave-keepers That Keep the Innocent in Bondage, Apostates* (1737), introduces the tropes of contamination that energize later activists. Lay refers to products such as rum and molasses as "filthy stuff" "composed of Grease, Dirt, Dung, and other filthiness, as, it may be Limbs, Bowels, and Excrements of the poor Slaves, and Beasts," and claims that the circulation of these goods will "ruin the Country."[11] However, Lay's methods of protest throughout his life place him firmly in the free-labor movement's ethical camp. His commitment to the ethical education of a mixed-age public using radical pedagogy paves the way for the children's books produced by the movement.

Born in Pennsylvania, Lay spent his early adulthood as a sailor, then started a mercantile business based in Barbados. Observing the violence of slave-enabled capitalism led him to quit his business and return to Pennsylvania to sway others to end enslavement. Lay's protest methods, detailed in Marcus Rediker's biography, were theatrical and creative, targeting not only slave goods but also domestic cultures of consumption.[12] He snuck tobacco pipes into a Quaker meeting and destroyed them. He smashed teacups at an open-air market in Philadelphia to "protest the mistreatment of those who harvested the tea in Asia and those who produced the sugar in the Americas that sweetened it."[13] Although neither action was directed at children, both resonate with the object lesson, a nineteenth-century pedagogical practice using a physical object as a teaching aid. Fascinatingly, neither the pipe nor teacup protests targeted enslavers or slave goods; Lay instead destroyed the consumer goods through which people and families *used* slave products. Given that Lay's demonstrations entailed the violent smashing of household items into shards of glass in public settings, they did not have the goal of protecting white people from harm. His attacks aggressively targeted the domestic world of the consumer, which, he implied, was already contaminated by its connection with enslavement. When Lay spoke of innocence, it was to claim this quality for the enslaved, as implied by the reference to "the innocent in bondage" in his book title.

By drawing connections between teacup and sugar, tobacco and pipe, Lay sketched a relational web including consumers and enslaved workers, which later activists would aim to make visible to readers. He profoundly suggested that products produced by enslaved people were not the only products dependent on the slave economy and that many more people were implicated in the institution of slavery than enslavers. Andrew White gives an example of the range of products connected to enslavement: "With the rise of tea came an entire industry. A novel, exotic beverage required new utensils and containers: tea kettles, teapots (made of silver or porcelain), tea caddies, tea strainers, sugar bowls, sugar tongs, reamers, tea cups, spoon trays, saucers, slop bowls, and tea tables."[14] By drawing attention to how people supported the institution of slavery through myriad acts of consumption, Lay identified manifold avenues for change and forestalled the objection that it would hurt too many industries to protest the slave system, insisting that full-scale disruption was necessary.

Building on the shock value of his public demonstrations, Lay's most notorious protest act—the temporary kidnapping of a young neighbor—suggests that he saw the growing sentimentality around childhood as hypocritical given widespread public support of the slave economy. An early biographer tells the story:

> This [neighbor] man had an interesting child, a boy of six years old, whom Lay sometimes met at a distance from the dwelling of his parents; on one of those occasions he succeeded in decoying him to his cave, about one mile distant . . . [T]he afflicted parents, apprehensive that they should never recover their child, replied with anguish, "Oh Benjamin, Benjamin! Our child is gone, he has been missing all day." Lay paused, and said, *"Your child is safe in my house, and you may now conceive of the sorrow you inflict upon the parents of the negroe girl you hold in slavery, for she was torn from them by avarice."*[15]

While this incident is more extreme than Lay's destruction of the vessels for consuming slave goods, we might read the kidnapping as an extension of these actions, targeting the white child as another vessel for consumption inseparable from enslavement. Lay hinges his point on the changing economics of childhood, in which white children were coming to be valued for their sentimental worth rather than their labor. He unmasks the presumption of childhood innocence that accompanied this recalibration as, paradoxically, a marker of guilt, connected to the "avarice" driving enslavement. Childhood innocence carved out a space for those who benefitted from the system without threat to their safety, who were free to consume products without awareness of the cruelties that produced them. Lay's actions pierce the bubble of innocence, subjecting a child to (comparatively minor) harm to make the point that white families benefitted from the system of slavery. In so doing, he lays the intellectual groundwork for children's texts making young people aware of their role in supporting enslavement.

Lay's activism spread the free-labor boycott to some, though by no means all, Quakers in the United States. The movement then traveled to Britain and gained broad support in the 1780s and 1790s, including among families and children. Of the British movement, Julia Holcomb writes, "Nearly one-half million consumers abstained from slave-grown sugar, an unprecedented level of participation."[16] The most widely read publication on the subject, Baptist printer William Fox's *Address to the People of Great Britain on the Utility of Refraining from the Use of West India Sugar and Rum* (1791) builds on Lay's argument that consumers' liability equals that of enslavers. Fox argues that both are criminally responsible: "Can we suppose, that an injury of enormous magnitude can take place and the criminality be destroyed merely by the criminals becoming so numerous as to render their respective shares indistinguishable?"[17]

While the US movement remained small because it was associated with religious communities, the British movement focused on families, widely seen as embodying the values of the nation. Indeed, when Fox referred to "individual" sugar consumers, he meant families, whom he encouraged to be at the center of the protest: "The consumption of sugar in this country is so immense, that the quantity commonly used by individuals will have an important effect. A family that uses only 5 lb. of sugar per week . . . will, by abstaining from the consumption 21 months, prevent the slavery or murder of one fellow-creature."[18] As Sussman has shown, sugar was so tightly integrated into Anglo domesticity that it was touted as a ready substitute for breast milk, making childhood "the site of an 'agreement of taste' between colonial production and domestic consumption."[19] Cartoons such as James Gillray's "Anti-Saccharites; or John Bull and his Family Leaving Off the Use of Sugar" and Isaac Cruikshank's "The Gradual Abolition off [*sic*] the Slave Trade; or, leaving of Sugar by Degrees" picture Queen Charlotte trying to convince her daughters to abstain from sugar-sweetened tea. Both images lampoon the movement by making the queen a hag-like figure but show their creators perceived activists' emphasis on families as the key players in the national reckoning with enslavement.

Some writers, however, began to depart from an other-based ethical stance by implying that British families were facing a moral challenge not because of ties to enslavement but because the nation had been invaded by polluted goods. The follow-up to Fox's book, Andrew Burn's *Second Address* (1792), offers what he calls a "new" persuasion appealing to white consumers' sense of disgust. His slicker textual product claims that slave goods were not only metaphorically stained but also adulterated and unsanitary because of their contact with Black bodies. After banking on readers' racism by claiming that sugar literally contained blood, insects, and other "nauceous effluvia" found in enslaved Africans' hair, between their toes, and under their nails, he offers a climax: the story of an enslaved child's skeleton found in a hogshead of sugar.[20] Possibly, Burn is responding to another Gillray cartoon, "Barbarities in the West Indies" (1791), which shows an enslaved person being boiled alive while taking a "bath" in a vat of liquid sugar cane. His image of harm to an enslaved child contrasts with Lay's protest-via-kidnapping. Whereas Lay calls attention to the hypocrisy of white parents protecting their children, Burn conjures horror by depicting a Black child's body rudely intruding into the safe space where white children consume. Even if the intention is to protest enslavement, the dynamic resembles the "fantasy of violation" that Sara Ahmed argues feeds racial hate.[21] Continuities exist between Burn's hysteria and later protests that racialize contaminants; anti-vax writers have used insinuations of racial contamination since the nineteenth century.[22]

Tellingly, Burn equivocates over whether consumers of slave goods are "innocent or guilty."[23] While he implies that reading his book means that consumers can no longer be innocent unless they abstain from slave products, the suggestion that the ignorant *could* claim innocence means that his argument shrinks from any radical idea of primal ethical responsibility for the other. Burn implies instead that lack of knowledge might lessen consumers' responsibility. This message has proved powerful, especially when it comes to children.

The idea that consuming goods in a slave-enabled economy did not make a person automatically guilty is indicative of the British movement's friendlier position on consumerism in general, which enabled a wave of antislavery products, including children's books about the movement. Moving away from Lay's asceticism, an innovation of British activists was to create consumer objects conveying the aspiration to engage in *responsible* consumption.

The most famous such product was a medallion featuring a kneeling African man in chains asking, "Am I Not a Man and a Brother?" made by pottery manufacturer Josiah Wedgwood. The image was reproduced on objects that usually facilitated the consumption of slave products, including tobacco pipes, teacups, and snuff boxes, clearing these items of consumer guilt, if stuffed with free-labor goods. Contrasting with Lay's pipe destruction, it makes sense that Wedgwood, a maker of china used to imbibe and store tobacco and sugar, would have engaged in a consumer-friendly campaign. The image exhorts the users of these objects to take responsibility for enslaved people as if they are family, exploding relational ethics limited to white family members. Notions of "brotherhood," kinship, and interdependence later contribute to ethical protests involving collaboration among Black and white activists, such as the Civil Rights campaign. However, the image preserves the notion that family connection, rather than a responsibility to all others, is the precondition for ethical investment. Marilisa Jiménez García has shown that such rhetoric is easily appropriated in a colonial context to provide a paternalistic justification of control.[24]

Protest books for children were part of this trend of creating boycott-friendly substitutes for other consumer products—and the Wedgwood image became a frontispiece for several books, including Lydia Maria Child's *The Fountain for Every Day in the Year* (1836).[25] A similar, but not identical, image with the subject's chains removed adorns Charlotte Townsend's *Pity the Negro; or An Address to Children on the Subject of Slavery* (3rd edition, 1825), discussed later in this chapter. Like the Wedgwood-stamped pipes, boycott-related children's books leverage the existing consumer market by redesigning popular genres into virtuous products. Although activists were engaging in a creative and disruptive kind of capitalist innovation to attempt to remake the market, the texts carry on the legacy of Lay's teacup smashing in calling out popular genres of children's books for complicity with enslavement. They depart from Burn's inflammatory mode, as well as Wedgwood's appeal to the familiar, instead promoting critical reading and caring relationships across physical and social distance.

The texts experiment with ways of approximating encounters with people who are different, including, for instance, images of Black faces, stories from formerly enslaved people, and appendixes with runaway slave advertisements reassembled for the purpose of critique. Their makers seem to have perceived in childhood a chance for a broader ethical relationality. That these texts stayed on the fringes of the children's literature market, however, anticipates a lack of lasting engagement in ethical boycotts among white consumers.

Radicalizing Children's Street Cry Books

British boycott books, such as Priscilla Wakefield's *Mental Improvement* (published in three volumes from 1794 to 1797 by the Quaker firm Harvey and

Darton), had an audience spanning the Atlantic because of their republication by Quaker publishers in the United States. Some of the most striking, understudied sugar boycott texts for children, however, were published by Quaker publishers in US cities in the form of street cry books. The publishers were active entrepreneurs, using their products to disrupt the slave-driven economy. The foremost publisher of antislavery street cries, Samuel Wood, owned the first successful and enduring children's book shop in the United States, on Pearl Street in New York City. As recorded in a scrapbook made by his daughter-in-law Mary S. Wood, Samuel was an "active worker" in organizations protesting enslavement, "the Emancipation So[ciety] and the Manumission Society, both of which were to assist colored people to obtain work and to aid runaway slaves."[26] In 1808, Samuel published *The Cries of New York*, which emphasizes avoiding slave goods. Indicating that he viewed bookmaking as activism as well as entrepreneurship, Samuel aided circulation by carrying books in his pocket and handing them out to children for free "in New York and when travelling."[27] *The Cries of New York* must also have proved viable as a commercial endeavor, as it went through multiple editions and was lightly revised as *The Cries of Philadelphia* by Johnson and Warner in 1810. Fellow Quaker publisher Mahlon Day, who established another juvenile bookstore at 376 Pearl Street in New York, mimicked Wood's book with his *New-York Cries in Rhyme* in 1812.

Quaker street cries borrowed from an existing tradition, with a long relationship to activism. First associated with a middlebrow art tradition dating from the fifteenth century in which artists created etchings of street sellers, street cry literature would come to be a literary and pictorial genre featuring images, prose, and rhymes. In his history of the genre, Sean Shesgreen points out that street cry literature derives from the politically charged oral culture of street workers, which was resolutely pro-commerce but critical of worker mistreatment: "The metaphorical term 'Cries' identifies storied images that represent sounds silently, sounds and voices that, in life, were common, vulgar, transgressive, even threatening, socially and politically."[28] The earliest printed versions of the cries were public broadsides that maintained the workers' radical politics even as they translated sounds into pictures and text. They represent hawkers collectively on large panoramic sheets, allowing for communication and solidarity among workers.

Children's books came relatively late in the history of the genre, according to Shesgreen's survey of London-based texts, and had the effect of sidelining workers' voices by making literary interpretations of their voices into stock for young people's instruction. Children's *Cries of London*, which began to be published in 1754, herald for Shesgreen a triumph of the word, verbal literacy, and the isolated reader over sound, pictures, communal reading, and worker solidarity. The quaint illustrations bear little trace of the alterity of the marketplace, and their lilting rhymes in "proper English" lack the improvisations of street sellers. Such texts proved popular among middle-class readers for reasons distant from their original purpose, offering decontextualized lessons on "basic concepts in weights, measures and currency" and ethical instruction meant to "tempt or scare [readers] into toil, thrift, reputation or temperance."[29]

Scholarship on street cry literature, however, has neglected the American cries, which means that their difference from British children's street cry literature has been overlooked. Some US publications of the *Cries of London* continue the trend Shesgreen identifies. An 1805 version offers a moralistic adage at once emphasizing class hierarchy and a politics of respectability meant to cut across classes: "If we be desirous of obtaining a tolerable knowledge of the world, we must of necessity take a survey of every rank . . . remembering, that . . . virtue, piety, and integrity, are the only things that can ensure the blessing of Heaven, and render us truly respectable."[30] But while the Quaker versions capitalize on the popularity of such books and continue the practice of translating worker voices into children's books, they introduce ethical language that promotes responsibility for immediate and distant workers. In the context of the sugar boycott, they invite children to read their environments critically and cultivate awareness that will allow them to make ethical choices within the transatlantic economy.

In addition to publishing *The Cries of New York*, Wood (likely in collaboration with an anonymous children's author or others at the press) experimented with street cry literature by publishing an unusual version of *The Cries of London* in 1811. This edition avoids bland moralism in favor of pointed class-based critique, beginning with an excerpt from John Bancks's poem describing London as a place one could find "Riches, if one could heap 'em; / Of poverty a greater share far."[31] Although *The Cries of New York* is more positive about commerce in general, pointing out, "Nature has done much towards making [New York City] one of the most advantageous situations for extensive commerce in the universe," it introduces ethical questions about specific products such as (sugar-laden) gingerbread, as well as pears and sweet potatoes sold by African Americans.[32]

Even without looking at the text, the illustrations by engraver Alexander

Anderson imply that children should be invested in ethical questions related to labor because they are not separate from the market. Woodcuts show young people selling cherries, pears, corn, and radishes, and driving a clam wagon. They buy oranges, milk, and images (statues) and visit the scissor sharpener. Reflecting the tradition of street cry literature as a genre expressing middle-class morality, the text at first positions readers and workers as primarily united by their shared Protestant work ethic. For instance, consumers buy radishes from child sellers regardless of their need for them "in order to encourage the little ones in their laudable examples of application and industry."[33] Such statements are recognizable adages used to promote reading and other middle-class learning activities, though it is unusual to see such activities compared to manual labor.

Yet the text soon asserts a more radical formation of this prolabor argument, juxtaposing free labor with slave labor:

> We are formed for labour; and it is not only an injunction laid upon, but an honour to us, to be found eating our bread by the sweat of our brows, and not spend our time to profit, as Dr. Franklin . . . describes in relating the observations of a Negro. "Boccarorra (meaning the white man) make de black man workee, make de horse workee, make de ox workee, make eberty ting workee; only de hog. He de hog, no workee; he eat, he drink, he walk about, he go to sleep when he pleases, he libb like a gentleman." And now, I would ask my little friends, whether it is not more desirable and reputable to be like the little [radish seller] in the picture, doing good, by being engaged in some useful employment, than like the gentleman-hog, only live to eat, drink, and sleep.[34]

The reference to Benjamin Franklin comes from the tract *Information for Those Who Would Remove to America* (1794), in which he claims that members of the European working class should emigrate to the United States because Americans, unlike the European aristocracy, prefer to be seen as laborers, eliding the topic of US enslavement. Wood's text radically repurposes Franklin's text, using it instead to prompt children to differentiate between US workers and enslavers.

Other sections go beyond such philosophical questioning to point to practical issues, like how to discern which goods rely on slave labor. About gingerbread, the text reads, "How would these things taste to us, were they produced by the sweat of a dear father, or tender mother, a loved brother, or affectionate sister, an only son, or innocent daughter, torn from us, and from all that are near and dear, in this world; and could we suppose their oppressors or those who encourage them, innocent?"[35] Following Wedgwood's lead, this passage uses what was becoming a common motif comparing enslaved people to intimate family members. Such an expansion remains notable given the earlier formulation of children's ethical duties as limited to the family (discussed in chapter 1), though the passage excludes those who cannot be interpreted as family.

The text's setting in the marketplace, however, means that it more often presents interactions between strangers, giving readers clues for determining whether those relationships are ethical. In reference to the gingerbread passage, passages alerting the child to where the products come from—pears from New York, pineapples from the West Indies, sweet potatoes from South Carolina—take on more significance. In the case of these products, the text pushes beyond rationales for ethical engagement based on family metaphors and uses innovations in word-image interaction to approximate face-to-face encounters with workers. Many pages position child workers or consumers as looking at each other.

At first glance, it is tempting to see such encounters as relying, if not on familiarity or sameness, on a logic of reciprocity and equivalence—in other words, on the logic of capitalist exchange, wherein an encounter with another person is meant to resolve in an even transaction. From a Levinasian point of view, such economic transactions are not founded on ethics, which demand that responsibility for others be unlimited, but instead diminish this responsibility by replacing it with a limited engagement. Through economic transactions, otherness functions as a product absorbed by consumers. In this sense, it seems relevant that many of the products represented in Wood's texts are foods, exotic products that can be incorporated into the bodies of readers. Placing workers within the pages of a book could be read as a process of incorporating and neutralizing otherness, making it a product for sale.

And yet in providing readers with images and rhyming lessons that exceed economic transactions—meant to be read over and over by children and their caretakers—Wood's text indicates that an exchange of goods for money does not answer the ethical needs of the relationships underpinning the economy. About one-third of the way through the book, on the page with West Indian pineapples, we begin to see images of workers staring not in the direction of the characters buying their products but in the direction of readers. In this sense, we might consider the author's use of "crying" not just as selling but as begging for attention and asking others to recognize one's experience. More than a half dozen workers are positioned in a forward-facing confrontational

Figure 3.1. Illustration labeled "Baked Pears," from *The Cries of New York*. New York: Printed and sold by S. Wood, 1808. Courtesy of the American Antiquarian Society.

stance. Several illustrations depict skin color, including a Black girl selling pears (fig. 3.1), an unusual feature for books of this era that were not directly about enslavement.

The implications are twofold: in addition to making ethical demands through an approximation of an encounter with another person, the inclusion of skin color references specific communities of workers, rather than abstract, ideal versions. With these images, Wood's text anticipates a key aspect of Levinasian ethics: that the face-to-face encounter calls us to ethical action. At the same time, it is important to recognize that the face-to-face encounters in the book are mediated; we do not see the actual faces of African workers or hear their voices directly, missing an opportunity for a fully responsive labor politics.

The inclusion of important information such as race in the pictures as well as the text (or, in some cases, rather than in the text) is nonetheless a significant innovation reflecting Wood's ethical commitments. While narratives of most *Cries of London* do not depend on images, meaning that the images function primarily as illustrations, the interrelation of images and text produced by Wood's press takes an experimental form, resembling how comics and modern-day picture books put image and text in dialogue. This structure encourages readers to make connections and act ethically.

Pears, for instance, have a long connection with enslavement in New York City, with the bowery purportedly named for the "bouwery," the seventeenth-century garden of Director-Governor Peter Stuyvesant, which contained a prominent pear tree cultivated by "forty or fifty slaves" during his lifetime.[36] Although the publication of Wood's text in 1808 falls after New York's passage of gradual abolition in 1799, some people were still enslaved because of their birth before the 1799 cut-off date. Additionally, many formerly enslaved people were considered indentured servants for life or were carrying out a period of servitude. According to Shane White, one in three Black New Yorkers lived in white households and "performed duties similar to those of slaves."[37] The pear seller's stare invites readers to investigate, and ominous elements of the image emerge on closer investigation. The girl stands in a pit limiting her movement. Behind her, we see a tall brick wall, a dog, and a gate with large bars that leads into a garden.

These boundaries, notably, do not appear in William P. Chappel's painting of a Black woman selling baked pears in the Bowery neighborhood, *Baked Pears in Duane Park* (painted in the 1870s but dated 1810 on the back, presumably to indicate that the image was a memory of an earlier time). Chappel's rendition shows an unencumbered woman in front of a low picket fence surrounding trees, with wide open streets around her and a blue sky stretching in the background. Assuming these images refer to selling practices that continue over time, they use the sellers for different rhetorical purposes; Anderson's illustrations emphasize the girl's possible unfreedom, prompting readers to investigate her well-being, where Chappel's later version presents her through the sunny lens of nostalgia.

It is equally possible that the pear seller is a free Black person, an idea conversely insinuated in the text's insistence that selling pears "is an honest way to procure a living."[38] White notes that New York City was "either the largest or second largest center of free blacks in the United States," a situation resulting from gradual emancipation and from enslaved workers negotiating for themselves, with many securing favorable terms or provisions for independent work that accelerated their freedom.[39] Some enslaved people procured plots of land in the bowery and remained there despite "ongoing hostility between New York's white citizens and its black population (both free and enslaved)."[40] "Free blacks and slaves," White writes, "were heavily involved in selling goods in the streets and markets, many coming from Long Island and New Jersey to sell their produce."[41] Black sellers also appear in the illustrations of Day's *New-York Cries in Rhyme*, in an image of hot corn sellers.[42] By including an image of the pear seller in front of a large barred door, the creator of the *Cries* might have been concerned about another version of unfreedom; free Black workers, especially street sellers, were often accused of petty crimes and prostitution.[43] The text defends pear sellers, contrasting them with people "white or black . . . [who are] willing to live by . . . means that are not honourable and honest."[44]

A Black man appearing in the image of Sweet Carolina potatoes, differently, indicates that they are likely products grown by enslaved people, given that enslavement in North and South Carolina was not abolished until after the US Civil War. The narrator notes that although "some" people produce sweet potatoes closer by, possibly a free-labor alternative, the tubers require a "southern or warm clime, to bring them to perfection."[45] Savvy readers, primed by the gingerbread page, will understand that there is more to consider than the taste of these items when deciding whether to buy. The narrator's seemingly hypocritical support for Carolina potatoes and not gingerbread may point to complex economic factors, for instance, that people buy cooked sweet potatoes secondhand from (likely Black) "huxter women," who, like the pear sellers, are trying to make an honest living. With this kind of complexity, readers must stay open to making ethical deliberations in the marketplace.

The reputation of the cry books among readers and critics reflect differing purposes between the English children's cries Shesgreen discusses and the radical US ones. Citing a letter in which a mother gives *The Cries of London* to a child recovering from smallpox, Shesgreen claims that they were associated with "sedentary [feminine] amusements" such as "pictures" and "dolls."[46] By contrast, the American cries retained their connection with street workers and politics. An 1840 editorial by J. Cypress (a pseudonym for William Post Hawes) opines, "Every thing here is done by crying . . . The Worshipful Corporation of the City of New York . . . [has] established and honorably maintain[s], schools for 'Cries.' . . . A boy, in this republic, has got his education when he can hurrah, squeal, and scream at a political meeting, so as to be heard five miles off;—not before that maturity."[47] Though Cypress is being sardonic, the continuum he imagines between street crying and political rallying sounds like a welcome outcome for Quaker activists like Wood.

Tellingly, though, the street cry genre in the United States did not have the longevity of the English versions, for which there is still merchandise being created, including figurines and art prints. What are left at the end of the nineteenth century in the United States are a few ethnographic pieces for adult readership and a handful of musical recordings. The decline of the US cries, we might suspect, had to do with their critical stance on consumerism, which was at odds with Americans' rising taste for sugar. As Wendy Woloson points out, "By the early 1870s, the average American consumed almost 41 pounds of (mostly imported) sugar a year, over six times what his or her counterpart had eaten in the 1790s."[48]

Ethical Consumption as Connection—and Colonization

Writing related to the sugar boycott did not disappear, however. There was another surge of international activism in the 1820s–1840s, prompted partly by young people's political action during the earlier movement and desire to involve a new generation. Repurposing genres such as the runaway slave advertisement and the it-narrative, the books written during this wave of the movement take aim at other forms of print they imply are complicit in enslavement.

Pity the Negro, by British writer Charlotte Townsend, whose mother Lucy participated in the sugar boycott as a child, uses the essay format of addresses written for a general audience by Fox and Burn, adding a human angle. Rather than describing sugar as a criminal commodity or polluted product, the book recounts Townsend's experience talking with a formerly enslaved man who visited her family. The man is missing an eye because he was pushed into a vat of sugar by an overseer as a child, but the iconic image of the slave in the sugar vat is not presented as a disgusting detail to promote visceral disgust. There are, similarly, no traces of the prominent metonyms of blood and sweat—or worse, racist stereotypes involving jiggers and filth—that appear in writing for adult audiences. Enslavement, instead, is a "foul stain" on "the British character" that children have the chance to eradicate.[49] Townsend focuses on the man's feelings about his experience, making explicit overtures for her audience to understand the pain he remembers from his childhood, commenting, for instance, that "Black children, as well as white, will cry when either grieved or vexed."[50] The title of the work suggests that Townsend intends the book to produce "pity"—that patronizing emotion—but the move is also to humanize the stranger and to posit a cross-cultural understanding of childhood, even as this is predicated on positioning the man within Anglo norms.

For Townsend, forging relationships with enslaved people emerges partly as a requirement of empire. She evokes British colonial aims to promote readers' responsibility for enslaved workers, quoting from the epilogue to the play *The Padlock*, spoken by the character of Mungo, who asks for "the British negro, [to be] like the Briton, free."[51] The notion of responsibilities for others across distance was, for Townsend as well as other children's authors associated with the boycott, directed into the channels of empire.

Within an overall framework of empire, Townsend reflects critically on the interactions between the (international colonial) printing business and enslavement. Her appendix reprints a selection of newspaper advertisements featuring enslaved people for sale and runaways, including a "creole" girl who is only a little over four feet tall. As I discuss in chapter 4, such ads often appeared in Caribbean newspapers on the same page as children's book advertisements. Lissa Paul suggests that runaway ads can be read as a testament to enslaved children using what little agency they had to change their situations.[52]

As Townsend does not provide much commentary, it is difficult to know whether she went so far as to make this connection. Yet by repurposing and compiling the ads, which were a common feature of newspaper media at the time, Townsend calls on her readers to approach these and other representations of enslavement critically. Text included with an extra ad in the third edition of 1825 threatening to sell a man named William Hall, if not claimed by an owner, models the careful reading that she wants readers to do and the questions she wants them to ask: "Here we have a Negro man, claimed as a slave by no man, accused of no crime, but who is seized as a runaway, only because he is black, and put in jail . . . Where is he now, and what is his condition?"[53] Italicizing a portion of the ad mentioning that Hall traveled to England and lived independently before returning to Jamaica, Townsend prompts young people to investigate his circumstances.

Media literacy and reflexivity are hallmarks of protest books of this era. Amelia Opie's *The Black Man's Lament; or How to Make Sugar* (1826) and Charles Williams's *Adventures of a Sugar Plantation* (1836), written under the pseudonym Harry Harcourt, reimagine it-narratives about products circulating in the market, as well as nonfiction designed to teach young people about new industries, to critique narrative genres that promote capitalist innovations without acknowledging enslavement. Going beyond the direct criticism of enslavement in activist books for adults, these texts train readers to be skeptical of celebratory descriptions of products and manufactures.

Opie's subtitle, *How to Make Sugar*, references the genre of how-to books preparing young people to engage in new industries, such as *A History of Wonderful Inventions* (1839), *The Young Mechanic* (1843), and *Success in Life: The Merchant* (1850).[54] Although the text is delivered in the form of a sentimental poem, Opie draws from the nonfiction format used in such books by including technical engravings as well as prose footnotes. The footnotes include what appear at first to be celebratory or neutral educational details about sugar. One calls the sugar cane field "one of the most beautiful productions that the pen or pencil can possibly describe."[55] Opie also gives detailed descriptions of machinery, similar to books promoting knowledge needed to reproduce manufacturing methods. She does not focus only on the sugar vat—the most frequently pictured part of the sugar-making process—but on the ingenious "moulds" in which plants were grown, the mill, the boiling vessels, the coolers, and the curing process. Interspersed with these details, however, are explanations that enslaved people are overworked and driven to labor—even when ill or feverish—by the force of the "cart-whip."[56] Each image showing a step of the sugar-making process includes not only tools and machinery but enslaved workers. By juxtaposing technical prose with sentimental poetry, Opie equates her subtitle, *How to Make Sugar*, with her main title, *Black Man's Lament*, disallowing the separation of these two processes and genres. Through her transformation of the how-to industrial manual, Opie illustrates that other books in this category support industrial processes without concerns for ethics.

In its interweaving of details of the sugar-making process with the pain of African laborers, Opie's work resembles songs that Caribbean people have sung to memorialize the horrific experience of processing sugar cane, such as the folk song "Sugar Cane," written by Vernon Cadogan and recorded in 1964 by the Barbados Folk Singers. The song alternates details of sugar harvesting with a refrain pointing out that laborers cut the cane until it burns their hands.[57] The counterpoint between the refrain and the verses, one of which describes the sweat and exhaustion of a worker who can get only a momentary break while the sugar is boiling, ties the sugar-making process with painful, backbreaking labor that workers are forced to accept to support themselves. A pointedly ironic chorus jubilantly proclaims that the planters provide "money for one and all," revealing the sharp contrast between the brutality of sugar work and propaganda such as Joseph Addison's "The Royal Exchange" (1711) that depicted global economic exchange as utopic and reciprocal.

The images included in Opie's book are, strangely given her critique, aesthetically pleasing. The "moulds" and a slave ship are drawn symmetrically with attractive colors. We can understand the oddness of these images by taking a cue from the ironic chorus of the upbeat "Sugar Cane." The blend of propagandistic images with text describing graphic violence creates contrast and dissonance. For example, the slave ship image is accompanied by lines describing how enslaved people are ripped from their families and often consider suicide.[58] Opie's juxtapositions of seemingly neutral manufacturing tips and attractive images with details of horrible suffering imply that readers should scrutinize not only slave-enabled industries but also children's books that present sanitized educational information about their products.

By writing a story of sugar, Opie builds on the framework of it-narratives: books telling the life stories of anthropomorphized consumer products. Jennifer L. Roberts has argued that such narratives initially raised consumer awareness, allowing readers to "gain symbolic perspective on the global market economy . . . that remained too complex to be perceived by any one individual."[59] It-narratives for mixed-age audiences such as Charles Johnstone's *Chrysal; or, the Adventures of a Guinea* (1760–1761), according to Liz Bellamy, comment on changes to society as a result of commercialism, such as the way that economic transactions define "relationships within contemporary society," and invite ironic reflection on how objects circulating in the economy are exempt from the rules of personal interaction.[60]

Lynn Festa contends that children's versions, particularly in the nineteenth century when Opie and Williams were writing, retreat from such critical commentaries to teach lessons about manufacturing processes or the importance of caring for one's possessions.[61] Stories like *The Adventures of a Pin Cushion* (1780) imagine "affective relations between persons and their possessions" and reinforce "the rights, privileges, and obligations of ownership," rather than educating children about the human relationships that products facilitate.[62] Festa suggests that children's it-narratives avoid questions about consumerism and ethics.

Opie counters this trend by *not* telling the story of sugar as a first-person object narrative, as similarly titled it-narratives for children did. Instead, she formats her text as a poem from the perspective of an enslaved person. Opie thereby uses enslavement to challenge the subject-object binary on which it-narratives depend; she does not humanize an object to make a commentary on consumer ethics but instead shows how humans have become objects. Karen Sands O'Connor rightly notes that West Indians are still objectified, as "Opie's poem does not present the actual voice of a Black West Indian slave" but rather "an idealized Noble Savage."[63] Opie's assimilation of the Black worker to European expectations builds in limits to her demands for ethical treatment. Yet the speaker of her poem is effective in pointing to British hypocrisies that disallow treating workers who live in England as animals and objects, pointedly questioning, "Who dares an English peasant flog, / Or buy, or sell, or steal away?"[64]

Charles Williams's *Adventures of a Sugar Plantation* (1836) makes similar interventions as Opie's text; although the title recalls it-narratives like Mary Ann Kilner's *Adventures of a Pincushion* (1780), Williams's book does not personify sugar or the plantation, instead using it as a setting for discussing the work of African laborers following abolition. However, the book differs from Opie's in that it does not treat boycotting sugar as an urgent matter for its readers because of its publication after the abolition of enslavement in the British colonies in 1833. The text is instead set during the four-year apprenticeship period requiring those over six to remain on estates and labor. The text memorializes the antislavery movement, while continuing the boycott's critique of mainstream children's literature, which, as we will see, came to include celebratory narratives about the transformation of sugar making through steam technology. Despite these (overt) changes, the book highlights the limits of the free labor boycotts in creating lasting change and suggests that consumer vigilance is still needed, arguing that "it is a maxim of great wisdom, that we should consider nothing done while anything remains to be affected."[65]

Williams's argument for continued ethical engagement, however, becomes a rationale for the oversight of the British Empire. He combines images of Black childhood innocence and ingenuity meant to challenge the horrors of enslavement with racist ideas of Black criminality and buffoonery used to justify white colonial power, especially ethical education and reading instruction (discussed in chapter 4). He retells an anecdote of a missionary teacher working with a "black curly haired rogue infinitely better pleased when roaming among orange and mango groves, than in poring over 'Reading made Easy.'"[66] The anecdote tells of the child's determination to escape punishment:

One day the little urchin was brought to the school, after he had been taking one of his rambling excursions, when with all the authority of a pedagogue, I

demanded where he had strayed . . . Summoning as much penitence as he could
into his little roguish face, he looked at me with the most irresistible impudence,
and said, "Stop, Schoolmassa, make me speak, me not tell a lie, me know me do
wrong; but you see Schoolmassa you is one great big buckra man, me is one little neger; pose, Schoolmassa, you lock me up in the school all night, why dere
is no man in the de world can hinder you . . . Schoolmassa, dat you forgive me
dis once, why, Schoolmassa, dere is no man in de whole world can hinder you."[67]

Williams excuses the child's visit to the orange and mango groves (presumably because he likes the sweetness) by asserting his "shrewdness."[68] This
shrewdness, a reflection of the child's resistance, indicates his ability to become a productive British citizen—a process dependent on his acknowledgment of unchecked white male power in the colonial education system. The
boy's description as an adorable curly-haired imp with a Caribbean accent
makes him into a new kind of product for the consumption of white readers
elsewhere in the empire.

Williams's text, furthermore, is laced with prejudices against the African
cultures of the formerly enslaved, construing them as a different contamination threat facing children. He (wrongfully) claims that enslavement endan-
gered youth because of funeral practices among the enslaved: "The very children were instructed by their parents in many wicked arts . . . No sooner did
the spirit depart from the body of a relative or friend, than they indulged in
the most wild and frantic tricks, accompanied by the beating of drums and the
singing of songs."[69] Although musical practices have long been tied to ethical
action in the Caribbean (as discussed in the introduction and conclusion),
Williams links children's value to their status as a transitional generation
in which there is potential to erase these practices. Given such images, it is
not surprising that free Black children's activism went beyond the prominent
narratives of the sugar boycott.

African American Children's Antislavery Activism

In addition to "Christmas," one of Chandler's widely circulated poems was
"The Sugar-Plums," published in multiple periodicals as well as William
Lloyd Garrison's *Juvenile Poems*. The poem is in the voice of "Fanny," a white
girl who decides not to eat the gift of sugarplums her grandmother has sent
in the mail.[70] Following its prescriptions, children formed sugar-plum societies, groups that refrained from eating slave-farmed sugar and candy. The societies, interestingly, define themselves by what they are not, yielding a pal-

atable name for a subversive consumer activity. The cuteness of the name masks the resistant acts of its members, while a need to define them as "sweet" reflects friction between the idea of the educated activist and the innocent child—an example of the strange way that a movement against a product could be packaged to be not entirely unfriendly to that product.

What records we have of white American children's activities suggest that commitment to boycotting sugar could coexist with a relatively disconnected engagement with the cruelty of enslavement, as indicated by the records of a female Juvenile Anti-Slavery Society in Boston. This society is the source of a quote often used to illustrate children's activism: "Had quite a discussion on self-denial and on the use of sugar and butter and at last came to the conclusion that we would deny ourselves of something so as to contribute one cent weekly to the Society."[71] Following this somewhat tepid commitment, later entries in the same book suggest that the girls used their time debating ethical questions: "finished our discussion is it ever right to kill came to the conclusion that it is never right to kill The next subject for discussion is it right ever for a slave to run away." These discussions suggest a disconnect with the realities for enslaved people, in which violent rebellion might be necessary and running away was easily justifiable.[72]

In contrast, records of free Black children involved with antislavery movements suggest that they did not take their main inspiration from sugar boycott literature or even limit themselves to challenging enslavement alone. Rather, they often emphasize economic activism in support of African American intellectual activity, adding another dimension to Paul's point that we need to acknowledge Black youth as activists. In their article on the sugar boycott, Kathryn Gleadle and Ryan Hanley argue that children's agency "needs to be understood as a specific, historicized phenomenon," which means that we cannot assume that youth activism, even in traditional forms such as organizing societies, is monolithic.[73] Gleadle and Hanley recommend using case studies to understand the "intricacies of children's involvement."[74] Michaël Roy points out that "for [African American children] the fight to abolish slavery was systematically intertwined with a broader struggle against segregation, disenfranchisement, and violence and for education, civil rights, and social reform."[75]

A difficulty in studying these children's participation is that records are relatively scarce. For example, we do not know how many participated in the sugar boycott. Yet traces of related activism are available when it comes to the African American Juvenile Anti-Slavery Society formed in Pittsburgh by

George B. Vashon and David Peck, both of whom would grow up to be distinguished professionals as adults, with abundant paper trails.[76] Vashon would go on to be the first African American graduate of Oberlin College; the first practicing African American lawyer in New York State; an accomplished writer, editor, and poet; one of the first African American professors in the United States; a college president; and the first African American professor at Howard University. Peck was the first African American to become a medical doctor from a US medical school.

In November 1839, young Vashon and Peck wrote to the African American newspaper, *The Colored American*, presenting a donation collected by their society, which was likely an outgrowth of an African school organized by John B. Vashon (George's father) and Lewis Woodson, held in the basement of the Bethel African Methodist Church.[77] The first two lines of their letter distinguish the work of their Juvenile Anti-Slavery Society from others that pooled money that would otherwise be spent on slave products to contribute to the cause: "At a meeting of the Juvenile Anti-Slavery Society, held November 11, it was unanimously resolved that five dollars should be given to the support of the Colored American—a paper, which of all others we ought to support. We hope that this small donation may be the means of doing good, and we pray you in the name of the members of the Juvenile Anti-Slavery Society, to accept it as a small token of the esteem we have for your paper."[78] While these children presumably also refused to support the slave economy, their activism is about creating relationships that positively support African American community and expression. In addition to supporting an African American paper, the youth developed their intellects through public speaking: "The Society now consists of about forty members: several of whom have addressed the Society, at different times."[79] We get a taste, perhaps, of the children's verbal stylings in the final line of their letter, referring creatively to the funds they are sending to *The Colored American* as "mite" (a.k.a. a small bit of coin).

The children's speaking continues a relational practice that Woodson developed at the school of encouraging contributions by students and teachers alike, promoting listening among the different groups.[80] Indeed, the youth were encouraged in their activism by parents and elders, particularly fathers and male community leaders whom we can read as providing relational care. John B. Vashon was the agent selling *The Colored American* in Western Pennsylvania. Hired as the African school's teacher as well as serving as minster at the Bethel Church, Woodson was a frequent contributor to *The Colored Amer-*

ican under the name Augustine, claiming that African Americans needed to form their own institutions, including schools and newspapers, to collectively protest their subordination in US politics.[81] Woodson explains in one edition that he sees the paper as part of the "ORGANIZED and systematic effort" he thinks necessary for the moral elevation of African Americans: "Every youth should be educated . . . and a copy of the 'Colored American' should be put into the hands of every family."[82] Woodson's appreciation for *The Colored American* is additionally expressed in an 1838 letter printed as "Further from Pittsburgh." He writes that even though he gets seven papers, *The Colored American* is "of far more importance to me, and to us, than them all."[83]

The Colored American notably focused on African American lives in an international context. The paper regularly published articles from Haitian newspapers. The boys' engagement with the paper suggests they were encouraged to frame their antislavery actions as part of international movements recognizing Africans as sovereign beings, rather than dependents on colonial good will. The children at this school were not alone in being encouraged to understand politics; Mary Niall Mitchell examines letters by African American children at the Couvent School in New Orleans in the 1840s–1850s, arguing that they show signs of "a particular education designed to make free children of color . . . aware of the political events surrounding them."[84] However, the Pittsburgh community was perhaps forward thinking when it came to the use of newspapers to inform African American children's political understanding, in that Peck and Vashon wrote to *The Colored American* prior to the paper's establishment of a children's department in 1840. Nazera Wright writes, "Editors . . . hoped that lessons learned from the column might train a generation of black children to become full participants in their communities and to find viable solutions to disfranchisement by channeling their literacy toward political engagement"—work that the Pittsburgh children were already doing.[85]

Even before the juvenile society was formed in 1838, the editors of *The Christian Witness*, a paper published by the Western Pennsylvania Antislavery Society, referenced African American youth in Pittsburgh and expressed confidence in their ability to understand the nuances of debates over how sovereignty, equality, and inclusion might be achieved. In an essay questioning the merits of international colonization schemes that would end enslavement by coercively removing African Americans to their own country, the author quips, "Now let the boys at school answer this question. If the colonization society removes as many slaves in one year as are born in one week, how long will it require to remove them all?"[86] The implication is that the free Black children in Pittsburgh could easily ascertain that colonization based on the forced removal of African Americans was a bad solution.

George B. Vashon would later argue against this form of colonization, while David Peck became involved with Martin Delany's removal scheme of African Americans to Nicaragua, which differed from efforts headed by white activists in that it emphasized finding a home in the Americas rather than returning to Africa. Committed to hemispheric Black solidarity, Vashon became a teacher in Haiti, where he wrote a poem about the revolutionary Vincent Ogé. The poem envisions "chosen" men who will "cleanse their souls from every stain," not merely by abstaining from sugar, but by ridding the world of tyranny.[87]

The New Media of Consumerism

Boycott literature for children ultimately did not have such a widespread impact or goal. The power of childhood innocence to excuse consumer guilt meant that the genres it used to criticize consumer culture were quickly reclaimed. Showing the recuperation possible in the children's book market and the market at large, authors used the advent of steam technology and the abolition of enslavement to repackage the use of African people's labor as ethical, even as many abusive practices and horrific conditions continued. Following the logic of capitalist innovation that had spurred antislavery books, some writers construed their offerings as innovations in new media for children, reflecting technology, rather than boycotts, as the key to a more ethical world. One next-generation it-narrative, *The History of a Pound of Sugar*, sometimes bound in a book called *Rhymes and Pictures* (published in London by Griffith and Farran in 1860), includes a cover illustration of a group of children gathered around a magic lantern, a kind of early projector, casting an image of sugar cane on the wall (fig. 3.2).

While Townsend and Opie insisted that children needed to hear about sugar in the voices of enslaved people who had encountered the industry directly, even if mediated by text, *The History of a Pound of Sugar* fetishizes technological mediation, which creates the illusion of access to the workers pictured on the slides without the need to approximate their voices. This will be a *new* story of sugar production, the image implies, one appropriate for the innocent (white) children who operate the magic lantern. The image hinges on a fantasy of harmlessness, both of what the technology depicts and the technology itself. The boy inserting the slide into the lantern is dangerously

Figure 3.2. Cover of *The History of a Pound of Sugar*, in *Rhymes and Pictures*. London: Griffith and Farran, 1860–1863. Courtesy of the Baldwin Library of Historical Children's Literature, George A. Smathers Libraries, University of Florida.

close to burning his eye or hair on the lit part of the lantern, but no adult hovers to ensure safety and the image does not express any danger.

The story inside presents a parallel technological fantasy of non-harmful sugar making, construed as a collaboration among "negroes" (presumably freed but still subject to white oversight), a white planter, and the magical invention of the steam sugar mill.[88] Black workers are pictured cutting and carrying sugar cane, but their strain is transferred to the technology: "Whose iron limbs, with mighty strain, / Receive and press the stalk."[89] Even though such mills were first introduced in Jamaica in 1768 to increase the efficiency of workers during enslavement, the mill is portrayed as a godlike personified object that, unlike the sugar, needs no explanation or discussion from workers, the details of its operation obscured in favor of mechanical magic. The boiling house, in turn, is "quite still" and contains none of the torture or death contained in earlier images of this step. Although the rhetoric emphasizes the technology's efficiency and safety, with a veneer of concern for ethics, steam sugar mills were not inherently safe, with risks to workers including explosions, burns, and exposure to hazardous materials.[90] Their greater capacity demanded faster and more intense labor related to the other parts of sugar production, including the cultivating, harvesting, mill-feeding, and boiling stages. The book idealizes this work, maintaining that the sugar, not the workers, has "pass'd Through many a peril, pinch and scrape" before reaching consumers.[91]

In this technological fantasy, capitalism and consumption are rendered innocent. The final page misleadingly suggests that the grocer eats some of the food to live while sharing the rest:

> The Grocer's shop's a human hive,
> Of honeyed goods from many a land;
> A part the grocer eats, to live;
> The rest he shares with liberal hand.[92]

In a fascinating repurposing of the dead-child-in-a-hogshead image Burn used to disgust consumers, a child hangs over the side of a barrel gobbling up the sugar (fig. 3.3). Through its connection to innocent-appearing child consumers, the disturbing image has been neutralized.

Disturbing insinuations about Black bodies persist, however. In addition to allowing consumers to imagine that products like sugar are produced without pain, the transition to steam means that fears of intrusion and contamination are replaced with new colonial fantasies of ownership and control. One British magic lantern company with a deep racist catalog, J. Theobald & Co., hawked a "steam dancing engine" that young people could use to make a minstrel-style figure dance for the "greatest fun and excitement ever known."[93] The mechanization allows for there to be no ethical concern about the suffering of a person being made to move without consent.

Countering the ways that boycott authors imagined a new kind of children's literature, authors writing about the new technology also claimed the need for new stories. In *Aunt Martha's Corner Cupboard, Or Stories About Tea, Coffee, Sugar, Rice, Honey &c.* (1875) by Mary and Elizabeth Kirey, the title character is unsure how to entertain her two nephews until she turns to the items in her cupboard, which "were sure to have something to relate that the boys had never heard of."[94] The stories Aunt Martha tells about "her china, her tea, her coffee, her sugar" are construed as innovative.[95] The children "were thoroughly acquainted with 'Jack the Giant-Killer,' and entertaining as he had once been, they were by this time a little tired of him. They knew 'Cinderella' and 'Little Red Riding Hood' by heart, and they did not want to hear them over again."[96] But just as the steam technology was not new in the late nineteenth century, stories of products date at least from Bar-

Figure 3.3. Page from *The History of a Pound of Sugar*, in *Rhymes and Pictures*. London: Griffith and Farran, 1860–1863. Courtesy of the Baldwin Library of Historical Children's Literature, George A. Smathers Libraries, University of Florida.

bauld's *Lessons for Young Children* (original editions 1778–1808, revised edition 1841) (discussed in my introduction). What *is* new is a description of technology that denies connection with other humans: "A great giant called Steam helps to make the sugar now, and does more than all the black people put together."[97] Departing from boycotters' attempts to endow sugar with human content, the Kireys imagine Steam as a powerful nonhuman being of fantastical origin.[98]

Although the fetishization of the machine obscures its relationships with human politics and the potential for human suffering, we see a trace of those relationships in the declaration that the steam sugar mill can do more than "all the black people."[99] Furthermore, Afro-Caribbeans continued to be pictured engaging in hard agricultural labor. At the time that these books were published, British colonizers were also bringing indentured laborers from India, China, Portugal, and elsewhere to the Caribbean to supplement free Black workers. This indenture system increased rather than decreased labor concerns. In denying the interdependence of workers and consumers, children's new media books stepped away from the ethical responsibility that the children's boycott books had promoted.

Critical perspectives are ultimately rare in comparison to consumer worries about contamination and recuperative pro-capitalist tales. Nonetheless, the ethical imperative to intervene in the lives of the enslaved represented by the boycott books meant that children's literature became a tool for promoting colonial relationships within a transatlantic, and ultimately global, framework. As I discuss in the next chapter, the first global children's literature might be children's literature promoting hard labor for the purposes of education—a labor only sometimes understood as separate from manual labor. This ideal circulated to the captive audience of colonized and enslaved children in the Caribbean in the guise of ethical intervention, meeting with resistance as well as strategic use by Afro-Caribbean children, parents, and teachers.

CHAPTER 4

The Ethics of Circulation in the Enslaved and Colonized West Indies

As antislavery activism gained traction in Britain, the emphasis on responsibility for others across distance, among other economic, social, and political motivations, yielded aspirations for children's literature to intervene directly in enslaved children's lives. A variety of would-be influencers—including missionaries, government officials, educators, and even some enslavers—promoted books and literacy to teach Afro-Caribbean children Christian virtue-based ethics, which they insisted were universally applicable around the world. The 1815 annual report of the British and Foreign School Society (BFSS), an organization spreading English children's books and Lancaster (or monitorial) teaching techniques, boasted that reading instruction had created "good subjects, good servants, good husbands, good wives, and good parents," proposing similar methods be adopted across the British colonies, including Canada.[1] As the possibility that the Caribbean islands would shift from slave societies to colonies of free people inched closer to reality, those who feared this transition and those agitating for it viewed education, especially in reading, as a way to address the impacts of enslavement.[2]

The assumption that children's literature was a moral good that could transform people harmed by the institution of slavery into "good subjects" narrowed ethical questions regarding the social and material impacts of enslavement to matters of book distribution and educational access. This focus on literacy fit with long-standing tropes of Caribbean children in English-language children's books. An early impulse had been to portray creole youth, even white creoles, as deprived of children's literature. In A. Selwyn's *The Little Creoles* (1820), readers are asked to sympathize with the white protagonists because they have lived without the trappings of middle-class European childhood, including children's books: "Francis had been taught to read by his father's book-keeper, but he never had been amused by any of those charming little narratives, with which the French and English languages are now graced; the delightful stories of Miss Edgeworth, or Berquin, were utterly unknown to him; he had scarcely opened any book but Vyse's Spelling Book."[3] This description of a culturally impoverished child anticipates later images of needy children from around the globe used to motivate Western generosity, which Kathryn Bond Stockton refers to as "kid Orientalism."[4] Selwyn's sentimental appeal resembles the glossy images of children's faces now appearing in UNICEF advertisements, which Stockton argues block the responsive ethical engagement Emmanuel Levinas claims is inherent in the face by creating the fiction that these children desire Western intervention. It obscures more than it reveals.

Children's books were, in fact, available in the English-speaking Caribbean, arriving via merchant ships and donations to missionary groups.[5] Caribbean newspaper advertisements suggest that spelling books like Charles Vyse's *New London Spelling Book* (1823) had wide circulation, as they did elsewhere, but children's storybooks also came to the Caribbean in significant numbers.[6] Despite its mention by Selwyn as unavailable, Arnaud Berquin's *L'ami des enfants* (1782–1783), usually translated into English as *The Children's Friend)* was advertised in two newspapers, in Bermuda and Trinidad, respectively.[7] Access to such books was uncomplicated for white children of means. Missionary educators also circulated school and storybooks to a limited but significant number of Afro-Caribbean children for various aims, including the maintenance of slave systems and education for a free labor economy. The circulated books contain purportedly universal lessons, built on Anglo-Christian ethics.

Given this reality, we can unmask the claim that books were not available as the product of a hypocritical colonial mindset, which touted the British mainland as the natural setting for childhood while forcing its ideals on children elsewhere. Later books by Caribbean authors such as Louise Bennett-Coverley's *Jamaican Maddah Goose* (1981) and John Agard and Grace Nichols's *No Hickory No Dickory No Dock* (1995) pointedly respond to the ways that children's literature in English (including nursery rhymes) came to dominate children's lives, inspiring these authors' lifelong projects of celebrating and validating Afro-Caribbean language and folklore.[8] The real ethical issue, we now know, was not lack but influence, efforts to promote the superiority of English-speaking (British, but increasingly US) cultures through literary transmission. Bringing missionary records and colonial newspapers together with rare firsthand accounts and school materials produced by Afro-Caribbeans, this chapter attempts to reconstruct Afro-Caribbean people's experiences as this was happening.[9]

Given that children's books from Britain and the United States emphasized Anglo-American language, knowledge, and viewpoints—and promoted Christianity over African and Indigenous beliefs—it almost goes without saying that the influx of English-language children's literature figured into what Norrel London calls a massive attempt by colonizers to "silence (forever in some cases) . . . indigenous ways of knowing and living," a position echoed by Cynthia James.[10] It is well known that English-language children's literature was a part of similar processes around the world. Yet it is worth historicizing when, where, and how these ambitions took hold—and what ethical claims underlie them. The drive to educate and Christianize the Caribbean population, we will see, had an ambiguous relationship to antislavery efforts. The circulation of English-language books, furthermore, notably replaced earlier efforts to translate works into Creole languages, which relied on cooperation between missionaries and native speakers and allowed for responsiveness to local circumstances. By contrast, English books prioritize global knowledge as defined by colonial powers, promoting docility during enslavement followed by self-sufficiency meant to lessen colonizers' ethical responsibility. By tracing their spread from the British Caribbean into areas occupied by other colonial powers, including the Dutch Creole-speaking Danish Caribbean, we can see how evangelical and imperial ambitions take the place of local responsiveness, paving the way for the global circulation of English children's literature.

Educators justified their global aspirations with ethical coating. For example, while working in Danish St. Croix, US Moravian missionary William Warner claimed to the Young Men's Missionary Society (YMMS) in Pennsylvania that their donation of English books to replace earlier Creole ones would have global ethical significance: "Surely from Greenland's icy mountains and from India's coral strand, many thanks . . . is offered up for such benefactors."[11] Twenty years later, free Black children in St. Croix received English-language tracts, originating in circumstances far removed from any connection with Caribbean people. This evolution, I argue, decreases possibilities for children's books to engage in a responsive relational ethics.

In examining how Caribbean circulation fed into global visions of children's literature, I build on scholarship by Nina Christensen, Charlotte Appel, and M. O. Grenby in *Transnational Books for Children, 1750–1900*.[12] This scholarship proposes that much of early children's literature was transnational—comprising adaptations of popular texts and formats, such as the ABC book, tailored to different local and national contexts in Europe and elsewhere. My research shows that books available in the Caribbean came to be far less transnational—that is, translated and tailored to specific local contexts and languages—than what I call "global-imperial": books created with the aspiration of being used universally for children's improvement.[13] Like Stockton's glossy images, this global-imperial children's literature flattens ethical relations into what is valuable to colonizing interests, attempting to reproduce in Afro-Caribbean children what Selwyn wanted to avoid for the white creoles: a childhood tied to hard, repetitive schoolwork and labor rather than leisure or fun. It was arguably this version of childhood that gave rise to the first and widest global children's literature.

The presence of enslaved and colonized readers, however, would push a minority of publishers and writers with global-imperial aspirations to account for their existence. Furthermore, threads emphasizing relational ideas such as interdependence occasionally surface in the emerging global children's literature. I offer a reading of a Religious Tract Society title circulated by the Moravians for which we have more circulation data than usual: *The Traveller: Or, A Description of Various Wonders in Nature and Art* (1838). Outlining the context of this book's travel to St. Croix post-emancipation, I argue that it presents a strikingly different vision of the world than books fetishizing the English climate (discussed in chapter 1), instead depicting global variety, multiplicity, and difference. Although this book aims to spread a universally applicable Christian ethics, it also introduces themes of ethical relationality and proto-multiculturalism, speaking obliquely to its secondary readers in the colonies.

Differently pushing against the incursion of the global, a map created by a nineteenth-century Afro-Caribbean teacher trained at the Moravian normal school in Fairfield, Jamaica, demonstrates the persistence of ethical values forged in anticolonial revolution. The route the map travels reverses the direction of colonial book circulation, entering an epistolary exchange between Moravian missionaries and their young US supporters in the YMMS. Referencing the history of the Maroons in relation to the landscape, the map expresses Shalini Puri's point (about the later Grenada Revolution) that the "land is an archive," making "an argument for the specificity and situatedness of [Afro-Caribbean] experience."[14] The YMMS's subsequent use of the map in their missionary museum speaks to the acquisitiveness underlying nineteenth-century multicultural education, but its copious details point to Afro-Caribbean ethical viewpoints.

Reading as Labor

Many British evangelicals considered the spread of English-language books to enslaved children an ethical intervention necessary for the end of enslavement. Responding to a letter from Baptist missionary Thomas Knibb in Jamaica, the 1825 annual report of the BFSS declares that literacy will "confer incalculable benefits on the slave population, and prove one of the best preparatives for their freedom."[15] Knibb had a broad idea of freedom. The Jamaican Baptist mission was founded by George Liele, an emancipated African American who arrived in 1782 and appealed for assistance from British missionaries. Through Knibb's interactions with the mission, he came to understand Afro-Caribbeans' need for spiritual *and* material sustenance.

The BFSS, though supportive of abolition, saw freedom as contingent on Afro-Caribbean people's willingness to sign on as compliant subjects of a benevolent British monarch, responding to Knibb: "Nor can your Committee imagine a better preparative for that universal emancipation which must one day be granted, than the establishment of a system of early scriptural instruction: for he who in childhood has been taught to 'fear God,' will not in mature age refuse to 'honour the King.' "[16] A specimen book of Jamaican children's writing sent by BFSS-trained instructor Jabez Tunley shows how educators attempted to manifest these sentiments even after abolition. A page of copywork by Benjamin Sharp dated 1844 repeats the phrase "Honour the Queen" nine times, reflecting the coronation of Queen Victoria in 1837, though another page repeats "Kings Must Die," perhaps a reference to the death of William IV or to biblical events.[17] It is unclear whether rebellious meaning can be inferred—and it is unlikely, given that the page appears without comment. As Hilary E. Wyss observes about similar handwriting samples from American Indians in mission schools, this writing has "the illusion of depth," but the emphasis is mostly on the "discipline and dexterity that they display, not … their meaning."[18]

Missionaries had started the process of evangelizing to enslaved people beginning in the mid-eighteenth century, occasionally providing literacy instruction.[19] Between this period and abolition, the British government's goals of amelioration and eventual emancipation, combined with continued colonization and the desire to extend British subjecthood (without its full rights) to people in the Caribbean, led to efforts to increase English-language reading instruction among enslaved children. While a great many children on these islands did not have the opportunity to learn owing to enslaver opposition, formalized at various points in slave codes, the government increasingly tracked missionary efforts to teach enslaved youth to read, which were uneven and probably often interrupted. The British *Quarterly Journal of Education* summarizes a report specifying "how many . . . pupils of each class are able to read well, or are learning to read," presented to Parliament in 1832 in preparation for emancipation, which was passed in 1833 and took effect in 1834 with the start of an apprenticeship system wherein those over age six would continue to labor until 1838.[20]

The percentage of enslaved people learning to read is low compared to the general population of the islands, but the numbers are surprisingly high. Just one missionary group in Antigua, "the Wesleyan Methodists," had "established three Sunday-schools, in which there are 1305 children taught, of whom 32 are free, the rest slaves; among the number 204 can read with tolerable fluency, and 395 are learning the alphabet . . . the books used are . . . Sunday School Union and Universal Spelling Books, Church and Watt's Catechisms, &c."[21] These numbers reflect the use of the Lancaster system, the BFSS classroom management method whereby a schoolteacher could instruct a large group of students with the assistance of student "monitors." Missionaries had been building up to these numbers. In 1826, William Knibb in Kingston (a brother to Thomas, who trained at the BFSS and took his place in the Baptist mission after his death), oversaw a school with 224 scholars, including 65 enslaved youth. By the start of apprenticeship, the Baptists claimed 1,300 children, 900 of whom were enslaved.[22]

We can determine what children read in such schools by consulting missionary diaries and letters, as well as (in rare cases) their own recollections. The 1823 BFSS report reprints a letter from John Wray of the London Missionary Society, who worked in Berbice, Guyana:

> I think at least *forty* repeated each a hymn to His Excellency, out of Dr. Watt's
> Divine Songs and the Fitzroy Hymn Book . . . [O]ne of the classes said the whole
> of a catechism on the duties of servants and slaves, chiefly in Scripture language,
> with great propriety, mentioning the chapter and verse; some of these children
> are only about nine years old . . . A very handsome medal was given to a little
> Black girl, named Flora, aged seven years, for industry; she read well in the
> New Testament; said the catechism on the duties of servants correctly; also
> answered several questions out of the Bible: she likewise teaches a class, and

on the Sabbath instructs some of the adults in reading . . . A second medal was given to a little boy, a slave to the crown, aged seven years; he reads the best of his age and size in the sixth class, and can repeat a great many of Watts's hymns, and texts of the Scripture.[23]

Missionary efforts accelerated as abolition was debated; Wray wrote again in 1826 to request "spelling books" and reading books "published by the Sunday-school union" so that the "country-slaves" could teach each other.[24]

Using such materials was often forbidden by enslavers; in 1846 Moravian missionary Edward E. Reinke relays memories from formerly enslaved people in Jamaica that "to be found reading a book was certain death."[25] Yet other recollections attest to (limited) access. Matthew Josephs, an Afro-Caribbean writer and poet who trained as a teacher in post-abolition Jamaica, recalls that his father, who was taught to read for his job as "headman," "endeavoured to teach my brothers and myself to read. Books were then scarce; Fenning's and Dilworth's spelling-books were then, by us, thought of the highest excellence."[26] Josephs also remembers reading the New Testament and William Guthrie's *Geography* while enslaved. Mary Prince (discussed in chapter 2) recalls learning to read at a Moravian school, where she caught on "very fast" and was able to practice with a copy of Sarah Trimmer's *Charity School Spelling Book* (1798–1799).[27]

As these records suggest, missionaries distributed a range of reading materials designed for children, suggesting that they were eager to view the young people made into property within the transatlantic economy as *children*. By examining the titles and types of books that came to dominate children's reading experiences in the Caribbean, we can identify the type of childhood that missionaries imagined: a school-oriented childhood in which young people would work tirelessly to achieve virtue as defined by colonizers and would look to books to understand their economically subordinate place in a globally connected world of people and information.

The most easily recognized book in Wray's letter, Isaac Watts's *Divine Songs* (a poetry book published by the Religious Tract Society as well as other outlets), reinforces the idea that children must devote themselves to hard work and a Christian method of accounting for ethical behavior. Watts's book appears across the British Caribbean in newspaper ads—in St. Christopher (now St. Kitts) in 1800, 1826, 1827, and 1829; Jamaica in 1822; Antigua in 1827; Trinidad in 1833; Bermuda in 1858; and Barbados in 1868.[28] The book is also included in an 1829 list of books "received by the district committee and available at the school room of the charitable institution" on St. Christopher, which was under the auspices of the (Anglican) Society for Promoting Christian Knowledge (SPCK).[29] The SPCK sent thousands of books to the Anglophone Caribbean for the purpose of educating enslaved children.

Watts's most famous poem, "Against Idleness and Mischief," promotes children's accounting of their ethical behavior with the lines:

> In works of labor or of skill,
> I would be busy too;
> For Satan finds some mischief still
> For idle hands to do.
>
> In books, or work, or healthful play,
> Let my first years be passed,
> That I may give for every day
> Some good account at last.[30]

Different from the transformative other-directed ethical accounting that Judith Butler advocates in *Giving an Account of Oneself* (2005) (discussed in my introduction), the poem emphasizes labor as the key to an ethical life, a colonial measuring stick for moral behavior that has been relentlessly applied to people of color in the Americas and around the globe.

Given that it was originally written for middle-class children in England, Watts's poem does not differentiate between different kinds of work, but gradations of child labor were coming to be debated in the context of enslavement. The idea that school, rather than home, would be the key setting for children's work was shaping what childhood was coming to mean in nineteenth-century Britain and the United States, though this had not been fully embraced by the public. Those who intervened in the Caribbean also were not in agreement about the relationship between enslavement, work, childhood, and schooling.

Some educators saw enslavement, including the expectation that enslaved children participate in manual labor, as thwarting their efforts, particularly English-speaking missionaries working on other islands after British abolition. US Moravians working in the enslaved Danish Caribbean in the 1840s, for example, saw enslavement as a major obstacle and opposed it to the extent that it conflicted with their educational aims (they did not, however, support the 1848 rebellion that led to emancipation on the Danish islands because of its insurrectionist methods). Moravian missionary M. Dammus, stationed in St. John, explains to the YMMS, "Every Saturday I visit some Estate or other to stir up the children. A great hindrance to the progress of the work is <u>slavery</u>."[31] Warner also claims that "our great hindrance on this island which keeps them behind the English islands is that baneful slavery which casts many stumbling blocks into our way."[32] This position was partly self-interested: the Afro-Caribbean population contributed money to missions on the emancipated islands, an act that Mary Turner argues gave them some agency in the missions' actions.[33] Reflecting emerging imperialistic US attitudes viewing contact with English and Christianity as general paths to freedom, not just membership in the British Empire, Warner insinuates that learning opens the door to an enlightened world.

This antislavery position was not shared by all missionaries. An equally popular expectation, particularly on the British islands before emancipation, assumed that Afro-Caribbean children would combine manual labor and schoolwork. Although Wray supported abolition if it was differentiated from rebellion, his program of education was designed to be compatible with enslavement. An 1812 series of letters responding to an uproar over an antislavery book, *Cushoo: A Dialogue between a Negro and an English Gentleman, on the Horrors of Slavery and the Slave Trade* (1790), demonstrate the balancing act that Wray did in setting up schools without offending enslavers.[34] One of Wray's fellows, John Davies, faced criticism because this book was given to (or found by) an enslaved child under his tutelage. When confronted by the colonial governor of Demerara (now Guyana), Davies claimed the book had accidentally appeared in a box of donations and eased tensions by showing the text the missionaries generally used, Lindley Murray's *English Reader* (discussed later in this chapter). Convinced of the missionaries' intention not to challenge enslavement, the governor allowed them greater access to enslaved children. In a subsequent letter to the BFSS, Wray mentions the children reading his catechism "on the duties of servants."[35] Wray was not the only one to emphasize servitude in children's education; John Shipman of the Wesleyan Missionary Society (WMS) adapted John Wesley's *Instructions for Children* for the enslaved in Jamaica, with three out of five sections "devoted to the duties of servants."[36] Under pressure from enslavers, Shipman had the children learn by rote rather than reading and later pushed WMS missionaries to adopt resolutions declaring that Wesleyan instruction was not antithetical to enslavement.

Whether learning by reading or rote, education could cause young people's labor to double or triple. Some missionaries arguing for freedom contended that the labor of schooling meant children could labor for money if freed. One of the few surviving educational artifacts made by nineteenth-century Afro-Caribbean children, a collection of Jamaican schoolchildren's handwriting samples sent to the BFSS by William Knibb in 1826, functions as a rhetorical object demonstrating the children's capacity for mental and physical labor. Although less than a third of the students at his school were enslaved, the item has come to be known as "The Slave Book" at the archive because of its use in antislavery conversations. Knibb used it to argue for enslaved children's educability and potential to succeed in a free workforce.

Unlike the US Moravians in St. Croix, Knibb supported active measures against enslavement. After an enslaved man trained as a Baptist deacon, Sam Sharpe, initiated a Christmas rebellion at one of their churches in 1831, Knibb was arrested under accusations that he had encouraged the enslaved to riot. Although Knibb was likely not involved in the planning, he refused to leave the island after released on bail; meanwhile, Sharpe's actions and his resulting execution, according to Rebecca Schneider, "hastened emancipation" by making "planter violence visible."[37] Knibb toured England and Scotland to expose enslaver practices, spoke against enslavement in Parliament, and argued against apprenticeship in favor of immediate freedom.

Although "The Slave Book" bears little trace of these radical agitations, it uses the children's labor to argue for Afro-Caribbean children's intellectual and economic promise. In its opening, Knibb includes the pointed note, "All the specimens, both of Writing and Needlework, are <u>entirely</u> the productions of the Children," implying their readiness for emancipation.[38] Despite this claim, the marks and stitches contained within are not "entirely" the children's productions as we would apprehend that word. They are the products of lessons taught in a disciplinary setting to young people who were not free. The children are presented as easily assimilable, similar to how Wyss characterizes the "Readerly Indian . . . standing at the ready for the mark of English civilization."[39] Wyss argues that "as passive consumers of English manners, such . . . students were celebrated only for reciting English lessons, not for bringing to bear their own thoughts or ideas."[40] Aside from a basic description of the school by an enslaved child named Sulliff, the samples are copied verbatim from source texts.

Although it is tempting to look for shreds of enslaved children's agency within the constrained forms offered to them by educators, these samples resist such an endeavor, instead telling us what educators wanted enslaved children to be and know. Twelve-year-old Caroline Porter, labeled a "slave," copied a stanza from Watts:

> Blessings for ever on the Lamb,
>
> Who bore the curse for wretched mans
>
> Let angels sound his sacred name
>
> And every creature say—Amen[41]

It is impossible to know how Porter might have felt about these lines or about her schooling. She, like many Africans in the Americas, might have found solace in Christian images of deliverance—and going to school must have required bravery, whether she found it inspiring or constraining. Yet her writing performs piety and writing competency in ways that serve the aims of abolition and colonial education, while failing to secure her freedom.[42] The lines instead signify Knibb's investment in a future in which enslaved youth might be free to inhabit this vision of childhood. The only deviation from Watts is a mistake: "mans" versus "man."

Although there is no opportunity to excavate Porter's perspective, that an enslaved child's copywork features Watts's poetry notably contrasts with Watts's vision of literary childhood, which limits the participation of children outside of Britain. If Porter read the whole of *Divine Songs*, she would have found lines disparaging the "East and West Indies" in favor of "British ground."[43] Educational practices allowing Afro-Caribbean children to inhabit the roles of child reader and copyist suggest that the fetishization of mainland Britain was coming to be replaced with the fetishization of English-language texts in the context of the British Empire. Thomas Babington Macaulay expressed this shift in an East Indian context in "Minute Upon Indian Education" (1835), in which he advocated for English-language instruction by offensively asserting that no person "could deny that a single shelf of a good European library was worth the whole native literature of India and Arabia."[44] Assigning Watts for copywork supports this privileging of European writing, though Porter's English writing skills may have had practical uses, as it did for English learners in the East Indies.[45] For instance, as I discuss in chapter 2, some enslaved people used writing skills to forge freedom and mobility documents. Others, as Haley North shows, employed writing to petition enslavers for manumission.[46]

Lines by enslaved sixteen-year-old Priscilla Brown further illustrate the uneasy fit between enslavement and British literary cultures of childhood.[47]

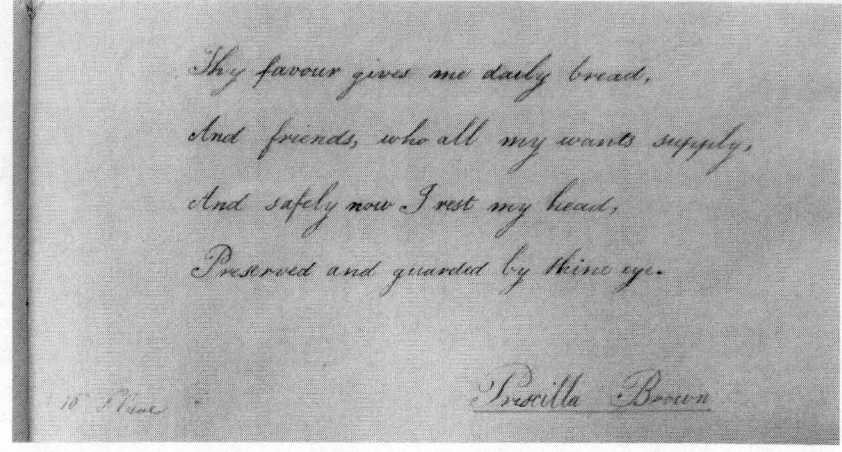

Figure 4.1. Passage copied by Priscilla Brown, in *Specimens of Writing &c.*, Lancasterian School, Kingston, Jamaica, 1826. Courtesy of Archives and Special Collections, Brunel University of London.

Brown copied a hymn that appears in many infant school publications (fig. 4.1):

> Thy favour gives me daily bread,
> And friends, who all my wants supply,
> And safely now I rest my head,
> Preserved and guarded by thine eye.[48]

These lines about safety contrast with the conditions in which enslaved youth lived—which included constant threats of sexual violence toward teenage girls—and there is no information to suggest that Priscilla was preserved from these threats while she was enrolled in school (as I discuss later, there were multiple cases of Afro-Caribbean children being sexually harassed at school). The words "friends who all my wants supply" and "safely now I rest my head" become ironic in the hand of an enslaved girl. The painstaking work of copying nonetheless connects Brown to recognizable Anglo cultures of childhood, including constraints of school life that also impacted white children. Copywork from British and US schools looks nearly identical to this. Knibb had reasons to lump enslaved youth in with schoolchildren, as it proved their readiness for freedom; for Brown, slave labor and the labor of childhood coexist with what was surely the heavy emotional labor of performing a freedom she deserved, but that was not safeguarded by friends or law.

Other infant school publications used in Caribbean schools present similarly idealized visions, while implying that colonial investments create social and economic obligations the children must repay. Warner reports that children on the "La Prince estate assemble together in the evening to sing hymns learned in school" and greet him in the morning singing, "School is a pleasure. Now unto our infant minds: Here we a treasure: Of heavenly wisdom."[49] Included in publications such as *The Glasgow Infant School Magazine*, this song was likely the product of a teacher involved in the infant school movement.[50] As Maria Ryan notes, singing, especially interesting songs, was a technique used to attract Afro-Caribbeans to missionary schools and churches.[51] Although the letter draws attention to the children's long day of working and schooling, the song emphasizes that learning is a pleasurable gift.

This gift is not free, however, but represents a balance they must repay, as implied in a subsequent stanza:

> We learn, the Holy Scriptures say,
> That we should honour and obey,
> And Do our utmost to *repay*
> Our Father and our Mother.[52]

Those teaching the hymn likely did not intend enslaved people to understand this verse as a reference only to their own parents but to the fifth commandment, "Honor thy father and mother," which many Christians associated with all authority figures. Subsequent stanzas repeat "we learn" three more times, drawing attention to the multiple kinds of learning the child will need to repay in the future. These demands were partly for assimilation, but a letter from Reinke in Jamaica attests to the expectation among Moravians that students would contribute materially to mission work post-emancipation: "The yearly subscriptions are not so large as might be expected," and the only "return" he gets for educating the 100 children in his school is "two or three hours of labor in our provision ground."[53]

Letters from missionaries to their home organizations, as well as annual reports, reinforce these expected economics of learning in the Caribbean by tallying the number of converted souls (and future workers) that justify investments from foreign (and local) subscribers.[54] The BFSS reports include accounts of children performing the roles of dutiful students, peer teachers, and religious dedicants, presumably with a canny awareness that such performances were expected. An 1832 examination by James Phillippo, a Baptist working in Spanish Town, Jamaica, claims that the schoolchildren's "knowledge of the Scriptures is accurate and extensive, and their enunciation in the English tongue natural and correct."[55] This acquisition is connected to their heavy reading: "Thirteen are reading the Grecian with other European Histories; six are pursuing lessons from the Scriptures in general; and the rest (excepting the first and second classes) are reading the New Testament writings."[56] These lessons are heavier than what was expected for children in Britain or the United States, where educators worried about the effects of overzealous learning on children when it came to rote memorization, recitation, and spelling.[57] In the colonial vision of childhood, the pressure to labor for education seems to have been unchecked. Colonizers frequently tried to make schooling compulsory or blend the labor of schooling with manual labor, plans that, after abolition, formerly enslaved people resisted in favor of lessons that would advance their economic opportunities beyond manual labor. Chelsey Smith writes, "Whether attendance at available schools . . . represented a new kind of compelled labor was an open question."[58]

At the beginning of the apprenticeship period in 1834, Lady Mico's Charity, an organization originally founded to liberate enslaved Europeans in Algiers, established official schools for the formerly enslaved that continued to use the BFSS curriculum designed for the working class, meant "to fit the rising generation . . . for the satisfactory and cheerful performance of their unavoidable duties."[59] E. A. Wallbridge, superintendent of the Mico Charity Normal School in Kingston, argues that reading will root out parental influence, by which he acknowledges the persistence of Afro-Caribbean practices of educating children.[60] Wallbridge complains specifically about the Maroons, claiming they teach their children warfare instead of sending them to school.[61] Meanwhile, in his time as superintendent, Wallbridge became aware of multiple cases of his teachers and those employed by other organizations sexually harassing Afro-Caribbean girls at school.[62]

After the Mico Charity folded owing to lack of funds in 1841, British schools continued to promote versions of childhood centered on educational and manual labor. A circular dispatch written by the colonial office in January 1847 argues that the government's goals are to "diffuse a grammatical knowledge of the English language as the most important agent of civilization" and to make readers aware that "the social lot of the coloured race" was labor in the interest of the mother country.[63] Kathleen Drayton's analysis of schoolbooks used in the nineteenth-century Caribbean shows that many emphasized the importance of a division of labor between working and propertied classes, and between men and women.[64]

Drayton suggests that Afro-Caribbean readers gradually gained purchasing power. She shows that, although individual books were cheaply priced because they were heavily subsidized by the organization, by 1828 the "coloured poor" in the Caribbean had bought a total number of books worth more than 500 British pounds sterling. There is some indication that enslaved and colonized readers came to expect more pleasurable and interesting material. Especially after enslavement ended, missionaries resorted to using books as Christmas presents to attract children to their schools, in addition to the rewards offered as part of the everyday functioning of the monitorial system. Newspapers attest to the circulation of works appropriated by the Caribbean public for the purposes of amusement, such as (Edmond) *Hoyle's Games* (1742), a source of Trinidad's national card game, all fours.[65]

Letters written after emancipation in the British islands are rife with complaints that Afro-Caribbean parents were unwilling to pay for books and expected their children to work for money rather than for an intangible future, reasonable expressions of a desire to choose what their children would do. E. Woolley writes from Jamaica in 1845, "Parents perhaps value education more than formerly—but value their children's labour, or their purse most."[66] Some explanation for this behavior might be found in the poverty of many Afro-Caribbean families and their need to labor for their support; Smith points out that "children were often central to . . . maintaining [families'] provision grounds and preparing to sell their products in the market."[67] Complaints also likely reflect resistance to colonial education, especially elements that resembled the labor of enslavement, with those resisting prioritizing their own languages, traditions, and stories.

Adding to Wallbridge's complaints about the Maroons' warlike teachings, missionaries refer to dancing traditions. Moravian Arthur Van Vleck describes Afro-Caribbean students in post-emancipation Barbados as suffering from an environment characterized by "heathenish dances, vice & immorality" and claims that "books would doubtless" prevent their slide into "eternal ruin."[68] (I discuss the very different role of dancing and other improvisational arts for Afro-Caribbean children in my conclusion.) Even post-independence, tensions between colonial and Afro-Caribbean forms of education continue to be reflected in many West Indians' resentment over the fact that they often learn English nursery rhymes before learning about Afro-Caribbean history and culture.[69] Contemporary Caribbean writers Agard and Nichols respond to this long history with anticolonial nursery rhymes, sardonically imagining a mouse who insists he did not run up the clock and a London bridge that is "broken down," mixed with culturally specific rhymes about Anansi and Mami-Wata.[70]

Gatekeepers of Childhood

The profusion of Anglo children's literature did not happen only through missionaries, for, as I argue in chapter 2, childhood was an idea that served enslavers as well. Children's books were part of the apparatus of colonization because, as James Raven puts it, "book imports were lifelines of identity" for colonists as well as "luxury goods."[71] Sean D. Moore argues that enslavement shaped colonial book circulation, as enslavers demanded emblems of cultural capital to legitimize their power.[72]

The earliest record of commercial children's book circulation in the Caribbean yielded by my research is an advertisement by Samuel Hurst of Bermuda hawking "Newbery books for children" in 1784, likely bought by enslavers for their families.[73] In 1788, Hurst posted another advertisement marketing Berquin's tales, a *Children's Miscellany*, and a "new" children's book by *Sandford and Merton* author Thomas Day, the *History of Little Jack: A Foundling* (1788).[74] Antiguan and Jamaican papers in the 1790s advertise "story books" as well as "children's spelling books."[75] By the 1810s and 1820s, newspapers in Grenada, Barbados, St. Christopher, and St. Vincent were also advertising "story books for children," "Christmas pieces," "entertaining books for children," "children's fancy books," and "children's books with coloured plates."[76]

It is not possible to know from the advertisements who, if anyone, bought the books, though we know who had the means and access to do so. Given that newspapers were mostly read by residents of means, the advertisements conjure a British audience with refined consumer tastes and ready money to spend on delicacies from abroad. The case of printer Henry James Mills gives a fuller picture of how enslavers and their sympathizers viewed children's literature. A supporter of both the enslaver class and the emerging West Indian literati, Mills is known for printing *Warner Arundell: The Adventures of a Creole* (1838), a contender for the first European-authored novel published in and about the Caribbean. Although Mills ran a robust business involving many kinds of publications, he seems to have had a special interest in "children's books," as these words were often capitalized and bolded in advertisements for his wider catalog. The *Port of Spain Gazette*, which Mills published from 1829 to 1843, advertised hundreds of children's books by name. In 1833, he ran an ad with a huge list of titles, including *Robinson Crusoe, New Year's Gift*, and *Girl's Own Book*.[77] His later imports include Anna Laetitia Barbauld's

Evenings at Home, Peter Parley's *Tales of Animals*, several books by Jacob Abbott, and a Family Library containing eighty-four volumes.

That Mills was publishing the paper primarily for an enslaver audience becomes apparent when we notice that he prominently advertises vacant estates and runaway enslaved people, sometimes on the same pages as his children's book advertisements.[78] That the paper sympathizes with this audience is obvious when we read the news and editorial section. The editorial content of many Caribbean newspapers had a pro-slavery bias. The same page of the *Bermuda Gazette* in which Hurst's advertisement for children's literature appears contains a letter from "Frugilegus," who claims it is good for enslaved people to labor: "Were they well employed at planting, in place of being a public nuisance, [it] would be a real advantage to the Island."[79] The editorial stance of Mills's paper supported the status quo or, failing that, *very* gradual rather than immediate emancipation. The paper highlights this as a point of difference from other local papers. An article in April 1833 threatens retaliatory violence against readers of a competing paper, the "Colonial Observer," which is "actually employed in communicating" "Anti-Colonial sentiments" "to the negroes."[80]

Mills's case points to factors that dogged the children's literature market in the Caribbean: elites tried to avoid bringing children to the islands and sent them back to Europe for school. Mills's sons, William Woodward Mills and Frederick Losh Mills, were born in the 1830s, when he started advertising children's books. Yet the printer appears to have subscribed to a common belief among wealthy colonists that the Caribbean was not a place for white children long term. He sent his sons to mainland Britain for school at a young age.[81] While Mills no doubt sold some children's books to younger boys and girls, the years that he prominently advertises them line up with years in which the British were debating abolition—a time when, according to Vasconcellos, planters became invested in the education of enslaved youth.[82]

An article Mills reprinted a few months before British abolition in his April 19, 1833, issue, which contains a large children's book advertisement, connects the paper's editorial position on enslavement with ideologies related to youth and education. The article contains excerpts from a speech by pro-slavery lecturer Peter Borthwick originally printed in the *Glasgow Herald*, which he gave on a tour protesting the British Anti-Slavery Society. The paper declares Borthwick to be an "interesting and accomplished speaker," repeating his false claims that enslavers who mistreat enslaved people are punished by the law.[83] The paper ratifies by reprint Borthwick's position that "it would [be] a heartless sin in the planter to [turn] the slave free" before "he was educated and able to provide for himself."[84] Borthwick also boasts of "what the planters ha[ve] been doing, silently, and humanely, for the benefit of the enslaved, since the year 1807, in order to bring him to that state of improvement."[85] This date coincides with the abolition of the slave trade and enslavers' use of education to portray themselves as benevolent and preserve their control. Implying that enslavement is good for children, the paper amplifies Borthwick's manipulative claim that "miseries . . . would inevitably follow to . . . the unprotected children" if enslavement were to end immediately.[86]

The paper's investment in enslavers' imagination of themselves as benevolent educators presents the possibility that Mills may have understood children's literature as having utility for island elites in transitioning from a slave society to a free one. Vasconcellos argues that enslavers increasingly cooperated with educators, owing to the sentiment that "education beat abolitionists at their own game. By teaching enslaved children to become good workers, these new and improved slaves would gradually replace the old. If abolition did come, the newly freed population would know their place and remain loyal."[87] Smith argues that enslavers clung to this vision after abolition by "insisting that schooling should shape [Afro-Caribbeans] into industrious, agricultural laborers, rather than encouraging them to dream beyond their station."[88]

Some of the books Mills imported contain sentiments that would have been appealing to planters trying to train a docile workforce during and after enslavement. *Murray's English Reader*, the textbook Wray and Davies used to convince the Demerara governor of their pro-slavery intentions, appears prominently in Mills's advertisements. The book was compiled by Lindley Murray, a US Quaker whose father had significant trade interests in the West Indies. Murray was involved in abolitionist efforts, donating to the African Institution to establish colonies for formerly enslaved people in Africa. However, his emphasis in his published works on morality, respecting social distinctions, and being a "humane and kind master" fit with the worldview of enslavers.[89] Some lessons from the reader include "Society, when formed, requires distinctions of property, diversity of conditions, subordination of ranks, and a multiplicity of occupations, in order to advance the general good" and "The chief misfortunes that befall us in life can be traced to some vices or follies which we have committed," ideas that deflect from white responsibility to address the harms of enslavement.[90] The *English Reader*, furthermore, established a canon of English works including writers such as "Blair,

Addison, Goldsmith, and Johnson," which bolstered colonizers' claims to cultural superiority.[91]

Mills also advertised heavy tomes and educational storybooks like those mentioned by the missionaries, who likely bought books and other school supplies when they had the requisite cash from donations or tuition fees.[92] A partial list from the advertisement on April 19, 1833, includes "an extensive Assortment of JUVENILE, SCHOOL, and other BOOKS, COMPRISING: Goldsmith's Geographical Grammar . . . Reading's Easy's and Primers, Mavor's and Fenning's Spelling Books . . . Watt's Songs . . . And a variety of other Works too numerous to detail."[93] Mills additionally stocked catechisms by David Blair, which appear on lists of books associated with mission schools.

It is unlikely that Mills intended the light-hearted books in his lists to be given to enslaved people or apprentices. Furthermore, without sale receipts or other records, like diaries, it is difficult to tell what was read and by whom. Some of the lighter books—like Jacob Abbott's nursery books—appear on lists of reward books used in mission schools in St. Croix. Yet promoting children's books, whether read by Afro-Caribbeans or not, reinforces the power of colonizers, in that the book lists present a catalog of knowledge the paper's editors implied was necessary to become part of the island's free population.

No bookseller, however, can control how books circulate and are read—and some of the books Mills stocked raise subversive potentials. For example, Barbara Hofland's *Africa Described* (1828, with a new edition in 1834) arrived at Mills's bookshop in 1836 during apprenticeship. This system meant that many free young people lived with adults and older siblings who were not free, while having access to education. Rooted in colonial occupation of Africa, Hofland's book was intended to interest European readers in missionary projects involving the continent. She problematically notes that Africa lacks the "enlightened mind and intellectual energy which give promise of renovation."[94] In the Caribbean context, however, the book may have been of interest to young people with access to literacy who wanted to compare memories of Africa passed down during enslavement with its "present state."[95] The book provides a level of detail about Africa unusual in children's books—and in short supply in the Caribbean, where teachers complained that children did not have books featuring topics relevant to them.

Readers catch a glimpse of the relational ethics of West Africans in a section on women emphasizing that they are kind to "those with whom they had no natural connection, and were, indeed, separated by religious opinions, colour, and the prejudices of their country."[96] The text goes on to measure the women's compatibility with European norms of motherhood by suggesting that their affection is finely tuned when it comes to their children—an assumption of feminist care ethics and, differently, of colonizers who wanted to promote this mindset in those they had enslaved. Yet the women's ethos of nondiscrimination breaks through Hofland's rhetoric and challenges the dominant ethical perspectives of European children's books, which emphasize family ties—and, increasingly, colonial investments—as preconditions for caring.

As abolition became imminent, the *Port of Spain Gazette* advocated for reparations to enslavers by casting them as victims of the "British Crown and Parliament," which they claim forced them into "the cultivation of the colonies by slave labor."[97] After this bid failed and apprenticeship began, the *Port of Spain Gazette* continued to print articles claiming formerly enslaved people were cared for as children. Yet Mills included ads for runaway apprentices bearing little difference from runaway slave notices.[98] He continued to promote children's items, but the ads eventually dwindle, perhaps with the realization that enslavers' control was waning.

A wide variety of popular English-language children's books appear in newspaper advertisements post-emancipation, including (Lydia) *Sigourney's Letters to Young Ladies*, *Paul and Virginia*, *The Lamplighter*, *Tom Brown's School Days*, *Arabian Nights*, *Pilgrim's Progress*, and *Don Quixote Boys' Edition*. This canon of children's classics has been slow to dislodge from the Caribbean in favor of books with local themes. As I suggest in the next section, the Caribbean was a crucible for English speakers to develop a global-imperial (or what they would have understood as a "universal") vision of children's literature, diminishing possibilities for a relational approach to global circulation.

From Colonial and Transnational to Global

English-speaking missionaries worked not only in the British Caribbean but also on islands held by other colonizing powers, taking part in a cultural imperialist expansion of English language and literature. In this context, there is a noticeable move away from children's books that respond to local circumstances toward books that promote the ethical values of Anglo-Americans as universal. US Moravians working in the Danish Caribbean, which was held by the British from 1801 to 1802 and became of interest to the United States as an imperial acquisition by the 1860s, shift from using children's books based on *local* creole culture and language, to books related to competing *colonial* cultures, and finally to children's books produced by British and US organizations with *global-imperial* aspirations, promoting hard work and financial independence as the universal ethical duties of children.

St. Croix was the site of colonial conflicts between Britain, France, Spain, and the Netherlands before it was bought by the Danish West India Company in 1733. German-speaking Moravians came to St. Thomas and St. Croix prior to this sale with the assumption that they would need to translate their tracts into the local language, Negerhollands, a now-extinct Creole resembling Dutch, with Danish, English, French, Spanish, and African (including Akan and Ewe) elements. Friedrich Martin, the leading missionary in the area, noted that his fellow, Brother Carstens, wanted to translate the New Testament into Creole but found it "very difficult" because the Creole "consists of too many languages."[99] The difficulty was part of the point; as North notes, "This linguistic innovation gave the enslaved a communication tool that could limit masters' access to their interactions."[100] The missionaries began communicating in the language anyway; Count Nikolaus Zinzendorf wrote a letter in Negerhollands that was circulated to enslaved people.[101]

A Negerhollands hymn appearing in a St. Thomas diary in 1755 appears to be meant for children as it contains the lines

> A small child I know I am
> And my strength is weak.
> To be a free child I have desire
> But do not know how to do it.[102]

These lyrics seem remarkably sensitive to the situation of enslaved children, but the song leverages the child's vulnerability for Christian educational purposes, suggesting that the speaker must follow Christ's example to be free. Although Schneider has shown that enslaved people interpreted Christian ideas to support agitation for freedom, including through rebellion, the Moravians in St. Croix did not endorse such measures.[103] The shift in the poem from the specific kind of freedom desired by enslaved people to the metaphorical freedom of Christian believers represents an early example of the tensions between a locally responsive, relational approach to creating children's books and the drive for a universally framed Anglo-Christian children's literature.

Missionaries moved toward circulating texts assumed to reflect such a universal ethics, but this was not a foregone conclusion. In 1765 the Moravians started their printing endeavors in Negerhollands with a prayer and hymn book, later creating ABC books and a grammar book.[104] A Creole speaker, possibly a white person (like Carstens) or an enslaved person, would have had to assist these efforts. The books, to some extent, reflect international educational publishing trends, as well as Christian literature.[105] The ABCs (printed in 1800 and 1825 in Germany) use the format Grenby has shown to be common among primers printed across Europe and elsewhere: a page of letters in upper and lowercase, followed by words of one syllable and so on.[106] A translation of three-syllable words in the 1800 book by Cefas van Rossem and Hein van der Voort reveals continuities with other Christian primers.[107] Compared with a 1777 New England primer, there are two overlaps—gratefulness/gratitude and holy/holiness.[108]

Yet the text gives a limited window into the culture and landscape of the Danish Caribbean. For instance, the word *pannekoek,* a specifically Dutch style of pancake common in former Dutch colonies, reflects the colonial culture. Although the format of an ABC book does not fully allow Creole to be represented, as Creole languages are more strongly marked by their syntax than their lexicon, the book contains words reflecting the Caribbean location, such as *Roenkert Je.* This word is not fully translated into English by Rossem and Vort; they approximate the translation as "buzzer" and remark that it could be a bee or hummingbird.[109] If the word is indeed hummingbird, this is striking, as hummingbirds are not European—at least not since antiquity—but native to the Americas and prevalent in the Caribbean. Hummingbirds, furthermore, are significant to local belief systems. Melissa García Vega notes that "across the Americas, the hummingbird is often linked to a spirituality among indigenous people that reflects a deep and systemic understanding of culture and the environment . . . Indigenous tribes throughout the Americas often feature the celestial hummingbird in stories."[110]

It is notable to have reference to Caribbean nature in an early children's book. An 1849 letter from Richard Rawle, the principal of Codrington College in Barbados, expressed worries that the books he was teaching did not reference the world around his students: "Our West Indian 'world' is too small and too much of a colour to supply children with a sufficient stack of fundamental ideas for the purpose of understanding the language of Books. Until some device of Education enlarges the horizon and endows the mind's eye with telescopic power to see things and customs and the social state of the country from which the books come . . . most little story books, meant particularly for the children's edification, appear as enigmas."[111] Although it does not seem to occur to Rawle that children might want to read about their own culture, his objection anticipates later concerns that books did not speak to Caribbean children's experiences. Twentieth-century Caribbean author Merle Hodge remembers that, as a child, her environment "did not seem real" compared to what appeared in books.[112]

Communicating in the language of a place, as the Moravians initially tried to do, allowed for the inclusion of words reflecting attempts to ethically address community concerns.[113] *Dienaarin* (female servant), *Mishandling* (mistreatment), and *Ongerecht* (injustice) may have been included in the 1800 ABC book because the Moravian Conference took ethical complaints and tried to solve conflicts between enslavers and those they enslaved.[114] The mission's activities, however, became more uniform in 1834 after abolition took effect in the British colonies. Governor-General Peter von Scholten responded to British abolition by contracting with the (by this point) English-speaking Moravians to make schooling mandatory for the enslaved Afro-Caribbean population on the Danish islands. The plan, called the Rural School Act of 1839, involved building eight schools, through which von Scholten hoped to discourage agitation for freedom and make steps toward gradual emancipation.[115]

Warner taught at the La Grande Princesse Rural School, located outside of Friedensthal. Attendance was compulsory, a rule Smith has shown Afro-Caribbean people resisted because of its resemblance to enslavement and intrusion on family life.[116] The Moravians took careful notes about who was absent owing to rain or sickness. One week, Warner notes that the children are "very wicked and troublesome," perhaps a sign of their resistance to lessons removed from their daily lives.[117] His lessons center on the Bible as a universally valuable source of ethical teachings, though he sometimes tailors them to local events. When one student, Elisabeth, dies at age twelve, he does a "lesson on the subject."[118]

Warner himself died only a few years later, but a notable shift happened in the time he was there; in 1843 he wrote to the YMMS, based in Bethlehem, Pennsylvania, explaining that since his arrival in 1840, the language of the mission had changed from Creole to English. This decision was made in Herrenhut, Germany, but Warner considered the change fortunate because he thought using the Creole prevented donations from English speakers. Following the decision, he enlisted teenagers in the YMMS to oversee the publication of a catechism, which he wanted not only to be in English but also "exactly the size of the English textbooks."[119] This design reflects the influence of books like *Murray's English Reader*.

Warner's request for an English book also indicates competition among colonial powers. The Danish government had asked the Lutheran Reverend

Bagger to write a nondenominational catechism for the schools, which Warner avoided adopting. He explains, "Tis true there already exist a number of Catechisms within our reach, but none adapted to our purpose."[120] Warner wants a Moravian book but requests that "Moravian" not be included in the title, as that would invite criticism from other denominations. The YMMS had the book printed in Philadelphia.[121] Warner claims the teenagers' donation of the English book will be globally meaningful, garnering thanks "from Greenland's icy mountains and from India's coral strand."[122]

After an 1848 rebellion in St. Croix led to emancipation on the Danish islands, the Moravians continued running schools for Afro-Caribbean children. Beginning around this time, the organization drew their staple texts heavily from British and US tract society catalogs. The register of the Friedensthal school in the 1850s contains an inventory of books in possession of the school, most of which come from tract publishers.[123] Another ledger from 1857–1858 shows expenses for "12 Bunyan Pilgrim's Progress, 2 Travellers for rewards, 12 Great Truths in Plain Words, [and] Freighted Sundry Books for London," plus standing orders for Miss Corner's *Play Grammar* (1847) and *Blair's Catechism* (1835).[124]

What makes these records extraordinary is that they not only attest that the books traveled to the Caribbean but also indicate the context in which they were distributed. An 1857–1858 record lists children's names with reward books they received and their prices: "John Griffith 1 Almanac 5 . . . Albert Potter Appeal to Young 5, Daniel Failkion ditto, Joseph Richard Traveller 50 cents, Benjamin Robert 1 bible 3 . . . Josef Perskey 1 Almanack 5, Benjamin Geography 3."[125] Story-based tracts the children received include *Four Seasons*, *Little Willy*, *Looking Unto Jesus*, *Daily Texts*, *Charlotte and Others*, *Sacred Story*, *Teardrops*, *Mary Prentice*, *Elspeth*, *Sweet Story of Old*, *Sabbath Day*, *Ki'an Queen*, and *Little Nazareth*.[126] Most can be identified among the publications of the Religious Tract Society or the American Tract Society. No context is given for the specific reward system, but the school likely employed the Lancaster system, commonly used in the English-speaking Caribbean, which allowed students to earn tokens for good behavior and academic performance, redeemable for prizes. Similar systems were used in British and US Sunday schools for memorizing Bible verses.

The history of Moravian education in St. Croix suggests that most, if not all, of the children appearing on this list were Afro-Caribbeans living under colonial government. They were born around the late 1840s, mostly too young to have been enslaved, but attended the Moravian schools established for enslaved children prior to emancipation. Names likely referring to these children appear on baptism and later census records, which do not include race, as first- or third-class laborers and apprentices.[127]

A sampling of the books the Moravians chose reveals how the supposedly ethical act of teaching formerly enslaved children served evangelical and imperial ambitions. Some, like *Great Truths in Plain Words* (full title: *Sunday Thoughts; or Great Truths in Plain Words*) and *Sweet Story of Old* (subtitle: *A Sunday Book for the Little Ones*), retell Bible stories in a straightforward way meant to yield universal Christian values. Others promote a fixation on work as the centerpiece of (poor) children's lives, reflecting a goal to produce global subjects whose self-sufficiency would ensure that they were not dependent on aid and whose willingness to do business in English might feed the wealth of English-speaking nations.

Some different facets of childhood emerge in the materials. The missionaries' grammar book of choice, *The Play Grammar* (1850), by Miss Corner, introduces maternal play-based education to the formerly enslaved population. The text was likely chosen, however, because it monetizes learning English in ways that were compatible with the Lancaster system. The characters learn parts of speech by playing a game with their mother that involves looking at pictures and naming the relevant parts of grammar for describing the scene. The book suggests that readers adopt the game, paying a forfeit for every word they do not name and gaining prizes for words they recognize. The emphasis on play contrasts with the idea of the hard-laboring schoolchild common in the Caribbean context, which was perhaps helpful in appealing to parents who wanted to avoid any semblance of enslavement for their emancipated children. *The Play Grammar* additionally reinforces the notion that people should be paid for effort, appropriate for a post-emancipation economy in which parents were seeking economic opportunities and needed their children to contribute to family earnings. Yet by tying economic gain to the willingness to adopt standard English, the text promotes assimilation and quells class conflict. Although Turner notes that "the meritocracy of the mission churches" was comforting in some respects to "the field slaves at the bottom of the plantation hierarchy and to all women who could not aspire to white mates," the idea that rewards follow merit distracts from systemic class stratification.[128]

A reward book given to a girl named Mary Duffy similarly promotes working for rewards, as well as accepting a laborious life that would not burden others. The book listed by her name is *Elspeth*, which almost certainly refers to *Elspeth Sutherland, Or, The Effects of Faith* (1823). This tract focuses on an orphan who takes pride in the "scanty support" she receives from her "laborious occupation," which allows her to pay rent without taking charity from her landlord.[129] When some of her neighbors criticize the rich for preferring to buy luxuries than give charity, Elspeth professes her belief in the fairness of the system: "Why, do not all their luxuries supply us with work?"[130] Such lessons would have been useful to elites in a post-slavery economy depending on impoverished people choosing to labor for low wages. Elspeth's antirelational views come under scrutiny when old age makes her unable to work. In a Caribbean context, this theme is relevant to ethical questions about the responsibility of colonizers to the enslaved who were too old or frail to work, as well as those who had been freed, but Elspeth turns to the divine, lessening that responsibility. She is "determined to maintain her independence by every means in her power," and then "trust[] God."[131]

Books such as this sideline local viewpoints in favor of those of cultures with greater economic power. Although neither Britain nor the United States had control over St. Croix at this time, the US Moravians further promoted Anglocentrism by using *Blair's First or Mother's Catechism*, a text that holds not religious knowledge but a compendium of colonial-capitalist ideologies billed as "common things necessary to be known at an early age."[132] This turns out to be which parts of the world have been claimed as British colonies, the history of the British Crown, the branches of British government, and the values of British money. The text invokes Caribbean readers only through the products of their labor. One exchange asks, "Q. What is sugar? A. Sugar is prepared from the sugar-cane, a plant that flourishes in the West Indies."[133] The book gives a basic education in British and US racist ideology, with questions like, "In what parts of the world are the greatest number of savages found?" and claims that there are "eight or ten" "varieties of men," organized by skin color.[134] Such passages might be seen, in a warped way, as an acknowledgment of the diversity of readers, but they are designed to produce an Anglocapitalist empire stretching around the globe and a reader that accepts the uneven distribution of power without making ethical demands.

The Travels of *The Traveller*

A more complex book on Moravian list is the "Traveller," which might have been a fairly common choice as a prize, as the school register mentions an order of "2 Travellers for Rewards."[135] Given that nearly all the books on the list were tract society standards, this book was almost certainly *The Traveller: Or, A Description of Various Wonders in Nature and Art* (1838), published by the London-based Religious Tract Society (RTS). The RTS claimed a circulation of 33,468 copies, making the book less popular than Watts's *Divine Songs* but more popular than many others the organization circulated internationally, including *Scripture Illustrations* (1827) and a children's version of *Wilberforce's Practical Christianity*.[136]

A fictionalized travel narrative, *The Traveller* presents lessons on science, geography, and religion with a framing dialogue recounting the storytelling sessions an English gentleman and his children have with a traveler who has circumnavigated the globe. Abandoning the focus on the English climate as the key to ethical rightness found in earlier children's books, the traveler offers a proto-multicultural form of education, emphasizing a world in a constant state of geological remaking, technological invention, and human motion. The text obsessively draws attention to scale, a concept Zachary Horton argues "names a set of relations" relevant to global expansion.[137] At the widest ring are the heavens, followed by global geographical phenomena, the RTS's evangelical mission, and British colonialism, which rests on the notion of a "vast empire on which the sun never sets."[138] The text additionally draws on Joseph Addison's familiar notion of multinational trade as the key to global peace.[139] In the face of these large-scale phenomena, the British boy characters lack understanding because they "have only been accustomed to ascend the hills of the surrounding neighbourhood" and "can form but a very imperfect idea of the high towering mountains of other countries."[140]

The traveler addresses the gap between children's small human scale and the larger scales relevant to his global vision by describing natural wonders. The overtly stated goal is a religiously tinged humility: "A man or a boy may be filled with pride so long as he moves among his fellow-creatures but when he goes forth into the wide world . . . he learns to form a more humble estimate of himself."[141] Although humility is arguably a basis for ethical consciousness, the text does not characterize relationships with natural phenomena as yielding any sort of ethical responsibility. Instead, the traveler gestures to ethical concerns via human scales containing people outside of England, such as a Mongol man who rides a horse without a saddle. Worrying that "the rider might [be] dashed to pieces in a moment," the traveler asserts that "the precipices of sin are a thousand times more dangerous," encouraging readers to imagine themselves on the mountain.[142] Although this lesson seems at first to (condescendingly) suggest that Britons have a responsibility to keep others around the globe from harm, it ultimately uses the dangerous setting for an abstract religious lesson.

Multiple questions underlie this discussion without being fully resolved: how to connect the human scale of the Mongol man with the large-scale universal ethics espoused by the traveler, how to determine children's responsibilities to others, and how to understand global difference. The traveler attempts in subsequent sections to knit together multiple global human scales. Although the premise is that the traveler's knowledge is necessary to broaden the children's understanding, the child ends up being a necessary contributor, as the text depends upon its embedded child listeners (and, by extension, child readers) to make the connections between small and large scales important for thinking about ethical responsibility. Although colonial children are not the privileged readers of the text, this structure makes space for them to further fill in these small scales, completing the text's global vision. This completion is messy, however, as the small scale introduces others with different ethical situations and needs.

The traveler's further lessons on natural disasters (earthquakes and hurricanes) traverse different human scales, yielding images of global interdependence that destabilize familiar tropes of Christian ethical interpretation and pedagogy found in other tracts and replace them with a positively framed large-scale evangelism. In many children's tracts, bad behavior or belief often leads to death through natural events like earthquakes or fires. The traveler's global scope complicates this interpretation by showing that these disasters cause such large-scale destruction that they impact people of various faiths. A section on earthquakes, for instance, depicts cultural difference and global interrelatedness. The English child characters are initially allowed to feel safe because the affected places "are a long way off."[143] Yet the traveler describes nearby earthquakes, including in Lisbon where worshippers died while celebrating holiday mass. Reflecting Christian ethical interpretations based on virtue, the children assert that Lisbon must be filled by "wicked people," and the traveler confirms that "Lisbon [is] a wicked place," a comment probably reflecting Protestant disapproval of Catholicism.[144] He points out, however, that effects were felt far from the center, in "Europe, Africa, and America," implying that the fates of people around the globe are intertwined.[145] Describing an earthquake in Aleppo, he notes that people of multiple religions were impacted, disallowing any easy narrative of God's punishment.

The global connections inherent in these large-scale events have ethical implications; as Horton argues, "Scale is . . . an *ethical ground* that binds individuals, groups and territories into interconnected milieus of interdependence and responsibility."[146] In acknowledgment of this, the traveler poses a positively framed universal evangelical ethics that unites the different scales, insisting that God's power over the large phenomena around the world leads to a universal realization of the "goodness of the creator."[147] The ubiquity and seeming randomness of natural disasters substantiates devotion to God because "an hour of pleasure may be an hour of peril."[148] The traveler includes litanies of natural phenomena to turn the child's mind to this universal scope, concluding with Psalm 150:6, "Let every thing that has breath praise the Lord."[149] However, the natural events that underwrite this universal ethics do not, in the traveler's hands, address small-scale human experiences, especially in places outside of Britain where the book was used as an evangelizing tool. For instance, in the earthquake section, we learn of "the earthquake of Jamaica, in 1692," in which "the town of Port Royal was buried in a gulf forty fathoms deep," but not about any human involvement in the event.[150]

With a striking bit of dialogue that we can read as a turning point in the text, the child emerges as a figure equally necessary as the traveler for connecting the small scale and large. This moment, I argue, makes children key to the completion of the text's global vision, while also moving closer to a practical ethics, addressing the disaster of enslavement. Building on the expectation in much of children's literature to this point that children engage ethics in a relational way, as well as on gospel verses emphasizing the wisdom and holiness of children, one of the English child characters, Gilbert, interrupts the traveler's description of hurricanes to bring up (and, implicitly, to ask him to explain) enslavement. Gilbert observes in response to the traveler's comment that "plantations are destroyed when hurricanes strike" that "the West Indies is where the negroes work in the sugar plantations."[151] In a sense, Gilbert's interruption can be seen as another attempt to reassert a Christian ethical interpretation in which natural events punish bad deeds like enslavement, but it also presses the issue of ethics on a human scale that has been hovering over many of the discussions without being addressed. Reaffirming his investment in universal divine ethics, the traveler argues that God has driven antislavery efforts: "Yes; let us thank God that in a few years they will have their freedom."[152]

Although this reply does not sufficiently account for the ethical harms of enslavement, the child has pushed the discussion in a different scalar direction than the traveler has been traversing to this point, fulfilling the problem the text sets forth of connecting large and small. The Bible verses underpinning the interruption, Psalm 8:2, "Out of the mouth of babes and sucklings hast thou ordained strength," and Matthew 21:16, "Out of the mouth of babes and sucklings thou hast perfected praise," emphasize God's ability to work through the smallest, most insignificant means. The traveler continues discussing the global impact of hurricanes on wider circuits of property, nature, and trade. However, the text incorporates smaller human scales into the discussion of disasters, adding the story of a milkmaid whose pail and hat are carried away by a whirlwind, suggesting that the child has played an important role in connecting the global and local. Reflecting Jacqueline Rose's argument that childhood is often evoked to simplify complex issues, the child has solved a problem—and yet the solution reflects relational messiness by raising a conflict between the outlooks of the child and adult traveler, as well as an awareness of enslaved people. An ethics of the small scale poses the challenge of difference.

Arguably, the text's secondary colonial child readers, in St. Croix and presumably elsewhere, are also necessary for drawing together its large global vision with human experiences on the small scale. Another way the traveler tries to knit together human scales around the globe is through human inventions, which are relevant to the book's circulation path in the Caribbean. The traveler marvels, for instance, at the global dissemination of the book trade: "When we look at the multiplication of copies of the holy Scriptures, and the millions of religious tracts scattered through the earth by means of the printing-press, we may well consider printing to be one of the most important inventions of the world."[153] Colonial readers, this passage implies, continue the text's work of knitting together large and small. Although the English child characters are undeniably privileged in text's imagination, the text's comprehensive global ambition means that its understanding of childhood is broad enough to support missionaries' attempts in the Danish Caribbean to turn formerly enslaved children into children of the world. Readers with knowledge of enslavement might have gained a small sense of inclusion from Gilbert's acknowledgment, though, importantly, the book does not give them a point of view, meaning that the relation between small and large remains incomplete.

Although for the most part *The Traveller* does not reflect the lives that Afro-Caribbean children were living, its treatment of Africa would likely have been of interest. On its face, the book reinforces colonial prejudices against the continent; Gilbert comments that he "had rather go to any part to the world than to Africa."[154] Yet the book's investment in a book trade that ventures around the globe brings with it an awareness that new ways of depicting the world are needed. The Africa section pushes against European prejudices by calling attention to Christians on the continent and suggesting that Africa has offerings that also connect people across the globe. For instance, the text points out that scissors were first made in Africa, anticipating the multicultural children's books of today that emphasize the contributions of multiple cultures to readers' lives.[155] While this brief acknowledgment of African contributions stems in part from another thread emphasizing that the entire world participates in trade, resembling Addison's "Royal Exchange," it also shows that global book circulation put pressure on ideas valorizing a single culture to the exclusion of others.

It is difficult to tell what such moments might have meant to the text's Afro-Caribbean readers, especially as they are insufficient to create true inclusion. Drayton opines that colonization was a "success" in that "many West Indians willingly and voluntarily rejected their own cultural heritage."[156] She notes that when Anansi stories were included in J. O. Cutteridge's *Nelson's West Indian Readers* in the 1920s, Caribbean people attacked this decision, in part because they included stereotypes but also because they believed Black children needed "knowledge of the white man's world" to compete with white children.[157] These shrewd arguments were no doubt the product of decades of indoctrination and painful choices to assimilate, in part, to the colonizing culture. However, we can trace alternative points of view that point to the persistence of Afro-Caribbean ethics.

Persisting Afro-Caribbean Traditions

We know that local traditions survived the incursion of globally oriented English children's literature because Afro-Caribbean oral stories continue to circulate, including in the late nineteenth and early twentieth centuries, when they were included in textbooks. An alternate education likely existed in the nineteenth century that made some youth aware of figures who engaged in resistance, such as the Jamaican maroon leader Queen Nanny (appearing, as discussed in chapter 2, in a story collected by Martha Beckwith in 1920). Traces of this education are scarce because many archives are attached to missionary organizations and schools, though as I discuss in my conclusion, some missionaries became interested in collecting Anansi stories from schoolchildren in the early twentieth century.

Afro-Caribbean people also became involved in schooling, forming educational groups using curricula supplied by religious organizations like the SPCK. For example, the Ladies' Branch Association for the Education of Female Children of the Coloured Poor on the Principles of the Established Church in England, composed of "free coloured women," started a school in Barbados in 1826, enrolling 144 girls (sixty-one free, eighty-three enslaved) by 1828.[158] This initiative was part of the expansion of schooling in Barbados that began with the establishment of the first SPCK school in 1818. Further efforts were made by Bishop William Coleridge, a former secretary of the SPCK who, according to Seton S. Goodridge (a later Anglican bishop of the Windward Islands), was largely interested in educating Afro-Caribbeans to suppress their traditions, especially funeral practices. This account of Coleridge's motivations raises the question of how the women's perspective might have differed from his. Unfortunately, as Shirley C. Gordon notes in *A Century of West Indian Education*, "the mass of people concerned have not left us their views."[159]

Other Afro-Caribbeans interested in education, many of them young adults, trained in missionary institutions as teachers. As Smith points out, the monitorial system used by most schools meant that youth with access to education often taught others as assistant teachers, though as Turner notes, Afro-Caribbeans were sometimes banned from religious teaching.[160] Emancipation made training Afro-Caribbean teachers more important and possible; the Mico Charity instituted four normal schools throughout the Caribbean in the 1830s. Smith estimates that by 1837, "teachers of color made up about [40 percent] of the total number of teachers working in Jamaica," and 50 percent of the Afro-Caribbean students admitted to the Mico normal school in Kingston in 1836 "were already working as teachers or teaching assistants" by 1838.[161] Admittees had to be recommended by ministers, which means that those chosen "had to present qualities or mannerisms that white missionaries lauded."[162] In 1839, the Moravians promoted three such students to the Mico training school in Kingston, before opening their own school at Fairfield, Jamaica, in 1840 to train fourteen-year-old boys as teachers. Another Moravian school in Antigua trained boys under age ten from different islands to become teachers and "native ministers."[163] Girls were incorporated into these programs later. The organization supported their training efforts with printed material from the Sunday School Society, the BFSS, and the RTS, the latter of which sent a "lending library" in 1844.[164]

These programs were largely meant to reproduce European and Christian knowledge in new bodies, frequently with some version of manual labor. About such training programs Barbadian educational reformer P. A. Edwards points out, "That they contemplated only the 'moral education' of the negroes, is an indication of how deeply imbued all Caucasians were with prejudices which labelled the negro as inevitably and eternally inferior."[165] Children and teachers were taught to recite hymns and recapitulate lessons as the culmination of their Anglicization.[166] Reflecting the persistent view that "returns" were needed to repay missionaries' investment in children's education, as well as planters' continued interest in agricultural education for those they had enslaved, the Fairfield school incorporated "Manual Labour time" in which pupils worked "a flower, fruit, and general produce garden (coffee)" in the "ground immediately surrounding the School House."[167]

Smith argues that the presence of Afro-Caribbean teachers nonetheless "pushes us to recognize that the teaching that actually took place . . . did not simply mirror the plans of British MPs, abolitionists, missionaries, or planters."[168] Unfortunately, little evidence remains to differentiate the work that these teachers did from the general work done by the organizations, even in reports by observers. Inspectors in British Guiana note that teachers "profess" to follow a certain system of education without following it, but these criticized teachers are not identified by race.[169] Rare accounts from Afro-Caribbean teachers yield insight; Matthew Josephs's autobiography suggests he was chosen because he showed an aptitude for geography, but he also modeled a love of language and creative expression for his students through his poetry. Writing to the YMMS, a Black Moravian teacher, Archibald Clarke, shrewdly advocates for his students by praising Reinke as his mentor, noting that the missionary is now serving God in "the new rich World America!"[170] Resembling charity materials positioning global children as needy children, Clarke notes that when Reinke was there, "the school enjoyed much of the riches of the New World, but latterly . . . we are still needy and even more so."[171] In his request for funding, he portrays his students as "pretty obedient and attentive . . . able to read fluently from any book—to write little letters to their friends—to cipher . . . Some also learn Geography."[172]

Clarke may or may not be the source of a remarkable hand-drawn map of Jamaica held at the Moravian Historical Society Museum in Nazareth, Pennsylvania, which contains traces of the preservation of Afro-Caribbean culture by a Black Jamaican teacher in the nineteenth century. In general, geography is a common thread in writing about Caribbean education because colonizers were invested in positioning Afro-Caribbean students and teachers within their wider global agenda; as Martin Brückner points out, maps "were a highly effective accomplice in the creation of empires and nation-states[,] . . . the aide of choice for maintaining power and social control."[173] Clarke shows his understanding of this agenda with an appeal to "new rich World America." Missionaries too had global interests, which influenced the maps made and solicited for educational use showing the Holy Land and mission stations around the world. Mid-nineteenth-century reforms in Lancaster schools, furthermore, incorporated map study more deeply into the curriculum, with children reciting geographical knowledge.

For Caribbean students, there were often gaps between the places they were expected to memorize and their immediate surroundings, though teachers may have adopted a Lancaster practice of using students' "personal knowledge of local topography . . . as the foundation of comparative and analytical thinking."[174] The Jamaica map was possibly the result of the creator's engagement in such an exercise, as well as a school culture encouraging productive use of leisure time. Walter Badhaus notes in his report on Fairfield that "free time is not devoted to play or bodily exercise[,] . . . but most draw or paint maps, pictures, or practice on the Harmonium."[175]

Whatever its exact origin, this rare example of an Afro-Caribbean teacher's work suggests the survival of responsive relational ethics based in rebellion, appropriate to preserving Afro-Caribbean history and promoting solidarity after enslavement. Notable for its artistry and detail, the map inscribes English names and boundaries atop the island: at its farthest reach, Cornwall (the Jamaican home of Matthew Lewis and the namesake of the same county in the south of England), Middlesex, and Surrey, then the parishes of St. James, Trelawney, St. Ann, St. Mary, and so on, in smaller lettering. Plantations are labeled in smaller writing, along with small features of the landscape likely known mainly to Afro-Caribbean locals: wells, holes, peaks, hills, and paths, as well as towns. About such landmarks, Hazel V. Carby observes that while enslavers sought "to manipulate and police how space was inhabited and traversed," "the colonized maintained and preserved routes where they were out of sight: paths that led to and from their provision grounds; tracks trodden quietly at night to attack the Spanish and British settlers[;] . . . routes of escape on which to run."[176]

While certainly not all such spaces are included on the map, the creator has labeled the best known, the "Maroon Old Path" approaching Old Nanny Town, a stronghold of the Maroons (fig. 4.2). The Maroons—as a mixed group of enslaved, free Black, and Indigenous people who began to congregate during Spanish settlement of the island—resisted British attempts to take over,

Figure 4.2. MHS 0328 "Jamaica." Courtesy of the Moravian Historical Society, Nazareth, Pennsylvania.

some by fighting and others by retreating into the interior. After the British succeeded, they carried out raids to liberate enslaved people, others of whom ran away to Maroon areas to seek asylum. Although the Maroons collaborated with the British at times, a key element of maroonage, according to Russell "Maroon" Schutz, is resistance to "direct integration into the surrounding oppressive settler colonial communities . . . [A] maroon was one who not only rejected oppression but also went further to help establish an alternative."[177] Maroon ethics present an alternative to Anglo-Christian colonialism and universalism.

Geography was crucial to this resistance. A key strategy of the Maroons entailed occupying several mountain fortresses on "cockpits," which Angelita Reyes summarizes as "precipitous rocks often covered with thick and thorny bushes," where they could form autonomous societies and use the terrain to evade capture.[178] As Carla Gardina Pestana puts it, "Maroonage arose in locations where geography cooperated, flourishing in topography that granted runaways places not only to hide but to carve out permanent habitations away from their former masters."[179] The town in question, built around 1723, became a place where Maroons ran their own society modeled on Ashanti culture, a safe haven for the enslaved as well as their children. It was named after Queen Nanny, an eighteenth-century Ashanti woman who became legendary for leading the resistance and liberating around 800 people. Called the Great Negro Town by the British, Old Nanny Town was taken into British control multiple times during First Maroon War (1728–1740) but repeatedly recaptured. The war ended in 1740 with a peace treaty, in which the inhabitants received land from the British to create New Nanny Town, later called Moore Town, motivating them to leave Old Nanny Town behind. By including "Old Nanny Town," the map makes Maroon resistance a persistent feature of the landscape.

The map also bears marks of revolutionary social changes happening in the 1830s–1840s, which presented different alternatives for Afro-Caribbeans. After emancipation, Baptists James Phillippo, Thomas Burchell, and William Knibb established free villages, in which the church assisted formerly enslaved people in obtaining land, allowing them to subsist without relying on planters, many of whom had vowed not to sell land to them. Other free villages, such as Martha Brae, were created by Afro-Jamaicans. Smith notes, "As freedpeople fled plantations in response to the planters' demands and intimidation tactics, some . . . found refuge by purchasing freeholds and settling in these villages."[180] Knibb estimates forty-three free villages in just the parish of St. Ann's by 1845; as such, the map does not contain them all.[181] Martha Brae is marked, along with Sandy Bay, founded by the Baptists in the 1830s. The map also includes Maidstone, a free village established by Moravians who purchased the former plantation in 1840 and "sold [land] to ex-slaves on generous terms, allowing them to escape the high rents charged by planters."[182] These towns made laudable efforts to materially improve the lives of Afro-Caribbeans, allowing them to build community and economic power, though missionaries emphasized the chance to better educate and "civilize" them through proximity to the church.[183]

The map was ultimately sent to the YMMS, the same organization that Warner had contacted in Bethlehem, Pennsylvania, and displayed as part of a collection at a museum they created from missionary donations.[184] That the map was used in this way suggests that it was considered a testimony to the success of Moravian methods. In turn, the youth were participating in the familiar looting of places through imperialism. The teens charged admission, thereby appropriating the labor of the Afro-Caribbean teacher for YMMS profit. Likely, they imagined that such endeavors contributed to their education about other places in the world—though this education was filtered through the acquisitive logic of colonialism. As Mahshid Mayar points out, US children were encouraged to see geography as a "leisurely practice through which the bourgeoisie browsed, sampled, and appropriated allegedly less civilized spaces away from home."[185]

At the same time, the map can be read as a powerful statement against the ethnocentrism of the teachings imposed on Afro-Caribbean children from abroad. This statement becomes even more significant when we consider that geography books and maps were some of the donations most frequently requested by missionaries in the Caribbean. These items often pointed *away* from the Caribbean toward places of importance to colonizers. For instance, a similar hand-drawn map of Palestine resides in the Mico Charity archive in Oxford. The Jamaica map can be read as a challenge lobbied by an Afro-Caribbean teacher to these attempts to center places of European or Christian significance, asserting Afro-Caribbean knowledge and ethics.[186]

In my next chapter, I continue to explore the emergence of what I'm calling global-imperial children's literature in connection with the Caribbean by analyzing books in tract society collections and Around the World libraries. I investigate how these texts brought Atlantic relations into global circulation, using them to promote the assimilation of people around the world to a universal Christian ethics based on respectability. I consider the transformation of English children's literature's versions of relationality in a Bengali translation of *Sandford and Merton*, which reorients the story of the "grateful Black."

CHAPTER 5

Traces of Atlantic Relations in Early Global Children's Literature

In *The Jubilee Memorial of the Religious Tract Society* (RTS), which documents the organization's efforts from 1799 to 1849, William Jones describes the religious publisher's attempts to expand into China and the East Indies after Britain acquired portions of the area. He presents the following story as a testament to their success:

> A Buyong youth received the Malay tract, "Moses, the Pious Negro," which deeply affected his mind. "I have not been able to sleep much in the night," he remarked to the missionary, "since I heard of this religion. I read the Gospel you gave till the middle of the night, while lying down on the mat and fell asleep with it on my breast; and even in my dreams I think on what I have heard and read of Jesus." He was asked, "How do you feel towards your countrymen around you?" He replied, "Every night I collect them together, and read to them the tract 'Pious Moses,' and tell them not to steal, or do any harm to others, but to follow that which is right." He translated, of his own accord, the tract that impressed his mind, from the Malay into the Buyong language.[1]

As I will discuss, this story—which features a receptive young person among what Jones calls the "poor and almost unimpressible" Indigenous Malay people of Singapore—has a more complicated origin and publishing history than appears at first glance.[2]

However, the tale indisputably presents the RTS's aspirations to create a global network for disseminating English books in translation to foreign youth, who could act as cultural mediators in areas of economic interest to the British government. RTS involvement in Malaysia and Singapore was tied to British competition with the Dutch East India Company and efforts to open trade and cultural influence in China. The story dubiously characterizes this intervention as an ethical endeavor, accompanied by the colonialist assumption that Indigenous people need training in a universal ethics of not stealing, avoiding harm to others, and following "that which is right."[3] The tract the Indigenous youth reads, *Moses the Pious Negro* (1827), casts its enslaved main character as a version of the biblical Adam to promote just such a universal adoption of Christian virtue ethics, based on conversion, hard work, and allegiance to foundational concepts of Western liberal society (namely, property). This chapter considers how such efforts to promote universal ethics around the globe build on the unethical relations of enslavement—and foreclose potentials for a relationally oriented global children's literature.

The RTS efforts in the East were part of the broader spread of children's books in English, of which the circulation of books to enslaved and colonized people in the Caribbean was only a small part. The globalization of children's literature has a longer history than is usually acknowledged. M. O. Grenby shows that by the time Jones was writing *The Jubilee Memorial*, the global circulation of children's books had been developing for more than two centuries.[4] Grenby demonstrates that cheap, formulaic texts such as primers, alphabet books, and religious tracts were the mainstay of the global book trade, making forms originally designed to educate children a major driver of the development of world literature in its most basic definition as texts that circulated globally.[5]

The nineteenth century saw an escalation of global circulation. Evangelicals developed visions for "what we today would call mass media and globalization," David Paul Nord argues, expanding tract societies into international enterprises with auxiliary societies around the world.[6] In the East, missionary organizations were the first to print Western books, sometimes in translation, often using printing presses from the Society for Promoting Christian Knowledge (SPCK). The *Jubilee Memorial* records the RTS's involvement in more than eighty countries and regions authoring tracts, raising funds, working with illustrators and translators, and forming groups to coordinate distribution. By the early nineteenth century, the RTS had established enough of a transcontinental network of religious schools, printers, translators, churches, and auxiliary groups that they were experimenting not only with the publication of tracts teaching basic biblical literacy, but also with what they hoped would become global literature, with stories for children an important subdivision of this category. By the late nineteenth and early twentieth centuries, the RTS celebrated the fruits of these endeavors in the titles of their annual reports: *Round the World with the Printed Page, For All Nations and Peoples,* and *For All the World.*

This formation of global children's literature has meant that not every country or region of the world has had the opportunity to contribute equally to the catalog of world literature. As Emer O'Sullivan puts it, "there is no equal exchange of texts" to this day.[7] I characterize the push to spread English children's literature as "global-imperial"—with aims driven by colonization and capitalism—rather than truly global in the sense of mutual respect, relational connection, and participation among the parts of the globe. This global-imperial culture often uses ethics as a front—asserting imperatives to educate and ethically intervene in situations portrayed as harmful to youth from the perspective of colonizing forces.

As I discuss in chapter 4, enslavement accelerated the development of a model of children's literature that silences local cultures in the name of a purportedly universal ethics, even if small acknowledgments of a potentially diverse colonial audience made their way into books like *The Traveller.* Practices developed to control the enslaved reverberate through tract publishers' globalizing efforts.[8] Jones, for instance, quotes an unnamed missionary who was so persuaded by the success of religious tracts in teaching Afro-Caribbeans Christian habits in Bermuda that he concluded "no missionary should go on a foreign mission without a good number of these little paper preachers to accompany him."[9]

The books that I discuss in this chapter incorporate characters their creators understood as foreign to prime the global relations they were trying to will into being. *Moses the Pious Negro* depicts a conversation with an enslaved African. Another book, Legh Richmond's *The Negro Servant* (1815, sometimes titled *The African Servant*) was closer to the heart of the RTS's juvenile publication efforts, which began with the designation of books for youth in 1809 and continued in 1817 with several books added by Richmond, better known for *The Dairyman's Daughter.*[10] Anticipating the RTS's overall direction, Richmond's vision for creating his children's tracts was global and, in his verbiage, "universal," casting the RTS as a nimbler and therefore more ubiquitous counterpart to the British East India Company. The RTS was to be "a united company of merchants, not merely trading to the East Indies, but to every part of the enlightened and unenlightened universe."[11] The "Buyong youth" story about the reception of *Moses* attests to the organization's success in publishing tracts in what had been the territories of the British East India Company's rival, the Dutch East India Company or Vereenigde Oost-

Indische Compagnie, widely understood as the first transnational corporation. *The Negro Servant*, for its part, circulated to India, as well as Syria, Persia, Egypt, and South Africa, expanding Richmond's vision into the Middle East, an area that Britain did not rule but considered key to the nation's political and economic aspirations.

This global-imperial technique for creating children's literature is reflected in a different way in nineteenth-century commercial publishers' creation of so-called global libraries: series books that purportedly feature global content. These series define world literature *as* British and US literature, while incorporating a handful of characters originating elsewhere in an early version of insufficient multiculturalism. One such series, The Round the Globe Library, was created in the 1870s by British publisher Frederick Warne, a major contributor to the Golden Age better known for debuting the work of Beatrix Potter, Frances Hodgson Burnett, Randolph Caldecott, Kate Greenaway, and Walter Crane.

The name of the Round the Globe series is puzzling, as many books take place in England—even London—but the name reflects an appetite among publishers of this era for broader content and circulation to match the expansion of Anglo power around the globe.[12] Some such content is evident in Warne's publication of Sarah Schoonmaker Baker's *The Babes in the Basket* (1859), unique for its Afro-Caribbean female protagonist, Daph. As we will see, Baker's novel creates a muddy ethical landscape that combines an interest in Black people's well-being with expectations of Christian respectability, echoing Harriet Beecher Stowe's *Uncle Tom's Cabin* (1852). *Babes in the Basket*, like Stowe's novel, became part of an early wave of global children's literature; according to Baker's daughter Louise Beckman, the novel was "translated into a great number of languages," including Swedish, German, and Arabic.[13]

Given the circumstances of their creation and circulation, characters like Moses and Daph function as vehicles for universalizing Anglo-American values and Christian religious beliefs, but they also reflect other relational potentials and realities. I argue that these texts are haunted by repressed possibilities that exist primarily as absences or traces, producing a sense of ethical insufficiency or incompleteness. These traces point toward what was missed as universalizing "pathological alternatives" to ethical relationality became dominant in global children's literature. We see a lack of ethical closure in these texts that gestures, though faintly, toward the ongoing potential for a just global ethics and an equitable global children's literature.

I end this chapter by turning to translation to excavate alternative potentials. As Shih-Wen Sue Chen has argued, international versions of Anglo-American books should be viewed not simply as cultural imperialist but as "hybrid transcultural" texts—an idea that Grenby also endorses.[14] I discuss an example of a hybrid text: *Kathataranga*, a Bengali translation and adaptation of Thomas Day's *Sandford and Merton* by Madhusudan Mukhopadhyay. Mukhopadhyay's adaptation, which transforms the relational ethics of Day's text, offers a chance to consider an ethics relevant to the Global South, with its history of colonial oppression and global marginalization.

Pious Blackness for Global Youth

As might be expected, neither *Moses the Pious Negro* nor *The African Servant* constitutes an authentic representation of Afro-Caribbean, African American, or Black British experience. Both instead use references to Atlantic relations to address perceived cultural differences between Anglo-American and global readers, producing stereotypes that reveal their grounding in white, Christian, colonial, and capitalist interests. Not originally designed as a children's book, *Moses the Pious Negro* (often nicknamed *Pious Moses*) was initially considered an all-purpose tract adaptable to multiple situations by missionaries or educators. The RTS seems to have believed that it would have wide appeal. According to a list of nearly 200 "tracts which have obtained a large circulation," *Pious Moses* was in the top thirty.[15] Somewhat unusually, the text was not written by a member of the RTS but taken from a supposedly nonfictional, probably fabricated, article frequently reprinted in the US press.[16] Once adopted by the RTS, the text circulated (at the very least) to Italy, Switzerland, Batavia (part of the Dutch East Indies, now Indonesia), and China.[17] Though the RTS used the book to support British political and economic aims, it may also be identified as an early example of the cultural imperialism that has characterized US influence around the world.

The story contains several elements that likely contributed to its appeal among Britons working to colonize Asia. An unnamed narrator visiting the rural US South finds an African American man named Moses working on a farm. The narrator calls attention to the man's hard work—which we are not told is due to enslavement, but which would have been, based on the location and year—commenting that Moses is "enduring the curse pronounced on fallen man."[18] This opening succinctly presents a core Christian logic, whereby toil is the expected and called-for product of sin. While the biblical reference establishes Moses as an Adam, or everyman, countering racist interpretations of Genesis tracing enslaved Africans back to Ham, the reference to Adam's punishment naturalizes the extraction of labor from enslaved people as part of God's plan. The book uses enslavement—characterized as ordinary work—to offer a story of their supposed destiny for labor.

Considering that the RTS chose this tract to be circulated to the far reaches of British influence, we can see it as an attempt to universalize this message to include colonized people who might contribute their labor to increase Western wealth. The African as everyman—standing for the people of the world—is a hard laborer working for the benefit of someone else. The "Buyong youth" story notably puts the text in the East Indies between 1830 and 1870, when the Dutch were establishing an agricultural policy called *tanam paksa* (forced plantation), in which local farmers were forced to surrender crops, including sugar and coffee, to the government as a tax, creating famines for the local population.

While the reference to Adam's sin would seem to suggest that work is the shared destiny of all people, the narrator, a self-described "worldly" man who encounters Moses while taking a joyride, stands apart from the enslaved man. Moses's world is pastoral; the narrator only visits this rural space, moving freely and undaunted by borders. Thus, while the narrator is interested in Moses, he cannot share Moses's feelings. When Moses says he would not relinquish his faith even if it meant losing his wife, children, or health, the thought of such sacrifice causes "a tear" to fall "down his cheek."[19] The narrator comments, "What would I give for such tears, and for such heavenly love and gratitude."[20] Beyond encouraging extreme sacrifice on the part of Black people, this moment turns Moses into a spectacle, framing his tears as a commodity the narrator covets. It defines the narrator not only through his ability to condescendingly ratify Moses as a good example of Christian humanity but also through his inability to relate to him.

The RTS depiction of their universalizing mission in the East might be understood as deriving from such a pathological inability to relate. In *The Jubilee Memorial*, Jones reflects on the day that the British took over Hong Kong at the end of the First Opium War, comparing it to the emancipation of enslaved Africans: "The news has quickened us all into new life. The treaty is something like an emancipation act. I thought myself happy to live in the day when the chains of the negro were broken, but thrice happy to live in the day when five ports, on the very coast, itself, are open to the efforts of the

Church of Christ."[21] This comment conflates freedom for the enslaved, whose contributions to global culture go unrecognized, with the identification of new audiences for Christian proselytizing.

Pious Moses seems to have been considered particularly useful in the Asian theater of which Hong Kong was a part. The Jubilee report chronicles that the tract traveled to China and the East Indies in the 1820s–1830s.[22] The chain of events that would produce the edition of the tract read by the "Buyong youth," described in the opening to this chapter, began before the First Opium War, when British missionaries faced restrictions because of Chinese opposition to Christianity. They moved into Malacca (modern-day Malaysia and Indonesia), Singapore, and the Dutch East Indies to stay near a potential Chinese audience. The missionaries brought tracts translated into Chinese (possibly including *Pious Moses*); set up printing presses in Malacca and the Dutch East Indies capital city of Batavia (now Jakarta); and published approximately 35,000 translated tracts in Dutch, Javanese, and Malay per year during the mid-nineteenth century. When China and Hong Kong began to open after the war, missionaries abandoned some of these posts, but not before putting books intended or adapted for children into circulation, including *Stories from Switzerland* (1837), translated into Dutch, and Mary Martha Sherwood's *Little Henry and His Bearer* (1814). The Malay version of *Moses the Pious Negro* referenced in the "Buyong youth" anecdote may have been published by the man who originally authored the anecdote, Benjamin Peach Keasberry, an India-born British missionary, translator, and educator who arrived in what would soon become the crown colony of Singapore in 1839 and ran a prolific mission publishing house using a press from the London Missionary Society.[23]

Although the "Buyong youth" story appears at first to be a straightforward account in which the tract was read by a young person, discrepancies in the recounting of the story reveal a layer of colonial fantasy parallel to the fantasy in the tract itself. It almost goes without saying that this account obscures many elements of the missionary enterprise; anecdotes were usually sent to tract societies to encourage donations. Yet its veracity is especially uncertain, as it differs from earlier stories of the same event appearing in two missionary publications, *The Evangelical Magazine and Missionary Chronicle* (1841) and *The Missionary Repository for Youth* (1842). The former names the original source as a journal written by Keasberry. Both earlier versions reference a "Buyong man" instead of a youth.

Although in Keasberry's account "Buyong" appears to refer to a people and language, the meaning of the word is unclear from modern-day language use. One potential translation from a 1901 glossary is "a boy, a youth, a servant—when it is desired to avoid mentioning their names."[24] This possible meaning lends credibility to the idea that the person in question was a youth, and Keasberry is said to have trained boys at a boarding school he established, employing them as print-shop apprentices who were taught "printing, lithography, book binding and typecasting to provide them a means of living after graduation."[25] Yet the flexibility of the name encapsulates the ways that colonizers stereotyped the colonized as childlike (meant, like Moses, for servitude). *Moses the Pious Negro* appears in *The Jubilee Memorial* among a list of children's books printed in Chinese, suggesting intended use among children in Asia.[26] Still, no "Buyong youth" may have existed as such—and, to my knowledge, no copies of the reported Indigenous Malay translation of *Moses the Pious Negro* are extant.

The "Buyong youth" story, rather than giving us access to Asian children's reception of *Pious Moses*, represents an evolution of the ideal colonized reader from adult to child. An Indigenous man may have been reimagined as a youth because adapting books for children was coming to be considered an effective way of changing the habits of colonized cultures via children's perceived malleability, contrasting with what Keasberry considers adults' "almost un-impressib[ility]."[27] Although the child in the story learns basic ethics common to many worldviews—including Islam, which was popular in Singapore at the time—it is relevant that the first adage he learns is to respect property by not stealing, which is not an overt lesson in *Moses in the Pious Negro*. Rather, Moses's status *as* property undergirds the entire narrative. Not violating property is a key tenet of capitalism and a foundation of freedom in the classical liberal politics used to legitimize the global spread of Western economic ventures. Property rights, meanwhile, rationalize the system of slavery and the seizing of Indigenous lands and livelihoods.

The shift to the colonial child as ideal reader accompanies changes to the RTS's cataloging of texts from adult to children's literature, due to ongoing efforts to break into, or in some areas create, a market for youth literature.[28] Attractive children's books, the society believed, would introduce "a taste for reading, and a disposition to buy books" that would last for generations.[29] In this way, *Pious Moses* is a metaphorical Adam, seeding the world with a universal model of hard work and assimilation meant to reproduce itself through the children's book trade.

Richmond's *The Negro Servant,* which was written for children, is narratively similar to *Pious Moses* in that it features a white narrator's conversations with a pious African, framed to be of use to a global audience. *The Negro Servant*, however, takes an overtly abolitionist viewpoint. The book was frequently bound with *The Dairyman's Daughter* in a compilation called *Annals of the Poor* (1814), dedicated to the antislavery activist and Anglican evangelist William Wilberforce. Although Richmond supports Wilberforce's pursuit of abolition in footnotes celebrating the end of the slave trade, he was arguably influenced more by Wilberforce's argument in *Practical View of Christianity* (1797) that Britain must spread the Christian religion "to the most distant regions of the earth."[30]

Like *Moses the Pious Negro*, Richmond's text promotes the universal spread of Christianity, but its repetitive catechizing structure suggests it is haunted by the idea that creating new converts might yield difference rather than universal agreement. While the opening and ending chapters of the book treat this difference largely as a problem that needs to be investigated and resolved, a middle scene set in an ocean cove introduces the potential for a deeper relation among people who have different subject positions in a world characterized by war, enslavement, and violence. Cueing us to the text's simultaneous interest in universality and a competing response grounded in relationality, some early reprint editions include Josiah Wedgwood's famous image, *Am I Not a Man and a Brother?* as a frontispiece.[31] The text is structured as an extended inquiry into the universal humanity (manhood) and relatedness (brotherhood), of its main character, a formerly enslaved man from Jamaica named William who has been freed but remains a "servant" on a visit to the Isle of Wight circa 1803.

Although William has become a Christian, the narrator probes him with continued catechizing in various settings, human-made and natural, to make sure that he coheres with the narrator's expectations of a Christian and an ethical person. He begins his first conversation with William by interrogating him about why he wishes to become a Christian, before moving on to deeper questions such as, "Tell me what is faith? What is your own faith?"[32] This session gives way to two more sessions of intense questioning.

On the one hand, while questioning is a part of the conversion process, this continued inquisition can be attributed to a refusal on the part of the narrator (and author) to see William as a fully equal human being, which results in multiple attempts to assimilate his difference. Taking inspiration from Fred Moten's notion of Black life as characterized by hybridity, intersubjectivity, and plurality rather than existing as "a single being" (a phrase he borrows from Édouard Glissant), we might read William's unassimilable difference as indicating Afro-Caribbean reticence to be fully incorporated into a Christian universality defined by British colonizers. On the other hand, the extra repetitions point to traces of the narrator's longing not only to complete the process of assimilation but also to continue relating—and possibly even to address white complicity with the slave system by relating better. These traces get submerged within the drive for conversion as the cornerstone of a global universal ethics, and the text overrides this longing by removing William from England.

Reflecting Wilberforce's *Practical View of Christianity*, the text opens with a cartographical image of the world, using Blackness as a metaphor for pockets of heathenry around the globe:

> If a map of the world, instead of being colored, as is usual, with many gay and brilliant tints . . . were to be painted with darker or brighter hues corresponding with the spiritual character of the inhabitants, what a gloomy aspect would be presented to the eye of the Christian geographer, by the greater portion of the habitable globe!—How dark would be the shade thus cast over the larger districts of the vast continents of Asia and America! And what a mass of gloom would characterize the African quarter of the world![33]

As in *Pious Moses*, Blackness becomes globally significant, but in this case through a more familiar and troubling equation of Blackness with sinfulness. The "darkness" that dominates the globe includes "the iron reign of Mahometan superstition and Pagan idolatry," but its darkest "mass" is in Africa, which Richmond identifies with the "descendants of Ham" supposedly cursed into slavery.[34] The narrator problematically claims that these areas produce people who engage in ethically questionable behaviors; "the dark places of the earth are full of the habitations of cruelty."[35]

The first section of the text offers the chance for this purported difference to be addressed through the universal adoption of Christian ethics. William, who has supposedly left ethically questionable behaviors behind, models this process. The man who enslaved him says he used to be "very unruly and deceitful; but for the last two years he has been quite like another creature."[36] However, William's ethical reform is treated with suspicion by the narrator; he tests William's resolve by subjecting him to questioning, with William confessing in a white-authored version of dialect that he recognizes himself in the descriptions he has heard of sin. The focus on sinfulness may reflect some resistance to this concept among the enslaved; Mary Turner notes that enslaved people "proved resistant to the basic Christian concept of sin; it tended, when first confronted, to intensify their feelings of inferiority induced by the slave system."[37] Maria Ryan further suggests that Afro-Caribbean people maintained their "own religious practices and beliefs" alongside Christianity and "often def[ied] missionary ideas of conversion."[38] William's acceptance of sin affirms his conversion while reinforcing the racist logic presented in the opening image, providing hope that the Blackest areas—and people— can be transformed through universal Christian ethical teaching.

Yet the questions give William an opening to tell his life story, which throws the narrator's map into question by drawing attention to the unethical behavior of white people during enslavement. William explains that a white man enslaved him when he was a small child collecting seashells. White people have also called him names, such as "black hypocrite," but like Jesus, he has learned to respond to such insults with serenity.[39] At the end of this round of questioning, the narrator affirms William's commitments but wishes to "inquire more minutely."[40] Contrasting with the narrator's questioning in *Pious Moses*, which makes Moses into an idealized figure with whom he cannot relate, this narrator's continued queries seem to be driven by at least two impulses: a lack of satisfaction with his degree of integration into a standard Christian worldview and a desire to keep talking with William, to understand his experiences.

In its second section, the text goes into a pattern of repetition that reprises its basic structure of sketching a map of the world then questioning that map, but with a difference. The section begins with the narrator walking along the shoreline and meditating on the ships as they go by, which allows him to create a mental map of their travels. Perhaps influenced by William's commentary on British enslavement, he thinks "of the concerns of empires, the plans of statesmen, the fate of nations, and the horrors of war," connecting engagement in trade with international aggression.[41] He confesses discomfort with his ability to detach from the violence while still benefitting from it: "We sit every man under his vine and fig-tree, tasting the sweets of a tranquility unknown to most other nations in these days of conflict and bloodshed!"[42]

This vision of peacefulness at home while war rages recalls the tranquility that Jenny Peace promotes in the insulated space of *The Governess* (discussed in chapter 1), but in this case it is revealed to be a costly peace that comes from global privilege. This reflection departs from the narrator's earlier ethical map, as well as from Joseph Addison's popular ideology of trade as a means of promoting peace in "The Royal Exchange" (1711). While Addison argues that the needs of trade lead to global peace because nations cooperate with each other to obtain goods they cannot produce, Richmond exposes this ideal as fictive and mentally confronts the horrors that have resulted from prioritizing global economic interests over ethical ones.

Although he is disturbed by these reflections, the narrator comforts himself with the reflection that those who go to sea and take part in international wars experience "the works of the Lord, and his wonders in the deep"—which conjures a divine solution to global trauma, recalling the large-scale Christian universal ethics pursued by *The Traveller* (discussed in chapter 4).[43] This utopian vision of the sea as an antidote to suffering contrasts with the disturbing images of the Atlantic Ocean and its creatures discussed in chapter 1, which I argue reference the brutalities of enslavement. Thinking of William, however, forces the narrator to depart from this solution and see the ocean as a witness to violence:

> Perhaps, thought I, some of these ships are bound to Africa, in quest of that most infamous object of merchandise, a cargo of Black slaves . . . Perhaps these very waves which are now dashing on the rocks at the foot of this hill, have, on the shores of Africa, borne witness to the horrors of forced separation between wives and husbands, parents and children, torn asunder by merciless men, whose hearts have been hardened against the common feeling of humanity by long custom in this cruel trade.[44]

The narrator is, in many ways, still in the realm of universal ethics (as well as white saviorism), as he claims the moral high ground to condemn the slave trade. However, the blackened global map of the opening chapters has given way to a reflection on "merciless" white enslavers.[45] This global crisis is not primarily a crisis of difference, which drives Christian efforts to convert, but a crisis of connection: the potential for relationships to be torn apart by enslavement. The narrator seems to be on the verge of a revelation that Africans should be in his sphere of ethical obligation not just because they are potential Christians but because they have been subject to genocide.

In an unlikely coincidence characteristic of nineteenth-century plotting, the narrator's reflections are interrupted when he comes upon William in an ocean cove, offering a chance—in a natural setting "shut out from human intercourse and dwellings"—to relate to William outside of existing institutions.[46] The description of the encounter, in contrast to the repeated attempts to assimilate William's difference in section 1, emphasizes that difference through a starkly bifurcated image in which "the black color of his features contrasted with the white rocks beside him," though his difference is also muted by having him be caught in the act of reading a Bible.[47] Once again, questioning ensues. Given the opening to the section, the scene seems to offer a chance to tackle the specific harms done to William in enslavement, but, as we will see, this need is overridden by the universalizing goals of Christian evangelism.

In many ways, the overriding of relationality is a foregone conclusion; as modern readers we are immediately aware that William, like Moses, is a pawn in the book's propagandistic campaign for a universal Christian worldview. Yet there are significant differences from *Pious Moses*. When the narrator speaks to William, the servant, like Moses, debases himself by talking of his great sin, expressing a desire to be like the narrator. But unlike the narrator in *Pious Moses*, the narrator points out that they are *both* sinners. The narrator's belief in his own sinfulness, while not surprising from a Christian perspective, makes this a more honest articulation of universal Christian ethical ideals than a colonial one that exempts white people from ethical judgment. At the same time, the white sin of enslavement goes unacknowledged. Instead, it hangs over the scene, undermining the characters' supposed equivalence. A footnote says that William calls the narrator "Massa" because that word "seemed most familiar to him."[48]

The text does not challenge this remnant of enslavement, likely because it is compatible with the text's grounding in white saviorism and the gratitude it supposedly elicits. Instead, the scene moves away from reckoning with enslavement and addresses William's difference with an articulation of relationality between the two men built on familial references and metaphors. William expresses concerns for his parents—who, notably, are not enslaved. Abandoning his ethical concerns about the slave ships, the narrator interests William in extending global Christian citizenship to the world by telling him one of the ships on the horizon might carry missionaries on their way to save his parents' souls.[49] The narrator and William pray together for this evangelical outcome, and the section ends with the narrator "lean[ing] upon [William's] arm with the feelings of a *brother*."[50] Overall, this scene evokes Wedgwood's *Am I Not a Man and a Brother?* image but with a greater emphasis on mutuality owing to the replacement of the enslaved African kneeling with a Black and white man standing together.

Yet this idealized version of quasi-familial connection comes from substituting the ethical concerns of Wedgwood's image with the evangelical goals of universal incorporation. The narrator says that he no longer considers William a "stranger and a foreigner" but a "fellow-citizen with the saints."[51] This common citizenship, it is important to point out, is dependent on an assumption of sameness rather than concern for others on their own terms. The natural location implies that even outside of the church, William can be made to cohere to its teachings, rather than rebounding into difference. His status as a man and brother is contingent on his adoption into a global Christian family. Reflecting continuity with the violence of enslavement, Richmond's language of relationality is infected with the language of ownership. Following his declaration of William as a brother, the narrator says, "It was a relationship I was happy to own."[52]

In this way, *The Negro Servant* anticipates a dynamic that Marilisa Jiménez García has noted in her work on later US children's writers' depictions of imperial relationships among its territories, including Mary Hazelton Wade's Little Cousin primer series and *Greater America: Our Latest Insular Possessions* (1900), the latter of which casts Puerto Rican children of color as "brothers."[53] Jiménez García notices that "the greater the perceived threat of uprising and overthrow, tied to deep-seated fears about a strong Black Caribbean population, the more kinship language shifts to denoting a closer relation."[54] Although no such fears appear directly in *The Negro Servant*, the narrator's worries about the nation's embroilment in wars through trade could include slave rebellions in the Caribbean. A low-level anxiety seems to underlie many of the narrator's interactions with William. In the end, William does not apparently pose enough of a possibility for co-citizenship, or enough of a threat, to be portrayed as a brother for long. He is memorialized as "the Negro Servant" in the book's title, indicating a continued tension between his difference and his incorporation.

This tension, along with the text's competing drives for conversion and connection, leads to a lack of ethical closure. In part 3, the narrator and William reprise the question-and-answer format with formal catechism questions in front of the whole church, in which William affirms (in the author's version of pidgin English) the narrator's first map by saying that he has been brought from "de land of darkness to . . . de land of light."[55] A poem written in William's voice called "The Negro's Prayer" confirms that Christians' obligations to the rest of the world are limited to salvation by equating chattel slavery with slavery to sin. The speaker claims to be "A slave to man, a slave to sin, / A slave to Satan too," before insisting that Christianity has made him "free" and wishing that God will grant this "freedom" to his parents, who were never enslaved.[56] In this replacement of specific ethical concerns about enslavement with the universal ethical goal of conversion, William is finally aligned with the narrator's view of the world. But at the end of the section, William leaves on a ship with his enslaver, even though he has supposedly been freed. William is not fully assimilated, which would ensure the victory of Christian ethics, and the narrator never addresses his complicity in enslavement, meaning that he fails to truly connect with William or become accountable to him.

At least a handful of readers investigated the status of William (and Richmond's other characters), with an interest in the ethics of writing declared as their purpose. As Cynthia S. Hamilton describes, these investigations emerged when some reviewers questioned whether *The Dairyman's Daughter* was a true history or fiction, causing the American Tract Society to write a rebuttal saying it was against their policy to "publish fiction in the style of truth."[57] James Milnor, the rector at St. George's Church in New York, defended Richmond's tracts by sharing accounts of his trip to the Isle of Wight, where he claims to have visited "the cottage where the Dairyman's Daughter died . . . and the place where Rev. Mr. Richmond met and prayed with the African servant under the rocks."[58]

Tellingly, Milnor focuses on whether William was drawn from life, not his eventual fate. He comments upon viewing the cove that "nothing could be more true to nature than the surrounding scenery as [Richmond] describes it in that tract."[59] Milnor's journals "inspired a number of American visitors to follow his itinerary."[60] That tract tourists focused on the cove scene as the most iconic part of *The Negro Servant* to the point of verifying that the setting was portrayed accurately, but did not concern themselves with seeking a human story to go with the version in the tale, demonstrates the power of the scene but its detachment from relational obligation. Modern readers might feel a different longing when considering William's character and the assertion that he was based on a real person; what was William's life really like? At the same time, we are never assured that William truly existed. If he were not a real person, could he have been an allegorical figure named after Richmond's hero, William Wilberforce, standing in for the potential of converting the world? Even if this is the case, the text seems to be haunted, still, by the narrator's failure to connect.

In addition to inspiring travel in its readers, the tract traveled. *The Negro Servant*'s focus on relational possibilities among those with shared religious sensibilities seems to have made it suitable for parts of the world with existing Christian populations, such as Christians in the Middle East, portrayed in

RTS documents as suffering under Islamic rule. Jones mentions that following Greek independence from the Ottoman Empire in 1821, which the British government supported so as not to allow for greater influence of France or Russia in the region, the RTS made a push to translate tracts in the area, including "eleven thousand juvenile works."[61] Greece was used, along with the nearby crown colony of Malta, as a base for promoting Christian community; a Greek priest in Malta translated *The Negro Servant* into Arabic "for Christians inhabiting Syria, Palestine, and Egypt."[62] The phrasing of this description does not assign conversion as a main goal of the text but rather suggests that it was considered helpful for consolidating Christian subjects as a group. This aligned with British policy for the region, which was driven by support for Christians under majority-Islamic governments and protection of access to trade routes and economic opportunities for British subjects.

Editions of *The Negro Servant* are also extant in Cherokee, Marathi, Bengali, and Zulu, in addition to Welsh, Russian, Spanish, French, and German, suggesting aspirations for creating new Christians in addition to existing ones. In addition to being a Christian ethical goal, conversion was a tool for social control imposed by empire. Although the text offers a brief critique of the violent extraction of resources in a way that perhaps rang true for some global readers, the dates associated with its publication connect to economic goals of empire. *The Negro Servant* appears in Bengali and Marathi in the 1840s–1850s as the British claimed control over India and used it as a base for the opium trade into China. The text was translated into Zulu by Reverend Josiah Tyler around the time of the diamond rush and quest for cheap Black labor in South Africa, establishing exertions of power and hierarchies that eventually resulted in apartheid.

The Relational Potential of Black Dolls

When I began my research, I had hoped to discover a surviving children's text that had persisted in the Caribbean as evidence of the circulation of English-language books. I was therefore thrilled when in the library of the University of the West Indies in Barbados I found an inscribed copy of *Babes in the Basket; Or Daph and Her Charge* (1859)—a book sometimes attributed to the British author C. E. Bowen but written by US author Sarah Schoonmaker Baker. Although it took an embarrassingly long time, I eventually realized that the copy in question was given to a young girl as a reward book in Christ Church, *England*, not Christ Church, Barbados, as the book's location led me to believe. I do not know the story of how the book got to Barbados but suspect it was purchased as part of the university's West India collection because it includes a Caribbean character.[63] Although the book does not provide documentary evidence of the nineteenth-century circulation of books to the Caribbean, it prompts us to think about how images of Afro-Caribbean people figured into the creation of global series by nineteenth-century publishers.

The book—which features an enslaved woman named Daph fleeing a slave rebellion with her enslavers' children Louise and Charlie in tow and forming a new family configuration in the multicultural city of New York—is global-imperial in multiple respects. A 1915 inscription in the 1859 copy by Baker's daughter Louise Beckman claims that it was her mother's "most famous book . . . translated into a great number of languages."[64] She mentions that Baker found it translated into Swedish when she emigrated later in life. Editions in German and Arabic remain extant.[65] Perhaps most notably, the book was chosen for Frederick Warne's Round the Globe Library around 1875.[66]

Warne's approach to this series seems to have been choosing books already circulating globally, including *The Dairyman's Daughter* as well as books by established authors with a transatlantic following like Susan Warner and Sarah Trimmer. The press also made minimal attempts to choose books that reflected foreign people and places, such as *The Italian Boy and Industrial Men of Note* (1875), *The Peasants of the Alps* (circa 1869), and *Pride and Principle, or, The Captain of Elbedon School* (1879), featuring a mixed-race Jamaican protagonist attending school in England. Other books offered accounts of the world, such as *The Earth We Live On* (circa 1875), or international excursions, such as *Uncle John's Adventures and Travels* (circa 1887). Most books in the series, however, are set in mainland Britain.

Baker's *The Babes in the Basket* was a clear fit for the series, in that many books share its classification under the subject of Christian life, but it was also unique for beginning in the Global South, on a "Southern island" (in some editions, "a Caribbean island"). That *The Babes in the Basket* is, to my knowledge, the only book in the series featuring a woman of color as a protagonist demonstrates the book's innovations—and indeed such a protagonist is rare in nineteenth-century literature in general. But as we will see, its universalizing elements also reflect Warne's whitewashing of the globe.

There is another reason why Baker's book is unusual. Unlike *Pious Moses* and *The Negro Servant*, which claim to be based on real people, another Beckman inscription explains that *Babes in the Basket* was "written by my Mother about dolls in my dolls house."[67] The text does not overtly state its connection to dolls, but there are clues that subtly convey this origin. One chapter title,

"The Red House with the Blue Shutters," draws attention to the markedly small house in which the characters reside in New York City.[68] There is a scene in which Daph outfits the children's room with dollhouse-like furniture: "The bright yellow chairs, adorned with the wonderful roses and tulips were first set aside, then followed a little table, painted in the same fanciful manner, and lastly, a good-sized trundle bed, of a somewhat less gaudy appearance."[69] Baker may have been nodding toward her daughter's dollhouse when she notes the source of these items, a "cabinet maker," also the source of most dollhouses in the nineteenth century.[70] A later edition from circa 1884 includes small illustrations of windows and rooms, making the book dollhouse-like.[71]

It is possible that the text got its origins in play between the young girl and her mother. In the same copy inscribed by Beckman, an earlier gift inscription to Anna W. Baker (Sarah S. Baker's sister-in-law and Beckman's aunt) for "Christmas 1858" notes that the book is from a "small author," perhaps a sly hint that Louise, then six years old, participated in creating the story—or, alternatively, a recognition of the role played by the doll itself.[72] If we take these inscriptions together, we can read the book as a manifestation of maternal care and ethical training. Baker, a Northern white Christian woman, may have been using her nurturing relationship with her daughter to inculcate a shared commitment to aiding Africans to become Christians, the outcome of Daph's transit north. The story prescribes this role for white women through the character of Rose Stuyvesant, a Christian who befriends Daph and defends her against prejudice.

Because the book turns out to have been based on a children's toy, it prompts us to examine how white children and their parents experienced transatlantic relationships on a material level—and to unpack the fantasies of universality, relationality, and familiality that hover around these material connections. It also invites comparison with slightly later Black doll narratives that circulated globally, including Bertha and Florence K. Upton's *The Adventures of Two Dutch Dolls and a Golliwogg* (1895), featuring a minstrel-inspired doll, and José Martí's "An muñeca negra," created for his *La edad de oro* (1889), a magazine dedicated to "los niños de América," encompassing Latin America and the Caribbean as well as the United States.[73]

Upton's book features interactions between two Dutch dolls, a name for wooden peg dolls originally produced in the Italian Alps, and a male Black cloth doll named Golliwog whom she describes as a "horrid sight" and a "gnome."[74] Born in the United States to British parents, Upton first published her book in London, taking advantage of a preexisting vogue for minstrel performance and helping to popularize US minstrel culture to a new generation of international readers. The book, which contains numerous hijinks in which the Golliwog doll suffers—for instance, by falling on ice and needing rescue by the Dutch dolls—gave rise to a series expanding on this theme, as well as merchandise.

Martí's "La muñeca negra" is a comparatively progressive text, in which a young girl named Piedad has a beloved Black rag doll, which she refuses to replace when her parents give her a white porcelain doll for her birthday. Miguel Cabrera Peña has noted that the story was inspired by *Uncle Tom's Cabin*; Piedad loves the doll because her parents do not love it, similar to the way that Eva expresses love for Topsy.[75] Jorge Camacho argues that the story aspires to antiracism but ultimately promotes white saviorism and imposes limits on Africans' aspirations: "If no one loves the black doll, it is also the case that the black doll wants nothing. Her poverty keeps her from aspiring to the things the other doll wants, which is why Piedad prefers her."[76] Baker's story is strikingly different from both later doll narratives, in part because it does not explicitly characterize its main character as a doll. It makes its Afro-Caribbean character the central human actor, rather than a funny sidekick or a pitiable bundle of rags. Baker therefore interacts with the ways that African-descended people have been made into objects (an idea Robin Bernstein claims is inherent in nineteenth-century doll play) and considers what ethical demands emerge when that transformation is reversed.[77] Daph, I argue, brings together exoticization, identification, emotional investment, and practice making ethical decisions—all relational possibilities opened up by children's relationship with dolls—though she most strongly reflects Baker and possibly Beckman projecting their feelings onto a figure of Black womanhood.

Baker moves her doll-turned-woman through competing narrative conventions, yielding creative possibilities that exceed, even as they are sometimes forced to fit, the racist narratives of the time. As I will discuss, the book reprises, though it also transcends, the genre of the faithful slave narrative. The title, however, more directly evokes the ubiquitous children's story, *The Babes in the Wood*, in which two children are abandoned in the woods by their wicked uncle. They die and are covered up with leaves by the birds, evoking readers' pity and ethical judgment. Louise and Charlie, conversely, are separated from their parents and threatened with death but saved by Daph, who like the wicked uncles and stepmothers of old poses a complication to the functioning of the family, but Daph turns out to be better-intended and more easily incorporated than an evil relative.[78] She shepherds the children onto a ship bound for New York City, where they stay with a sailor's widow. While there, Daph faces the widow's prejudice, cares for her in sickness, and sells cakes on the street to support the blended family. In the end, there is a chance encounter with the children's parents, who made a last-minute escape from the island before the rebellion. Daph is not reenslaved but continues to live with the children and their parents. She learns to read the Bible, and the book ends with her death and ascendance to heaven.

Although the context that Beckman's inscription provides is thin, we might sensibly posit that Louise's dollhouse supplied the basic ingredients for the story: a white boy, a white girl, two parents, perhaps a basket with infant dolls, and, most importantly, a Black doll. Such a doll would likely have been the product of transatlantic circulation; most dollhouse dolls were made by German, French, or English manufacturers, which mass-produced Black dolls prior to US companies. Black dolls made by enslaved women also traveled from the US South and Caribbean in the nineteenth century; for instance, the Moravian Young Men's Missionary Society received at least two dolls from missionaries to the West Indies, which they displayed in their missionary museum in Bethlehem, Pennsylvania, not far from Baker's home in New Jersey.[79] Although the origin of Louise's doll and dollhouse are not known, Baker incorporates a notion of Black dolls as world travelers into her story.

To the extent that the story gives us a window into the kinds of play nineteenth-century mothers and children engaged in with dollhouses, it is rare, for as Frances Armstrong points out, information about such play is scarce in records and material evidence, because "the survivors are often the failures, playthings that were not enjoyed to the point of extinction."[80] The international scope of Baker's text, if reflective of play, challenges a prevailing interpretation of dollhouse play scenarios as intensely domestic and isolated from the wider world. Armstrong, for instance, claims that "early dollhouse play" usually had a "private familial nature."[81] She writes, "Until about 1850, baby-houses were usually large family heirlooms, and how a girl played with them may have been influenced more by family tradition than by games played by her contemporaries. Even after dollhouses began to be mass-produced, they usually remained at home, and the dolls at home within them, each miniature household living its individualized and often idiosyncratic existence."[82] Armstrong's conclusions, though, do not preclude the possibility of creative parents like Baker dreaming up play scenarios depicting foreign people and places. The foreignness of the doll is related to the story that Baker wants to tell of Christian conversion, dovetailing with missionaries' global circulation of children's books.

Beckman's Black doll was probably made for white consumption and use. Bernstein shows that material aspects of Black dolls embedded scripts based on enslaver practices and minstrel representations. For instance, many Black dolls were made of soft or indestructible rubber materials, which prompted their white girl owners to beat them and hang them upside down, becoming a part of the apparatus of white supremacy. Upton's depiction of roughness toward the Golliwog character reflects these practices.

Bernstein discusses dollhouse dolls only briefly, quoting from Georgianna Hamlen's 1885 memoir that "very small dolls of black china were *supposed to be the proper thing for servants* in doll houses."[83] Other memories and surviving evidence confirm that dominant dollhouse scripts equated Blackness with enslavement and servitude. A retrospective account written in the 1900s about a dollhouse owned by the Philadelphia-based Cadwalader family records the writer's experiences of the house between 1850 and 1861: "I think there was also an open hearth in the kitchen . . . [A] coloured cook, her head covered with a once-bright bandanna, stood waiting, and a coloured butler also waited in the dining-room."[84] This account squares with what Armstrong has discovered by examining surviving dollhouses: Black dolls, she claims, were almost exclusively mammy-type dolls, deriving from the Anglo-American myth of enslavement as a benevolent institution: They "almost always seemed to be called Dinah and to be relegated to the kitchen."[85] Importantly, Black dolls in dollhouses belonging to white children did not live in their own houses or with other Black dolls, which discouraged play scenarios in which they had their own families and communities.

Baker's text reflects this history. Her heroine is described at the beginning of the text as a stereotypical mammy living in a white family. She is "Dark Daph," "a short, strongly-built woman, whose Black face and gay turban . . . formed a striking contrast to the fair children in their loose, white night-dresses."[86] She uses crude dialect that represents the US author's warped hearing—or imagination—of Black speech, likely aided by minstrel representations. Baker ventriloquizes racist views into the mouth of the character, as minstrel shows did using blackface performers, a potential that Bernstein connects to doll play in which "white girl[s] spoke in dialect from behind a black doll" making "the doll function[] as the minstrel mask."[87] In the first two pages, Daph performs the white gaze on herself. She catches a glimpse of herself in a mirror and chastises herself for being a "foolish Darky" for "looking at [her] own ugly face!"[88] Building on this racist association of Blackness with ugliness, Baker makes Daph the mouthpiece for a racialized coding of ethics. Describing the planned slave rebellion to the captain, Daph simplifies and color codes the ethical question of retaliatory violence by saying, "Dey told Daph deir secret, as if dey thought she was all Black, inside and out."[89]

Although Daph derives from the mammy stereotype, Baker complicates the stereotype of African women as all-purpose servants for life, reflected in most dollhouses' inclusion of only one Black servant. She notes that Daph is not the children's usual female caretaker but the cook. Once the characters leave the Caribbean, Daph is no longer in the kitchen serving others but uses her cooking skills to start her own business.[90] The rapid departure from the islands means that most of the story takes place in a city where, by this time, African Americans lived in freedom, perhaps reflecting Baker's experiences as a Northern woman. There was a relationship between the Caribbean and the Northern US, with US citizens and some free Africans traveling between the two places, and Baker may have had contact with West Indians in New York City and New Jersey, where she lived.[91]

While mainstream doll culture replicated race relations in the US South, other traditions of doll collecting create configurations of people from around the globe, a simplified blend of cultures faintly mimicking the multicultural urban society emerging in Northern US cities. Doll collectors sought dolls from multiple places. This practice appears in doll fiction such as Julia Charlotte Maitland's *The Doll and Her Friends, Or, the Memoirs of Lady Seraphina* (1862) and, later, *Raggedy Ann Stories* (1918), which includes a nursery of dolls of different nationalities. Although there was recognition and, to some degree, celebration of cultural differences, these were often collections of stereotypes and could promote appropriation and feelings of ownership, an ethos echoed in Warne's insufficiently multicultural global series.

Dolls signifying Blackness, overall, invite the replication of exploitative relationships in children's play on a small scale, but these materials also present flexible relational possibilities, by virtue of being combined with white dolls in a contained space without definitive instructions on how to negotiate the coupling. As children have shown, breaking stereotypes is often more enticing as a play scenario than upholding them. The grounding of *Babes in the Basket* in material culture and play seems to have offered Baker flexibility to shift between multiple narrative forms, at times drawing and other times diverging from the plantation mythology that influenced mainstream doll-house culture to consider different configurations of social life where people of multiple cultures coexisted. If we use Beckman's inscription to discern that the story is taking place in one dollhouse, we see the house morph from a plantation house to an urban boarding house to what Baker calls a "happy home" of blended families.

The text's opening in a plantation house demonstrates Daph's complex positioning within available narrative conventions for enslaved characters. Daph is, in this space, an enslaved person, but the text plays with inverting her relationship with the children of her enslavers. Daph enters the bed-room of the two children, Charlie and Louise (presumably named for Baker's daughter), to find them "sleeping in their curtained beds, like birds in pretty cages."[92] Through this image of children confined within a "lavish" space that befits the dollhouse origins, Baker refuses a romanticized vision of the plan-tation and disrupts the implicit hierarchy in ethical lessons using animals as metaphors for the enslaved (discussed in my introduction and chapter 1).[93] The image echoes the grateful Black's perspective in *Sandford and Merton* (1783–1789) that white people are dependent and helpless, a critique that underwrites narratives both of Black ethical righteousness and sacrifice. The image complicates the house as a place of Daph's confinement—and it is not to be for long. The remainder of the scene references—and inverts—accounts in slave narratives of child kidnappings in Africa, found, for instance, in Olaudah Equiano's autobiography. Cast as a threatening "dark intruder," Daph drugs the two children and puts them in a large basket, but the text moves away from this othering of Daph to reveal her good intentions.[94]

Although the text allows its Afro-Caribbean character humanity and eth-ical rightness, it also assimilates her by making her actions reflect white Christian ethical values, rather than an Afro-Caribbean antislavery ethics in which rebellion could be justified. We see these twin impulses in the scene in which Daph calls herself ugly. Baker depicts her heroine looking in a mir-ror, which positions (what were likely her white) readers inside Daph's per-spective and even inside her body. This device presents Daph as simulta-neously other and same, forcing readers to confront her (negatively framed) physical difference in a kind of literary blackface, while framing her within a white gaze with expectations for universal Christian ethical behavior. In one sense Daph produces affect in this scene as a comical figure, eliciting a flat form of condescension; in another, she prompts a fuller range of feelings, identifications, and connections. These are tied (problematically) to her ethical quandary, which results in her decision to save the white children based on Christian ethical decision making, rather than join the slave rebellion, the latter a choice more consistent with the history of Afro-Caribbean women's ethics during enslavement (consider Queen Mary, discussed in my introduction, or the unnamed enslaved storytellers in chapter 2).

By featuring an enslaved woman who remains faithful to her enslavers despite the possibility of freedom, this text fits uneasily into a racist genre called the faithful slave narrative. Faithful slave narratives appeared en masse in Anglo-American children's books and periodicals of the eighteenth and nineteenth centuries, written by authors such as Lydia Maria Child and Mary Pilkington. Although the stories differ in their emphases, some taking a cautious abolitionist perspective and others a pro-slavery stance, they generally accept the myth that enslavement could in some circumstances be happy and that owners could be benevolent. Particularly after the US Civil War, such stories became part of the plantation tradition: songs and stories that implied enslavement was at worst tolerable and at best idyllic. The stories could introduce complex ideas—for instance, faithful slaves' choice to defend their masters was offered as evidence that they possessed universal ethical qualities like disinterestedness and virtue, which should have qualified them to become citizens and be enslaved no longer. However, they also reinforce the myth of enslavement as a great patriarchal institution and the plantation as a family. The text's use of these conventions reminds us that the very act of including a Black doll in a dollhouse with a white family promotes plantation mythology by suggesting that Black women were without families of their own. As Hazel V. Carby argues, this insidious myth results in Black women's caregiving being defined "through their employment (or chattel position) as domestics and surrogate mothers to white families rather than in relation to their own families."[95]

The Babes in the Basket diverges from the faithful slave tradition in important respects. The genre usually involves an enslaved person demonstrating their faithfulness by preventing a slave rebellion or attempt on an enslaver's life, but this plot is usually tacked on at the end of the text. The rebellious plot is deflected, the enslaved person chooses to remain enslaved owing to the enslaver's benevolence, and the instability of the slave system is quickly resolved. Baker instead extends the slave rebellion scenario by making it the raison d'être of the text. Even if she does not go so far as to imagine a nation, like Haiti, in which enslaved people take over and declare themselves free, the book dwells for the majority of its pages on an Afro-Caribbean woman, made autonomous if not literally freed, who takes the family's children and forms a new household with them in a different place. Daph is a faithful slave in that she sacrifices for the white children and remains with them; in other ways, she is a runaway. It is significant that she heads for the free US North, not the much closer South. Daph sells cakes on the street to support a blended family composed of her, the children, the widow Mrs. Ray, the widow's daughter Mary, and friends she has made, including a sea captain and her wealthy customer Rose. The text thereby gives the slave rebellion much more disruptive power than it is usually given in texts for children.

Baker also develops Daph's character with greater emotional depth and sensitivity than the typical faithful slave story. It seems possible that this aspect of the text derives in part from the character's origin in doll play, where doll figures are meant to inspire empathetic attachments. A more overt doll narrative from the period, Maitland's *The Doll and Her Friends*, recognizes the capacity of dolls to encourage empathy in children when the narrator, who is a dollhouse doll, says that the "power of inspiring strong attachment" is essential to the work of dolls.[96] Yet many doll narratives insist on the doll's (and particularly the Black doll's) insensibility, raising questions about how relational attachment overlaps with ethical responsibility. Maitland's Seraphina suggests that dolls cannot feel "pain, sickness, or fatigue."[97] Yet in turning the Black doll into a human protagonist, Baker endows her with precisely these feelings. Important scenes show Daph getting seasick (a condition that Baker notes can "only be appreciated by those who have experienced its miseries"); dealing with taunting from "idle boys"; experiencing "dread" when she sees the house where they are to board; encountering the prejudice of Ray, the white boarding house proprietor, confiding her worries about parenting the children to Rose (whose "tears . . . made Daph feel that she had found a true friend"); and managing family tensions for the Ray and her daughter Mary.

Daph's interactions with Ray expand readers' sense of Daph's personal ethics beyond the commentary about the slave rebellion put into her voice, while initially minimizing questions of white responsibility toward her. Ray refuses to help Daph because she does not want to "take a Negro" as a lodger.[98] She refers to Daph as a "queer one" even once she has accepted her into the house.[99] Yet Daph treats this stranger with kindness and cares for her when she becomes sick. Daph's ethics, which allow for ethical responsibility to those who are *other* in addition to those who are the same, are sounder and more comprehensive than the ethics of the narrators of *Moses the Pious Negro* and *The Negro Servant*, which support kind relationships only to those who can be assimilated to the narrator's worldview. Yet they also manifest as self-sacrifice in a way that fits white fantasies of Black women, demonstrating the influence of ideologies developed in enslavement on relations at a remove from the slave system.

Daph's superior but self-sacrificial ethics are compatible with the racist hierarchy of society. When making a drink for the sick widow, Daph naturalizes Africans' labor by saying, "White folks isn't used to such hard work. You just can't bear it, dats it."[100] We are shown that there is a clear cost to these dynamics for Daph; she feels despondent at her life in the boarding house because of the widow's "harsh voice" and other factors.[101] Ray comes to regret her behavior, and although the arrangement she makes with Daph entails her ironing for the boarders, Ray also supports Daph's burgeoning cake-making business, giving Daph a measure of autonomy. Particularly striking illustrations in a 1773 edition mix images showing Daph's emotional depth and independence (fending off sailors, buying furniture) with scenes of her working and providing emotional labor (ironing, comforting the widow's daughter).[102]

The reimagination of the dollhouse from a plantation to a New York City boarding house opens possibilities for interracial solidarity, which build on communal scenes in doll culture. Maitland's Seraphina explains doll collectors' propensity to combine and play with dolls from multiple cultures: "Dolls . . . have a natural sympathy with each other . . . Besides plenty of pretty English damsels I was introduced now to a Turkish sultana, now to a Swiss peasant . . . another day to an Indian rajah."[103] Although Daph's experiences are not so exotic, she meets sympathetic female characters in New York, including Rose and Mary. Daph's experience goes beyond the frivolousness implied in Maitland's text; in a later scene, Maitland's characters do not even notice when Seraphina is hung upside down and trapped. Baker's characters, conversely, help Daph when a busybody sees that she has gold chains and has her arrested for theft. White advocates help defend Daph to Ray. Rose's father, Diedrich Stuyvesant, lectures the widow, "What have you to bring forward in comparison with the heroism and self-sacrifice of this poor woman, whom you despised?"[104]

Although the text's visions of relationality draw from the idea of the diverse doll community, they shift away from these origins. The society of the text, like the composition of Warne's Round the Globe Series, does not ultimately represent diverse global cultures coming together; instead, Daph is assimilated into a group of white women and their families. A telling illustration places Rose in the foreground and Daph in the background, implying that Daph's care of the children is only an approximation of Rose's care—even as it alludes to the truth that Black women were, in many cases, involved with raising white children (fig. 5.1). Carby points out that such assistance from an empowered to a disempowered individual or group "far from transforming or destroying institutionalized inequality, actually reinforce[s] such inequality, because the power of the patron is secured at the same moment that those subjected to patronage are confirmed in their powerlessness."[105] While there is a progressive ethical intention in the text's extension of subjectivity and humanity to the enslaved, it is ultimately based on white and Christian universalizing notions of humanity (similar to those that Saidiya Hartman sees in the progressive politics of Northern cities fifty years later and contests in *Wayward Lives, Beautiful Experiments*).[106]

In light of Moten's argument that Black people occupy a position of thingliness or fugitive in-betweenness when it comes to subjecthood and objecthood, we could imagine a version of the story in which Daph's doll origins might allow the character to resist full incorporation into this limited Christian idea of universal humanness, of which she never has a full share.[107] However, the thingly origins of the character are erased in this white progressive fantasy, leaving mainly negatively framed traces of difference as inferiority. As the in-betweenness is removed, we are left with what is incorporated into whiteness and what is left over, Blackness as ontological death.

The recognition of Daph's humanity is finally tied to her assumption of roles considered respectable by white readers; she becomes a quasi-maternal caregiver, then a Christian. Daph's embrace of Christianity extends her earlier expressions of Christian ethics—and ends up making her relatable to those who enslaved her. The text's experiments with extrafamilial sociality end with the return of the children's parents, who have made a last-minute escape from the island. There is never a moment that reasserts Daph's enslavement. Yet we would be remiss if we did not read the myth of the happy plantation family in these scenes. Daph lives with her former enslavers in a new house where Daph has her own room and is purportedly "best loved and most cared for."[108] The family hierarchy maintains the structures associated with Anglo-American enslavement even after it has ended.

The text does not narrate any new adventures for Daph after her enslavers arrive but instead rushes to her ascendance to heaven. This ending represents a version of what Russ Castronovo calls "necro-citizenship," or the par-

Figure 5.1. Illustration labeled "The Visit of Miss Rose Stuyvesant," from *The Babes in the Basket, or, Daph and Her Charge*. London: S. W. Partridge & Co., c. 1873. Courtesy of the Baldwin Library of Historical Children's Literature, George A. Smathers Libraries, University of Florida.

adox by which African Americans could attain full freedom only via death.[109] In death, she becomes a figure not only free of her former enslavers but also whose ethics can be identified as universal and pure. This outcome has obvious limitations for anyone invested in the stories about Daph's life, business, and friendships that drive the plot of Baker's narrative. The text is irretrievably impacted by the faithful slave story, as Daph's greatest obligation is, always, to the children she saved. This fact reminds us that Baker's daughter, Louise, was likely the first reader of the text, if not a cocreator, and the first intended beneficiary of the lessons it presents. Daph's ascendance to heaven fashions her narrative into the expectations of a didactic model of children's literature that presents a religious lesson for white readers (I found no evidence to consider what the text might have meant to readers outside of this audience).

Babes in the Basket is, consequentially, not a very progressive book by today's standards. The progress that it does make is rare; most books in Warne's nineteenth-century Round the Globe series feature white European protagonists. Baker, though, stops short of taking the step that some of her contemporaries did in using Black dolls to protest enslavement. Martha Katz-Hyman and Kym Rice have discovered that some abolitionists used dolls "to raise public awareness about slavery and to generate empathy" that would lead to action.[110] Some Black rag dolls intended for this purpose have been found at Bronson Alcott's Utopian community, Fruitlands. Baker's text does seem to be in the spirit of some practices involving these abolitionist dolls; Hyman and Rice note that "Philadelphia Quakers" located near Baker's home in Princeton, New Jersey, "sent Black dolls . . . dressed in traditional Quaker Clothing, to Friends in Britain, perhaps as testimony to free Blacks' piety and respectability."[111] However, the book does not encourage children to investigate conditions for the enslaved or understand why rebellions were happening. In the end, it is difficult to shake the notion that Baker moves Daph through multiple narrative conventions as one might move a doll through a dollhouse.

The inclusion of *Babes in the Basket* in Warne's Round the Globe series is an example of how relational dynamics deriving from Atlantic enslavement became incorporated into a global-imperial children's literature canon. As a model for global relationships, the relationship between Daph and Rose envisions active roles for the colonized and colonizers to support each other in ways that are construed as ethically motivated and caring, while demanding that the colonized accept white definitions of care and respectability. By including only texts in English by Anglo authors, Warne's series does not allow for a very relational or reciprocal global children's literature, which would be open to the contributions of others around the globe.

A Bengali *Sandford and Merton*

By contrast, the Bengali Family Library, published in India by the Vernacular Literature Committee, includes multinational works, including stories translated from English, such as a version of Day's *Sandford and Merton*, and other European languages. The series combines translations with selections from Bengali periodicals and an original children's work, *Tale of Sushila: An Instructive Tale for Bengali Girls* (1877). As a globally diverse series, the Bengali Family Library models openness to difference and attempts to understand the relationship between one's own perspective and the perspectives of others, taking a relational approach to global children's literature.

The significant spread of English on the Indian subcontinent leads Gauri Viswanathan to argue that "no serious account of [the] growth and development" of English literature can "ignore the imperial mission of educating and civilizing colonial subjects" there.[112] In Bengal, English texts circulated, often in translation, alongside the "languages and sciences" of the region.[113] Translations produced in this context, as "hybrid" texts, offer a different way to think about the relational possibilities of global children's literature. Published in 1865 as part of the Bengali Family Library, *Kathataranga*, a translation of Day's *Sandford and Merton* by Madhusudan Mukhopadhyay, features an African character who derives from but does not reproduce Day's grateful Black. Mukhopadhyay's text incorporates the British text, while embedding it in a new cultural context and refusing attempts to cast Anglo-Christian culture as universally applicable. In turn, it reshapes Day's character, excerpting and isolating a portion of his story of more relevance to colonized populations than white readers.

Kathataranga, the title of which Nivedita Sen translates as "Rippling stories," was solicited by the Indian Vernacular Literature Committee, established in 1851 to enrich the Bengali language.[114] Mukhopadhyay turns universalizing language back toward the colonizers by claiming that Mr. Barlow's lessons and pedagogical technique resemble those of Vishnu Sharma, the Indian author of the *Panchatantra*, who "had taught the princes the religion and ethics in disguise of general discussion."[115] This revision underscores Viswanathan's point that the Bengali upper classes saw a "symbiosis between

Oriental literature and English studies . . . [as] easily conceivable."[116] Comparing Jesus Christ to a "guru," and referring to "caste" and the "Dharma," Mukhopadhyay rejects the idea that British stories as universal by placing the story in an Indian context.[117] He articulates his own agenda as a translator: "[Mr. Barlow] taught them religion and ethics by reading the narratives, which were translated, so I named this book 'Sandford and Morton's Book of Words.' At once I pray to God that reading the translated book may benefit boys and girls."[118] "Book of Words" suggests that language learning, achieved by comparing the original and translation, may be one goal.

The text, meanwhile, deviates in multiple ways from Day's original. It confines Tommy Merton and Harry Sandford to an opening section, before diverging into a selection of fables and stories translated and adapted from Day's text. While Day's version includes interstitial sections with ethical discussions between the boys and their teacher, as well as a concluding section showing Tommy's transformation, *Kathataranga* does not narrate Tommy's transformation into an ethical person. It is implied by the frame narrative that he will be redeemed, but he remains unredeemed in the narrative itself—indicating perhaps that the child of British enslavers cannot easily achieve redemption in an Indian context.

Mukhopadhyay's translation indeed questions the assumptions of the original frame story. Day's version (as I point out in chapter 1) does not blame Tommy's enslaver father for his bad behavior, instead scapegoating Tommy's mother and enslaved caretakers for overindulging him. Mukhopadhyay, however, does not exonerate Tommy's father, clarifying that the "excessive indulgence" derives from both of Tommy's parents.[119] Additionally, while the original text claims that slaves were "forbidden" to contradict Tommy, treating the authority of the enslaver as self-evident, the Bengali version foregrounds the removal of their agency by British enslavers: "They did not have the power to stop him from doing illegal things."[120]

Tommy's father still makes the decision to have his son educated by Barlow, but his reasoning draws from Hindu philosophy. When Mrs. Merton, who is status conscious, questions Barlow's qualifications, Mr. Merton remarks, "It is good to be fond of some outward beauty and manners of the children of the rich, but all beauty is in vain if the heart is not beautiful. A person who receives the human gift and does not refine his intellect and religious instincts through learning and teaching the Dharma, his birth is like the birth of an animal."[121] Comparing Tommy to an animal in some ways dovetails with Day's use of animals to make Tommy aware of his weaknesses (discussed in my introduction), but it is more damning in its implication that Tommy, as a white colonizer, is a brutish and unenlightened creature—especially when we consider that it is enslaved people who are usually compared to animals in English-language children's literature (I have discussed exceptions to this general rule throughout the book). The comparison, furthermore, implies that Tommy's transition into an ethical person should follow a Hindu path of enlightenment.

As the text does not include Tommy and Harry after the first few chapters, Day's scene in which the grateful Black saves Tommy does not appear. However, Mukhopadhyay ends his text with a story told by "a slave" from Buenos Aires, which draws from a story the grateful Black tells. Without the baggage of his portrayal in Day's text, the enslaved man's ethical lesson is transformed. The story, in which a man imprisoned for a crime impresses the ruler of his country with his bull-slaying skills and achieves his freedom, appears in Day's text but is subsumed within the frame narrative where the grateful Black saves Tommy, insinuating that it is merely helpful knowledge for this end goal.[122] Mukhopadhyay's editing takes out the rescue and references to gratitude in Day's version, allowing the main outcome to be the man's advocacy for his freedom and successful release from enslavement. The story, therefore, jettisons the universal Christian focus on self-sacrifice promoted by global-imperial children's literature, instead advancing a lesson in antislavery (and implicitly anticolonial) action. Mukhopadhyay ends with this tale, giving the enslaved and colonized the last word.

In isolating the enslaved man's story of an imprisoned man asserting and saving himself, Mukhopadhyay identifies this action, rather than the grateful Black's sacrifice, as the ethical lesson relevant to his readers. The enslaved character claims it will help his audience "realize what man can do with courage and intelligence."[123] The imprisoned man's demonstration of virtue refuses the sacrificial dynamic too easily used to reinforce African and Asian subservience in an Atlantic and global context, implying instead that it is an ethical imperative to free oneself, even if it requires some violence—a fitting lesson for the colonized and oppressed. The man's value is not related to his utility for a white child but exists on his own terms. His ethics are not instantly recognizable as relational. Yet the story has applications for others who are oppressed. Additionally, it is *related*, in the sense of being a story, and promotes openness to difference and the specific needs of others, departing from the global-imperial texts offering Western Christian ethics as a universal standard. Although Mukhopadhyay laudably removes the frame narrative featuring white child listeners in favor of his own audience of Bengali boys and girls, we might frame its lesson as valuable for readers around the globe, as a chance to listen and understand.

———

The portions of Day's text that, I argue in my introduction, open up relational dimensions for white audiences are exposed for their limitations in Mukhopadhyay's translation. I conclude, then, with Mukhopadhyay's text as a thought-provoking example that suggests that those interested in an inclusive ethical perspective for children need to consider how colonized and enslaved people have articulated what ethical action means from their perspective. Adopting such a relational openness encompasses a commitment to interconnectedness and the belief that listening to and learning from others is the key to an ethical future for all. As I have discussed, this undertaking is difficult when it comes to historical people who have been oppressed, because of the limited colonial aims that shape the formation of archives. Yet archives can also yield unexpected opportunities to encounter and comprehend the experiences of those who have not been given the full opportunity to tell their stories, cultivating a more informed awareness of historical injustices and a commitment to equitable action. In my conclusion, I reflect on my research experiences and methodology to consider how scholars can ethically approach archives related to enslaved and colonized youth.

Relating Ethically in the Archives

As I have discussed throughout this book, archives represent a challenge for scholars interested in an ethics that bends toward justice. Because many archives are attached to state and academic institutions, the histories of which are bound up with enslavement and colonization, they often contain the preferred stories (and organizational schemes) of the powerful, even if valiant archivists and librarians call these stories into question when they present materials to students and the public.[1]

After the turn to an insufficient ethics promoting educational access, hard work, and universal ethics in the British Caribbean, the archives of missionary organizations include many biased records that proclaim the failure of Afro-Caribbean children to meet educators' universalizing aims and blame parents for inadequately receiving the global-imperial cultures of English literature and literacy. For example, a missionary teacher in Jamaica writes to the British Foreign and School Society (BFSS) in 1845: "I have often thought of writing to you, but not having anything of a very encouraging nature to communicate I have not been able to make up my mind before to do so . . . My own impression is that it will be many years before the people of Jamaica will be an educated people. The parents do not value instruction; and are, therefore, not only unwilling to pay a trifling sum for it, but very irregular in sending their children to school."[2] We can draw a line from such viewpoints to earlier ideas about the deficiencies of enslaved caregivers, such as Matthew Lewis's depiction of Goosee Shoo Shoo (discussed in chapter 2).

In the Goosee chapter, I suggest we look past the woman's depiction by an enslaver to consider how her story fits into a counternarrative of Afro-Caribbean education. Considering the bias of the BFSS archive—namely, that it does not include direct accounts from Afro-Caribbean children or parents—

we can similarly look for alternative ways to interpret the details presented in the aforementioned letter. Blaming Afro-Caribbean parents for a perceived rejection of colonial educational efforts, meant in part to clear European consciences, simplifies the story and excuses white descendants of enslavers from apprehending Afro-Caribbean children and parents on their own terms.

As Chelsey Smith has shown, Afro-Caribbean parents in Jamaica refused to invest in the education system not because they did not value education but because they did not agree with the aims of colonial education, increasingly understood as a way to provide industrial training "that . . . carried strong resonance with unfree agricultural labor."[3] Parents also relied on their children for help with planting, harvesting, and selling crops, forcing them to reconcile "their desires to gain access to the literacy they valued with the demands of life as peasant families who relied on returns from their provision grounds, freeholds, and engagement in the Sunday markets to survive."[4] Many families, Smith concludes, "engag[e] and disengag[e] tactically and practically with schooling."[5] Additionally, we can read this familiar, racist depiction of Black educational failure as a dubious way to conceal ongoing Afro-Caribbean expressive traditions involving youth, which look on colonial educational goals with a critical eye.

Traces of this counternarrative in the archive are faint, but not absent. Archives impose order and silence that are themselves forms of sugarcoating, but the approach of the researcher matters. Commenting on Jacques Derrida's *Archive Fever* (1995), John D. Caputo suggests that what Derrida calls "archive illness" is driven by the desire to impose on the archive an unethical universalism that "confus[es] one's own archive with an *arche* [origin] that is taken to be the law for everybody and to exercise absolute control over the archive of the other."[6] However, it is possible to take a more ethical approach that starts with the assumption that history is contested, rather than fully known or accepted, choosing to be guided by the search for different accounts, or what Caputo calls "the courage to recall 'dangerous memories.' "[7]

Derrida suggests that this ethical approach—one open to otherness and difference, and therefore open to meeting others on their own terms—is inherent in the archive in that it always contains a trace or memory of the past, rather than the origin (*arche*) itself, and therefore reflects multiplicity and variation. As Saidiya Hartman articulates in *Wayward Lives, Beautiful Experiments*, archival documents can be "br[oken] open," to "untether waywardness" and "refusal" "from their identification as deviance, criminality, and pathology," a discourse as relevant to Afro-Caribbean children in the years following enslavement as to the urban African American women Hartman studies.[8] Archives, especially when combined with attention to living traditions and people, can be key to writing histories that are not sugarcoated.

Taking an ethical approach to the archive raises the potential to do justice to historical people who are represented without the unconstrained ability to tell their own stories. To do this, we might take cues from relational ethics' emphasis on openness and interconnectedness. As I describe in this conclusion, being open to the difference and multiplicity that Derrida sees as inherent in the archive often leads to surprises that make it possible to gain a deeper understanding of historical others. Being aware of our interconnectedness, in turn, means noticing how our scholarly pursuits make us dependent on past and present actors, including the ways that materials are framed by authorized and unauthorized users of archives (categories that shift over time). In discussing my encounters with an engraving of nineteenth-century dancing children hanging on the wall of the Codrington College library in Barbados and an archive of Anansi stories collected by Jamaican schoolchildren in the early twentieth century, I attend to how the descendants of enslaved people vie with archivists *and* act as archivists in post-emancipation educational settings, challenging colonial narratives of educational failure and pushing against the universalism driving global-imperial forms of ethics (discussed in chapter 5) by maintaining their own ethical resources built on variation, multiplicity, and adaptability.

Dancing as Ethical Expression

I did some of the research for this book in the library of Codrington College, an Anglican academic institution founded on a working sugar plantation in Barbados at the behest of a member of the colonial elite, Christopher Codrington III, in 1710. Administered by the Society for the Propagation of the Gospel (SPG), the college was originally intended to aid in Christianizing the island's Afro-Caribbean residents, 300 of whom were forced to labor on the estate, in part by training missionaries who would proselytize in the Caribbean and Africa. However, when the college opened in 1745, it admitted only white students to its grammar school and upper level. Affiliates of the college gradually adopted practices for catechizing Afro-Caribbean youth, and eventually some Afro-Caribbeans attended the school and college after the abolition of British enslavement in 1833. About the school, Janice McLean-Farrell and Michael Anderson Clarke write, "Codrington College was a contested place/space. While it made some dynamic and innovative educational developments, these were all subservient to the role of being an ally in maintaining the status quo."[9] McLean-Farrell and Clarke critique the school's use of religion to "make [the enslaved on the estate] obedient and hardworking slaves, fully committed to the maintenance of colonial society, training them to believe that there was divine authority behind their enslavement" and its use of education as "a colonization tool wielded to aid Britain's expansion."[10]

As might be expected given this context, many written archival records depicting nineteenth-century Afro-Caribbean children's time at the school fall into the genre of white perceptions of ineptitude. As discussed in chapter 4, Richard Rawle, then principal of the college, worried about the children's ability to understand the world as conveyed by British books, suggesting that they might need some form of fantastical technology to understand and fit into universalizing expectations of childhood. We might read between the lines some resistance on his students' part—a refusal rather than an inability to understand. Another letter from Rawle in 1848 gives a further window into his attempts to discipline his students using music, a case revealing for the terms through which it defines their failure and success:

> A tune which the [British Sunday School] Union children used to sing to the Christmas hymn, "Hark, what mean" takes well with my [Afro-Caribbean students]; and I frequently hear them now singing it as they come down to the water, though "Cherry Ripe" to which I have adapted a marching rhyme, is superseding it. At first their attempts at a march were ludicrous, as though they had no innate ideas of time or step; but the bump of order must be developing, for they now go out of school in a steady pace, and always give some indication of the tune being in their heads, though it is not allowed to be used but on good behavior.[11]

This description employs familiar, offensive racist language casting young Africans as comical and the passage describes the institution's role in disciplining their natural movements into orderly marching—in other words, into a kind of movement that can be universalized and that befits the ideal of the hardworking schoolchild. The songs in question are classic British songs, likely meant to replace African musical traditions, which Jessica Swanston Baker notes were seen as "infectious for [their] repetitiousness, drive, tempo, rhythm" and thought to threaten "educated, decorous, and 'civilized' white subjectivity."[12] Rawle imagines that British music is successful in colonizing even the children's thoughts.[13] But even as Rawle's observations define failure and success from the viewpoint of colonizers, the passage reminds us that

Figure C.1. "Fete at Codrington College, Barbadoes," in *Illustrated London News*, October 26, 1850. Courtesy of University of Michigan Libraries.

white educational efforts were surrounded by Afro-Caribbean children's movements and voices, which have their own contexts not represented, perceived, or understood by Rawle.

Working in the library, I was surprised to find material on the wall illustrating that the children at the school exhibited a different kind of physical acuity, relating to Afro-Caribbean movement traditions. Posted over a student desk in a windowed nook, I found a framed cut-out of an engraving labeled a "Fete at Codrington College, Barbadoes," originally published in an 1850 edition of the *Illustrated London News* (fig. C.1).[14] The image, to which someone had applied color, shows a celebration on the campus with children participating in African-derived dancing, including stilt-walking, circle dancing, and bottle dancing.[15]

Made discoverable not through an official act of archival preservation but an informal act of archival presentation, this image has multiple layers relevant to the trajectory that I trace in this book. The *Illustrated London News* constitutes another example of the global-imperial literary culture of mid-nineteenth-century Britain, as it both visually represented areas around the globe and circulated to the British colonies. Although it was not specifically created for children, the newspaper named young people as a part of its audience. It was a vehicle for the developing British visual culture that would feed into children's book and magazine illustration, in that it contained engravings by John Greenaway (father to Kate Greenaway) as well as early efforts by Randolph Caldecott.[16] By compiling images from around the world, the paper creates a visual archive that mimics the acquisitiveness of the empire and appropriates the world to provide an education for white British youth. However, the children appearing in the image are archives of Afro-Caribbean practices with their own knowledge traditions and ethical strategies. The placement on the wall of the Codrington archives, presumably by a librarian or archivist, reverses the flow of the circulation of Afro-Caribbean culture as part of a sugarcoated version of colonial knowledge for white children and links the college to traditions of embodied knowledge and education uncontrolled by white educators.

Keeping with the two-shoe approach that I outline in the Goosee chapter, we can interpret the image in multiple ways to account for its meaning to different audiences. As a pictorial paper with global journalistic ambitions, the *Illustrated London News* represents various kinds of otherness for British readers in the mainland and larger empire, traversing class lines as well as racial and cultural ones. Ethical teaching, including generating empathy and compassion, are implicit goals, but as Peter W. Sinnema points out, the varying tone of economic critique in the paper establishes a "equilibrium between reformist and conservative tendencies" that he reads as an attempt to "manufacture . . . consensus" among readers.[17] This consensus view, he argues, issues a charge for readers to address symptoms of inequality "without seriously challenging the entrenched structures which underpin economic disparity," a limited framing of ethical obligation that we can connect to white civility and fragility (discussed in chapter 1), as well as to the narrowing of ethical responsibility to schooling and book distribution (chapter 4).[18]

Many of the images of the enslaved that appeared in the paper—including two images labeled "Brazilian Sugar Mill" and "Domestic Punishments of Slaves, on a Brazilian Sugar Farm" that appear on one page in March 1845—pair with writing meant to promote a deceptively balanced or sugarcoated view of enslavement, which banks on the assumption that readers are at a safe distance from this content. The news story accompanying these two images comments on new duties on Brazilian sugar imposed by Sir Robert Peel as a response to the abuse of the enslaved workers producing the product: "Many conflicting statements have been put forth, to show on the one hand the justness and humanity of his restrictions, and on the other, to depreciate them as partial, and founded on an hypocritical regard for sufferings which have no real existence. Both classes are, to some extent, in error ... The slaves are not so well off as the friends of the planters would have us believe; nor are they, on the contrary, so badly used as the anti-slavery party declared."[19] The images reflect this questionable attempt at a balanced view, with one showing a sunny, pastoral image of enslaved people loading a sugar mill and the other an enslaved woman getting her hand struck by both a lash and hammer, with white and Black children looking on. The news story lands on a tepidly negative view of enslavement by pointing to the slave trade as the "worst feature of slavery," while revealing the artificiality of this balanced perspective by noting that the paper has "purposefully kept" this feature "out of view."[20]

Like *The Lobster's Voyage* (discussed in chapter 1), the *Illustrated London News* story about Brazil alludes to Britain's ongoing economic benefits from the institution of slavery through trade deals, despite its legal abolition. The paper, however, often characterizes enslavement as a problem primarily affecting other countries, especially as its first edition appeared after the 1833 abolition of enslavement in the British colonies. As an example of this, text accompanying the image of the dancing children at Codrington is congratulatory, a representation of Britain's (narrow) ethical commitment to educating Afro-Caribbean youth in the years following enslavement. The author does name a couple of other ethical obligations, namely that "substantial rations of meat and other provisions were given to the labourers and old people of the Codrington estates," filtering material concerns through older ideas of benevolent enslavement.[21] The recipients are formerly enslaved people still working for little pay in the working sugar mill on the estate. The focus, however, is on championing Rawle for his "zealous exertion in the cause of Negro education," pointing to the "700 children" in attendance at the celebration as evidence of his success (the mixed feelings in his letters notwithstanding).[22] This emphasis on colonial education fits with Sinnema's suggestion that the paper encourages conventional and limited rather than radical and far-reaching solutions to inequality.

The choice to show Afro-Caribbean children enjoying a party rather than learning in a classroom is nonetheless unusual in its departure from the ideal of the hard-laboring schoolchild (discussed in chapter 4). The author comments on the "playground" as an important "educational department," perhaps trying to reconcile the school's interest in bodily discipline under Rawle's leadership with the children's physical acuity in what is largely an extracurricular space.[23] The depiction of the children's movements means, however, that alternative ethical perspectives are represented that deviate from the paper's moderate and conciliatory form of ethics, though their meanings are likely only accessible to an informed audience that does not strongly overlap with the main audience reading the paper.[24] The act of hanging the image on the wall of the Codrington archive brings the image closer to such an audience—as well as to researchers. Being open to the unexpected appearance of this image in the archive helped me absorb how the Afro-Caribbean music and dance contain embedded ethical meanings.

Although dancing presents challenges to scholars due to its ephemerality, dancing is never limited to one performance—or, in the case of the Codrington image, one (not-fully-informed) viewer's drawing of one moment in a performance. It is an ongoing practice. While the accompanying article in the *Illustrated London News* speaks of the dances as "amusing" activities and "races" that form part of the children's physical education, the children's movements have connections to longer-established holidays and dances that express Afro-Caribbean worldviews, as well as histories of resistance. Celebrations on the Codrington campus date from the time of enslavement. The basic form of the school celebration likely derives from the Harvest Home, which Jerome S. Handler and Charlotte J. Frisbie suggest was a holiday based on "the termination of the sugar cane harvest."[25] The holiday builds on both British and West African traditions and continues in the contemporary Barbadian festival called Crop Over. The earliest reference to the Harvest Home, Handler and Frisbie note, was on the "Codrington plantations," which would become the college.[26] The SPG, they claim, established the holiday around 1820—notably, within the 100-year period celebrated by the anniversary fete—as part of "an ameliorative policy in slave management and treatment."[27] But despite its function for enslavers as a way to ease the dejection of enslavement and prevent uprisings, Marcia Burrowes points out that the Harvest Home "was creolized by the many African-Barbadian Masquerade Traditions," which used music and dance to express Afro-Caribbean religious and social beliefs.[28] Holiday traditions, she argues, provided rare opportunities for enslaved people "to honour their ancestors," "perform the rituals for their dead," and express "world views and experiences that went beyond the dehumanising realities of slavery."[29]

Afro-Caribbean dance, a varied and multilayered set of traditions with more facets than are possible to unpack here, often takes the shape of "danced religion" and "embodied wisdom" in Brenda Dixon Gottschild's words, sources of knowledge and ethical perspectives at cross-purposes with British educational efforts, with their emphasis on orderly movement and hierarchy.[30] More specifically, the basic structure of a circle dance, which some girls perform in the Codrington image, references ways of knowing, being, and creation deriving from West African cultures, which democratically make room for contributions from various participants. As Gottschild puts it:

> In Africanist performance the circle reigns . . . The circle stands in contrast to the fourth-wall, proscenium stage of Europeanist performance that emerged from the medieval Christian mass and continues today in the tradition of the concert stage. In proscenium form . . . [t]he energy and focus are targeted in one direction: toward the stage, by the spectators, and to the house, by the performers. Where the circle rules, there is an abundance of energy, vitality, flexibility, and potential . . . [T]his is a democracy of structure that is characteristic of Africanist-based performance modes.[31]

Interestingly given Gottschild's comparison, an image appearing on the same page as the Codrington fete in the *Illustrated London News* shows a "concert at Her Majesty's theatre," with the precise European aesthetic she describes—perhaps, again, a manifestation of the paper's effort at balance.[32] Harewood and Hunte connect the circle-dancing tradition in Barbados to dances "where slaves would gather in a large circle; though everyone would move to the music, those who wished to dance entered the circle created by the crowd."[33] This dynamic promotes a relational connection between individuals (with their diverse ways of expression) and their community (with its shared ethos of cultural sustenance and resistance). Alan Lomax (who collected Caribbean children's games in the late 1950s), J. D. Elder, and Bess Lomax Hawes record multiple versions of such a circle dance in which a "brown girl" does her own motion, then hugs or dances with another child, who then takes her place.[34]

Another type of movement appearing in the image, stilt-walking, has "been a part of tribal dance ceremonies in Africa for as far back as records go," according to Roy Maloy, who notes that "one of the earliest references to stilt walking in African tribal life still survives to this day; known as the Moko Jumbie."[35] The Moko Jumbie, a protective stilt-walking figure appearing in Trinidadian Carnival, which Burrowes compares to Crop Over in Barbados, is often danced by children. With roots in West Africa, the Moko Jumbie represents ancestors or deities meant to tower over and protect the people and land, interceding with the spiritual world and performing powerful acts that are, in Maloy's words, "unexplainable to the human eye."[36] Some of the spirits embodied in this tradition have ethical significance as mediators of human concerns. According to Patricia T. Alleyne-Dettmers, drawing from the work of Molly Ahye, "In contemporary Trinidadian Carnival the word jumbie signifies a dead spirit, while Moko 'according to oral tradition . . . is known as the god of Vengeance. On the other hand, there is Omoko, an Ibo Ancestor spirit who is known as an appeaser of disputes.'"[37]

The idea of the stilt dancer as a mythical protector fits with other traditions of quasi-mythical figures engaging in ethical action to protest harm to Afro-Caribbean people, such as Nanny and Queen Mary (who both continue to be embodied in different ways). Alleyne-Dettmers notes that current performers talk about "taking on the actual spirit of the persona embodied by the costume," which she argues dates back to a time when enslaved people attempted "to literally come out of themselves to confront the mask of the oppressor."[38] This rebellious spirit was not limited to dancing; Susan Harewood and John Hunte argue that the Harvest Home and other dance festivals "gave slaves the opportunities to come together and plot rebellion."[39] As an acknowledgment of this, as well as an expression of colonizers' paranoia, musical activities including drumming have been banned at various points throughout the Caribbean.[40]

With limited information available about how the dancing children understood the fete depicted in the Codrington image, it is unclear whether its description of the dances as mere "amusements" is a misunderstanding on the part of the British writer, a reflection of how dances were appropriated in the educational environment, or an indication that dances were replaced by versions that educators considered safe. But even if the children were not doing authentically African dances at the pictured celebration, their activities attest to skills developed outside of the school context. Stilt walking does not happen in a day—and racing would have been impossible without prior experience. Furthermore, these movements were not excised by schooling; they resonate with Afro-Caribbean traditions that persist.

Children, indeed, remain an important part of the stilt-walking troupes that dance the Moko Jumbie figures in Trinidad, usually learning from adults outside of a school context. Alleyne-Dettmers reads their involvement in these traditions as a way to "configure their own sense of history and heritage, thereby forging a sense of identity for themselves" and becoming "elevated."[41] In one example that she considers, child dancers use images of fish to reclaim the Atlantic Ocean as "the medium for transcendence of the ordinary world to the realm of the extraordinary."[42] As one child performer of the Trinidadian Moko Jumbie puts it, "Being in the air" is to "have a sense of being free and knowing that anything is possible because I could walk up high."[43]

Combining these reflections with Fred Moten's arguments in *The Universal Machine* (2018) and *The Undercommons* (2013), we can understand historical and current Afro-Caribbean dancing as another answer to the ethical problem of suffering and as "study," which he defines as collective, creative, and critical interactions before and beyond formal education:

Study is what you do with other people. It's talking and walking around with other people, working, dancing, suffering, some irreducible convergence of all three, held under the name of speculative practice . . . The point of calling it "study" is to mark that the incessant and irreversible intellectuality of these activities is already present. These activities aren't ennobled by the fact that we now say, "oh, if you did these things in a certain way, you could be said to be have been studying." To do these things is to be involved in a kind of common intellectual practice. What's important is to recognize that that has been the case—because that recognition allows you to access a whole, varied, alternative history of thought.[44]

What kind of study does dancing allow? We cannot answer for the historical child dancers in the Codrington image, but dancing, as with other kinds of study, offers possibilities for "refuge, joy, and resilience."[45] Study is also a potent source of relational ethics; a description by the School of Commons suggests that "reserves of compassion . . . emerge from this kind of study."[46]

Many of my reflections about the image so far take us out of the archive, but this is what relational openness does; it makes room to follow threads, to connect with what others are telling us. Zeroing in on the act of archiving, though, presents another opportunity to consider relationality in my research. My insights about this image depend on an unseen act by an unknown librarian or archivist who decided to frame and hang the piece. Although my persistent efforts to learn more about who hung the image were not fruitful, it makes sense to consider that the person likely falls into the 90 percent of Barbados residents who descend from enslaved people. Even so, the unknowability reinforces Derrida's point that the archive does not capture a point of origin but rather traces and potentials that are left behind. The image's presence in the archive reminds us that, as a place of multiplicity and difference, the archive can be a space of ethics in which we look for and listen to the perspectives of others.[47] We cannot know this specific person's intentions, but we can make observations about how the image's new context brings into play different meanings than it does on the pages of the *Illustrated London News.*

As a point of departure, we might read this act of archiving through the lens Ellen Gruber Garvey proposes in *Writing with Scissors* (2012) for analyzing scrapbooking, a tradition in which people "collected, concentrated, and critiqued accounts from a press that they did not own, to tell their own stories."[48] Garvey's account interestingly dates the advent of scrapbooking to the decade of the 1850s when the *Illustrated London News* image was created, though it is likely this particular image was hung at a later time given its persistence today. A major element of "clipping and saving the contents of periodicals," Garvey notes, is "a form of active reading that shifts the line between reading and writing. Readers become the agents who make or remake the meaning and significance of their saved items."[49] Those who "write with scissors" change the audience, decide what to save and leave out, and create new juxtapositions that unlock hidden meanings. They are unconventional as archivists, in that their actions do not only preserve but also destroy, yet this can draw our attention to the selective politics of archives in general.

The person who hung the image preserves the title from the *Illustrated London News,* but the celebratory paragraph about Rawle is removed, meaning that the children's dancing is no longer described as part of the college's physical education and does not feature in a celebration of white intervention. Bright colors are applied to the dancing children's clothing, making them stand out as the central players, and their skin is colored brown, where whiteness is signified by a lack of color, perhaps indicating a lack of interest in the white figures. The main representation of colonial authority is a white teacher (probably Rawle) wearing a suit and mortarboard (colored black) in the foreground of the image, who condescendingly touches the head of a young girl.

This foregrounding of girlhood is striking in light of discourses of respectability around Black girls that have surfaced throughout my study. As Baker shows, the moralization of dance movements in the Caribbean frequently targets women and girls owing to sexualized and racialized notions of degradation, likely responding to the ways that women represent control over the future.[50] In the framed version, the girl's dress has been colored to match the blue dresses of the girls in the circle behind her, giving her added visual weight, as well as an implied connection to the democratic and communitarian potentials of the circle dance, which become an alternative to the hierarchy implied in the teacher's gesture.

Just as scrapbookers repurpose images and passages for new audiences, putting the framed image in the library of what is now a theological seminary serving primarily Afro-Caribbean students means that it addresses an audience more likely to have a context for understanding the children's movements than the white readers of the *News*, including the ability to perceive continuities with the contemporary Crop Over festival and its "celebration of life, heritage and Barbadian culture."[51] By framing the newspaper image, the unknown librarian has changed the image's ephemerality into (relative) permanence. Where in the *Illustrated London News*, the dancing is only one image of many that will be consumed and discarded quickly by many readers, in this new context, the news is discarded and the dancing preserved. In Garvey's words, the librarian has transformed "trash to riches and power, or at least to authority."[52]

At the same time, there are significant differences between a cut-out image on a wall and in a scrapbook. Putting the image in a public space is different from putting it in a personal album, in that it invites a greater number of viewers, who will forge various kinds of relationships to the historical subjects, the forms of ethics they represent, and the traditions that they embody. One possibility, given that the image appears on the wall of a school, is that this act of archiving has pedagogical implications, which work against the narratives of failure with which I began this conclusion. It is possible to read putting the children's dancing on the wall as part of a history of appropriation of their activities by the educational institution. However, I choose to read it as a validation of the children's dancing as a tradition of knowledge and ethical practice that was not (and could not be) fully recorded by the *News* writer and illustrator. Rather than attempting to control Afro-Caribbean children's movements, as Rawle claims he attempted to do, the unknown librarian invites their extracurricular forms of embodiment into the school environment, granting them enduring significance, including as preparation for ministering to an Afro-Caribbean population in a contemporary context.

A Children's Archive of Justice and Injustice

Although we know little about the Codrington librarian who chose to frame the image of the dancing children, we can probably assume that they were not a child when they made this choice. Materials related to children frequently appear in archives, especially of educational organizations, but children are usually not the archivists. As Mahshid Mayar points out, most records are produced by adults *about* or *for* children, rather than *by* children.[53] When materials are produced by children, they are often "records of childhood that have been created by children but for adults, ranging from records of how children fared in school science projects or at written exams and how they coped with work in factories or as newsboys to evidence that suggests that they practiced spelling in their diaries—practices and products that were often exacted, regulated, and ultimately evaluated by adults."[54] The materials I discuss in this section—Anansi stories drawn from a group of nearly 5,000 tales collected in the 1930s by 1,124 Jamaican schoolchildren for a story contest run by missionary and Jesuit priest Joseph J. Williams—fall into this category of texts created *by* children *for* adults. Yet the colonial setting introduces further complexity, as the children are navigating the expectations of adults inside and outside of school. Having encountered versions of the tales told by adults in their homes and communities, they are asked to translate those tales in the school environment. The children make choices that show their investment both in preserving and creatively interpreting the tales, making them archivists of a sort; meanwhile their renditions frequently diverge from schoolish expectations.

At Williams's request, local teachers assigned the writing project and gathered stories from students at ninety-seven Jamaican schools, religious and governmental, then sent them to Williams in Kingston or Boston for judging. First a student and then a teacher of anthropology, Williams was motivated to run the contest for his own research on Jamaican folklore, which he conducted largely for the purpose of outlining a holy war in which God and the devil were competing for souls. In *Psychic Phenomena of Jamaica* (1834), he interprets many Jamaican folk practices as devil worship.[55] This was an underlying belief shaping many missionaries' claims of educational failure—and it is striking that Williams solicited materials from schoolchildren as part of his research. His investments suggest that a "battle over childhood and youth" remains "at the heart of the colonial enterprise."[56]

As this archive represents stories that are varied in their telling, it resists the standardization and universalization inherent within colonial education. However, in discussing this archive, we should not forget that Williams is its compiler and organizer. His oversight is reflected in the ways that teachers in Jamaica packaged the stories, which express worry about educational deficiencies. One teacher writes that Williams has "roused the children to action," indicating concern about the children's lack of engagement in school prior to the contest.[57] Others suggest that the stories do not rise to the children's potential, providing reasons for elements that fall short of school standards, for instance that any deficiencies reflect the storytellers, referred to as nanas or grandmothers. A teacher at the Ocho Rios school writes, "Observe that in keeping with the children's idea that the 'Nanas' did not know English at all, they have not paid much attention to punctuation, etc."[58] Another teacher remarks that one child's stories are "close to the local style of narration" to explain its use of "apparent monotonous repetition."[59]

Most stories include Jamaican patois, contrasting with school lessons that derived mostly from British curricula in standard English. As Cynthia James notes, the occasional folk stories that "found their way into West Indian children's readers" were stripped of "the cultural and stylistic features that are inherent in their Creole orality" and rendered in Standard English to emphasize "functional literacy objectives."[60] Reflecting this trend, the teachers' excuses indicate that they think the children's (apparently assertive) decision to use dialect and ungrammatical prose is not what Williams is expecting. Some include glossaries in their letters to explain words the students have left untranslated. For his part, Williams does not explain his prize decisions, other than to say that he will give additional prizes to stories he has not yet encountered. This suggests that he was open to diversity, if only because it enhanced his own study of the tales.

Because of its size and diversity, this archive needs multiple scholars, particularly those with a cultural relationship to African-derived tales, to unpack the many tales it includes—and I hope that the following analysis of just a few tales will entice others to work with the collection more deeply. As a starting observation, the stories present a rich landscape of memories, values, ideas, and strategies presented to young people outside of school and remembered within it. Contrasting with the worry among teachers that the tales fall short of school standards, the writing constitutes an abundant record of intellect, expressive talent, critical awareness, and ethical thinking. Although we cannot say that the children have acted as archivists in a strict sense, as the stories are held in Williams's papers, their decisions have shaped the archive. Even if they might have been motivated, in part, by Williams's promise to give prizes to unique stories, their refusal to standardize, explain, or clarify the stories amplifies their variability and diversity, as well as their evasion of universal meanings.

Although the stories have no doubt been changed because of the necessity of translating improvisational performances involving storytellers and audiences with cultural understanding into static prose, they retain qualities of improvisation, especially when taken together. The interplay between recurring elements and creative changes signals a culture that values relationality and uses basic story structures to respond to the specific needs of a given situation or group of people. As I will discuss, the variations reflected in this archive not only refuse the idea of a colonial master narrative in a general sense but specifically take aim at the simplified versions of ethics taught and enforced by colonial educational and justice systems, such as ethical codes that uniformly condemn actions like lying and stealing but do not take enslavement and the lasting inequalities of colonial society into account.

The stories, as told by the children, indeed contain high degrees of "anarchy," a quality Emily Murphy associates with children's archives to describe their frequent blurring of boundaries that adults (at least in a colonial or school setting) might consider distinct.[61] Some of the ideas that get blurred in the children's Anansi renditions are social and antisocial behavior, destruction and creation, justice and injustice. The blurring is largely consistent with the tradition of Anansi tales told by adults outside of school, though we can identify the young tellers' commitment to the anarchy by noting that it was probably not fully welcome in the school environment. The actions of the Anansi character, in particular, do not cohere with the ethics taught in colonial schools, as he misleads and defrauds others, though usually for survival and sustenance. James notes that school texts appropriated the stories to "depict Anansi as a lazy cheat, who took advantage of weaker creatures, and thrived on eating at the expense of others."[62]

The children's renditions do not generally pass judgment on Anansi but invite us to read his actions as remnants of strategies of resistance developed during enslavement, a context signaled by their use against characters called "buckra" (slang for "white man"), "massa," or "gentleman." As Sage Adia Swaby writes, "Anansi's tricks worked against enslavers, plantation owners, and Jamaica's colonial government. His tricks were utilized by enslaved Jamaican people to push back against their inhumane treatment and resist the plantation structure."[63] Drawing from Ropo Sekoni's analysis of relational dynamics between trickster characters and audiences, Swaby points out that trickster stories invite a full range of responses, including the rejection of antihumanitarian behavior as well as identification with the trickster as a "victim of circumstances" who, through a willingness to transgress, finds inventive ways to challenge the status quo.[64]

A motif of characters consuming each other, as James mentions, is pervasive in the Anansi tales, resembling the consumption-driven atmosphere of Atlantic enslavement as portrayed in *The Lobster's Voyage to the Brazils* (1808) (discussed in chapter 1). As in *The Lobster's Voyage*, the objectification of others through consumption threatens ethical relationality—a bleak situation that is nonetheless played for humor—but in the Anansi stories collected by the children, what looks at first like unethical behavior on the part of the trickster often yields a shaky form of hope or resilience, tied not to immediate access to justice but to the ability to reimagine or reshape the world. In a story written/collected by B. Lorrell, age fifteen, Anansi tells some young fish that he will cure their blind mother using a spell but eats her instead, leaving only the bones.[65] The relentless focus on eating—including of anthropomorphized characters—in this and other Anansi stories reflects the dehumanization of enslavement and draws our attention to the inversion of morality within the system of slavery. As Swaby points out, "Slaves were poorly fed and were not given food to support their survival; Anansi taught them that in order to live, they had to steal" and exploit others.[66]

As a result of this implied context, Anansi's actions are not wholly demonized. Although on its face the story warns against trusting folk magical practices, coinciding with colonial discouragement of such practices, it presents Anansi as a creator/destroyer with real magical powers, rather than an unambiguously villainous swindler. To "pay for their mother," Anansi tells the fish children he will help them collect wood to burn him in retribution but then tricks them into jumping into the river and ocean to avoid being caught by a fisherman.[67] Through this chicanery, the fish children lose their significance as parties seeking justice and instead become common fish. However, the tale ends with an explanation that this is how fresh and saltwater fish originated, rendering Anansi a paternal replacement for the fish mother. Swaby notes that in an African context Anansi's "disregard of [traditional] societal and communal ideals" means that he "unintentionally creates new ones," making the community more resilient.[68] In this situation, immediate justice is not achieved, but Anansi's transgressions result in a different kind of world, in which the fish children have innumerable progeny.

As the just-so ending of this tale demonstrates, informational lessons sometimes appear in Anansi stories, but the children's versions mostly lack the educational elaboration that James sees in later textbook versions of the tales. They instead use the consumption-driven society as a training ground to survive using wits and humor. Singing and dance, in particular, emerge as useful tools for challenging colonial ideas of justice, escaping punishment, and showing the pervasiveness of injustice through new variations on common themes. Analyzing singing and dancing in these stories can help imaginatively fill in some of the ideas that may have informed children's dancing at Codrington and elsewhere in the Caribbean.

Like Anansi's trickery in the fish story, singing and dancing appear as means to avoid punishment, but they also destabilize ethical frameworks developed in the context of colonization and enslavement, such as those emphasizing the rights of property. For instance, in a tale written/collected by N. Williams, age twelve, a group of animals including Crawfish, Candle-Fly, and Pigeon attempt to steal corn from Nana, an old woman (nanas, as mentioned previously, are named as the source of the tales).[69] When a watchman sees the animals on Nana's land, Candle-Fly and Pigeon take flight, leaving Crawfish to be caught and set aside for Nana's dinner. Although there is a logic of ethical retribution in the watchman's decision to punish Crawfish, hunger as a consumptive desire yields an unethical and objectifying logic whereby characters deny others' equal sentience, as well as their needs and desires, in favor of competition for resources. The tale, however, calls attention to how property, rationalized through cultivation, facilitates the unequal distribution of resources. This is a common theme throughout the collection, and many stories take aim at characters with greater resources labeled "buckra."

Perhaps because she is not a buckra, or enslaver, Nana does not eat Crawfish right away but takes him with her to the river to wash her dishes. Contrasting with the ending of *The Lobster's Voyage*, in which Lobster escapes the stew pot only because he is English, Crawfish escapes through cunning, which is possible because of Nana's willingness to engage with him in an unconventional, non-disciplinary way. He convinces her to put him by the waterside, singing a humorous song about how "A pigeon bring me ya [here], Crawfish never thief."[70] As we will see, songs excusing oneself of theft and blaming others instead constitute a genre. Although the song seems like bald-faced mendacity at first, it draws attention to the complicated ethics of the situation; Crawfish has not actually stolen anything, as he was seen before they took any corn, so punishing him is unjust. Additionally, Pigeon contributed to the situation but escaped punishment, merely because he could fly and Crawfish could not. It would not be fair to punish Crawfish alone—and this applies also to the institutional legal apparatuses of the colonial justice system, which punish those who are caught regardless of the specific context and greater circumstances.

Although it is not stated explicitly, the inequality between Pigeon and Crawfish also impacts the animals' relationship with Nana; as a human, Nana has property and food, along with the rights and the ability to guard it, where the animals do not. Aiming to change this situation, Crawfish presents the song not merely to deny culpability but to "cheer [Nana's] heart," substituting the unequal competition over resources with an offer of emotional connection. In a moment not driven by competition, Nana dances alongside Crawfish. This allows him to dive into the river and hide under a rock (a subtle lesson about the Crawfish's habitat and its possible origin). This action reveals the song to be (in some sense) a trick, but it is unclear whether Nana regrets allowing Crawfish to make his well-earned escape, especially as Nana's name implies that she may be the source of the story.

The theme of singing and dancing to escape punishment stretches across the tales in the collection, appearing most commonly in a type of story told/collected by several children about Anansi stealing sheep from another buckra character. A similar story was also collected by Martha Beckwith in 1924 as "Tiger's Sheep-skin Suit," told by George Parkes of Mandeville, Jamaica.[71] Reinforcing Derrida's reading of the archive as a space of difference, the story, as told by multiple children, does not take a standard shape but exhibits creativity and improvisation, suggesting that a significant element may be its adaptability. In addition to some basic story elements, music and dancing are focal points, signaling an improvisational ethos. As with the Crawfish story, a running theme is a critique of the colonial justice system and how its universal ethics pin guilt on individuals without taking the unjust social structure into account.

A representative version of the sheep stealing tale is told/collected by I. Johnson, age twelve and a half (notably, Johnson also tells another version of the Talking Eggs story included in Matthew Lewis's 1834 *Journal of a West India Proprietor*, discussed in chapter 2). A white man has begged Anansi to care for his sheep, but Anansi decides to steal and eat some of the flock. When the white man notices some sheep have been eaten, Anansi offers to help find the culprit. Anansi proposes that he give a ball. Meanwhile, Anansi enlists Brother Monkey to play music for the event, for which he will need a suit. Anansi dresses Monkey in a sheepskin. At the ball, Anansi plays a song in which he reveals, "All de time me da tell bredda Monkey mind de Baca dem sheep," which is corroborated by Monkey playing a song, "Yunkutunkotung a monkey got de [s]kin."[72] As a result, the white man punishes Monkey; "tak' him raza' an' cut off him head."[73]

Music is a key part of this tale type, sometimes involving a drum, other times a tambourine or fiddle.[74] As the two friends are playing music and dancing at the ball, either Anansi or his friend sings a song, usually involving non-lexical vocals (sometimes mimicking the different instruments the characters play), that point to the sheepskin and signal that the friend is the thief. In this version, the friend is executed. In others, he is arrested and jailed.

Echoing the Crawfish story, as well as the 1924 Jamaican Cinderella story discussed in chapter 2, the central character's actions seem to be villainous at first not only from the perspective of colonial educators and law enforcement but also from a broader ethical stance of treating others fairly. Anansi not only steals sheep but also dishonestly blames his friend and, in Johnson's version, gets that friend killed. However, if we view Anansi as the victim of bad circumstances, he becomes more sympathetic, and the story's critique is revealed. That the main antagonist is a buckra (elsewhere, "massa" or a "gentleman") means that the story harks back to unequal relations of enslavement. The white man has begged—or coerced—Anansi to take care of the sheep, with no renumeration mentioned. It is therefore implied that Anansi takes the sheep partially out of necessity (some versions of the story make a differentiation between the meat and the skin, which Anansi can easily produce for the clothes because it is left over). Reading between the lines, we can posit that he steals because he has no other means of getting sustenance. When the white man seeks justice for the stolen sheep, Anansi is left with no option that would take his exploitation into account and indict the white man for the unequal division of labor and property. Indeed, if Anansi were to accept blame and punishment, it would seem as if justice were done from the perspective of the colonial system, but this would only compound the injustice.

Instead, Anansi cleverly draws attention to the unjust societal structure and invites critical reflection by showing how easy it is to single out and punish an innocent person, based on appearances no less. The singing and dancing, as expressive forms responding to a specific moment and circumstances, signal that Anansi's actions respond to the whole complicated ethical terrain of enslavement and its legacies. Anansi's trickery may not yield justice in the moment, but it has the potential to give rise to a truer execution of justice, as it calls attention to the flaws in the system and invites listeners to ponder how they can challenge it. Anansi ultimately makes a point about the relational interconnectedness of people and the ways that the system produces criminal acts; it is unjust to operate a justice system that singles out an individual person to be punished for stealing when inequality and the legacies of enslavement are the true causes.

The shift from tricking the Buckra to challenging an unjust system is subtle in most versions of the story, but a version told/collected by O. Bartley develops this theme by having Anansi rescue his friend from the miscarriage of justice. As an indication of the adaptability of the story, this version involves a friend named Dog rather than Monkey (other versions cast Tiger or Ram Goat in this role). After Anansi's song leads to Dog being arrested, Dog cries out for help, which leads to the following ending:

> Anancy say . . . me we make them let you go. So when them go a court get one lime and dig out the gut and catch one magich fly and shut up in the lime. When them try dog . . . Anancy open the lime the magich make noise the Judge could not hear him ears so him get vex and drive all of them out of court. So them say dog make obeah and it dey till now.[75]

This version of story targets colonial institutions as sites for injustice. Anansi's trick with the lime fits into a tradition of Obeah medico-religious practices that Danielle N. Boaz argues were used for resistance and thereafter suppressed by the colonial government. During Tacky's Revolt, a slave rebellion in 1760s Jamaica, Obeah men used a spell to convince the enslaved rebels that they were impenetrable to bullets, leading to the criminalization of the spell ingredients by colonial authorities.[76] In this fantastic version, the magical lime produces long-lasting results. In addition to allowing Dog and Anansi to escape punishment, the effects of the Obeah remain there "until now"—though it is unclear whether they have reformed the system entirely.

The multiple variations of the story imply that there is no overarching solution, failing wholesale change, but present creative responses to injustice as it involves individuals in specific circumstances. The various friends evoked in the tale—Monkey, Dog, Tiger, Ram Goat—seem to suggest that injustice can land on anyone in the unjust system run by the buckra. One variation explains that Anansi blames Ram Goat for the sheep stealing because he wants his house.[77] In others, jealousy is the motivation for targeting a particular friend; for instance, Dog is a better dancer, and more women flirt, kiss, or dance with him than Anansi. Sometimes the friend is involved in the stealing, but in a comparatively minor capacity.[78] The miscarriage of justice unfolds differently each time. Parkes/Beckwith end with Tiger sentenced to ten years in prison and Anansi married to an enslaver's daughter, an ending that recalls the headless man's marriage to a princess in the story attributed to Goosee Shoo Shoo (discussed in chapter 2).[79] Johnson's version has Monkey decapitated by the white man, an ending that recalls the *beginning* of Goosee's story, which I interpret as using headlessness to convey the injustice of being born into enslavement. Another version, by A. Hart, age fourteen, has Dog lop off his own tail out of shame, which is a lighter sentence with just-so appeal but also perhaps a metaphor for a lack of wholeness.[80] Positive outcomes are possible; the Ram Goat version compensates for Anansi's theft of Ram Goat's house by having him return it in the end.

These outcomes call for storytellers to stay vigilant and to use the ethical resources at their disposal, which, as framed by the story, are musical. In opposition to the universalized system of justice favored by the colonial government and enslavers, dancing and singing become tools for seeking a relational, context-driven form of justice. Notably, the songs that Anansi and his friend sing in the story variations have different words and sounds, which share common features (non-lexical vocalizations and/or nonsense syllables) but do not overlap. The sheer variety of lyrics, usually presented as song fragments without any accompanying scores, remind us, again, that the archive is not an origin and that some of the meaning of the stories relies on their performance to specific listeners within a specific situation and cultural context. There are undoubtedly meanings connected to the songs that remain elusive, at least to this researcher. But one reading of the diversity of songs is that this invites improvisation on the part of each teller, including the young tellers of this archive, prompting them to use their own sounds to create the song that Anansi sings and to embody his quest for a truer form of justice. This means that the fight against injustice can continue.

This book opens with the slave trade and the beginning of an ethical crisis. Finding ways to respond to the diverse and varied impacts of this crisis on individuals, groups, and institutions is important because the crisis is not over. The efforts at sugarcoating and the pathological alternatives to ethical engagement that I identify in this book persist, some in the form of the afterlives of slavery as defined by Saidiya Hartman: "If slavery persists . . . it is not because of an antiquarian obsession with bygone days or the burden of a too-long memory, but because black lives are still imperiled and devalued by a racial calculus and a political arithmetic that were entrenched centuries ago."[81] Others persist in a pervasive insularity, an expectation to not have to engage with others—to not be invaded by them, as some of the sugar boycotters (discussed in chapter 3) began to imagine—or the expectation (discussed in chapter 5) that people dealing with oppression conform to an Anglocentric universality, color blindness, sameness, or respectability. Ethics must then also be an ongoing pursuit because treating others ethically means being open to new needs and as yet unacknowledged differences. We might take cues from the variability and differences in these archives as we seek new ways to respond to myriad forms of injustice in the world that result from enslavement and colonization. It is my hope that this book inspires multiple pathways to ethical action.

Introduction • Enslavement and the Relational Ethics
of Children's Literature

1. *Port of Spain (Trinidad) Gazette*, Aug. 5, 1836, 1.

2. Ibid.

3. The simultaneous rise of children's literature and the growing reliance on enslavement means that, as Karen Sands O'Connor points out, "the rise of children's literature in Britain and the rise of anti-racism campaigning are tied together"—though a minority of children's books took part in antiracist efforts. See O'Connor, *British Activist Authors Addressing Children of Colour* (Bloomsbury, 2022), 18. See Deborah de Rosa, *Domestic Abolitionism and Juvenile Literature: 1830–1865* (State University of New York Press, 2003) for discussion of abolitionist literature for children.

4. Wilma King, *Stolen Childhood: Slave Youth in Nineteenth-Century America* (Indiana University Press, 1997), xx.

5. William Boelhower, *Atlantic Studies: Prospects and Challenges* (Louisiana State University Press, 2019), 31. The Atlantic world represents a vast complex of relations. As Bernard Bailyn summarizes, "By mid-century 1,000 ships a year were involved in England's transatlantic traffic," including ships transporting slaves as well as "459 ships across the Atlantic to transport colonial goods," which included children's books in English. See Bailyn, *Atlantic History: Concept and Contours* (Harvard University Press, 2005), 86. These vessels and goods were the material means through which the Atlantic world, as David Armitage theorizes, came to function as "a particular zone of exchange and interchange, circulation and transmission." Armitage, "Three Concepts of Atlantic History," in *The British Atlantic World, 1500–1800* (Palgrave Macmillan, 2002), 16. For discussion of how childhood gets transformed in its connection with enslavement, see Anna Mae Duane, *Suffering Childhood in Early America: Violence, Race, and the Making of the Child Victim* (University of Georgia Press, 2010).

6. See Colleen Vasconcellos, *Slavery, Childhood, and Abolition in Jamaica, 1788–1838* (University of Georgia Press, 2015); and Sasha Turner, *Contested Bodies: Pregnancy, Childrearing and Slavery in Jamaica* (University of Pennsylvania Press, 2017).

7. Vasconcellos, *Slavery, Childhood, and Abolition*; and Turner, *Contested Bodies*.

8. Ebony Elizabeth Thomas, "Shadow Books: Considering Enslavement and Its Legacy in Children's Literature," *School Library Journal*, January 2022, 27.

9. Ibid.

10. It is interesting given its rich—and thorny—ethical landscape that children's literature of the early period has been largely neglected by two otherwise excellent publications on children's literature's ethics, Lisa Sainsbury, *Ethics in British Children's Literature: Unexamined Life* (Bloomsbury, 2013) (focusing on postwar children's books); and Claudia Mills, ed., *Ethics and Children's Literature* (Routledge, 2014) (primarily covering post–Golden Age literature, though with attention to earlier influences).

11. Ebony Elizabeth Thomas, Debbie Reese, and Kathleen T. Horning, "Much Ado About a 'Fine Dessert': The Cultural Politics of Representing Slavery in Children's Literature," *Journal of Children's Literature* 42, no. 2 (2016): 6–17.

12. "Relation" and "relationality" are multivalent terms that have produced a growing body of scholarship sometimes describing itself as a "relational turn." A focus on relation means framing a phenomenon in terms of the interactions its creates or requires between various actors. A framework of relationality typically, though not always, adds that relation yields ethical demands.

13. Early books for children were produced and popularized during a time when the dominant ethical systems were coming to imagine themselves as universal. Prominent forms of Christian ethics (sometimes called "virtue ethics") claimed that humans could develop moral character because they were made in the image of God, while Enlightenment approaches outlined by thinkers like John Locke, Jean-Jacques Rousseau, and Immanuel Kant (sometimes called "universal ethics") focused on reason as an all-purpose way to determine ethical actions. Building on truth claims about God, the human mind, and nature, these ethical approaches argue that the duty to act ethically stems from unchangeable, divinely engineered circumstances, such as the creation of the universe by a Christian God, the arrangement of nature, and the endowment of humans with reason. Although they emphasize freedom, universal reason-based ethics have been insufficient for addressing Atlantic slavery and its legacies. Kant, Locke, and Rousseau fail to address the realities of British enslavement but instead use slavery as a metaphor to describe monarchical tyranny and European work conditions. As Huaping Lu-Adler has shown, "The passages involving slavery" in Kant's *Groundwork of Morals*, "either do not concern modern, race-based chattel slavery or at best suggest that Kant mentioned it as a cautionary tale for labor practices in Europe." Lu-Adler, "Kant and Slavery—or Why He Never Became a Racial Egalitarian," *Critical Philosophy of Race* 10, no. 2 (2022): 263–264. Locke in *Two Treatises of Government* (1689) uses enslavement metaphorically in his claim that "slavery is so vile and miserable an estate of man . . . that it is hardly to be conceived that an Englishman, much less a gentleman, should plead for it." John Locke, *Two Treatises of Government*, ed. Ian Shapiro (Yale University Press, 2003), 7. Rousseau condemned "slavery" as a concept but was silent on race-based enslavement. See John Christman, "Rousseau's Silence on Trans-Atlantic Slavery: Philosophical Implications," *European Journal of Philosophy* 30, no. 4 (2022): 1458–1472.

14. Although enslaved people quickly applied European ethical arguments about natural rights to their lives, many critics argue that universal rights discourses have failed to lead to full equality, because they are not truly inclusive. The continued violations of Black people's basic human rights by those who profess to be committed to universal rights led Franco-Caribbean philosopher Frantz Fanon to argue for an anticolonial ethics incorporating actions considered unethical from the perspective of a

Eurocentric universal ethics—namely, anticolonial violence. See Fanon, *The Wretched of the Earth* (Penguin, 1967). Sylvia Wynter points out that the rational model of humanity has been a way to "invent, label, and institutionalize . . . Black Africans as the physical referent of the projected irrational/subrational Human Other." Wynter, "Unsettling the Coloniality of Being/Power/Truth/Freedom," *CR: The New Centennial Review* 3, no. 3 (2003): 281–282. Scholars interested in children's rights, such as those included in *The Routledge Handbook of International Children's Rights Studies* (Routledge, 2015) argue that children too are othered by age-based restrictions on so-called universal rights. Yet Western children's literature is a product of universal ethical traditions. Many English-language children's books are driven by the promise to fulfill universal ethical goals by teaching young people, no matter their circumstances, to be good rational (and capitalist) citizens of the world as defined by Western liberal thought, a goal that reflects the legacies of colonialism and ongoing cultural imperialism. This universality competes, and interweaves, with children's literature's relational strands.

15. Parvati Raghuram, "Race and Feminist Care Ethics: Intersectionality as Method," *Gender, Place & Culture: A Journal of Feminist Geography* 5 (2019): 629, 617.

16. Sarada Balagopalan, "Precarity and the Question of Children's Relationalities," *Childhood* 28, no. 3 (2021): 329.

17. Simone Drichel, "Prospectus," *Relationality: A Symposium*, November 18–20, 2015.

18. Anne Helen Petersen, "White Celebrity and Rituals of Civility: Taylor Swift, Brittany Mahomes, Kate Middleton, and Culture Study," *Culture Study*, September 15, 2024. See also Daniel Coleman, *White Civility: The Literary Project of English Canada* (University of Toronto Press, 2006) for a discussion of how British ideas of white civility inform how people, including children, come to understand their relationships in a colonial context.

19. Robin DiAngelo, *White Fragility: Why It's So Hard for White People to Talk About Racism* (Beacon Press, 2018).

20. Lissa Paul, "The Enslaved in Late-Enlightenment Stories for Children: The Real and the Imaginary," *Transnational Books for Children 1750–1900*, ed. Charlotte Appel, Nina Christensen, and M. O. Grenby (John Benjamin, 2023), 334–355.

21. Emer O'Sullivan, *Comparative Children's Literature*, trans. Anthea Bell (Routledge, 2005), 70.

22. Édouard Glissant, *Poetics of Relation*, trans. Betsy Wing (University of Michigan Press, 1997). Betsy Nies and Melissa García Vega, eds., *Caribbean Children's Literature, Volume 1: History, Pedagogy, and Publishing* (University Press of Mississippi, 2023), 7.

23. Paul, "The Enslaved in Late-Enlightenment Stories," 336.

24. Fred Moten, *The Universal Machine (consent not to be a single being)* (Duke University Press, 2018).

25. See Martin, "Brown Girl Dreaming of a New ChLA," *The Lion and the Unicorn* 41, no. 1 (2017): 98–99.

26. Barbauld did not invent this form. It derives from catechisms and other books for a mixed-age audience. Penny Brown traces the evolution of the initially French form from adult to children's literature. See Brown, "'Girls Aloud': Dialogue as a Pedagogical Tool in Eighteenth-Century French Children's Literature," *The Lion and the Unicorn* 33 (2009): 202–218.

27. Jacqueline Rose, *The Case of Peter Pan, or The Impossibility of Children's Literature* (Macmillan, 1993), 53.

28. Kimberley Reynolds, *Children's Literature: A Very Short Introduction* (Oxford University Press, 2011), 116.

29. Significant contributions include work by O'Connor; Paul; and Marilisa Jiménez García, author of *Side by Side: US Empire, Puerto Rico, and the Roots of Youth Literature and Culture* (University of Mississippi Press, 2021); as well as Nies and Vega's two-volume edited collection, *Caribbean Children's Literature.*

30. Rose, *The Case of Peter Pan*, 1. For alternate theories, see Marah Gubar, "The Hermeneutics of Recuperation: What a Kinship-Model Approach to Children's Agency Could Do for Children's Literature and Childhood Studies," *Jeunesse: Young People, Texts, Cultures* 8, no. 1 (2016): 291–310.

31. Rose, *The Case of Peter Pan*, 2, 8–9. Karín Lesnik-Oberstein echoes this critique. See Lesnik-Oberstein, *Children's Literature: New Approaches*, ed. Lesnik-Oberstein (Palgrave, 2004), 4. Some scholars of color have argued that dismissing ethical questions about the books given to children as a legitimate form of scholarship fails to recognize the importance of this question for marginalized people. In early 2020, Gabrielle Owen posted a call for papers for an MLA session addressing the "ethical turn in children's literature and childhood studies," sparking a debate on the Syllabus Swap: Children's and YA Literature Facebook group about whether ethics was indeed a new focus in the field. Debbie Reese, whose work focuses on representations of Indigenous people, argued that children "are persons who take the contents personally. They can be thrilled by what they see but they can also be damaged," noting that her work has been unjustly criticized for this focus. Laura Jiménez concurred, noting that "the fact that readers' histories, culture, language, and identity matter [in determining how books impact them] has been talked about by marginalized scholars for years."

32. Marah Gubar, *Artful Dodgers: Reconceiving the Golden Age of Children's Literature* (Oxford, 2010).

33. Rose, *The Case of Peter Pan*, 2.

34. Ibid., 2.

35. Jessica Wen Hui Lim, "Barbauld's Lessons: The Conversational Primer in Late Eighteenth-Century British Children's Literature," *Journal for Eighteenth-Century Studies* 43, no. 1 (2020): 102.

36. John Locke, *Some Thoughts Concerning Education* (W. Baynes, 1800), 211. Kant also adds a relational component to his otherwise context-adverse ethics by claiming that young people can perceive the value of ethical righteousness by watching adults: "When one represents an upright action as it is carried out with a steadfast soul . . . separate from every intention for any advantage in this or in another world, it leaves far behind and eclipses every similar action which is affected even in the slightest with an alien incentive. Even moderately young children feel this impression, and one should never represent duty to them otherwise than this." Immanuel Kant, *Groundwork for the Metaphysics of Morals: With an Updated Translation, Introduction, and Notes*, translated by Allen W. Wood (Yale University Press, 2018), 46. Kant does not dwell on the relational foundation of ethics implied in this claim and overall emphasizes adult ethical deliberations rather than children's ethical learning.

37. See Marianna Papastephanou and Zelia Gregoriou, "Locke's Children? Rousseau

and the Beans (Beings?) of the Colonial Learner," *Studies in Philosophy and Education* 33, no. 5 (2014): 463–480.

38. John Wall points out that the field of ethics has largely neglected exploration of children as ethical subjects in favor of seeing them as ethical objects. See Wall, in "Childism: The Challenge of Childhood to Ethics and the Humanities" in *The Children's Table: Childhood Studies and the Humanities* (University of Georgia Press, 2013), 61. Looking at children not only as *objects* of ethical or unethical behavior on the part of adults, but also as ethical *subjects* and as *objects* within other children's ethical learning thus opens up new pathways in scholarship. Modern relational ethicists seem to create more space for children as ethical actors with their insistence that the foundations of ethical behavior are " 'pre-reflective,' 'pre-rational' and embodied." Marjan De Coster, "Towards a Relational Ethics in Pandemic Times and Beyond: Limited Accountability, Collective Performativity and New Subjectivity" in *Gender, Work, and Organization* 27, no. 5 (2020): 749. Scholars in childhood studies have made the argument for children's actions being ethically consequential along these lines. Robin Bernstein, for example, argues that white children living in the late nineteenth century, while not fully autonomous, act as bad ethical agents by using doll play to reproduce violent racial scripts. See Robin Bernstein, "Children's Books, Dolls, and the Performance of Race; or, The Possibility of Children's Literature," *PMLA: Publications of the Modern Language Association of America* 126, no. 1 (2011): 160–169. The ageist bias of philosophical discourse, however, has meant that children still often appear in modern discussions of ethics as objects of ethical behavior or metaphors for aspects of intersubjectivity, rather than as participants in ethical action. It is ultimately children's literature that explores the ethical potential of the child most fully, even as many books exploit the child's perceived limitations to foreclose ethical responsibility.

39. Clémentine Beauvais, *The Mighty Child: Time and Power in Children's Literature* (John Benjamins, 2015), 3.

40. Gabrielle Owen, *A Queer History of Adolescence: Developmental Pasts / Relational Futures* (University of Georgia Press, 2020), xvi.

41. Ibid., xvi.

42. Lim, "Barbauld's Lessons," 105.

43. Anna Laetitia Barbauld, *Lessons for Children, in Four Parts* (London, 1841), 76–77.

44. Lim, "Barbauld's Lessons," 106.

45. Barbauld, *Lessons for Children*, 75.

46. Ibid.

47. Joseph Addison, *The Spectator*, no. 69, May 19, 1711.

48. Addison's sentiment was popular in British culture and appears in other children's books, though often tempered with a more realistic sense of inequality. For example, Quaker reformer Priscilla Wakefield imagines a universally beneficent force directing trade: "Providence . . . leaves not the most obscure corner of the globe without its peculiar riches." Yet she argues that the effective functioning of trade depends on children's energetic entrance into economic activities due to global competition. See Wakefield, *Mental Improvement: Or the Beauties and Wonders of Nature and Art*, 4th ed. (Philadelphia: Benjamin Johnson, 1819), 13. For instance, she notes that the inventors of China pottery "are extremely secret, and so jealous of the eye of strangers,

that they will not allow the Europeans to go beyond the suburbs of the cities where factories are established" (152). Although this stereotype of the Chinese as possessing exotic knowledge is problematic, Wakefield provides a more accurate representation of actions that the British were taking on an international scale than Addison's fantastical vision of trade. Worried about the popularity of Chinese products like tea and silk—and the resulting unevenness of British and Chinese trade—the British used India as a base for spreading opium to China, leading to the First Opium War, events that prove Addison's vision of trade as creating worldwide peace to be naive at best. At other points, Wakefield acknowledges the impacts of enslavement, writing that Africans are "snatched from their own country, friends, and connections, by the hand of violence, and power" (74). Because trade cannot assuage inequality, Wakefield argues that global society must be structured in hierarchical relationships that promote feelings of mutual obligation in the face of economic disparities (138).

Anglican philanthropist Sarah Trimmer presents a pithier expression of the assumptions underlying Addison's vision: "Every country produces something that does not grow any where else." Trimmer, *An Easy Introduction to the Knowledge of Nature, and Reading the Holy Scriptures* (London: T. Longman and O. Rees, G. G. and J. Robinson, 1799), 89. Trimmer's text, however, does not suggest that this leads to reciprocity or peace; she writes that sugar causes enslaved Africans "undergo severe hardships" (100). She instructs her readers to respect differences: "You must not despise the people of other countries because they do not speak, act, and dress, as we do, for to them we appear as strange as they do to us" (90). Yet Trimmer's sequel reveals that caring for others, in a transatlantic context, could feed into colonial hierarchies. See Trimmer, *Sequel to Mrs. Trimmer's Easy Introduction to the Knowledge of Nature* (London: F. C. and J. Rivington, 1818), 47. She celebrates the end of the slave trade and advocates action to "improve the slaves already in our possession," asking her female child listener whether she would like to become a teacher in Jamaica. This response prioritizes English expectations that enslaved children learn virtue, rather than have needs mutually agreed upon through relationship.

49. The seeming reciprocity in Addison's statement presents a mythology that has been valuable to global capitalism: the idea that free trade allocates benefits in ways that will eventually be reciprocal. Adam Smith's well-known idea of the "invisible hand," in which participants in the market promote positive good without making a conscious effort, extends this basic notion that preexistent, largely unseen forces guide the operations of trade and produce positive effects.

50. Karl Marx and Friedrich Engels, *The Communist Manifesto*, ed. Jeffrey C. Issac (Yale University Press, 2012), 77.

51. Marx and Engels name the global circulation of literature, in which children's literature would play a key part, as one outcome of this exploitation: "The intellectual creations of individual nations become common property . . . from the numerous national and local literatures, there arises a world literature." Ibid., 64.

52. John Aiken and Anna Laetitia Barbauld, *Evenings at Home; Or, the Juvenile Budget Opened* (London: Cornish and Co., 1839), 445. This book was originally published in 1796 in multiple volumes.

53. Ibid., 163.

54. Ibid., 445.

55. See Ibid., 164.

56. Ibid., 446.

57. Ibid., 446–447.

58. Ibid., 447.

59. Ibid., 270.

60. Michelle Levy, "The Radical Education of *Evenings at Home*," in *Eighteenth-Century Fiction* 19, nos. 1/2 (2006–2007): 140.

61. Beauvais, *The Mighty Child*, 4.

62. Quoted in Mary Jeanette Moran, "Making a Difference: Ethical Recognition Through Otherness in Madeleine L'Engle's Fiction," *Ethics in Children's Literature*, eds. Claudia Mills and Claudia Nelson (Routledge, 2016), 76.

63. Wesley S. Jacques, "Reading Relational in Mildred D. Taylor: Toward a Black Feminist Care Ethics for Children's Literature," *Research on Diversity in Youth Literature* 2, no. 2 (2020): 7.

64. While the text's view of motherhood differs from feminist ethicists' view of caring maternal relations as strong grounds for relational ethical development, it supports Nel Noddings's point in *Caring: A Feminine Approach to Ethics and Moral Education* (University of California Press, 1984) that care as an ethical ideal can be diminished by education that discourages empathy. As I will return to in chapter 1, this feminization and racialization of bad care means that Day largely excuses Tommy's enslaver father for his son's behavior, downplaying the unethical everyday treatment of enslaved Africans.

65. Thomas Day, *The History of Sandford and Merton: A Work Intended for the Use of Children* (Philadelphia: William Young, 1793), 200.

66. Day was engaging in his own practical experiments by helping fellow pedagogue Richard Lovell Edgeworth educate his son.

67. John-Jacques Rousseau, *Émile; or, On Education*, translated by Barbara Foxley (Everyman Paperbacks, 1993), 10.

68. Rose, *The Case of Peter Pan*, 51.

69. Isaac Watts, *Divine Songs Attempted in Easy Language for the Use of Children* (Boston: Printed by S. Kneeland and T. Green, for D. Henchman, in Cornhill, 1730), 21.

70. Judith Butler, *Giving an Account of Oneself* (Fordham University Press, 2005), 50.

71. Ibid., 100–101.

72. Ibid., 101.

73. Day, *Sandford and Merton*, 52.

74. This tension between ethical standards and their effects converses with Smith's *Theory of Moral Sentiments* (1759), which offers an analysis of ethical decision making based on the operation of a "moral sense," defined quasi-relationally. The moral sense, Smith claims, derives from an individual's perception of society's reaction to their behavior, mediated by what he calls an "impartial spectator"—a hybrid universal-relational construction we might contrast with Virginia Held's relational ethics of care starting "with the moral claims of particular others." Adam Smith, *The Theory of Moral Sentiments*, ed. Knud Haakonssen (Cambridge University Press, 2002), 184, 30; Virginia Held, *The Ethics of Care: Personal, Political, and Global* (Oxford University Press, 2006), 10. Beyond this section, several passages strikingly emphasize Tommy "look[ing] foolish," to particularized (though stereotyped) global spectators, a topic Rose discusses at

length. For instance, although Tommy asserts that the Greenlanders are inferior to English gentlemen, Barlow imagines them scolding Tommy when he loses his temper because his friends laugh at his attempts to make a dogsled. See Day, *Sandford and Merton*, 222. Although Barlow romanticizes these international figures, in part to teach Tommy that knowledge of the world is a crucial acquisition to avoid weakness, Barlow's imagination of their reaction takes a small step toward accountability to specific others.

75. Although relational ethical approaches are most often linked to modern-day feminist care ethics, they have been in development for centuries in diverse forms. Some derive from moral sense-based ethical systems explored by David Hume, Hutcheson, and Smith, which reject reason as the ground for ethics and propose important roles for feelings, senses, and "natural virtues" such as benevolence. Others have roots in classical traditions such as stoicism, which imagines that people will develop their ethical consciousness by moving through concentric circles of care. For a discussion of the influence of Stoicism on early modern ethics, see Benjamin Parris, *Vital Strife: Sleep, Insomnia, and the Early Modern Ethics of Care* (Cornell University Press, 2022).

76. Jeremy Bentham, *Introduction to the Principles of Morals and Legislation* (Oxford: Clarendon Press, 1907), 1.

77. John Locke, *Some Thoughts Concerning Education* (London: Printed for A. and J. Churchill, 1693), 51–52. Locke argued against corporal punishment and rewards for this reason.

78. Day, *Sandford and Merton*, 247.

79. Ibid., 95–96. There is, of course, a vast scholarly critique of sentimental feeling as a response to enslavement, but this is not how Tommy ends up relating to the grateful Black. See Marcus Wood, *Slavery, Empathy, and Pornography* (Oxford, 2002).

80. Bentham, *Introduction*, 311.

81. Brigitte Fielder, "Animal Humanism: Race, Species, and Affective Kinship in Nineteenth-Century Abolitionism," in *American Quarterly* 65, no. 3 (2013): 487–514; and Spencer Keralis, "Feeling Animal: Pet-Making and Mastery in the 'Slave's Friend,'" *American Periodicals* 22, no. 2 (2012): 121–138.

82. In "Force of Law," Jacques Derrida suggests that the ongoing pursuit of ethics means that "Nothing [is] less outdated than the classical emancipatory ideal . . . The examples closest to us would be found in the area of laws on the teaching and practice of languages, the legitimization of canons, the military use of scientific research . . . and so on, without forgetting, of course, the treatment of what one calls animal life." Derrida, *Acts of Religion*, ed. Gil Anidjar (Routledge, 2002), 258.

83. The text does not fully commit to the ethical approach in "Androcles and the Lion." Harry follows the tale with a different story containing a more common formulation of the slave-animal metaphor in which a domesticated jackass stands in for the enslaved, yielding a more limited moral that leaves ownership intact: "If [the animal] was his father's ass, [the child] should not use it ill." This version is relevant to Tommy's situation in that one goal of his education is to keep him from abusing the people his father enslaves, but it misses that ownership contributes to enslaved people's suffering. Its ethics rely not on kindness to increasingly diverse and disconnected strangers (like the animals in Bentham's metaphor), but on an assessment of familiarity and sameness. Harry concludes that the ass should not be mistreated because we are "all God's creatures." Day, *Sandford and Merton*, 51.

As Harry's revision reveals, fables have the drawback of dealing in the abstract or generalizable. This is also a feature of some versions of utilitarianism, which has been criticized for failing to promote responsibility for others in all circumstances. For example, while Bentham was skeptical about imperial conquests, his follower John Stuart Mill used a modified notion of the end justifying the means to excuse despotism as "a legitimate mode of government in dealing with barbarians, provided the end be their improvement." He tied this argument to what he saw as children's and colonial others' inability to be treated as free beings, claiming they were in "backward states of society in which the race itself may be considered as in its nonage." John Stuart Mill, *On Liberty* (Andrews UK, 2011), 26. Such end-based considerations reduce people to symbols, rather than individuals who might express their specific needs.

84. Day, *Sandford and Merton*, 373.

85. Ibid., 370.

86. Ibid., 370.

87. Ibid., 385.

88. Ibid., 385.

89. See, for instance, Maria Edgeworth's short story, "The Grateful Negro" (1804).

90. Raghuram, "Race and Feminist Care Ethics," 623, 628. In the first instance, Raghuram is quoting Chris Cuomo, *Feminism and Ecological Communities: An Ethic of Flourishing* (Routledge, 1997), 14.

91. García, *Side by Side*, 39–40.

92. One piece of evidence as to the radical nature of the grateful Black's argument is that *Sandford and Merton*, while popular in Europe, does not appear to have been advertised in the Caribbean, in contrast to Day's *The History of Little Jack*, which depicts its hero becoming a soldier, Christian, and colonist to India. The latter appeared on a bookseller's list in Bermuda in 1788. See *Bermuda Gazette, and Weekly Advertiser* (St. George's, Bermuda), December 6, 1788, 3. However, as not all Caribbean newspapers are extant or available digitally, it is possible that an advertisement for *Sandford and Merton* may yet be found.

93. Joseph Roach, *Cities of the Dead: Circum-Atlantic Performance* (Columbia University Press, 1996); Diana Taylor, *The Archive and the Repertoire: Performing Cultural Memory in the Americas* (Duke University Press, 2003).

94. Saidiya Hartman, *Lose Your Mother: A Journey Along the Atlantic Slave Route* (Farrar, Straus and Giroux, 2008); Marisa Fuentes, *Dispossessed Lives: Enslaved Women, Violence, and the Archive* (University of Pennsylvania Press, 2018); Lisa Lowe, "History Hesitant," *Social Text* 33, no. 4 (2015): 85–107.

95. Kate Capshaw and Anna Mae Duane, eds. *Who Writes for Black Children? African American Children's Literature Before 1900* (University of Minnesota Press, 2017), x.

96. Ibid., xi. Angela Sorby, "Conjuring Readers: African American Poetry and the Imagined Black Child Reader, 1850–1890," in *Who Writes for Black Children? African American Children's Literature Before 1900*, eds. Kate Capshaw and Anna Mae Duane (University of Minnesota Press, 2017), 5–32. For children's literature written by African Americans after enslavement, see Michelle M. Martin, *Brown Gold: Milestones of African-American Children's Picture Books, 1845–2002* (Routledge, 2004).

97. Audra Diptee and David V. Trotman, "Atlantic Childhood and Youth in Global

Context: Reflections on the Global South," *Atlantic Studies, Global Currents* 11, no. 4 (2014): 441.

98. Vasconcellos, *Slavery, Childhood, and Abolition,* 66.

99. Moten, *The Universal Machine.*

100. Ibid., 9.

101. Ibid., 53.

102. Janus August Garde, "Publication," *St. Thomas Avis* 80 (October 1878): 2.

103. *The Illustrated Times (Illustreret Tidende),* November 3, 1878, Worker's Museum (Arbejdermuseet), https://www.arbejdermuseet.dk/wp-content/uploads/2018/10 /illustrated-times-about-the-riot-1878.pdf.

104. Garde, "Publication," 3.

105. "A Woeful Ballad," Worker's Museum (Arbejdermuseet), accessed April 22, 2022, https://www.arbejdermuseet.dk/wp-content/uploads/2018/10/chapbook-song -about-the-riot-in-1878.pdf.

106. Mary Thomas prison records, Worker's Museum (Arbejdermuseet), accessed April 22, 2022, https://www.arbejdermuseet.dk/wp-content/uploads/2019/06/mary -thomas-prison-records.pdf.

107. "Folksong About the Riot," Worker's Museum (Arbejdermuseet), accessed April 22, 2022, https://www.arbejdermuseet.dk/wp-content/uploads/2018/10/folk song-about-the-riot-in-1878.pdf; Maud Cuney-Hare, "History and Song in the Virgin Islands: The Latest Gift of Folk Music to the United States," *The Crisis* (April 1933): 83–84.

108. Review by C. G. Woodson, *The Journal of Negro History* 29, no. 1 (1944): 101.

109. Regan Macaulay and Frances-Anne Solomon, *Literature Alive,* Season 1, Episode 13, "Miss Lou Then and Now," aired December 29, 2005, on Bravo! Canada.

110. Cuney-Hare presents a fascinating theory of the "bang-a-lang" aspect of this song, pointing to the use of drums to spread news of the 1848 Proclamation of Freedom that ended enslavement in the Danish West Indies—and the slang term "Queen" for drummers.

111. See Leonard Harris, "Insurrectionist Ethics: Advocacy, Moral Psychology, and Pragmatism," in *Ethical Issues for a New Millennium,* ed. J. Howie (Southern Illinois University Press, 2002).

112. Tami Navarro, *Virgin Capital: Race, Gender, and Financialization in the US Virgin Islands* (State University of New York Press, 2021), 52.

113. Roger Hill, *Clear de Road: A Virgin Islands History Textbook* (US Virgin Islands Department of Conservation and Cultural Affairs, 1983), 149.

114. Ibid., 164–165.

115. Ibid., 167.

116. Various Artists, *Zoop! Zoop! Zoop! Traditional Music and Folklore of St. Croix, St. Thomas, and St. John,* New World Records, 1993, compact disc.

117. DaraMonifah Cooper, "Gladys A. Abraham Elementary School Cultural Choir—Queen Mary," YouTube video, posted by DaraMonifah Cooper (DaraMonifah), October 3, 2010, 3:00, https://www.youtube.com/watch?v=93yCzZ-G1pY.

118. See La Vaughn Belle and Jeannette Ehlers, "I Am Queen Mary," accessed October 18, 2023, https://www.iamqueenmary.com/.

119. Butler, *Giving an Account of Oneself,* 4.

Chapter 1 • Early Children's Literature and White Civility

1. Karen Sands O'Connor, *Soon Come Home to This Island: West Indians in British Children's Literature* (Routledge, 2008), 10. As O'Connor puts it, "Market forces, which proscribed a 'need' for children's literature in the first place, likewise prescribe a 'need' for British involvement in the West Indies. Empire, colonization, and white superiority are thus directly linked to the early development of children's literature."

2. Sarah Fielding, *The Governess; Or Little Female Academy*, 2nd ed. (London: A. Millar, 1749), 22.

3. The text does not mention whether Jenny had an inheritance from her parents that might have contributed to her tuition. On the one hand, it seems likely that she would have, given her parents' diligence and care, but, on the other, her father died when she was young and we do not have an indication of Jenny's mother's income. It is unlikely that Jenny would have been entirely insulated from her aunt's business in the West Indies.

4. Mary Sherwood, who revised the novel in 1820, left her out entirely, though Sherwood herself had experience in the East Indian colonies.

5. Given the destination of Jenny's relatives, it is an interesting coincidence that the name Newman would come to be associated with one of London's premier grocers and importers of Jamaican produce, Abram Newman. Trading under the sign of the Three Sugar Loaves and Crown, Newman's company, Davidson, Newman, and Co., which dates from 1660 and which he joined in 1759, sold tea to the American colonies (most famously supplying the tea for the Boston Tea Party) and imported sugar, coffee, chocolate, rum, and fruits from Jamaica, allowing the firm to purchase a 4/18 share of a Jamaican estate in 1789. Although this Newman is too late to be an inspiration for Jenny's relatives, his activities provide an illustration of the sphere in which Fielding's characters circulated—or, in Jenny's case, did not circulate.

6. Sarah's brother, Henry, reports on the activities of Admiral Edward Vernon, who is stationed in Jamaica, and the escalation of fighting with Spain over colonial territory. See Henry Fielding, ed. *The Champion: Containing a Series of Papers, Humorous, Moral, Political and Critical*, vol. 2 (London: J. Huggonson, 1740), 60.

7. Edward Said, *Culture and Imperialism* (Knopf, 1993), 62.

8. Ibid., 87.

9. Ibid., 96.

10. Daniel Coleman, *White Civility: The Literary Project of English Canada* (University of Toronto Press, 2006), 9.

11. Ibid., 10.

12. Simone Drichel, "Relationality," *Angelaki: Journal of the Theoretical Humanities* 24, no. 3 (2019): 1–2. Drichel borrows this phrase from Niobe Way, Alisha Ali, Carol Gilligan, and Pedro Noguera, *The Crisis of Connection: Roots, Consequences, and Solutions* (New York University Press, 2018).

13. Simone Drichel, "Call for Papers for Relationality: A Symposium," accessed August 31, 2016, https://relationality2015.com/.

14. Fielding, *Governess*, 12.

15. Joseph Addison, *The Spectator*, no. 69 (May 19, 1711).

16. Mary V. Jackson, *Engines of Instruction, Mischief, and Magic* (University of

Nebraska Press, 1989), 208. Referencing the French word for "butterfly," "papillonade" resembles "Robinsonnade," books that build on the popularity of Daniel Defoe's *Robinson Crusoe*.

17. Fielding, *Governess*, 3.

18. Ibid., 4.

19. Ibid., 7.

20. Ibid., 8–9.

21. Ibid., 12.

22. Ibid., 16.

23. Ibid., 19.

24. Mary Jeanette Moran, "Making a Difference: Ethical Recognition Through Otherness in Madeleine L'Engle's Fiction," in *Ethics in Children's Literature*, eds. Claudia Mills and Claudia Nelson (Routledge, 2014), 76. Key thinkers in this tradition are Carol Gilligan, Nel Noddings, and Virginia Held.

25. Fielding, *Governess*, 19.

26. Ibid., 19, 20.

27. Ibid., 20.

28. Ibid., 20.

29. Jenny derives many of her arguments from stoicism, a philosophy that links happiness to the emotional endurance of individuals. See Pamela L. Cheek, *Heroines and Local Girls: The Transnational Emergence of Women's Writing in the Long Eighteenth Century* (University of Pennsylvania Press, 2019), 137.

30. Anne Helen Petersen, "White Celebrity and Rituals of Civility: Taylor Swift, Brittany Mahomes, Kate Middleton, and Culture Study," *Culture Study*, September 15, 2024, https://annehelen.substack.com/p/white-celebrity-and-rituals-of-civility.

31. Susan Dwyer Amussen, *Caribbean Exchanges: Slavery and the Transformation of English Society, 1640–1700* (University of North Carolina Press, 2007), 107.

32. Fielding, *Governess*, 22.

33. Daniel Livesay, *Children of Uncertain Fortune: Mixed-Race Jamaicans in Britain and the Atlantic Family, 1733–1833* (University of North Carolina Press, 2018).

34. The only further reference to Harriet is that she is "quite impatient" to see Jenny again when she returns to England, which could subtly imply she lacks Jenny's talent in regulating her emotions (Fielding, *The Governess*, 141). Impetuousness would later be established as a common problem of English children who had contact with enslavement. Another character named Harriet is described as "gay and coquettish"— words sometimes used to demean Afro-Caribbean creole women—but if Fielding meant us to parallel the characters, there is no indication of it beyond the recycled name. Fielding simply is not interested in imagining Harriet in detail.

35. Parvati Raghuram, "Race and Feminist Care Ethics: Intersectionality as Method," *Gender, Place & Culture: A Journal of Feminist Geography* 5 (2019): 629.

36. Elizabeth Dillon, "The Secret History of the Early American Novel: Leonora Sansay and Revolution in Saint Domingue," *Novel: A Forum on Fiction* 40, nos. 1/2 (2006–2007): 83.

37. Ibid., 84.

38. Ibid., 85.

39. See Amussen, *Caribbean Exchanges*.

40. Fielding, *Governess*, 46.

41. Ibid., 46.

42. Fielding essentially appropriates the mantra "Britons never shall be slaves" (from the popular song "Rule Britannia," written nine years earlier, in 1740, about the war in the Caribbean with Spain) as applicable to white British women and children, even if servants.

43. John Locke, *Two Treatises of Government: And a Letter Concerning Toleration*, ed. Ian Shapiro (Yale University Press, 2003), 7.

44. Fielding, *Governess*, 112.

45. Ibid., 113.

46. Ibid., 168.

47. Amussen, *Caribbean Exchanges*, xiv.

48. Fielding, *Governess*, 25.

49. Ibid., 37.

50. Ibid., 32.

51. Ibid., 32.

52. Ibid., 41.

53. Ibid., 32.

54. Ruma Chopra, "The Royalist Maroons of Jamaica in the British Atlantic World, 1740–1800," *Varia Historia, Belo Horizonte* 35, no. 67 (2019): 213.

55. Ibid., 218.

56. Fielding, *Governess*, 38.

57. See, for instance, Thomas Bellamy, *The Benevolent Planters. A Dramatic Piece* (London: J. Debrett, 1789).

58. Fielding, *Governess*, 74.

59. See Caroline Levander, *The Cradle of Liberty* (Duke University Press, 2006), for an analysis of how the British and their descendants in the United States connected their freedom to "Anglo-Saxon" blood. The Welsh context makes the notion of Anglo-Saxon blood complicated, as the Celtic Britons of Wales originally fought the Anglo-Saxons and Normans, but the text likely banks on a generalized understanding of Anglo-British ancestry as antithetical to enslavement.

60. At the same time, Jenny's final act—writing letters to the girls—represents how her influence traveled transatlantically via Fielding's book. Typical of many eighteenth-century books, *The Governess*'s transatlantic movements flow from London through major American urban centers and port cities. If the book moved on from these places, records are not easily found. Despite trying, I have not been able to determine that Jenny Peace ever did go to the Caribbean inside the pages of *The Governess*, though it is possible that this book was among the "story books" listed in eighteenth- and nineteenth-century Caribbean newspaper ads (discussed in chapter 4). The book does appear in shop and circulating library catalogs in Philadelphia, Boston, and Portsmouth. Mary Sherwood's version, which omits Jamaica and Jenny's family entirely, came to New York and Philadelphia in 1827. See Sherwood, *The Governess; Or Little Female Academy* (Hartford: J. J. Harper, 1827). "Barbarico and Benefico" was published on its own in Boston in 1768, followed by the full text in Philadelphia in 1791. In *Imaginary Citizens: Child Readers and the Limits of American Independence, 1700–1868* (Johns Hopkins University Press, 2013), I propose that the stand-alone publication of "Barbarico and

Benefico" prior to the American Revolution might have been interesting to US readers as a rationale for revolution. If so, Mrs. Teachum was right to worry that readers needed instruction in how to read the text as an allegory for internal and familial rather than external and global struggles. But although the date of the publication of "Barbarico and Benefico" suggests that readers may have read more rebelliousness in the text than its pedagogue character advocates, I have found no evidence that readers applied its denouncement of captivity to British enslavement. A more faithful version of Jenny's intended role in the lives of US readers might be gleaned from her appearance in Isaiah Thomas's version of John Newbery's *The Mother's Gift*. In addition to using the name "Teachum" for another (male) teacher, the text includes the story of a naughty girl named Emily who disciplines herself by "sit[ting] down and read[ing] some of the Stories in Mrs. Teachum" proclaiming "those Misses, especially Miss Jenny Peace, are good Examples for me." Newbery, *The Mother's Gift* (Worcester, MA: Isaiah Thomas, 1787), 40.

61. Frances Hodgson Burnett, *A Little Princess* (Fingerprint Classics Reprint, 2022), 139.

62. Ibid., 11.

63. Ibid., 41. Burnett compares Sara's leadership style with Lavinia, who leads because she can make herself "extremely disagreeable if the others [do] not follow her," where Sara leads "not because she could make herself disagreeable, but because she never did."

64. Ibid., 74.

65. Ibid., 157.

66. Ibid., 143–144.

67. Ibid., 213.

68. Ibid., 241.

69. Amussen, *Caribbean Exchanges*, xv.

70. Livesay, *Children of Uncertain Fortune*, 295.

71. O'Connor, *Soon Come Home to This Island*, 13.

72. Thomas Day, *The History of Sandford and Merton: A Work Intended for the Use of Children* (Philadelphia: William Young, 1793), 386.

73. This text clearly interested publishers and readers in the United States in addition to those in England; *Sandford and Merton* went through at least fourteen editions in the United States from 1788 to 1818, extending beyond the reach of the usual publishing centers and port cities of Boston, New York, and Philadelphia to Baltimore, Maryland; New Brunswick, New Jersey; and Carlisle, Pennsylvania. The publication dates roughly coincide with gradual abolition in these areas, suggesting *Sandford and Merton*'s balance between arguing against enslavement and not demonizing characters who continue to engage in the practice might have appealed to those in the United States who wanted to aid in the process of recovering from American enslavement, even as it continued in other parts of the country.

74. This copy is Barbara Hofland, *The Barbados Girl* (London: Printed for A. K. Newman and Co., 1840), call number W.I.C. 26.

75. Hofland ran a boarding school similar to the fictional one run by Mrs. Teachum.

76. Barbara Hofland, *Matilda, Or the Barbadoes Girl. A Tale for Young People.* (London: A. K. Newman and Co., 1816), 10–11.

77. Ibid., 38.

78. Hofland's later children's book, *The Captives in India* (1836), anticipates Burnett's book even more strongly by telling the similar story of an Anglo-Indian girl who comes home to England to learn English manners—though, unlike Burnett's heroine, she must return to India to find her kidnapped father before finding her way to British society permanently. See Supriya Goswami, *Colonial India in Children's Literature* (Taylor & Francis Group, 2012).

79. Hofland, *Matilda*, 99.

80. Ibid., 56.

81. Ibid., 46.

82. Ibid., 47.

83. Chimamanda Ngozi Adichie, "The Danger of a Single Story," TED Talks, accessed February 27, 2025, https://www.ted.com/talks/chimamanda_adichie_the _danger_of_a_single_story?language=en.

84. Ibid.

85. See Jules Gill-Peterson, *Histories of the Transgender Child* (University of Minnesota Press, 2018).

86. Hofland, *Matilda*, 100, 101.

87. Ibid., 102.

88. O'Connor, *Soon Come Home to This Island*, 11–12.

89. Hofland, *Matilda*, 14.

90. Ibid., 127

91. Ibid., 135.

92. Ibid., 136.

93. Ibid., 188.

94. Ibid., 141.

95. Ibid., 178.

96. Ibid., 179.

97. Robin DiAngelo, *White Fragility: Why It's So Hard for White People to Talk About Racism* (Beacon Press, 2018), 2.

98. Hofland, *Matilda*, 183. Emphasis mine.

99. Ibid., 192.

100. *The Barbadoes Girl* became popular in the United States in the context of impending abolition. Existing copies suggest the book had significant circulation, concentrating around its first release and then starting up again in the 1840s–1860s, with at least two editions printed in the antebellum United States. The University of Florida's Baldwin Library of Historical Children's Literature contains three editions, one published in London (call number 15h4610). The other two were published by Francis and Co. in New York in 1849 (call number 23h21493) and in Boston in 1863 (call number 23h21494). Both US copies contain inscriptions by their owners—the first contains dedications to two girls, Mary Nusik and Louise Buck, and the second a handwritten inscription by Josie S. Parker.

101. A. Selwyn, *The Little Creoles; Or the History of Francis and Blanche* (London: William Cole, 1820), 17.

102. Hazel V. Carby, *Imperial Intimacies: A Tale of Two Islands* (Verso, 2021), 256–257.

103. Of the texts in this chapter, *The Little Creoles* and *The Lobster's Voyage to the Brazils* are the only ones that do not appear to have been republished in the United States.

104. Selwyn, *Little Creoles*, 16.

105. Ibid., 29, 35.

106. Ibid., 54.

107. Ibid., 21.

108. Ibid., 21.

109. Ibid., 67.

110. Richard De Ritter, "The Feast of the Fishes: Satire, Slavery and Romantic-Period Children's Literature," *Romanticism* 28, no. 3 (2022): 257–258.

111. Daniel Froid, "Satirical Conservatism in Catherine Ann Dorset's Papillonades," *Women's Writing* 25, no. 1 (2017): 1.

112. Jackson attributes *The Lobster's Voyage* to Tyro. There is some similarity between the two texts in their disturbing references to enslavement, but *Feast of the Fishes* more closely resembles blatantly racist texts that present the motif of Black people being eaten in a humorous way, while *The Lobster's Voyage* aims its humor at British hypocrisy.

113. Theresa Tyro, *The Feast of the Fishes; Or, the Whale's Invitation to his Brethren of the Deep* (London: J. Harris, 1808), 5.

114. De Ritter, "The Feast of the Fishes," 259.

115. Ibid., 262.

116. Ibid., 261, 262.

117. *The Lobster's Voyage to the Brazils* (London: J. Harris, 1808), 3.

118. Ibid., 4.

119. Ibid., 4.

120. Ibid., 5.

121. Ibid., 6.

122. Ibid., 6.

123. Ibid., 6.

124. Ibid., 7.

125. Ibid., 8.

126. Ibid., 10.

127. Ibid., 10.

128. Spencer Keralis, "Feeling Animal: Pet-Making and Mastery in *The Slave's Friend*," *American Periodicals* 22, no. 2 (2012): 124.

129. Ibid., 122.

130. Ibid., 124.

131. Christina Sharpe, *In the Wake: On Blackness and Being* (Duke University Press, 2016), 40–41.

132. *The Lobster's Voyage*, 13.

133. Lynn B. Harris, "Maritime Cultural Encounters and Consumerism of Turtles and Manatees: An Environmental History of the Caribbean," *International Journal of Maritime History* 32, no. 4 (2020): 789–807.

134. Ibid.

135. *The Lobster's Voyage*, 16.

136. Ibid.

137. Ibid.

138. Related to the rationalization of human actions, like fishing and eating, that might harm animals, researchers are still debating whether fish can feel pain. See Lynne U. Sneddon and Jonathan A. C. Roques, "Pain Recognition in Fish," *Veterinary Clinics of North America: Exotic Animal Practice* 25, no. 1 (2023): 1–10. Brian Key, "Fish Do Not Feel Pain and Its Implications for Understanding Phenomenal Consciousness," *Biology & Philosophy* 30, no. 2 (2015): 149–165.

139. See advertisements in Samuel Bentley, *Mamma's Lessons for Her Little Boys and Girls* (London: J. Harris, 1840), n.p.; *Johnny Gilpin* (London: Dean and Son, c. 1940), back cover; and *The Giant Hands, or, the Reward of Industry* (London: G. Routledge and Co., 1857), back cover.

140. Lewis Carroll, "Entry for January 17, 1856," in *The Diaries of Lewis Carroll,* vol. 1, ed. Roger Lancelyn Green (Greenwood Press, 1954), 74.

141. See *The Butterfly's Ball* (London, c. 1860), held by the Baldwin Library of Historical Children's Literature (call number 39h1733); and *The Butterfly's Ball* (New York: MacLoughlin Brothers, c. 1867–1870). The former uses Carroll-esque imagery, such as a mushroom made to look like a table, upon which an anthropomorphic bug sits, calling to mind John Tenniel's illustration of the Caterpillar in *Alice in Wonderland* (though Tenniel uses a different composition).

142. Edward Wakeling, ed., *Lewis Carroll's Diaries: The Private Journals of Charles Lutwidge Dodgson (Lewis Carroll)*, vol. 3 (Lewis Carroll Society, 1995), 120; and Edward Wakeling, ed., *Lewis Carroll's Diaries: The Private Journals of Charles Lutwidge Dodgson (Lewis Carroll)*, vol. 4 (Lewis Carroll Society, 1995), 287.

143. F. J. Harvey Darton, *Children's Books in England: Five Centuries of Social Life,* 3rd ed. (Cambridge University Press, 1982), 199. Originally published in 1932.

144. Lewis Carroll, *Alice in Wonderland* (New York: D. Appleton and Co., 1866), 149.

145. Ibid., 149, 152.

146. Ibid., 153.

147. Ibid., 152.

148. Ibid., 157.

149. Ibid., 158.

150. Ibid., 160.

151. Harris, "Maritime Cultural Encounters."

152. Carroll, *Alice in Wonderland*, 54, 82.

153. Ibid., 86–87. Sea creatures, for what it is worth, continue to appear in writing that probes the ethics of capitalist consumption; most famously, David Foster Wallace's "Consider the Lobster" identifies lobsters as creatures on the flimsy boundary between human and animal, debunks the dubious claims about a supposed lack of pain receptors that undergird cruel practices involving them (boiling them alive for eating), and explores the lengths that people will go to avoid tackling the "troubling questions" of their ethical treatment. See Wallace, "Consider the Lobster," *Gourmet*, August 2004, 64. Madeline Orton, an undergraduate at Pitt, explored more recent attitudes toward crustaceans, learning that crabs and lobsters often represent capitalist desire and its ill effects (consider Tamatoa from Disney's *Moana*). Lobsters, as ambiguous figures of both power and otherness, tend to unflinchingly reflect the unethical and deeply destructive

entanglements of Atlantic (and global) trade—calling for comparatively radical solutions. A more positive version of the lobster appears in Serena Lane Ferrari's picture book, *Saving Tally*, which calls attention to unethical costs of global commerce with its story of a turtle getting trapped in a plastic bag until a lobster can cut her out. See Serena Lane Ferrari, *Saving Tally: An Adventure into the Great Pacific Plastic Patch* (Serena Ferrari, 2019).

154. Marah Gubar, "Lewis in Wonderland: the Looking-Glass World of Sylvie and Bruno," *Texas Studies in Literature and Language* 48, no. 4 (2006): 372–394.

155. Carroll, *Alice in Wonderland*, 22.

156. Ibid., 15.

157. Ibid., 34, 36.

158. Kyla Wazana Tompkins, *Racial Indigestion: Eating Bodies in the 19th Century* (New York University Press, 2012), 1.

159. Ibid., 1.

160. Ibid., 8.

Chapter 2 • Afro-Caribbean Stories in the Battle over Childhood

1. My references to the Goosee letter refer to its reprint in Matthew Lewis, *Journal of a West India Proprietor, Kept During a Residence in the Island of Jamaica*, ed. Judith Terry (Oxford University Press, 1999), 253.

2. Ibid., 253.

3. *The History of Little Goody Two-Shoes* (London: J. Newbery, 1765), 3.

4. Lewis, *Journal*, 253.

5. Ibid., 253. "Mother Goose" was used in eighteenth-century children's literature to refer to a peasant woman who told rhymes and stories, especially in efforts to translate these oral cultures into book form.

6. Ibid., 255.

7. Kelly Wisecup and Toni Wall Jaudon use this phrase to describe colonial writing about Obeah in "On Knowing and Not Knowing About Obeah," *Atlantic Studies: Global Currents* 12, no. 2 (2015): 129–143.

8. It is difficult to uncover much about the woman (or women) who may have inspired Goosee. Lewis's portrayal of her is inconsistent even within the brief letter. He refers to her both as a "little old woman" and "an irresistible little woman," making her age obscure. The most consistent feature, her littleness, refers as much to her story as her person: "her pretty little story." Slave registers from Lewis's two estates, St. Thomas in the East and Westmoreland, help only minimally. Out of more than 1,000 enslaved people listed in 1817, these records document 176 women age thirty or over (a mix of Africans and creoles), 19 if we count only those sixty or older. None obviously fit the Goosee description. See Matthew Gregory Lewis, "Registers for St. Thomas in the East (1817) and Westmoreland (1817)" in *Former British Colonial Dependencies, Slave Registers, 1813–1834*, T 71/145 and T 71/178, National Archives of the UK, Kew, Surrey, England.

9. Hartman, "Venus in Two Acts," *Small Axe* 12, no. 2 (2008): 2. Hartman writes, "What has been said and what can be said about Venus take for granted the traffic between fact, fantasy, desire, and violence" (5).

10. Lewis, *Journal*, 255.

11. Ibid., 254–255.

12. Ibid., 254.

13. Ibid., 261.

14. Ibid., 254–255.

15. Ibid., 254. Lewis's *Journal* is mostly an autobiography, not a collection of Anansi stories. Such a collection was later published by Mary Pamela Milne-Home, a white writer who grew up in Jamaica. In her *Mamma's Black Nurse Stories* (1890), she similarly suggests that the tales were children's stories: "Old women . . . keep the children quiet with these tales." Milne-Home, *Mamma's Black Nurse Stories* (Edinburgh: William Blackwood and Sons, 1890), 2.

16. The recipient of the letter's identity is unknown. As far as the *Journal*, although pedagogues recommended that children read travelogues, I have not found evidence that children read Lewis's text. Lawrence Needham does a rare close reading of the stories in the letter and *Journal*, arguing that they would have appealed to a sophisticated readership fascinated with "the 'primitive.'" Needham, "'Goody Two-shoes' / 'Goosee Shoo-shoo': Translated Tales of Resistance in Matthew Lewis's *Journal of a West India Proprietor*," in *Between Languages and Cultures: Translation and Cross-Cultural Texts*, ed. Anuradha Dingwaney and Carol Maier (University of Pittsburgh Press, 1995), 110–111.

17. Cynthia James, "From Orature to Literature in Jamaican and Trinidadian Children's Folk Traditions," *Children's Literature Association Quarterly* 30, no. 2 (2005): 165.

18. Ibid., 166.

19. Lewis, *Journal*, 72. Lewis's registers for St. Thomas in the East (1817) and Westmoreland (1817) contain 109 children between ages two and twelve who could have been part of the audience. Although Lewis gives no indication of when they could have listened to stories, he mentions at least five places that children occupied on his plantation. As babies, they are with their (working) mothers; Lewis mentions a woman dropping her baby when the knot holding the child on her back fails. At Lewis's imposed age of fifteen months, they go to the "weaning house." Lewis also mentions that very young children spend time on the lawn with old women but does not describe what sort of care they receive. Shirley G. Gordon writes about such situations: "[Children] were usually put in the care of an elderly woman as early as possible to release their mothers for work . . . [O]ne suspects that African songs, stories, dances, and games may well have been passed on to these little children to while away the long day." Gordon, *A Century of West Indian Education: A Source Book* (Longmans, 1963), 10. Lewis describes older children working in a group, romanticizing their labor as like that British children might perform on a farm. These children occasionally make their voices heard by singing, as I discuss. Finally, Lewis mentions teenagers working in roles similar to those of adults.

20. Jennifer L. Morgan, in "Partus Sequitur Ventrem: Law, Race, and Reproduction in Colonial Slavery," *Small Axe* 22, no. 1 (2018): 1–17, traces the earliest American iteration of this idea to the Virginia slave codes of 1662.

21. Colleen Vasconcellos, *Slavery, Childhood, and Abolition in Jamaica, 1788–1838* (University of Georgia Press, 2015), 8.

22. Audra Diptee and David V. Trotman, "Atlantic Childhood and Youth in Global Context: Reflections on the Global South," *Atlantic Studies, Global Currents* 11, no. 4 (2014): 438.

23. Vasconcellos, *Slavery, Childhood, and Abolition*, 66.

24. Shalini Puri, "Beyond Resistance: Notes Toward a New Caribbean Cultural Studies," *Small Axe* 7, no. 2 (2003): 23–38, for a discussion of the latter two terms as they feature in analysis of Caribbean people.

25. "Why Anansesum?," *Anansesem*, accessed January 30, 2017, http://www .anansesem.com/p/why-anansesem_24.html. There is a strong Anansi tradition in Britain, due to the immigration of Afro-Caribbean people. For instance, Anansi occupies an entire room of the Oxford Story Museum, which reconstructs children's stories in visual tableaux.

26. This reclamation of Goosee's story is offered in the spirit of Hartman's vision of writing to "illuminate the contested character of history, narrative, event, and fact, to topple the hierarchy of discourse and to engulf authorized speech in the clash of voices." Hartman, "Venus in Two Acts," 11–12.

27. Ibid., 4.

28. Lewis misses this ethical call of the stories, but they can engage us along the lines of Christina Sharpe's queries: "What happens when we look at and listen to these and other Black girls across time? . . . This looking makes ethical demands on the viewer; demands to imagine otherwise; to reckon with the fact that the archive, too, is invention." Sharpe, *In the Wake: On Blackness and Being* (Duke University Press, 2016), 51.

29. Simon Gikandi, "Rethinking the Archive of Enslavement," *Early American Literature* 50, no. 1 (2015): 84.

30. Ibid., 92.

31. Lewis, *Journal*, 42.

32. Gikandi, "Rethinking the Archive of Enslavement," 92–93.

33. Ibid., 100.

34. Sasha Turner, *Contested Bodies: Pregnancy, Childrearing and Slavery in Jamaica* (University of Pennsylvania Press, 2017), 248.

35. Marah Gubar, "Risky Business: Talking About Children in Children's Literature Criticism," *Children's Literature Association Quarterly* 38, no. 4 (2013): 450.

36. Marah Gubar, "On Not Defining Children's Literature," *PMLA* 126, no. 1 (2011): 209–216; Sarada Balagopalan, "Introduction: Children's Lives and the Indian Context," *Childhood* 18, no. 3 (2011): 291–297.

37. Lewis, *Journal*, 6.

38. Following earlier informal schooling, in 1813 "a person residing at Antigua . . . organized a School of 1000 persons to learn to read, being Negroes and their Children." *1814 Report of the BFSS* (London: Richard and Arthur Taylor, 1814), 20. This report refers to the first schoolroom for educating the enslaved, the Bethesda school established by British missionary Charles Thwaites and his free colored wife, Elizabeth Hart Thwaites, along with enslaved headman, Vigo Blake. See John Horsford, *A Voice from the West Indies* (London: Alexander Heylin, 1856).

39. As I discuss in chapter 4, William Knibb, a Baptist missionary, sent a collection of enslaved "children's" writing to the BFSS in 1826.

40. Maria Edgeworth, *Popular Tales*, vol. 3 (London: J. Johnson by C. Mercier and Co., 1804), 193. This ideology touting the mutual interdependence of enslaved and enslaver had long-lasting circulation. A 1957 US textbook insisted that "a strong tie existed between slave and master because each was dependent on the other. The master needed the work and loyalty of his slaves. The slave was dependent for all his needs on the master." Francis Simkins, Sidman Poole, and Spotswood Hunnicutt, *Virginia: History, Government, Geography* (New York: Charles Scribner's Sons, 1957), 373. The copy I examined is held by Special Collections, University of Virginia.

41. Turner, *Contested Bodies*, 222–223.

42. Vasconcellos, *Slavery, Childhood, and Abolition*, 73.

43. Mary Turner, *Slaves and Missionaries: The Disintegration of Jamaican Slave Society, 1787–1834* (University of Illinois Press, 1982), 8.

44. Ibid., 14.

45. Rebecca Schneider, "Black Literacy and Resistance in Jamaica," *Social and Economic Studies* 67, no. 1 (2018): 52.

46. Lewis, *Journal*, 113.

47. Ibid. Competition among religious groups was fierce, causing later educators to write fiery letters denouncing other groups for stealing their students. Mico Charity teacher Samuel Edgerly accused the National School teachers of "abducting" eighty of their students by going door to door, sparking an inflammatory newspaper war between him and the president of that school. See Samuel Edgerly, Manuscript Letter to the Mico Charity Organization from Montego Bay, Jamaica, October 15, 1839, Oxford, Bodleian Libraries, Mico Charity Papers, Mss. Brit. Emp. S.20/E1/1 1835–1839.

48. Lewis, *Journal*, 88–89. Andrew Bell pioneered the Madras system of education; a monitorial system imported from the Indian colonies to educate large numbers of children. A similar BFSS system, the Lancaster system, was used throughout the Caribbean, including in Baptist schools established for Afro-Caribbean children in Jamaica in the 1820s.

49. Ibid., 101.

50. Haley North, "Forgery for Freedom: Enslaved Literacy and Resistance in the British Caribbean" (master's thesis, Carleton University, 2023), 75, https://carleton.scholaris.ca/items/00b099e8-3cc3-4102-9010-407099343234.

51. Ibid., 59, 61.

52. Lewis, *Journal*, 55.

53. See ibid., 140.

54. Ibid., 76–77.

55. Turner, *Contested Bodies*, 213.

56. Ibid., 248.

57. Vasconcellos, *Slavery, Childhood, and Abolition*, 66.

58. Lewis, *Journal*, 87. Whaunica likely refers to a twenty-two-year-old woman listed on the aforementioned 1817 register for Westmoreland, which is where Lewis lived in Jamaica, though there was also an eleven-year-old named Whaunica on his St. Thomas in the East estate.

59. Ibid., 109, 147.

60. Ibid., 254.

61. Ibid., 254.

62. Mary Ellen Lamb, *The Popular Culture of Shakespeare, Spenser and Jonson* (Routledge, 2006), 48.

63. Interestingly, Goody Two Shoes is not a nursery or fairy tale figure but a character from what Andrew O'Malley identifies as a disciplinary children's book with "chapbook residue." O'Malley, *The Making of the Modern Child: Children's Literature in the Late Eighteenth Century* (Routledge, 2004), 32.

64. Missionaries from multiple denominations wrote to the BFSS beginning in the early nineteenth century to plead for schoolbooks and children's books (the latter used for rewards) and to thank them for parcels already received.

65. Lewis, *Journal*, 254.

66. Lara Putnam, "Global Child-Saving, Transatlantic Maternalism, and the Pathologization of Caribbean Childhood, 1920s–1940s," *Atlantic Studies / Global Currents* 11, no. 4 (2014): 491–514.

67. Elizabeth Dillon, "The Secret History of the Early American Novel," *Novel* 40, nos. 1/2 (2007): 87.

68. Lewis, *Journal*, 105.

69. Ibid., 256.

70. Ibid., 260.

71. Ibid., 260.

72. Turner, *Contested Bodies*, 253.

73. Lewis, *Journal*, 79.

74. Ibid., 260.

75. Ibid., 260.

76. "Just Received," *The Kingston Chronicle*, April 15, 1819, 4; "Murray's English Reader," *American Annals of Education*, November 1837, 516.

77. Lindley Murray, *The English Reader* (New London: W. & J. Bolless, 1836), 25. This book would become what I call "a super-spreader" in the Caribbean, appearing in newspaper ads in Jamaica, St. Vincent, Grenada, and Trinidad between 1824 and 1837. See *Jamaica Journal* (Kingston, Jamaica), November 6, 1824, 8; *Royal St. Vincent Gazette and Weekly Advertiser* (Kingstown, St. Vincent), July 29, 1826, 1; *Grenada Free Press; and Weekly Gazette* (St. George's, Grenada), April 9, 1828, 1; and *Port of Spain (Trinidad) Gazette*, February 3, 1837, 1.

78. S. R. Toliver, *Recovering Black Storytelling in Qualitative Research: Endarkened Storywork* (Taylor & Francis, 2021), xv.

79. Ebony Elizabeth Thomas, "We Have Always Dreamed of (Afro)Futures: The Brownies' Book and the Black Fantastic Storytelling Tradition," *The Journal of the History of Childhood and Youth* 14, no. 3 (Fall 2021): 396.

80. Virginia Held, *The Ethics of Care: Personal, Political, and Global* (Oxford, 2006), 10.

81. See Julia Kristeva, *Powers of Horror: An Essay on Abjection* (New York: Columbia University Press, 1982). Thank you to an audience member at the Society for the History of Children and Youth Conference in 2015 for helping me make this connection between Goosee's story and abjection.

82. Lewis, *Journal*, 157.

83. Ibid., 255.

84. Derek Walcott, *The Poetry of Derek Walcott: 1948–2013* (Farrar, Straus and Giroux, 2014), 185.

85. Lewis, *Journal*, 253.

86. Onyefulu, who is Nigerian, claims he based *Chinye* on a West African folk story. San Souci's *The Talking Eggs* derives from the US South. As Patricia Glinton-Meicholas argues, the legacy of the diaspora "has created a shared cultural grammar or, at least, a mutual intelligibility among the traditional canons of communities where African descendants predominate or are significant." Glinton-Meicholas, "'M'Riddle, M'Riddle, M'Yanday, O': Folktales of the Bahamas as Signposts of Heritage and as Children's literature," in *The Routledge Companion to International Children's Literature*, ed. John Stephens (Routledge, 2018), 313.

87. Maria Tatar, introduction to *The Classic Fairy Tales* (W. W. Norton, 2016), 2.

88. See William Bascom, "Cinderella in Africa," *Journal of the Folklore Institute* 9, no. 1 (1972): 54–70. In *The Classic Fairy Tales* (Oxford University Press, 1980), Iona and Peter Opie identify a tale by Charles Perrault called "Diamonds and Toads" that resembles one of the stories in Lewis's text (98).

89. For discussion of Strabo's version, and its similarities and differences from the broader Cinderella tale type, see Joshua J. Mark, "The Egyptian Cinderella Story Debunked" in *World History Encyclopedia*, last modified March 23, 2017, https://www.worldhistory.org/article/1038/the-egyptian-cinderella-story-debunked/.

90. Harry G. Lefever, *Turtle Bogue: Afro-Caribbean Life and Culture in a Costa-Rican Village* (Associated University Presses, 1992), 182.

91. See Hazel V. Carby, *Cultures in Babylon: Feminism from Black Britain to African America* (Verso, 1999), 188.

92. Glinton-Meicholas, "'M'Riddle, M'Riddle, M'Yanday, O,'" 316.

93. According to S. Turner, enslavers considered ages twelve to sixteen good years for breeding, but 1823 imperial reforms considered "a view of childhood innocence" when it came to girls as a way to "change the character and habits of the slave population." Turner, *Contested Bodies*, 217. These reforms had little effect on the enslaved children's treatment, however. The 1826 Consolidated Slave Law in Jamaica protected girls under ten but was short lived.

94. Gordon, *A Century of West Indian Education*.

95. Fairy tales did not always inspire rebellion; they also distracted from the realities of children's lives. Giselle Rampaul discusses "how irrelevant cultural myths and fairy tales . . . contributed to the definition of social norms in colonial societies and to the shaping of the ideological perspective the child character is encouraged to assume." Rampaul, "'How the Mirror Broke': Deconstructing Colonial Fairy Tales in 'I Remember Pampalam,'" in *The Child and the Caribbean Imagination*, ed. Giselle Rampaul and Geraldine Elziabeth Skeete (University of the West Indies Press, 2012), 81.

96. Lewis, *Journal*, 156.

97. Ibid., 157.

98. Glinton-Meicholas finds this "Cinderella reward system recompensing good characters and meting out humiliation to the antisocial ones" in Bahamian stories. See Glinton-Meicholas, "'M'Riddle, M'Riddle, M'Yanday, O,'" 21.

99. Mary Prince, *The History of Mary Prince, a West Indian Slave*, 3rd ed. (London: F. Westley and A. H. Davis, 1831), 1.

100. Ibid., 8.

101. Lewis, *Journal*, 105.

102. Lewis, Registers for St. Thomas in the East (1817) and Westmoreland (1817).

103. Lewis, *Journal*, 241.

104. Ibid., 156.

105. Nazera Sadiq Wright, *Black Girlhood in the Nineteenth Century* (University of Illinois Press, 2016), 12.

106. Lewis, *Journal*, 185. A version of this story appears in Ruth Manning-Sanders's children's book, *A Book of Enchantments and Curses* (Dutton Books for Young Readers, 1977). In that version, "neger" has been replaced by "beggar," making the story even more Cinderella-esque.

107. Lewis, *Journal*, 184.

108. Vasconcellos, *Slavery, Childhood, and Abolition*, 26.

109. Lewis, *Journal*, 26.

110. Emily Zobel Marshall, *Anansi's Journey: A Story of Jamaican Cultural Resistance* (University Press of the West Indies, 2012).

111. Vasconcellos, *Slavery, Childhood, and Abolition*, 33.

112. Lewis, *Journal*, 187.

113. "Andrew Coltart," *Antigua Weekly Times*, June 20, 1851, 4. Similar ads for storybooks appeared in Jamaica, not always listing specific titles. Contrary to what we might assume—that these books were only for white children—the books may have circulated among Afro-Caribbean audiences. One potential venue was in missionary schools, where children were given books as rewards of merit. Moravian missionary Arthur Van Vleck writes to the Young Men's Missionary Society (YMMS) from Barbados in 1850, "As other schools, besides our own, distribute presents, we must do it also." A. Van Vleck, Manuscript Letter, Letter to the YMMS from Barbados, Records of the Young Men's Missionary Society (hereafter cited as YMMS), no. 107, Moravian Archives, Bethlehem, Pennsylvania (hereafter cited as MAB).

114. See Errol Hill, *The Jamaican Stage: 1655–1900: Profile of a Colonial Theatre* (University of Massachusetts Press, 1992), 108. The same play ran in Barbados in December 1872 as a Christmas play at Spacious Hall and again at a different theater in 1874. The *Barbados Agricultural Reporter* contains this advertisement: "The Great Fairy Burlesque CINDERELLA . . . will be produced with new Scenery, Effects, and A GRAND DISPLAY OF PARLOUR FIREWORKS BY MR. M. J. BLANK, AND THE FARCE OF SKETCHES IN INDIA." *Barbados Agricultural Reporter* (Bridgetown, Barbados), April 28, 1874, 2.

115. Quoted in Mervyn Morris, *Miss Lou: Louise Bennett and Jamaican Culture* (Signal Books, 2014), 44. Morris translates the line, "I wonder if it's England or Jamaica I am in?"

116. Simon J. Bronner, *Following Tradition: Folklore in the Discourse of American Culture* (Utah State University Press, 1998), 259. While Beckwith espouses problematic ideas of Jamaican culture as primitive, Bronner points out that she emphasized "the influence of culture and history," such as British and US contributions to the poverty of African-descended people, "over racial or mental characteristics." Beckwith, furthermore, contributed to an emerging idea of American culture as diverse and transnational, and saw "gender as a significant social category for the production of folklore" (253).

117. Ibid., 256.

118. Jean D'Costa comments that "European folktales adapted into the Creole cycle change so much in form that even 'Mr. Bluebeard' resembles the original only in the basic plot outline . . . [A]t the end of the Anancy story, unlike at the end of the European folk fairy tale, the hero's great triumph usually consists in staying alive." D'Costa, "Bra Rabbit Meets Peter Rabbit: Genre, Audience, and the Artistic Imagination—Problems in Writing Children's Fiction," in *Caribbean Literary Discourse: Voice and Cultural Identity in the Anglophone Caribbean*, ed. Barbara Lalla, Jean D'Costa, and Velma Pollard (University of Alabama Press, 2014), 116–117.

119. Martha Beckwith, *Jamaica Anansi Stories* (New York: American Folk-Lore Society, 1924), 131.

120. This motif also appears in European tales, especially the story of Rhiannon in the Welsh *Mabinogi*. See *The Mabinogion*, trans. Sioned Davis (Oxford, 2007).

121. Henrice Altink, "Imagining Womanhood in Early Twentieth-Century Rural Afro-Jamaica," *The Journal of Caribbean History* 40, no. 1 (2006): 64–91.

122. Deborah Gabriel, "Queen Nanny of the Windward Maroons Has Largely Been Ignored by Historians," *Jamaica Magazine*, August 8, 2004, http://jamaicans.com/queennanny/.

123. Quoted in Mel Cooke, "Story of the Song: 'Black Cinderella' Developed from a Poem," *The Jamaica Gleaner*, June 28, 2009, http://old.jamaicagleaner.com/gleaner/20090628/ent/ent9.html.

124. The song appeared on a record released by the Fi-Me-Time label in 1972.

125. "Sister Carol, Mother Culture," *Irie Magazine*, 3, no. 3 (2017): n.p.

126. The song appeared on the album *Black Cinderella* (1984) released from Jah Life Music.

127. Lewis, *Journal*, 142. Cecily Jones writes about singing as resistance in "Youthful Rebels: Young People, Agency, and Resistance Against Colonial Slavery in the British Caribbean Plantation World," in *Child Slaves in the Modern World*, ed. Gwyn Campbell, Suzanne Miers, and Joseph C. Miller (Ohio University Press, 2011).

128. "The 2018 Phoenix Picture Book Award Recipients," *Children's Literature Association Newsletter* 24, no. 2 (2017): 9.

129. Robert San Souci, *Cendrillon: A Caribbean Cinderella* (Aladdin, 2002), 39.

Chapter 3 • Taking Responsibility for the Other in Sugar Boycott Books

1. Benjamin Lundy, *The Poetical Works of Elizabeth Margaret Chandler* (Philadelphia: T. E. Chapman, 1845), 124.

2. Julie L. Holcomb notes, "Free produce was the first consumer movement to transcend the boundaries of nation, gender, and race in an effort by reformers to change the condition of production. Even when they acted locally, supporters embraced a global vision." Holcomb, *Moral Commerce: Quaker and the Transatlantic Boycott of the Slave Labor Economy* (Cornell University Press, 2016), 3–4.

3. Dennis Denisoff, "Small Change: The Consumerist Designs of the Nineteenth-Century Child," in *The Nineteenth-Century Child and Consumer Culture* (Ashgate, 2008), 2.

4. As Mitzi Myers points out, a "maternal persona" was a key way female children's authors framed their ethical interventions. See Myers, "Impeccable Governesses,

Rational Dames, and Moral Mothers: Mary Wollstonecraft and the Female Tradition in Georgian Children's Books," *Children's Literature* 14 (1986): 34. See Deborah C. De Rosa, *Domestic Abolitionism and Juvenile Literature: 1830–1865* (State University of New York Press, 2003) for further discussion of maternal postures in antislavery activism.

5. Some activists and writers, of course, mix both viewpoints.

6. Charlotte Sussman, "Women and the Politics of Sugar, 1792," *Representations* 48 (1994): 50.

7. See Conrad, "'Polluted Luxuries': Consumer Resistance, the Senses of Horror, and Abolitionist Boycott Literature," *American Literature* 90, no. 1 (2018): 3. The poem appeared in Benjamin Lundy's abolitionist newspaper, *Genius of Universal Emancipation*, in 1832, then in the Ladies' Department of Garrison's *Liberator* a month later, suggesting its audience was adult women.

8. Elizabeth Chandler, "The Sugar-Plums," *Juvenile Poems: For the Use of Free American Children, of Every Complexion*, ed. William Lloyd Garrison (Boston: Garrison and Knapp, 1835), 19.

9. Fred Moten, *The Universal Machine (consent not to be a single being)* (Duke University Press, 2018).

10. Simone Drichel, "Prospectus," *Relationality: A Symposium*, November 18–20, 2015.

11. Benjamin Lay, *All Slave-Keepers That Keep the Innocent in Bondage, Apostates* (Philadelphia, 1737), 34–35.

12. Marcus Rediker, *The Fearless Benjamin Lay: The Quaker Dwarf Who Became the First Revolutionary Abolitionist* (Beacon Press, 2017).

13. Ibid., 106. These acts drew counterprotest. In the case of the teacups, Lay was carried away, and the cups salvaged by a crowd before he could smash them all.

14. Andrew White, "A 'Consuming' Oppression: Sugar, Cannibalism, and John Woolman's 1770 Slave Dream," *Quaker History* 96, no. 2 (2007): 15.

15. Roberts Vaux, *Memoirs of the Lives of Benjamin Lay and Ralph Sandiford* (Philadelphia: Solomon W. Conrad, 1815), 28–29.

16. Holcomb, *Moral Commerce*, 37.

17. William Fox, *An Address to the People of Great Britain, on the Propriety of Abstaining from West India Sugar and Rum*, 10th ed. (London: Daniel Lawrence, 1792), 9.

18. Ibid., 4.

19. Sussman, "Women and the Politics of Sugar, 1792," 49.

20. Andrew Burn, *A Second Address to the People of Great Britain* (Rochester: W. Gillman, 1792), 7.

21. Sara Ahmed, *The Cultural Politics of Emotion*, 2nd ed. (Edinburgh University Press, 2014), 44.

22. See Paula Larson, "The Inherent Racism of the Anti-Vax Movement," *The Conversation*, July 15, 2021, https://theconversation.com/the-inherent-racism-of-anti-vaxx-movements-163456.

23. Burn, *A Second Address*, 5.

24. Marilisa Jiménez García, *Side by Side: US Empire, Puerto Rico, and the Roots of American Youth Literature and Culture* (University of Mississippi, 2021), 39–40.

25. Lydia Maria Child, *The Fountain for Every Day in the Year* (New York: R. G. Williams for the American Antislavery Society, 1836).

26. Mary S. Wood, Scrapbook Made for Her Granddaughter Mary Underhill Wood, Wood Family Papers, RG5 192, Friends Historical Library at Swarthmore College, 6. The scrapbook contains correspondence between Wood's press and abolitionists throughout the United States.

27. Ibid., 152.

28. Sean Shesgreen, *Images of the Outcast: The Urban Poor in the Cries of London* (Manchester University Press, 2002), 11.

29. Ibid., 153.

30. *The Cries of London* (Philadelphia: Benjamin Johnson, Jacob Johnson, and Robert Johnson, 1805), 4. This text is written in neoclassical verse with street workers as symbols for virtues. For example, its scissors sharpener symbolizes honing the truth, which the author claims as his calling too: "Sharp be their edge, as edge of sharpest knife, / That in these moral pages to the life / I may descry, and closely trim each truth, / And be the whetstone to the rising youth" (11).

31. *The Cries of London* (New York: Samuel Wood, 1811), n.p. Wood leaves out Bancks's most radical line criticizing consumer products: "Gaudy things enough to tempt ye, / Showy outsides, insides empty."

32. *The Cries of New York* (New York: S. Wood, 1808), 4.

33. Ibid., 16.

34. Ibid., 17.

35. Ibid., 31.

36. U. P. Hedrick, *The Pears of New York* (Albany: J. B. Lyon Company, 1921), 49. One theory is that bowery comes from *bouwerij*, an Old Dutch word for "farm."

37. Shane White, "'We Dwell in Safety and Pursue Our Honest Callings': Free Blacks in New York City, 1783–1810," *The Journal of American History* 75, no. 2 (1988): 452.

38. *The Cries of New York*, 22.

39. White, "'We Dwell in Safety,'" 447.

40. James Nevius, "The Ever-Changing Bowery: New York City's Oldest Street Is More Than Its Skid Row Reputation," *Curbed New York*, October 4, 2017, https://ny .curbed.com/2017/10/4/16413696/bowery-nyc-history-lower-east-side.

41. White, "'We Dwell in Safety,'" 456.

42. *The New-York Cries in Rhyme* (New York: Mahlon Day, 1812).

43. White, "'We Dwell in Safety,'" 454.

44. *The Cries of New York*, 22.

45. Ibid., 20.

46. Shesgreen, *Images of the Outcast*, 152.

47. J. Cypress, "The Cries of New York: An Unpublished Chapter of Mrs. Trollope, Addressed to the Printer," in *Sporting Scenes and Sundry Sketches* (New York: Gould, Banks & Company, 1842), 126.

48. Wendy A. Woloson, *Refined Tastes: Sugar, Confectionery, and Consumers in Nineteenth-Century America* (Johns Hopkins University Press, 2002), 6.

49. Charlotte Townsend, *Pity the Negro; or An Address to Children on the Subject of Slavery*, 3rd ed. (London: Francis Westley, 1825), 12.

50. Ibid., 4.

51. Ibid., 12.

52. Lissa Paul, "Agency and the Children's Crusade Against Slavery: 1791–1833" (presentation, "Books for Children: Transnational Encounters 1750–1850 Conference," Cotsen Children's Library, Princeton University, October 31–November 2, 2019).

53. Townsend, *Pity the Negro*, 16.

54. *A History of Wonderful Inventions* (London: Chapman and Hall, 1839); John Frost, *The Young Mechanic* (Auburn: Alden & Markham, 1848); Louisa C. Tuthill, *Success in Life: The Mechanic* (Cincinnati: H. W. Derby, 1854). That one such book, *Francis Lever, The Young Mechanic* (London: John Harris, 1835), circulated to the Caribbean is evidence of the ubiquity of these manual-like texts. *Port of Spain (Trinidad) Gazette*, January 5, 1836, 2.

55. Amelia Opie, *The Black Man's Lament, Or How to Make Sugar* (London: Harvey and Darton, 1826), 3–4.

56. Ibid., 17.

57. The song was released by the Barbados Folk Singers on a self-titled album, volume 1, in 1964. See also Sato, "Songs for Bajan Opera," *Pictures and Materials of Season 2000*, accessed March 22, 2023, https://crs-sato.tripod.com/bajanopera.html.

58. Opie, *The Black Man's Lament*, 5.

59. Jennifer L. Roberts, *Transporting Visions: The Movement of Images in Early America* (University of California Press, 2014), 29.

60. Liz Bellamy, "It-Narrators and Circulation: Defining a Subgenre," *The Secret Life of Things: Animals, Objects, and It-Narratives in Eighteenth-Century England*, ed. Mark Blackwell (Bucknell University Press, 2007), 124.

61. Lynn Festa, "The Moral Ends of Eighteenth- and Nineteenth-Century Object Narratives," *The Secret Life of Things: Animals, Objects, and It-Narratives in Eighteenth-Century England*, ed. Mark Blackwell (Bucknell University Press, 2007).

62. Ibid., 309–310.

63. Karen Sands O'Connor, *Soon Come Home to This Island: West Indians in British Children's Literature* (Routledge, 2008), 35.

64. Opie, *The Black Man's Lament*, 22.

65. Charles Williams, *Adventures of a Sugar Plantation* (London: Sunday School Union, 1836), 134.

66. Ibid., 135.

67. Ibid., 135–138.

68. Ibid., 135.

69. Ibid., 31.

70. Modern-day ethical vegans, who struggle with how to deal with food gifts and with meals made by noncomprehending family members, might recognize this situation.

71. Juvenile Anti-Slavery Society records, Massachusetts Historical Society, 1837–1838, https://www.masshist.org/collection-guides/view/fa0427.

72. Other accounts, including a sample meeting of the Chatham Street Chapel Society contained in *The Slave's Friend*, depict children hearing prepared speeches delivered by adults, reading letters from adults, and reading aloud from *The Youth's Cabinet* (in the case of the Boston society, while knitting or sewing items to sell for the cause). See "Juvenile Antislavery Society," *The Slave's Friend* 2, no. 5 (May 1, 1837): 102.

73. Kathryn Gleadle and Ryan Hanley, "Children Against Slavery: Juvenile Agency

and the Sugar Boycotts in Britain," *Transactions of the Royal Historical Society* 30 (2020): 97.

74. Ibid., 97.

75. Michaël Roy, *Young Abolitionists: Children of the Antislavery Movement* (New York University Press, 2024), 7.

76. The Pittsburgh group, which was founded in the 1838 as the first Juvenile Anti-Slavery Society west of the Appalachian Mountains, may have been the first Black-led society to use this title. As Roy has shown, groups run by African Americans were the earliest of any antislavery societies but "did not always use 'antislavery' in their names" despite their commitment to abolition, as they foregrounded broader issues like "education and racial uplift." Ibid., 82–83. Roy identifies the Juvenile Garrison Independent Society, founded in Boston in 1831, as the earliest juvenile antislavery society in the United States using this broader definition.

77. David Peck and George B. Vashon, "The Boys of Pittsburgh Against the World," *The Colored American* 3, no. 35 (November 23, 1839): 3. George B. Vashon and David Peck were students at the school—as was Martin Delany, who was a bit older than they were.

78. Ibid.

79. One reason the Pittsburgh children may have resorted to speaking as a pastime is found in the records of the adult Pittsburgh antislavery society, where the adult leaders complain that lecturers cannot be had so far west. See March 16 and May 2, 1837, entries in the Pennsylvania Anti-Slavery Society Western District, 1837–1838 Minute Book, MFF 0197, Heinz History Center, Detre Library & Archives.

80. See Augustine, "The Sabbath School," *The Colored American* 2, no. 24 (August 4, 1838).

81. In inspiring the Pittsburgh boys to write to *The Colored American*, Woodson and other adult activists fulfilled the parenting philosophy printed in the newspaper. An article republished from the London Sunday School Magazine exhorts parents to "be what the children ought to be" and "do what the children ought to do." "Thoughts for Parents," *The Colored American* 2, no. 20 (July 17, 1841): 4. Peck's and Vashon's parents were active and extensive contributors to African American independence and inclusion. In addition to forming the African school with Woodson, the elder Vashon was the proprietor of Pittsburgh's first bathhouse, which was used as a station on the Underground Railroad, and a founding member of Pittsburgh's adult antislavery society, as well as its chief fundraiser. David's father, John Peck, was a businessman, a preacher at the African Methodist Church, and a delegate to state and national antislavery conventions.

82. Augustine, *The Colored American* 1, no. 48 (December 2, 1837).

83. Augustine, "Further from Pittsburgh," *The Colored American* 2 (March 15, 1838), 31.

84. Mary Niall Mitchell, "Madame Couvent's Legacy: Free Children of Color as Historians in Antebellum New Orleans," in *Who Writes for Black Children? African American Children's Literature Before 1900*, ed. Katherine Capshaw and Anna Mae Duane (University of Minnesota Press, 2017), 62.

85. Nazera Wright, "'Our Hope Is in the Rising Generation': Locating African American Children's Literature in the Children's Department of the *Colored American*," in

Who Writes for Black Children? African American Children's Literature Before 1900, ed. Katharine Capshaw and Anna Mae Duane (University of Minnesota Press, 2017), 148.

86. James Shaw, "For the Christian Witness," *The Christian Witness*, May 31, 1837.

87. "Appendix 3: Two Poems by George B. Vashon; 'Vincent Ogé' and 'A Life Day,'" in *The WPA History of the Negro in Pittsburgh*, ed. Laurence A. Glasco and J. Ernest Wright (University of Pittsburgh Press, 2004), 369.

88. Many children's how-to books were dedicated to steam technology. See Elizabeth Hoiem, *The Education of Things: Mechanical Literacy in British Children's Literature, 1762–1860* (University of Massachusetts Press, 2024). The Young Men's Missionary Society (YMMS) in Bethlehem, Pennsylvania, held John Bourne's *A Catechism of the Steam Engine* (New York: D. Appleton and Company, 1850) in their library. See Alphabetical List of Books in the Library, YMMS, no. 24, Moravian Archives, Bethlehem, Pennsylvania.

89. *The History of a Pound of Sugar*, in *Rhymes and Pictures* (London: Griffith and Farran, 1860), 5.

90. Ibid., 6.

91. Ibid., 11.

92. Ibid., 12.

93. "J. Theobald and Co.'s Specialties," *The Illustrated London News*, December 6, 1886, 15.

94. Mary and Elizabeth Kirey, *Aunt Martha's Corner Cupboard, Or Stories About Tea, Coffee, Sugar, Rice, Honey &c.* (London: T. Nelson and Sons, 1875), 14.

95. Ibid., 14.

96. Ibid., 16.

97. Ibid., 63.

98. In an inverse of the paradigm discussed in chapter 1 where the English landscape is the cure for the excesses of enslavement, the object stories cure the white boys of laziness: "The next morning, Charley and Richard, instead of spending every moment in play, walked up and down the garden-walk, talking about the clay, and the glaze, and the enamel—things they had known nothing about before" (ibid., 41).

99. Consumer boycotts persist around the world despite these stories of neutral or innocent capitalism. Today, protests are waged over exploitative labor practices, the inclusion of dangerous chemicals, and even a company's choice to advertise to children. Relegated to a niche market and published by small publishers rather than mainstream presses, ethical vegan children's books such as Ruby Roth's *That's Why We Don't Eat Animals: A Book About Vegans, Vegetarians, and All Living Things* (North Atlantic Books, 2009) and *V Is for Vegan: The ABCs of Being Kind* (North Atlantic Books, 2013) carry on the legacy of nineteenth-century children's protest writers.

Chapter 4 • The Ethics of Circulation in the Enslaved and Colonized West Indies

1. *Report of The Committee to the General Meeting of the BFSS, November 1814* (London: Richard and Arthur Taylor, 1815), 55. This section of the report is a reprint of Mr. Bromley's *Report of the Royal Acadian School, established at Halifax Nova Scotia, July 31, 1813.*

2. See Chris Bischof, "Liberal Subjects: Elementary Education and Native Agency in the British West Indies, c. 1834–1860," *Slavery & Abolition* 40, no. 4 (2019): 750–773.

3. A. Selwyn, *The Little Creoles; Or the History of Francis and Blanche: A Domestic Tale* (London: William Cole, 1820), 34.

4. Kathryn Bond Stockton, "The Queer Child Now and Its Paradoxical Global Effects," *GLQ: A Journal of Lesbian and Gay Studies* 22, no. 4 (2016): 516.

5. James Raven writes, "The ships taking books from Britain and payment and orders back were powered by the northeast trade winds and the difficult westerlies . . . Those on the 'sugar route' made their way south to Madeira or the Canary Islands and then sailed to the Caribbean." Raven, *London Booksellers and American Customers: Transatlantic Literary Community and the Charleston Library Society, 1748–1811* (University of South Carolina Press, 2002), 11.

6. The robust circulation of spelling texts can be substantiated by the books that have survived the years, the climate, and poor resources (perhaps also poor motivation) for preservation, such as a copy of *An Introduction to Spelling and Reading* (1818) that I saw on display at the Barbados Museum in 2017.

7. See *Bermuda Gazette, and Weekly Advertiser* (St. George's, Bermuda), December 6, 1788, 3, and *Port of Spain (Trinidad), Gazette*, January 5, 1836, 2. To track circulation, I examined missionary records along with advertisements published by booksellers and other merchants in the largest digitized collection of eighteenth- and nineteenth-century newspapers, the *Caribbean Newspapers*, series 1, *1718–1876*, which includes ninety-eight titles in English from twenty-three locations. In this corpus, 21.8 percent of pre-emancipation and 23.2 of post-emancipation newspapers advertised children's literature at some point in their years of publication. This number provides a limited picture, because some newspapers are represented by only one or two extant issues in the database, artificially inflating the total number of newspapers. Another way of gauging circulation is to track unique locations represented with advertisements. There are twenty-three locations represented by English-language newspapers in the database pre-emancipation and twenty post-emancipation. Children's literature was available for sale in at least 10 of the locations pre-emancipation, or 43.5 percent, and seven post-emancipation, or 35 percent. The data skews toward places with established print cultures, which were more likely to have long-running newspapers. In many cases, though, purveyors of children's books did not specialize in bookselling but sold books alongside foods, fabrics, medicines, tools, and other paper products (including bills of sale for enslaved people). An advertisement from the *St. George's Chronicle and Grenada Gazette* includes the following goods alongside the books: "pickles, mushrooms, ketchup . . . Harvey's sauce, Salad oil, capers, fresh olives, Durham mustard, Hyson tea." *St. George's Chronicle and Grenada Gazette* (St. George's, Grenada). February 11, 1837, 1. Overall, these sources indicate that children's literature had significant circulation to the Caribbean beginning in the eighteenth century.

8. Louise Bennett-Coverley, *Jamaican Maddah Goose* (Jamaica School of Art, 1981); John Agard and Grace Nichols, *No Hickory, No Dickory, No Dock: Caribbean Nursery Rhymes* (Candlewick Press, 1995).

9. Tracing a broad picture from multiple sources is a methodology meant to account for the impact of colonialism on the historical record. Because of the legacies of colonial

recordkeeping, most archives associated with the historical Caribbean do not reside there, where they might be considered en masse and put into a context involving anti-colonial resistance. They are instead housed in British and US archives, often in the papers of evangelical operations that accompanied and supported colonial rule. Although critical reframing by current archivists, curators, and scholars is possible, these archives are, in the words of the creators of the Early Caribbean Digital Archive, "deeply entwined with colonial European capitalist modernity and a knowledge regime that racializes bodies with the aim of extracting labor, land, and capital." The curators of that archive argue that "revis[ing] the colonial knowledge regime" requires a practice of "re-archiving (remixing and reassembling) materials from existing archives." "Decolonizing the Archive: Remix and Reassembly," *The Early Caribbean Digital Archive,* accessed October 16, 2018, https://ecda.northeastern.edu/decolonizing-the-archive/. I too reassemble data. In addition to presenting my findings in this chapter, I used them to create digital maps for a collaborative project, *Round the Globe: Travel Routes of Children's Literature,* https://roundtheglobe.omeka.net.

10. Norrel London, quoted in Cynthia James, "From Orature to Literature in Jamaican and Trinidadian Children's Folk Traditions," *Children's Literature Association Quarterly* 30, no. 2 (2005): 165.

11. William Warner, Manuscript Letter to the YMMS, Friedensthal, St. Croix, August 13, 1842, YMMS, no. 109, Moravian Archives, Bethlehem, Pennsylvania (hereafter cited as MAB).

12. Charlotte Appel, Nina Christensen, and M. O. Grenby, eds., *Transnational Books for Children 1750–1900* (John Benjamins, 2023).

13. Religious Tract Society books in the Caribbean, for instance, were only available in the colonizing languages of English, Spanish, and French.

14. Shalini Puri, *The Grenada Revolution in Caribbean Present: Operation Urgent Memory* (Palgrave MacMillan, 2014), 19–20.

15. *20th Report of the BFSS* (London: Richard Taylor, 1825), 28. English books were supposedly enticements for young people to relinquish the vice-filled books distributed by competing colonizers. Pierre André writes to the BFSS from Haiti: "One thing which I apprehend may for a long time paralyse the progress of moral instruction among the youth here, is the sale of obscene books which our commerce with France has introduced in great quantities." "Extract of a Letter from Mr. Pierre André, Port-au-Prince, Feb. 3, 1823," *18th Report of the BFSS* (London: Richard Taylor, 1823), 129. André implied that English publications, in contrast, were good vehicles for the distribution of morals.

16. *21st Report of the BFSS* (London: J. B. G. Vogel, 1826), 28.

17. Specimen book from Jabez Tumley, Jamaica, 1844, BFSS/1/5/1/8/4/52, Archives and Special Collections, Brunel University of London.

18. Hilary E. Wyss, *English Letters and Indian Literacies: Reading, Writing, and New England Missionary Schools, 1750–1830* (University of Pennsylvania Press, 2012), 40.

19. For example, the Moravians arrived in Jamaica in 1754.

20. *The Quarterly Journal of Education,* vol. 5: *January–April* (London: Charles Knight, 1833), 266.

21. Ibid., 269. See Rebecca Schneider, "Black Literacy and Resistance in Jamaica," *Social and Economic Studies* 67, no. 1 (2018): 57.

22. Mary Turner, *Slaves and Missionaries: The Disintegration of Jamaican Slave*

Society, 1787–1834 (University of Illinois Press, 1982), 87. The Baptist mission claimed 3,000 Afro-Caribbean children and adults, most enslaved, could read by 1832.

23. *18th Report of the BFSS* (London: Richard Taylor, 1823), 132.

24. *22nd Report of the BFSS* (London: J. B. G. Vogel, 1827), 124.

25. Edward E. Reinke, Manuscript Letter to the YMMS, Fairfield, Jamaica, April 26, 1846, YMMS, no. 106, MAB.

26. Matthew Josephs and Robert Gordon, *The Wonders of Creation, and Other Poems* (London: F. E. Longley, 1876), 11. Chelsey Smith explains that the designation of "headman" "meant that during the period of legal slavery, he was expected to play a role in the organization of labor and scheduling shifts during times of harvests." Smith, "A Generation Rising: Education for Freedpeople in Post-Abolition Jamaica, 1834–1872" (PhD diss., University of Pittsburgh, 2024), 131.

27. See Mary Prince, *The History of Mary Prince: A West Indian Slave*, ed. Sarah Salih (Penguin Books, 2000), 29.

28. See *St. Christopher Gazette; and Charribbean Courier* (Bassaterre, St. Christopher). November 8, 1800, 4, and September 18, 1827, 4; *Saint Christopher Advertiser, and Weekly Intelligencer* (Basseterre, St. Christopher), April 11, 1826, 1, and January 2, 1829, 1; *Royal Gazette* (Kingston, Jamaica), May 8, 1822, 14; *Antigua Weekly Register* (St. Johns, Antigua), December 24, 1827, 1; *Port of Spain (Trinidad) Gazette*, April 19, 1833, 2; *Royal Gazette* (Hamilton, Bermuda), February 16, 1858, 1; *The Times* (Bridgetown, Barbados), July 8, 1868, 2.

29. *St. Christopher Gazette; and Charribbean Courier*, January 2, 1829, 1.

30. Isaac Watts, *Divine Songs Attempted in Easy Language for the Use of Children* (Boston: S. Kneeland and T. Green, for D. Henchman, 1730), 21.

31. M. Damus, Manuscript Letter to the YMMS, Emmaus, St. Johns, June 7, 1847, YMMS, no. 117, MAB.

32. William Warner, Manuscript Letter to the YMMS, Friedensthal, St. Croix, April 14, 1841, YMMS, no. 109, MAB.

33. Turner, *Slaves and Missionaries*, 86.

34. See Thomas Rain, *The Life and Labours of John Wray, Pioneer Missionary in British Guiana* (J. Snow, 1892), 65–72, for a reprint of the exchange.

35. *18th Report of the BFSS*, 131.

36. See Turner, *Slaves and Missionaries*, 86.

37. Schneider, "Black Literacy and Resistance in Jamaica," 58.

38. William Knibb, Specimens of Writing &c., Lancasterian School, Kingston, Jamaica, 1826. BFSS/1/5/1/8/4/3, Archives and Special Collections, Brunel University of London.

39. Wyss, *English Letters and Indian Literacies*, 50.

40. Ibid., 50.

41. Knibb, Specimens of Writing &c., n.p.

42. Ibid. In *A Century of West Indian Education* (Longmans, Green, 1963), vii, Caribbean educational historian Shirley Gordon points out that "apart from a few secondary school pupils who wrote to newspapers, the children have not been in a position to have their say." She is right; samples like this do not tell us what children thought or believed. Even after emancipation, when some of the material Afro-Caribbean children copied seems more meaningful and apt, it is difficult to read intentions into their

words. For instance, in the Mico Charity papers, there is a writing sample from Andrew Lathon, a fourteen-year-old "coloured" boy in Trinidad who copied the line, "Poor freedom is better than rich slavery." Letters Received by the Mico Charity, 1835–1842, vol. 4, Oxford, Bodleian Libraries, Mss. Brit. Emp. S20/E1/4. This line appeared in multiple educational texts, especially in the United States, and appears to not have originally had any connection to chattel slavery. Although the line's repurposing is interesting, it does not necessarily represent Lathon's views. Another fourteen-year-old, Paul Birotte, copied the same line, suggesting this was a lesson. The two boys copied the same, less immediately meaningful line, "Calico printing invented," directly above the freedom/slavery quotation.

43. Watts, *Divine Songs*, 6.

44. Thomas Babington Macaulay, "Minute by the Hon'ble T. B. Macaulay," in *Bureau of Education: Selections from Educational Records*, part 1: *(1781–1839)*, ed. H. Sharp (Calcutta: Government Printing, 1920), 109.

45. See Gauri Viswanathan, *Masks of Conquest: Literary Study and British Rule in India* (Oxford University Press, 1989), 13, for an example of how Indians strategically used English learning.

46. Haley North, "Forgery for Freedom: Enslaved Literacy and Resistance in the British Caribbean" (master's thesis, Carleton University, Ontario, 2023), 45.

47. A seventeen-year-old girl named Priscilla appears on a register of enslaved people at the estate of Hamilton Brown in St. Ann's Parish, 1826. This is approximately the correct age but not the correct location, as the school was in Kingston. Slave Register for Hamilton Brown in *Former British Colonial Dependencies, Slave Registers, 1813–1834*, T 71/46, National Archives of the UK, Kew, Surrey, England.

48. Knibb, Specimens of Writing &c., n.p.

49. William Warner, Manuscript Letter to the YMMS, Friedensthal, St. Croix, June 28, 1842, YMMS, no. 109, MAB.

50. *The Glasgow Infant School Magazine: Containing a Selection of Lessons Generally Used in Infant Schools* (Glasgow: Alex. Colville, 1832), 37.

51. Maria Ryan, "'The Influence of Melody upon Man in the Wild State of Nature': Enslaved Parishioners, Anglican Violence, and Racialized Listening in a Jamaica Parish," *Journal of the Society for American Music* 15 (2021): 176.

52. *Glasgow Infant School Magazine*, 37. Emphasis mine.

53. Reinke, Manuscript Letter to the YMMS, Fairfield, Jamaica, April 26, 1846, YMMS, no. 106, MAB.

54. A staple item in annual reports is a table with the number of students, male and female, at each school.

55. *27th Report of the BFSS* (London: Longman and Co.; J. Nisbet, 1832), 87–88.

56. Ibid., 87–88.

57. See my discussion in chapter 5 of *Imaginary Citizens: Child Readers and the Limits of American Independence, 1700–1868* (Johns Hopkins University Press, 2013).

58. Smith, "A Generation Rising," iv.

59. Colonial Office Papers, 1847, quoted by Barbados Museum and Historical Society exhibit on education, 2017.

60. Quoted in the *34th Report of the BFSS* (London: J. Rider, 1839), 121.

61. E. A. Wallbridge, Manuscript Letter to John Trew, Kingston, Jamaica, June 9,

1838, Oxford, Bodleian Libraries, Mico Charity Papers, Mss. Brit. Emp. S.20/E1/1 1835–1839.

62. In one wide-ranging scandal, a teacher in Jamaica named Samuel Edgerly got into a lengthy newspaper battle with teachers from the National School, an organization that produced anxiety among Mico teachers about their charity's future because it was free to attend. The battle began with an essay Edgerly wrote about the National School "abducting" their students and using the children's preexisting learning to tout their own success. In subsequent publications, he charged members of the school with attacking him violently at school, embezzling money Afro-Caribbean workers had given them for advocacy, and sexually violating students. They, in turn, accused him of shooting neighbors' pigs, hating the "negroes" he was employed to teach, and issuing legal notices on Sunday. See Mr. Samuel Edgerly, Letter to E. A. Wallbridge from Montego Bay, Jamaica, October 15, 1839, Oxford, Bodleian Libraries, Mico Charity Papers, Mss. Brit. Emp. S.20/E1/1 1835–1839.

63. Colonial Office, *Circular Dispatch Enclosing a Suggested Scheme for Industrial and Normal School in the Colonies*, Jan. 26, 1847, quoted in Gordon, *A Century of West Indian Education*, 58.

64. Kathleen Drayton, *"Politics of Textbooks*: School Books and the Making of the Colonial Mind" (paper presented at the First Biennial Cross-Campus Conference on Education, April 3–6 1990, Kingston, Jamaica), 3.

65. This book was advertised in the *Jamaica Journal* (Kingston, Jamaica), November 6, 1824, 8; *Port of Spain Gazette*, April 19, 1833, 2; and *Antigua Weekly Register*, September 15, 1857, 1.

66. See E. Woolley, Letter to Henry Dunn, from Jamaica, February 3, 1846. BFSS/1/5/1/8/4/65, Archives and Special Collections, Brunel University of London.

67. Smith, "A Generation Rising," 134.

68. A. Van Vleck, Manuscript Letter to the YMMS, Barbados, March 13, 1850, YMMS, no. 107, MAB.

69. Efforts have been made to change this persistence of colonial culture, but I found Barbadians eager to complain about how they learned "Jack and Jill went up the hill" in school when I visited Bridgetown in May 2017.

70. Agard and Nichols, *No Hickory, No Dickory, No Dock*, 9, 28–29, 37, 42.

71. Raven, *London Booksellers and American Customers*, 7, 13, 8.

72. Sean D. Moore, *Slavery and the Making of Early American Libraries: British Literature, Political Thought, and the Transatlantic Book Trade, 1731–1814* (Oxford University Press, 2019).

73. *Bermuda Gazette, and Weekly Advertiser*, July 10, 1784, 2.

74. *Bermuda Gazette, and Weekly Advertiser*, December 6, 1788, 3.

75. See *Antigua Gazette* (St. John's), February 14, 1799, 4; and *Jamaica Mercury* (Falmouth), January 17, 1798, 4.

76. See *St. George's Chronicle and Grenada Gazette*, May 12, 1810, 1; *Barbados Mercury, and Bridge-Town (Barbados) Gazette*, June 7, 1814, 1; *The Saint Christopher Advertiser* (Basseterre), November 16, 1824, 1; and *Royal St. Vincent Gazette, and Weekly Advertiser* (Kingstown), July 29, 1826, 1. Children's book advertisements in Caribbean newspapers are a microcosm of nineteenth-century children's book advertisements in general, with recognizable gambits for selling, including foregrounding popular titles

or steady sellers, advertising books as Christmas or New Year's presents, and highlighting special features such as colored plates or illustrations.

77. *Port of Spain (Trinidad) Gazette*, April 19, 1833, 2.

78. For example, on page 2 of the October 3, 1829, edition of the *Port of Spain Gazette*, near an advertisement for "Reading Books for Schools, Spelling and Children's Books," the following notice appears: "Runaway from Terre Promise Estate . . . a Negro named Josh, and registered by the name of Joseph Rosade. He is a creole of this Island; aged 25 years; Is five feet three inches high, and has marks of Iota in his face; his colour is Cob."

79. *Bermuda Gazette, and Weekly Advertiser*, July 10, 1784, 2.

80. *Port of Spain (Trinidad) Gazette*, April 30, 1833, 2.

81. In a handwritten account of the City of London School, Frederick writes, "Like most creole children I was sent at an early age to England to be educated." Reprinted in Terry Heard, "Two Brothers—and Was There One More?," *The Gazette: The Magazine of the John Carpenter Club* 293 (Summer 2008): 12–13. Frederick entered the school in 1844, when he was seven years old. His older brother William was also educated at the City of London School, then attended Oxford. William became a teacher, a priest, and finally an inspector of schools in Norfolk; his portrait appears in the National Portrait Gallery.

82. See Colleen Vasconcellos, *Slavery, Childhood, and Abolition in Jamaica, 1788–1838* (University of Georgia Press, 2015), 8.

83. *Port of Spain (Trinidad) Gazette*, April 19, 1833, 3.

84. Ibid.

85. Ibid.

86. Ibid.

87. Vasconcellos, *Slavery, Childhood, and Abolition*, 76.

88. Smith, "A Generation Rising," 81.

89. Lindley Murray, *Memoir of the Life and Writings of Lindley Murray*, 2nd ed. (York: Thomas Wilson and Sons, 1827), 229.

90. Lindley Murray, *The English Reader* (New London: W. & J. Bolless, 1836), 15, 14.

91. "Murray's English Reader," *American Annals of Education* (November 1837): 516.

92. For instance, letter from James McMurray working for the Mico Charity in post-emancipation Jamaica attests to the multiple channels through which teachers sought books:

> Agreeably to the plan I proposed to you I cause the children to pay for their own Sch. Requisites and in order to give no trouble to Mr. Wallbridge, I went to Jercesem [*sic*] and Osbourne's and purchased them on <u>my own account</u> but I found the materials for writing so bad that I thought I should write to you to know whether I could get a few reams of such writing paper as you used to supply me with at the Globe, it would be very valuable and if the Kildare Place Society would supply me with good paper and spelling books . . . I think the Tract Society would give you a small Library for us.

McMurray, Manuscript Letter, August 23, 1837, Oxford, Bodleian Libraries, Mico Charity Papers, Mss. Brit. Emp. S.20/E1/1 1835–1839.

93. *Port of Spain (Trinidad) Gazette*, April 19, 1833, 2.

94. Barbara Hofland, *Africa Described, in Its Ancient and Present State* (London: A. K. Newman and Company, 1834), 9.

95. Ibid., 9.

96. Ibid., 200.

97. *Port of Spain (Trinidad) Gazette*, May 31, 1833, 3.

98. See *Port of Spain (Trinidad) Gazette*, May 19, 1837, which includes this notice on page 2: "From the Matilda Estate, Quarter of Savanna Grande, three indented Africans, named, Lanois, Philippe, and Marcelin, they were seen in Port of Spain during the present week, and are supposed to be lurking about the neighbourhood."

99. Quoted in Cefas Van Rossem and Hein Van der Voort, *Die Creol Taal: 250 Years of Negerhollands Texts* (Amsterdam University Press, 1996), 27.

100. North, "Forgery for Freedom," 15.

101. Rossem and Van der Voort, *Die Creol Taal*, 26.

102. Ibid., 104. Enslaved children's access to hymns was likely limited, but some attended Sunday schools. As on the British islands, enslavers on some Danish estates were willing to have missionaries talk with slaves, especially after the end of the slave trade, which happened for the Danish-related colonies in 1792.

103. Schneider, "Black Literacy and Resistance in Jamaica."

104. The Danish Lutherans, who had been in the area since the late seventeenth century but did not start a mission for the enslaved until 1756 when the islands became a Danish state colony, created an ABC book (and others) in Negerhollands in 1770, a bit earlier than the Moravians. See Johan Christopher Kørbitz Thomsen Kingo, *A, B, Buk* (St. Croix 1770). These innovations were likely a result of competition between the groups. Despite this win on the Lutheran missionaries' part, the mission struggled from lack of funds and ended in 1799.

105. White children often learned Negerhollands from their caretakers, and the language was widely spoken by island inhabitants. Others spoke English or English Creole, while few people spoke Danish. Negerhollands was primarily an oral language, printed through missionary efforts. The Moravians initially helped transcribe the language so that speakers could communicate; Zinzendorf (who was antislavery) took letters from enslaved people to his connections in the Danish government.

106. *ABC-Boekje voor die Neger-Kinders na St. Thomas, St. Croix en St. Jan.* (Barby 1800); *ABC-Boekje voor die Neger-Kinders na St. Thomas, St. Croix en St. Jan* (Gnadau, 1825).

107. See Van Rossem and Van der Voort, *Die Creol Taal*, 184.

108. *The New-England Primer* (Edward Draper, 1777), 12.

109. Van Rossem and Van der Voort, *Die Creol Taal*, 184.

110. Melissa García Vega, "Ecopedagogy and Aesthetics in Caribbean Children's Literature," *Caribbean Children's Literature*, vol. 2: *Critical Approaches*, ed. Betsy Nies and Melissa García Vega (University Press of Mississippi, 2023), 219.

111. Richard Rawle, *A Report of the Assembling of Church Schoolmasters at Codrington College* (Barbados: Barbadian Office, 1849), 63–64.

112. Quoted in Liz Gershel, "Merle Hodge: Crick Crack Monkey," *A Handbook for Teaching Caribbean Literature*, ed. David Dabydeen (London: Heinemann), 83.

113. Van Rossem and van der Vort show that Danish Lutheran Negerhollands

grammar books from an earlier period include more elements of the culture, including proverbs and snippets of conversation.

114. See Van Rossem and Van der Voort, *Die Creol Taal*, 184.

115. Jan Hüsgen, "The Recruitment, Training and Conflicts Surrounding 'Native Teachers' in the Moravian Mission in the Danish West Indies in the Nineteenth Century," *Itinerario* 40, no. 3 (2016): 451–465. Van Scholten planned that slavery would cease in 1859.

116. Smith, "A Generation Rising," 129.

117. Manuscript Records from LaGrande Princesse Rural School, 1841–1846, Friedensthal, St. Croix, Records of the Moravian Church in the Eastern West Indies Province (hereafter cited as EWI), no. C.9.3, MAB.

118. Ibid.

119. Warner, Manuscript Letter to the YMMS, Friedensthal, St. Croix, August 13, 1842, YMMS, no. 109, MAB.

120. Ibid.

121. William Warner, Manuscript Letter to the YMMS, Friedensthal, St. Croix, February 1, 1843, YMMS, no. 109, MAB.

122. Warner, Manuscript Letter to the YMMS, Friedensthal, St. Croix, August 13, 1842, YMMS, no. 109, MAB.

123. Manuscript School Records: Friedensthal Day School Various Lists etc. 1859–60, EWI, no. C.32.3, MAB.

124. Manuscript School Records: List of Day School Children, Accounts, Catalog of Books, etc., 1857–1858 of the Friedensthal Day School, EWI, no. C.32.1, MAB.

125. Ibid.

126. Ibid. The missionaries at this school also requested several books from the American Sunday School Union, because George Weihs, a member of the YMMS turned missionary, had received the Sunday School and Family Library No. 1, a set of tracts published by the American Sunday School Union, when working in St. John's. The library was donated by the YMMS in 1847. See Weihs, Manuscript Letter to the YMMS from Nisky, St. Thomas, April 28, 1851, YMMS, no. 110, MAB.

127. See, for example, the baptism record for Albert Potter on May 18, 1845 by the United Brethren, U.S. Virgin Islands: Virgin Islands History Associates (VISHA); Fredericksted, U.S. Virgin Islands; St. Croix, U.S. Virgin Islands, Slave and Free People Records, 1733–1930; Box Number: 27. See also the census records for Potter and John Griffith, born around 1844, in the 1860 Danish West Indies Census, The Danish National Archives-Rigsarkivet; København, Danmark; 1841–1901 Dansk Vestindiske Folketælling. Both are listed as apprentices, Potter a Moravian and Griffith living on an estate owned by the Moravians.

128. See Turner, *Slaves and Missionaries*, 85.

129. *Elspeth Sutherland, Or, The Effects of Faith* (Edinburgh: Thomsons, Brothers, 1823), 2.

130. Ibid., 7.

131. Ibid., 20.

132. David Blair, *Blair's First or Mother's Catechism. Containing Common Things Necessary to Be Known at an Early Age*, 75th ed. (London: William Darton, 1835). Although this book is attributed to Blair, it is possible that it was ghostwritten by Eliza

Fenwick, who ran a school in Barbados. See Lissa Paul, *Eliza Fenwick: Early Modern Feminist* (University of Delaware Press, 2019).

133. Ibid., 47.

134. Ibid., 36, 42.

135. Manuscript School Records: Friedensthal Dayschool 1857–1858, EWI, no. C.32.1, MAB.

136. William Jones, *The Jubilee Memorial of the Religious Tract Society* (London: Religious Tract Society, 1850), 657.

137. Zachary Horton, *The Cosmic Zoom: Scale, Knowledge, and Mediation* (University of Chicago Press, 2021), 4.

138. George Macartney, *An Account of Ireland in 1773 by a Late Chief Secretary of that Kingdom*, cited in Kevin Kenny, *Ireland and the British Empire* (Oxford University Press), 72.

139. Reflecting Addison's *The Royal Exchange*, in which each nation contributes something that is needed by the whole, resulting in peaceful coexistence, the title character of *The Traveller* gives the boys a fantasy account of a world in which "different nations might benefit each other, not by wars and bloodshed . . . but by arts of peace . . . China may barter her tea, Russia her furs, Spain and Portugal their wines, America her timber, and Africa her gold, for the manufactured articles of England." *The Traveller: Or, A Description of Various Wonders in Nature and Art* (London: Religious Tract Society, 1839), 59. A section of various inventions reinforces this vision, as does the section on printing, which makes clear that the tract publishers consider Christianity to be Britain's most valuable export. See *The Traveller*, 160.

140. Ibid., 2.

141. Ibid., 3–4.

142. Ibid., 21, 30.

143. Ibid., 48.

144. Ibid., 50.

145. Ibid., 51.

146. Horton, *The Cosmic Zoom*, 6.

147. *The Traveller*, 1, 13.

148. Ibid., 5.

149. Ibid., 110.

150. Ibid., 48.

151. Ibid., 104.

152. Ibid.

153. Ibid., 160.

154. Ibid., 71–72.

155. Ibid., 132.

156. Drayton, "Politics of Textbooks," 5.

157. Ibid.

158. *First Annual Report of the Ladies' Branch Association for the Education of Female Children of the Coloured Poor on the Principles of the Established Church of England* (Bridgetown, 1827). For enrollment figures, see Seton S. Goodridge, *Facing the Challenges of Emancipation: A Study of the Ministry of William Hart Coleridge, First Bishop of Barbados, 1824–1842* (University of the West Indies Press, 2014), 61. See also Jerome S.

Handler, *The Unappropriated People: Freedmen in the Slave Society of Barbados* (University of the West Indies Press, 2009).

159. Shirley C. Gordon, *A Century of West Indian Education: A Source Book* (London: Longman, 1963), vii.

160. For instance, the 1816 slave code in Jamaica denied the "right of slave converts to preach and teach." Turner, *Slaves and Missionaries*, 89.

161. Smith, "A Generation Rising," 110, 113.

162. Ibid., 198.

163. Oliver G. Maynard, *A History of the Moravian Church Eastern West Indies Province*, 1968, 51.

164. Ibid., 70. As Inge Dornan notes, some Afro-Caribbeans went to the BFSS school near London for training. See Dornan, "Conversion and Curriculum: Nonconformist Missionaries and the British and Foreign School Society in the British West Indies, Africa and India 1800–50," *Studies in Church History* 55 (2019): 410–425.

165. P. A. Edwards, *Education for Development in the Caribbean* (Bridgetown, Barbados: Caribbean Ecumenical Consultation for Development, 1971), 7.

166. Reflecting perhaps years of training and implementation of Moravian educational ideas, a different unnamed teacher's lesson planner from 1870s St. Croix focuses daily reading lessons on hymns, Bible passages, English history, (likely Eurocentric) geography, grammar lessons, and natural history featuring nontropical animals such as the ass, the raven, the swan, and the owl. See School Records: Fragment of Class Record Book, 1870, EWI, no. C.32.7, MAB.

167. Walter Badhaus, *Report of Fairfield Training School*, Fairfield, Jamaica, 1840–1845, MissJmc Jamaica Papers, no. 50, MAB.

168. Smith, "A Generation Rising," 109.

169. *Report of the Inspectors of Schools, British Guiana*, 1853. The complaint that a "former cartman" has been "allowed" to be teacher based on his ability to wear glasses, look smart, speak pleasantly, and say (not read) the Lord's Prayer might be a remark on his race, but it is not overtly so. The Moravians' records criticize their trainees for wasting their power in "passion for awkward show; while what is needed is show and conviction, and a quietness which tells of a depth of feeling, and a reserve of power." Badhaus, *Report of the Fairfield Training School*. Other potential sources of information are autobiographies by white residents of the Caribbean, such as Henry Bleby, *A Missionary Father's Tales* (London: Wesleyan Mission House, 1876), who discusses an Afro-Caribbean teacher, Christopher James.

170. Archibald Clarke, Manuscript Letter to the YMMS, April 24, 1854, from Bethabara, YMMS, no. 112, MAB.

171. Ibid.

172. Ibid.

173. Martin Brückner, *The Social Life of Maps in America, 1750–1860* (Omohundro Institute of Early American History & Culture, 2017), 27.

174. Ibid., 366.

175. Badhaus, *Report of the Fairfield Training School*.

176. Hazel V. Carby, *Imperial Intimacies: A Tale of Two Islands* (Verso, 2021), 261, 259–260.

177. Russell "Maroon" Shoatz and Lisa Guenther, "Maroon Philosophy: An Inter-

view with Russell 'Maroon' Shoatz," in *Death and Other Penalties: Philosophy in a Time of Mass Incarceration*, ed. Lisa Guenther, Scott Zeman, and Geoffrey Adelsberg (Fordham University Press, 2015), 62–63.

178. Angelita Reyes, *Mothering Across Cultures: Postcolonial Representations* (University of Minnesota Press, 2002), 80.

179. Carla Gardina Pestana, "The Jamaica Maroons and the Dangers of Categorical Thinking," *Commonplace: The Journal of Early American Life*, accessed December 20, 2023. https://commonplace.online/article/vol-17-no-4-pestana/.

180. Smith, "A Generation Rising," 166.

181. See Sidney Mintz, *Caribbean Transformations* (Columbia University Press, 1989), 161.

182. "An Original 'Free Village,'" *The Gleaner* (Jamaica), September 24, 2010, https://jamaica-gleaner.com/gleaner/20100924/news/news41.html.

183. See Smith, "A Generation Rising," 163.

184. We can identify the map as part of the museum because it appears in a spreadsheet of YMMS museum items compiled by the Moravian Archives. The YMMS museum contained other Caribbean items—namely, Black dolls, coins, and shells. While later Caribbean dolls exist at the current Moravian Historical Society in Pennsylvania, the whereabouts of most of the specific items received and shown by the YMMS are now, unfortunately, unknown.

185. Mahshid Mayar, *Citizens and Rulers of the World: The American Child and the Cartographic Pedagogies of Empire* (University of North Carolina Press, 2023), 31.

186. Other Afro-Caribbean challenges to this orientation appear in subtle ways in the archive—for instance, in misunderstanding. A BFSS report about a school in Salter's Hill, Jamaica, remarks, "The subject in geography was the British Colonies . . . but the lessons did not seem to have been well understood." *56th Report of the BFSS* (London: J. & W. Rider, 1861), 88. Some teachers appear to have tried to innovate by asking for natural history plates and samples of European plants and animals to supplement lessons on geography. Other teachers encouraged the children to connect to the natural features around them, an activity that subtly shifts the ability to produce knowledge away from the colonizers. A letter to BFSS mentions beautiful watercolors of the islands made by young boys in Demerara: "Any manifestation of artistic taste and skill made by the boys of this country is particularly pleasing, for it suggests the possibility of native artists rising up to copy the forms and colours of the wonderful variety of birds and flowers which sparkles around their house." *57th Report of the BFSS* (London: J. & W. Rider, 1862), 20. However, these kinds of activities appear infrequently in records.

Chapter 5 • *Traces of Atlantic Relations in Early Global Children's Literature*

1. William Jones, *The Jubilee Memorial of the Religious Tract Society* (London: Religious Tract Society, 1850), 506.

2. Ibid.

3. Ibid.

4. M. O. Grenby, "Spreading the Words: Global Networks and the Circulation of Cheap Instructional and Religious Children's Print," *Transnational Books for Children 1750–1900* (John Benjamins, 2023), 18–45. Areas central to enslavement, such as the

Caribbean, figured comparatively marginally in the development of these global publishing and distribution efforts, when measured against Asia. For instance, I have found no evidence that the SPCK sent printing presses to any Caribbean islands, though they sent books and funding. RTS activity featured the translation of books into multiple languages (including more than a dozen languages in India alone), but translation was sparse in the Caribbean because British enslavement created barriers for Afro-Caribbeans' preservation of their native languages, and the possibility for slave rebellions created anxieties around language use.

5. See Grenby, "Spreading the Words." The RTS is a part of this history. *The Jubilee Memorial* gives a history of publishing that begins with circulating and translating simple books "called 'Abeis,' that is, A-Bs," which "contained the Alphabet, the Paternoster, the Ave-Maria, etc." Jones, *Jubilee Memorial*, 110.

6. David Paul Nord, *Faith in Reading: Religious Publishing and the Birth of Mass Media in America* (Oxford University Press, 2004), 39.

7. Emer O'Sullivan, *Comparative Children's Literature*, trans. Anthea Bell (Routledge, 2005), 65.

8. See Courtney Weikle-Mills, "Book Publishing and the British Sphere of Influence in the Eighteenth and Nineteenth Centuries," in *The Routledge Companion to Children's Literature and Culture*, ed. Claudia Nelson, Elizabeth Wesseling, and Andrea Mei-Ying Wu (Routledge, 2023), 429–440.

9. Jones, *Jubilee Memorial*, 597.

10. Ibid., 124. The books for juveniles included versions of Christian and tract society mainstays such as Isaac Watts's *Divine Songs* (1715), James Janeway's *A Token for Children* (1671), Philip Doddridge's *Principles of the Christian Religion* (1777), *Persuasives to Early Piety* (1799), *Pilgrim's Progress* (1678), and *Poor Joseph* (1822); children's books by Legh Richmond and Mary Martha Sherwood; children's magazines; and educational volumes on topics such as Greek and Roman history. These texts were circulated by the society, the hawkers with which it contracted, and "wholly unconnected" booksellers, who made them into "little books, with neat covers and coloured prints" (124).

11. Ibid., 81.

12. In this early venture after separating from his former partner George Routledge in 1865, Warne seems to have drawn on Routledge's business model, which according to Catherine Golden involved popularizing what he considered quality literature. See Golden, "Frederick Warne and Company," in *British Literary Publishing Houses, 1820–1880: Dictionary of Literary Biography*, vol. 106, ed. Patricia J. Anderson and Jonathan Rose (Gale Research, 1992). Marketing practices involved grouping books into series via pricing and thematic groupings, including groups of stories from different cultures coming to be in vogue in the mid-nineteenth century. Warne's catalog for 1874 lists several series incorporating stories set in foreign lands, such as the *Hopeful Enterprises Library* (combining *Robinson Crusoe* and *The Swiss Family Robinson* with titles like *Wild Sports and Savage Life in Zulu Land*) and the Star of Hope series (including *The Son of the Pyrenees* and *Life of a Berlin Doll*). See *Frederick Warne and Co.'s General Catalogue of Choice New Illustrated Works, Juvenile Publications, Reference and Useful Books, Issued at Popular Prices* (London: Frederick Warne and Co., 1874). Warne's "global" model appears to have been at least somewhat effective in encouraging circ-

ulation outside of Britain; Maria Eulália Ramicelli shows his books were available at a circulating library in Rio Grande, Brazil. Ramicelli, "British Fiction in the Far South of Brazil: The Nineteenth-Century Collection of the Rio-Grandense Library," in *The Transatlantic Circulation of Novels Between Europe and Brazil, 1789–1914*, ed. Márcia Abreu (Palgrave Macmillan, 2017), 249–270. The idea of seeking stories about multicultural characters for the Round the Globe Library would not fully crystallize until a later incarnation in the 1940s, which included books about Japan, Fiji, South America, India, Poland, Alaska, and other "exotic" locations. The twentieth-century incarnation is more international, but narratives by diverse creators are glaringly missing.

13. Beckman's note appears in the copy held by the Bancroft Library at the University of California, Berkeley (call number PZ6.B25 B22 1852).

14. Shih-Wen Sue Chen, *Children's Literature and Transnational Knowledge in Modern China: Education, Religion, and Childhood* (Palgrave Macmillan, 2019), 25; Grenby, "Spreading the Words," 20.

15. According to the appendix of *The Jubilee Memorial*, 468,170 copies of the tract were in circulation by 1849. For comparison, *The Negro Servant*'s distribution was 360,621 copies, when considering its inclusion in *The Annals of the Poor* as well as its circulation as a single tract.

16. See "Moses, the Pious Negro," *Christian Secretary* 2, no. 25 (1839): 2; "Moses the Pious Negro," *Zion's Herald* 4, no. 20 (May 17, 1826): 1; "Moses the Pious Negro," *Western Recorder* (May 2, 1826): 1; "Moses the Pious Negro," *Christian Watchman* 7, no. 23 (1826): 1; "Moses the Pious Negro," *Western Luminary* 2, no. 50 (1826): 785. The story was published in another wave of US papers in 1839 and continued to circulate into the 1860s.

17. An anthology by the Glasgow Religious Tract Society also includes the story in Scottish Gaelic. See *Pamphlet Volumes of Tracts in Gaelic*, no. 16 (Glasgow Religious Tract Society, 1800–1899).

18. *Moses the Pious Negro* (Religious Tract Society, 1827), 1–2.

19. Ibid., 3.

20. Ibid.

21. Jones, *Jubilee Memorial*, 492.

22. The tract also circulated in Italy and Switzerland, which may have influenced the spread to the Dutch East Indies owing to the closeness in language to Dutch, a reason given for translating a different tract, *Stories from Switzerland*, for use in the East Indies.

23. Keasberry's publications included works for children, including a translation of Bible stories from T. H. Gallaudet's *The Picture Reading Defining Book*, as well as steady sellers such as *Pilgrim's Progress*. See "Benjamin Keasberry," *Singapore Infopedia*, National Library Board of Singapore, accessed July 5, 2021, https://www.nlb.gov.sg/main/article-detail?cmsuuid=f65a75d3-057e-44ca-adf8-cd8c68c15214. See also Leona O'Sullivan, "The London Missionary Society [LMS]: A Written Record of Missionaries and Printing Presses in the Straits Settlements 1815–1847," *Journal of the Malaysian Branch of the Royal Asiatic Society* 57, no. 2 (1984): 61–104.

24. R. J. Wilkinson, *A Malay-English Dictionary* (Singapore: Kelly and Walsh, 1901), 136.

25. "Benjamin Keasberry."

26. Jones, *Jubilee Memorial*, 491.

27. Ibid., 506.

28. Other accounts suggest that missionaries did not limit themselves to the children's list when selling or giving books to young people around the world. *The Jubilee Memorial* mentions an Afro-Caribbean girl reading Boston's *Fourfold State*, which is "not a child's book certainly, and yet read by this Ethiopian convert with delight and profit" (ibid., 195).

29. Ibid., 433.

30. William Wilberforce, *A Practical View of the Prevailing Religious System of Professed Christians, in the Higher and Middle Classes in the Country, Contrasted with Real Christianity* (Boston: Crocker and Brewster, 1829), lix. Somewhat surprisingly given its dry content, the RTS circulated Wilberforce's *Practical View* as a children's book.

31. See *The Negro Servant* (Kilmarnock: Printed for the Booksellers, c. 1825), held by the Bodleian Library at Oxford University (call number Firth f.73).

32. Legh Richmond, *Annals of the Poor* (New York: Crocker and Brewster, 1829), 170.

33. Ibid., 161.

34. Ibid., 162.

35. Ibid.

36. Ibid., 164.

37. Mary Turner, *Slaves and Missionaries: The Disintegration of Jamaican Slave Society, 1787–1834* (University of Illinois Press, 1982), 71.

38. Maria Ryan, "'The Influence of Melody upon Man in the Wild State of Nature': Enslaved Parishioners, Anglican Violence, and Racialized Listening in a Jamaica Parish," *Journal of the Society for American Music* 15 (2021): 275.

39. Richmond, *Annals of the Poor*, 168–169.

40. Ibid., 170.

41. Ibid. 173–174.

42. Ibid., 174.

43. Ibid., 175.

44. Ibid., 175–176.

45. Ibid., 176. A footnote in later editions attributes the end of the slave trade to "the triumph of the cause of Christ over the powers of darkness," but this is a significant realignment of Richmond's opening map.

46. Ibid., 177.

47. Ibid., 178.

48. Ibid.

49. Ibid., 186.

50. Ibid.

51. Ibid., 184.

52. Ibid., 186.

53. Marilisa Jiménez García, *Side by Side: US Empire, Puerto Rico, and the Roots of American Youth Literature and Culture* (University of Mississippi, 2021), 39–40.

54. Ibid.

55. Richmond, *Annals of the Poor*, 194.

56. Ibid., 201.

57. Quoted in Cynthia S. Hamilton, "Spreading the Word: The American Tract Society, *The Dairyman's Daughter*, and Mass Publishing," *Book History* 14 (2011): 38.

58. "Tract Meeting in New York," *Western Recorder* (Utica, NY) 7, no. 48 (1830): 190.

59. "Dr. Milnor's Visit to the Isle of Wight," *Christian Secretary* (Hartford, CT) 9, no. 46 (1830): 181.

60. Hamilton, "Spreading the Word," 45–46.

61. Jones, *Jubilee Memorial*, 377. Jones also mentions the circulation of *The Negro Servant* to Malta; majority-Catholic countries Portugal and Ireland; and the Netherlands, Prussia, and Armenia, places with established connections to the church.

62. Ibid., 373.

63. The book may have had some life in the Caribbean, but if it did, the archives I examined yield silence on this point. Nineteenth-century children's storybooks do not appear to have survived there in large numbers or to have been preserved by readers, making it necessary to use historical accounts and ads rather than surviving copies to establish circulation.

64. See the edition held by Bancroft Library.

65. Archived copies also allow us to trace its Anglo-American circulation. Four copies inscribed to British children were awarded to Emily Rodgers for good attendance at Christ Church Sunday School, Leeds, on New Year's Day 1874; Edith Rogers at the Bestwood Road Besthesda Sunday School in Hucknall Torkard, for reciting on the anniversary of the church in May 1880; Alice Jones at the Clint Road Board School in Liverpool, as part of an 1894 geography exam; and Charles Collins from Trecoyse Sunday School in Cornwall in 1900. It is Emily's book, published by Frederick Warne and Co., that resides in the West India collection at University of the West Indies (call number PS1059.B3 B3). Alice's book was published in London by T. Nelson and Sons in 1892 and is held by the British Foreign and School Society (BFSS) Archive at Brunel University (call number SWBook/14). Edith's was published by George Routledge and Sons, and Charles's by Milner and Company; both are held by the Baldwin Library of Historical Children's Literature at University of Florida's George A. Smathers Libraries (call numbers 23h3703 and 15h647). Three other Baldwin copies have inscriptions to girls living in the United States from family members, an uncle (Frederick Warne, 1875, call number 23h3674), a grandmamma (S. W. Partridge and Co., call number 23h3707), and an aunt (S. W. Patridge and Co., call number 23h3701). We can explain these inscriptions by pointing to the influence of educational institutions like the RTS, the American Sunday School Union, and the BFSS on book circulation in Britain and the United States, as well as other parts of the world.

66. Sarah Schoonmaker Baker, *The Babes in the Basket; or Daph and Her Charge* (New York: Anson D. F. Randolph, 1859), 5. All citations to the text in this chapter are to this first edition, unless noted. The Warne version is *The Babes in the Basket* (London: Frederick Warne and Company, 1875). A copy can be found at the Baldwin Library of Historical Children's Literature, University of Florida (call number 23h3674).

67. See the edition held at the Bancroft Library.

68. Baker, *Babes in the Basket*, 53.

69. Ibid., 70–71.

70. Ibid., 70.

71. Sarah Schoonmaker Baker, *The Babes in the Basket* (London: S. W. Partridge and Co., c. 1884).

72. See the edition held at the Bancroft Library. The dedication is to Anna W. Baker, Sarah Baker's sister-in-law and Beckman's aunt, on "Christmas 1858."

73. Golliwog stories had a large circulation and even influenced doll culture in the Caribbean. I saw Golliwog dolls on display at the Barbados Museum when on a research trip there in 2017.

74. Bertha Upton (author) and Florence Kate Upton (illustrator), *The Adventures of Two Dutch Dolls and a Golliwogg* (London: Longmans Green and Co., 1895), 23.

75. Miguel Cabrera Peña, "Harriet Beecher Stowe in José Martí's 'The Black Doll,'" *Islas: Quarterly Journal of Afro-Cuban Issues* 4, no. 13 (2009): 50–58.

76. Jorge Camacho, "'Compassion' and Blacks in a Story by José Martí," *Islas: Quarterly Journal of Afro-Cuban Issues* 24 (2013): 65–68.

77. Robin Bernstein, *Racial Innocence: Performing American Childhood from Slavery to Civil Rights* (New York University Press, 2011).

78. See Patricia Crain, *Reading Children: Literacy, Property, and the Dilemmas of Childhood in Nineteenth-Century America* (University of Pennsylvania Press, 2017), for an analysis of the multiple versions of *Babes in the Wood* circulating in the eighteenth- and nineteenth-century United States.

79. Unfortunately, these dolls cannot be identified among the current collection of the Moravian Historical Society.

80. Frances Armstrong, "The Dollhouse as Ludic Space, 1690–1920," in *Children's Literature* 24 (1996): 26.

81. Ibid., 25.

82. Ibid.

83. Bernstein, *Racial Innocence*, 205. Emphasis added by Bernstein.

84. Mickey Herr, "Archaic Expectations: Freeing Female Roles from a Dollhouse in Society Hill," *Hidden City Philadelphia*, February 1, 2019, https://hiddencityphila.org /2019/02/archaic-expectations-freeing-female-roles-from-a-dollhouse-in-society-hill/.

85. Armstrong, "The Dollhouse as Ludic Space," 47. If Beckman's dollhouse had a similar doll to that of the Cadwalader family, the headscarf might have been a prompt for connecting the doll to the Caribbean for, as Elizabeth Dillon argues, the headscarf was strongly connected to creole culture. See Dillon, "The Secret History of the Early American Novel," *Novel* 40, nos. 1/2 (2007): 87.

86. Baker, *Babes in the Basket*, 6.

87. Bernstein, *Racial Innocence*, 212.

88. Baker, *Babes in the Basket*, 7.

89. Ibid., 19.

90. Ibid., 31.

91. Irma Watkins-Owens writes, "In the nineteenth century and earlier, the United States attracted small communities of Caribbean intellectuals, churchmen, and students . . . These individuals were mainly men who came with exceptional educational and other skills and found opportunities within the African American community." Watkins-Owens, "Early-Twentieth-Century Caribbean Women: Migration and Social

Networks in New York City," *Island in the City: West Indian Migration to New York*, ed. Nancy Foner (University of California Press, 2001), 27.

92. Baker, *Babes in the Basket*, 5.

93. Ibid.

94. Ibid., 6.

95. Hazel V. Carby, *Cultures in Babylon: Feminism from Black Britain to African America* (Verso, 1999), 79.

96. *The Doll and Her Friends; or Memoirs of the Lady Seraphina* (London: Griffith and Farran, 1862), 2–3.

97. Ibid.

98. Baker, *Babes in the Basket*, 61.

99. Ibid., 65.

100. Ibid., 95.

101. Ibid., 88.

102. See Sarah Schoonmaker Baker, *The Babes in the Basket* (London: S. W. Partridge and Co., 1873).

103. Baker, *Babes in the Basket*, 41–43.

104. Ibid., 168.

105. Carby, *Cultures in Babylon*, 110.

106. Saidiya Hartman, *Wayward Lives, Beautiful Experiments: Intimate Histories of Riotous Black Girls, Troublesome Women, and Queer Radicals* (W. W. Norton, 2019).

107. Fred Moten, *The Universal Machine (consent not to be a single being)* (Duke University Press, 2018).

108. Baker, *Babes in the Basket*, 119.

109. Russ Castronovo, *Necro Citizenship: Death, Eroticism, and the Public Sphere in the Nineteenth-Century United States* (Duke University Press, 2001).

110. Quoted in Emily Madsen, "Phiz's Black Doll: Integrating Text and Etching in Bleak House," *Victorian Literature and Culture* 41, no. 3 (2013): 428–429.

111. Quoted in ibid., 428–429.

112. Gauri Viswanathan, *Masks of Conquest: Literary Study and British Rule in India* (Oxford University Press, 1989), 2.

113. Ibid., 43.

114. Nivedita Sen, *Family, School and Nation: The Child and Literary Constructions in 20th-Century Bengal* (Routledge, 2015), 27. In a conversation with me, Sreemoyee Dasgupta explained, "Katha means spoken words, or speaking. For example, if I want to say, 'I am speaking,' I would say 'katha bolchi.' But in certain oral storytelling performance forms, *katha* also translates into 'stories.' *Taranga* is 'waves.'"

115. Thomas Day, *Sandford and Merton*, translated by Madhusudan Mukhopadhyay as *Kathataranga* (Calcutta: Calcutta School Book and Vernacular Literature Society, 1865), 17. I quote from an English translation I commissioned by Saquib Ahsan.

116. Viswanathan, *Masks of Conquest*, 44.

117. Mukhopadhyay, *Kathataranga*, 13, 16.

118. Ibid., 17.

119. Ibid., 1.

120. Ibid.

121. Ibid., 16.

122. Thomas Day, *The History of Sandford and Merton: A Work Intended for the Use of Children* (Philadelphia: Printed by William Young, 1793), 373.

123. Ibid., 310.

Conclusion • Relating Ethically in the Archives

1. As Ellen Gruber Garvey points out, "By the later twentieth century, the collecting policies of many institutions changed to reflect greater interest in history from the ground up. Archives more often seek to include materials documenting the lives of ordinary people and members of subordinated groups, rather than the relics of great men. Yet the guidelines that were once used to decide what to accept or acquire have left an enduring mark on what is available for study today. Although government archives may hold material on marginalized people as they ran up against the law, for example, they won't contain the materials those people themselves saved and organized." Garvey, *Writing with Scissors: American Scrapbooks from the Civil War to the Harlem Renaissance* (Oxford University Press, 2012), 209.

2. Manuscript Letter to the BFSS from Fuller's Field, Jamaica, September 5, 1845. BFSS/1/5/1/8/4/151, Archives and Special Collections, Brunel University of London.

3. Chelsey Smith, "A Generation Rising: Education for Freedpeople in Post-Abolition Jamaica, 1834–1872" (PhD diss., University of Pittsburgh, 2024), 19.

4. Ibid., 21.

5. Ibid., iv.

6. John D. Caputo, *The Prayers and Tears of Jacques Derrida: Religion Without Religion* (Indiana University Press, 1997), 265.

7. Ibid.

8. Saidiya Hartman, *Wayward Lives, Beautiful Experiments: Intimate Histories of Riotous Black Girls, Troublesome Women, and Queer Radicals* (W. W. Norton, 2019), xiv.

9. Janice McLean-Farrell and Michael Anderson Clarke, "Missions in Contested Places/Spaces: The SPG, Slavery, and Codrington College, Barbados," *Mission Studies* 38, no. 3 (2021): 337.

10. Ibid., 330, 340.

11. Letter from Rawle to an English Friend in Staffordshire, February 1848, quoted in Shirley Gordon, *A Century of West Indian Education* (Longmans, 1963), 62.

12. Jessica Swanston Baker, *Island Time: Speed and the Archipelago from St. Kitts and Nevis* (University of Chicago Press, 2024), 61.

13. Maria Ryan shows that missionaries and educators thought music could have this role beginning during enslavement. See Ryan, " 'The Influence of Melody upon Man in the Wild State of Nature': Enslaved Parishioners, Anglican Violence, and Racialized Listening in a Jamaica Parish," *Journal of the Society for American Music* 15 (2021): 276.

14. "Fete at Codrington College, Barbadoes," *Illustrated London News* 17, no. 452 (October 26, 1850): 333.

15. *The Illustrated London News* included color illustrations beginning in 1855.

16. Advertisements for educational books also appear in the newspaper's pages.

17. Peter W. Sinnema, "Constructing a Readership: Surveillance and Interiority in the Illustrated London News," *Victorian Review* 20, no. 2 (Winter 1994): 156.

18. Ibid.

19. "Slave Labour in the Brazils," *Illustrated London News* 6, no. 152 (March 29, 1845): 197.

20. Ibid., 198. Later issues did show elements of the trade, including a slave auction in Virginia. See *Illustrated London News* 29, no. 822 (September 27, 1856): 315.

21. "Fete at Codrington College, Barbadoes," 333.

22. Ibid.

23. Ibid.

24. For mainland British readers, the children's activities were likely a mix of familiar and exotic; stilts were a known (if antiquated) plaything, while bottle-dancing was uncommon. See "Toys," *Illustrated London News* 19, no. 528 (November 8, 1851), 579; and "Children's Games," *Illustrated London News* 219, no. 5873A (November 15, 1951), 33, which refer to stilt walking as a traditional children's game.

25. Jerome S. Handler and Charlotte J. Frisbie, "Aspects of Slave Life in Barbados: Music and Its Cultural Context," *Caribbean Studies* 11, no. 4 (1972): 11.

26. Ibid.

27. Handler and Frisbie note that the holiday may have been at cross purposes with antislavery efforts, as holidays "temporarily reduced the severity of the system for the slave, and by so doing helped to perpetuate the slave-system itself." Ibid., 12. Discussing similar holidays in Jamaica, Mary Turner notes, "The yearly festivals . . . became seasonal circuses in which the slaves provided the whites with exotic entertainment." Turner, *Slaves and Missionaries: The Disintegration of Jamaican Slave Society, 1787–1834* (University of Illinois Press, 1982), 52.

28. Marcia Burrowes, "Losing Our Masks: Traditional Masquerade and Changing Constructs of Barbadian Identity," *International Journal of Intangible Heritage* 8 (2013): 41.

29. Ibid., 41, 40.

30. Brenda Dixon Gottschild, "Crossroads, Continuities, and Contradictions: The Afro-Euro-Caribbean Triangle," in *Caribbean Dance from Abakuá to Zouk: How Movement Shapes Identity*, ed. Susanna Sloat (University Press of Florida, 2002), 5.

31. Ibid., 9.

32. "National Concert at Her Majesty's Theatre," *Illustrated London News* 17, no. 452 (October 26, 1850): 333.

33. Susan Harewood and John Hunte, "Dance in Barbados: Reclaiming, Preserving, and Creating National Identities," in *Making Caribbean Dance: Continuity and Creativity in Island Cultures*, ed. Susanna Sloat (University Press of Florida, 2010), 266.

34. See Lomax, Elder, and Hawes, *Brown Girl in the Ring: An Anthology of Song Games from the Eastern Caribbean* (Pantheon Books, 1997), 7.

35. Roy Maloy, *Stilt-Walking: A History and a How-To* (Mac Brothers Entertainment, 2008), 7.

36. Ibid., 7.

37. Patricia T. Alleyne-Dettmers, "The Moko Jumbie: Elevating the Children," in *Caribbean Dance from Abakuá to Zouk: How Movement Shapes Identity*, ed. Susanna Sloat (University Press of Florida, 2002), 266. See also Molly Ahye, *Golden Heritage: The Dance in Trinidad and Tobago* (Port of Spain: Heritage Cultures, 1978), 29.

38. Alleyne-Dettmers, "The Moko Jumbie," 272.

39. Harewood and Hunte, "Dance in Barbados," 267.

40. See Turner, *Slaves and Missionaries*, 75.

41. Alleyne-Dettmers, "The Moko Jumbie," 264.

42. Ibid., 276.

43. "Dance in Trinidad: Moko Jumbie On 9-Foot Stilts," YouTube video, posted by The New York Times, December 17, 2017, 3:20, https://www.youtube.com/watch?v=vHiUIHgPhus.

44. Fred Moten and Stefano Harney, *The Undercommons: Fugitive Planning and Black Study* (Autonomedia and Minor Compositions, 2013), 43.

45. "Study & Planning," School of Commons (SoC), accessed February 16, 2024, https://schoolofcommons.org/tags/study-and-planning.

46. Ibid.

47. I inquired via email who hung the image on the wall but was not able to get an answer.

48. Garvey, *Writing with Scissors*, 4.

49. Ibid., 47.

50. Baker, *Island Time*, 62.

51. "Mission Crop Over: The Only Guide You Need to Survive Barbados' Sweetest Summer Festival," Visit Barbados, accessed December 10, 2024, https://www.visitbarbados.org/mission-crop-over.

52. Garvey, *Writing with Scissors*, 49.

53. Mahshid Mayar, "'Playes Print the Letter': American Child(hoods) as Archival Present/ce," *The Journal of the History of Childhood and Youth* 16, no. 3 (Fall 2023): 365.

54. Ibid., 365–366.

55. Joseph J. Williams, SJ, *Psychic Phenomena of Jamaica* (New York: Dial Press, 1934).

56. Audra Diptee and David V. Trotman, "Atlantic Childhood and Youth in Global Context: Reflections on the Global South," *Atlantic Studies, Global Currents* 11, no. 4 (2014): 438.

57. "Correspondence," in Joseph J. Williams, SJ, Ethnological Collection, Anansi Stories, 1930–1931, Project Planning, 1930–1931, Correspondence, 1930–1931, MS2009_030_62957_0008, Digital Record, Burns Library Archival Collections, Boston College.

58. "Correspondence," MS2009_030_62957_0025.

59. "Correspondence," MS2009_030_62957_0039.

60. Cynthia James, "From Orature to Literature in Jamaican and Trinidadian Children's Folk Traditions," *Children's Literature Association Quarterly* 30, no. 2 (Summer 2005): 166.

61. Emily Murphy, "The Anarchy of Children's Archives: Citizenship and Empire in the Global 1930s," *Journal of American Studies* 57, no. 5 (2023): 677–699.

62. James, "From Orature to Literature," 167.

63. Sage Adia Swaby, "Radical Folk Heroes: Anansi & Br'er Rabbit's West African Origins & Their Forced Pilgrimages" (senior project, Bard College, 2022), 12.

64. Ibid., 7. See also Ropo Sekoni, *Folk Poetics: A Sociosemiotic Study of Yoruba Trickster Tales* (Greenwood Press, 1994).

65. B. Lorrell, Manuscript 486, in "Black River School, Church of England," in Joseph J. Williams, SJ, Ethnological Collection, Anansi Stories, 1930–1931, Parish of

St. Elizabeth, 1930–1931, MS2009_030_63030, Digital Record, Burns Library Archival Collections, Boston College. This story appears in multiple versions throughout this corpus.

66. Swaby, "Radical Folk Heroes," 22.

67. Ibid.

68. Ibid., 18.

69. N. Williams, Manuscript 2127, in "Annotto Bay Private School, Catholic," in Joseph J. Williams, SJ, Ethnological Collection, Anansi Stories, 1930–1931, Parish of St. Mary, 1930–1931, MS2009_030_63040, Digital Record, Burns Library Archival Collections, Boston College.

70. Ibid.

71. Martha Warren Beckwith, *Jamaica Anansi Stories* (New York: American Folk-Lore Society, 1924), 6.

72. I. Johnson, Manuscript 1129, in "Pisgah School, Moravian," Joseph J. Williams, SJ, Ethnological Collection, Anansi Stories, 1930–1931, Parish of St. Elizabeth, 1930–1931, MS2009_030_63033_0176, Digital Record, Burns Library Archival Collections, Boston College.

73. Ibid.

74. Drums were often made of sheep or goatskin, adding another layer of significance.

75. O. Bartley, Manuscript 1815, in "Airy Castle School, Government Undenominational," Joseph J. Williams, SJ, Ethnological Collection, Anansi Stories, 1930–1931, Parish of St. Thomas, 1930–1931, MS2009_030_63045_0138, Digital Record, Burns Library Archival Collections, Boston College.

76. Danielle N. Boaz, "'Instruments of Obeah': The Significance of Ritual Objects in the Jamaican Legal System, 1760 to the Present," in *Materialities of Ritual in the Black Atlantic* (Indiana University Press, 2014), 145.

77. L. Edwards, Manuscript 3039, in "Airy Castle School, Government Undenominational," Joseph J. Williams, SJ, Ethnological Collection, Anansi Stories, 1930–1931, Parish of St. Thomas, 1930–1931, MS2009_030_63045_0154, Digital Record, Burns Library Archival Collections, Boston College.

78. A version by F. McDonnough suggests that Tiger is wearing the sheepskin during the theft, because the sheep already recognize Anansi. Anansi takes advantage of this when the master comes, jumping out of the sheep pen and leaving Tiger to be caught (with help from a song). See F. McDonnough, Manuscript 4139, in "Chalky Hill School, Government Undenominational," Joseph J. Williams, SJ, Ethnological Collection, Anansi Stories, 1930–1931, Parish of St. Ann, 1930–1931, MS2009_030_63003_0072, Digital Record, Burns Library Archival Collections, Boston College.

79. Beckwith, *Jamaica Anansi Stories*, 8.

80. A. Hart, Manuscript 4311, in "Buckingham School, Jamaican Baptist Union," Joseph J. Williams, SJ, Ethnological Collection, Anansi Stories, 1930–1931, Parish of St. James, 1930–1931, MS2009_030_63035_0089, Digital Record, Burns Library Archival Collections, Boston College.

81. Saidiya Hartman, *Lose Your Mother: A Journey Along the Atlantic Slave Route* (Farrar, Straus and Giroux, 2008), 6.